THE
GREEK WORLD
IN THE 4TH AND 3RD CENTURIES BC

UNIWERSYTET JAGIELLOŃSKI
INSTYTUT HISTORII

ELECTRUM

Journal of Ancient History

Editor-in-Chief: Edward Dąbrowa

Assistant Editor: Sławomir Sprawski

VOL. 19 (2012)

THE
GREEK WORLD
IN THE 4TH AND 3RD CENTURIES BC

JAGIELLONIAN UNIVERSITY PRESS

Electrum, vol. 19 (2012)

COVER DESIGN
Barbara Widlak

Cover photography: 'The Pistiros Inscription', photo D. Graninger

TECHNICAL EDITOR
Jadwiga Makowiec

PROOFREADER
Małgorzata Szul

TYPESETTER
Wojciech Wojewoda

The publication of this volume was financed by the Jagiellonian University in Krakow – Faculty of History.

ISBN 978-83-233-3483-5
ISSN 1897-3426

The digital version of the "Electrum" (ISSN 2084-3909) – which counts as the original – is published in the journals section of the Jagiellonian University Press website (www.wuj.pl).

Number of copies: 250

www.wuj.pl

Jagiellonian University Press
Editorial Offices: Michałowskiego St. 9/2, 31-126 Krakow
Phone: +48 12 631 18 81, +48 12 631 18 82, Fax: +48 12 631 18 83
Distribution: Phone: +48 12 631 01 97, Fax: +48 12 631 01 98
Cell Phone: + 48 506006 674, e-mail: sprzedaz@wuj.pl
Bank: PEKAO SA, IBAN PL80 1240 4722 1111 0000 4856 3325

Contents

The journals *sigla* utilized are similar to the rules used in *L'Année Philologique*. The other abbreviations used in this volume are as follows:

Agora	–	*The Athenian Agora*, Princeton 1953–
CID	–	G. Rougemont *et al.*, *Corpus des inscriptions de Delphes*, 3 vols., Paris 1977–1992
FD	–	*Fouilles de Delphes*, III : *Épigraphie*, Paris 1909–1985
FGrH	–	F. Jacoby, *Die Fragmente der Griechischer Historikern*, Berlin–Leiden 1928–
I. Cret.	–	M. Guarducci, *Inscriptiones Creticae*, 4 vols., Roma 1935–1950
I. Délos	–	*Inscriptions de Délos*, 7 vols., Paris 1926–1972
I. Milet	–	P. Herrmann *et al.*, *Inschriften von Milet*, 2 vols., Berlin 1997–
IG	–	*Inscriptiones Graecae*
IGBulg	–	G. Mihailov, *Inscriptiones Graece in Bulgaria repertae*, 6 vols., Sofia 1958––1997
LGPN	–	*Lexicon of Greek Personal Names*, 7 vols., Oxford 1987–
SEG	–	*Supplementum Epigraphicum Graecum*
SGDI	–	H. Collitz, F. Bechtel *et al.*, *Sammlung der griechischen Dialekt Inschriften*, 5 vols., Göttingen 1884–1915
SIG³	–	W. Dittenberger, *Sylloge Inscriptionum Graecarum*, 3 ed., 4 vols., Leipzig 1915–1924

ELECTRUM * Vol. 19 (2012): 9–40
doi:10.4467/20843909EL.12.001.0742

Ctesias and the Importance of His Writings Revisited

Eran Almagor

Abstract: Following the recent attempts to rehabilitate the reputation of Ctesias and the information given in his works, this paper proposes to understand certain of the seemingly fanciful details that were associated with the physician and his writings. It tries to shed some light on several uncertainties connected with Ctesias (i.e., his sojourn in Persia) and the *Persica* (i.e., date, original style and sources of imagery). It argues that the pedestrian lists included in the work might have been later interpolations and that the minor works circulating under Ctesias' name might have been either sections of the *Persica* that were taken out to be presented as stand-alone volumes or else falsely attributed to him. The paper addresses the *Indica* and puts forward several possibilities concerning its relation with the *Persica*. The influence of Ctesias on the author Deinon is examined, and in the appendix the impact of the *Persica* on Xenophon's *Anabasis* is analyzed.

Keywords: Ctesias, *Persica*, *Indica*, Artaxerxes II, Xenophon, *Anabasis*, Greek Historiography, Photius, Plutarch, Deinon.

From Cnidos comes one of the more controversial and influential authors of Classical literature, namely Ctesias, a physician and a historian (probably *floruit* 401–392 BCE).[1] Ctesias seems not only to have been one of the first prose writers to dwell on his own personal experiences (in this case, at the court of the Great King Artaxerxes II), in what might be considered tantamount to a proto-autobiography,[2] but also to have developed a unique genre of historical writing, following Herodotus yet going beyond his model, in creating works situated between fact and fiction.[3] On the one hand, Ctesias seems to

---

[1] For a bibliography on Ctesias and his *Persica*, see the references in Alonso-Núñez (1996); Lenfant (2004); Wiesehöfer/Lanfranchi/Rollinger (2011). The fragments and testimonia of Ctesias presented here follow the accepted sequence of Jacoby (1958), as augmented by Lenfant (2004), and should be understood as *FGrH*, no. 688. See also Tuplin (2004a) for further references. The first full translations of all fragments was in Latin (Müller 1844), followed by the French ones of Auberger (1991), Lenfant (2004) and Nichols (2008). Fragments of the *Indica* were translated into English by McCrindle (1881) and Nichols (2011), those of the *Persica* by Gilmore (1881) followed by those of Llewellyn-Jones/Robson (2010) and Stronk (2010). In 1972 König published a German translation and commentary of the *Persica*. The text of Photius was translated by Henry (1947) into French and Wilson (1994) into English.

[2] Alongside fifth-century travel descriptions; cf. Momigliano 1971: 57.

[3] Cf. Lenfant 2004: XXVIII–XXXII.

have continued an already existing tradition of works called *Persica*, written by Dionysus of Miletus (*FGrH*, no. 687; Suda, s.v. "Διονύσιος", Delta, 1180: Περσικὰ Ἰάδι διαλέκτῳ), Charon of Lampascus (*FGrH*, no. 262, 687b; Περσικὰ ἐν βιβλίοις β) and by Hellanicus of Lesbos (*FGrH*, no. 4).[4] Ctesias followed in the footsteps of these works in providing colorful ethnographic depictions of Eastern cultures, mythologies and political history, yet his innovation was to do so with an internal, Persian, point of view.[5] The espousal of the Persian attitude to the past apparently opened the door for the inclusion of novelistic features in Ctesias' description, as well as for making it more disposed to the adoption of Greek literary techniques and allusions (see below). On the other hand, Ctesias combined his presentation with a story of a grand historical process, like Herodotus' "Great Event" but in a way that seems to have marginalized the Greco-Persian Wars into one event among many of the Persian Empire.[6] The new genre challenged generations of readers from antiquity, and continues to defy any well defined appreciation even today.[7] In antiquity, Ctesias' works were not highly regarded. Repeatedly regarded as untrustworthy and deemed a mythographer, whose accounts are sensational and full of pathos and whose details could not be relied upon,[8] Ctesias was thus said to have founded his own "liar school."[9] This attitude appears to be maintained among several scholars today.[10] Yet, both in ancient and modern times, this approach has not precluded Ctesias from being cited widely.[11] For instance, Plutarch uses him extensively in the biography of Artaxerxes, even though he shares this disrespect for the physician (*Art.* 1.4, 6.9, 13.5–7).[12] Indeed, recent years have seen an attempt at a Rehabilitation of

---

[4] See Lenfant 2009.

[5] Marincola 1997: 170.

[6] See Llewellyn-Jones/Robson 2010: 52, 58–68, 83.

[7] "Demetrius" (F T14a.215) calls Ctesias a poet (ποιητής). Cf. P. Högemann in *Der Neue Pauly*, s.v. "Ktesias": "Historiker dem lit. Genre, Romanschriftsteller modernen Kriterien nach." Cf. Jacoby 1922: 2033 and Whitmarsh 2008: 2: "romanticized Persian history"; cf. the attempts of Llewellyn-Jones/Robson 2010: they consider it something more than straightforward "history" writing (4), a melding of "the legendary aspects of Eastern history" with personal observations of recent events (6–7), a "court history" (66–68), a "novella" combined with history (69–76), a "creative dramatic history" (78) and a "melange of history, gossip, fantasy, and (tragic) poetry" (86). See the lengthy discussion in Stronk (2010: 36–51).

[8] See Antigonos of Caristos, *Hist. Mir.* 15; Luc. *VH* 1.3; cf. Gellius, *NA* 9.4.1; Strabo, 1.2.35 and 11.6.3. Most of the criticism was on the *Indica*. See Llewellyn-Jones/Robson 2010: 32–33.

[9] See Braun 2004: 123. On Herodotus in particular D. Fehling, *Herodotus and his "Sources"* (trans. J.G. Howie), Leeds 1989; originally published in German in 1971). See Momigliano 1958; Evans 1968; Pritchett 1993.

[10] Under the influence of Jacoby (1922: 2033, 2045–2047: "gleich Null"); cf. Burn (1962: 12); Momigliano (1975: 134); Cook (1983: 22); Sancisi-Weerdenburg (1983: 21; 1987: 35, 43); Briant (2002: 7, 265); Lenfant (2004: CXXIV–CXXVII). On Ctesias' love of sensationalism see Cizek, 1975: 547. On his many shortcomings as a historian see Bigwood 1976; 1978; 1980: 197; 1983 (errors, doubtful numbers, questionable geography, bias, simplification, confusion, duplications, anachronisms, etc.). Cf. MacGinnis 1988. A comparison with Herodotus is usually to Ctesias' disadvantage. Cf. Drews 1973: 103–116. The first publication of the celebrated epitome of Ctesias by Photius (see below), by Stephanus (1566) saw it appended to the text of Herodotus.

[11] See Arrian, *Anab.* 5.4.2: ἱκανὸς καὶ Κτησίας ἐς τεκμηρίωσιν. Cf. Karttunen 1997: 636.

[12] He also quotes Ctesias in *De sollertia animalium* (974de), where oxen in Susan carry only a hundred buckets of water each and it is impossible to make them fetch more; cf. Ael. *NA* 7.1 = F 34a. Stadter (1965: 53) assumes that Plutarch made direct use of Ctesias in *Mul. Virt.* 246ab, on Persian women, as this story also

Ctesias, his reputation and the information that he gives.[13] A clear judgment is difficult to obtain, since Ctesias' works have regrettably been lost and are only preserved in several fragments found in a few authors (like Plutarch). Thus, the original content cannot be fathomed with absolute certainty. What is clear is that through his influence upon his immediate readers, chief among them being Xenophon, Ctesias should be seen as one of the most significant and creative writers of the fourth century BCE.

Ctesias was born in the second half of the fifth century BCE,[14] in Cnidos (T 2–4, 7c, 11h, 12), one of the two centers of medical practice in classical Greece,[15] and the place where he presumably studied and practiced this occupation. His father was named Ctesiochus (T 1, 11h) or Ctesiarchus (T 1).[16] According to his own report, he was taken prisoner and brought to the Persian court because of his medical expertise (Diod. 2.32.4). His departure from Persia involved some sort of trickery; according to Ctesias' report, he was apparently involved in mediation between the king on the one hand and Evagoras, king of Cyprian Salamis, and Conon, the Athenian admiral (and soon to become an admiral of the new Persian fleet) on the other, and made sure he would be assigned a diplomatic mission (Plut. *Art.* 21.1–4;[17] cf. F 30.72–4), an opportunity he used to bring about his escape from Persia and the service to the Great King (398/397 BCE, cf. Diod. 14.46.6); Ctesias departed on his way to Sparta, but somehow was detained in Rhodes (F 30.75).[18] He may have settled in Sparta or returned home, to Cnidus,[19] and may also have continued practicing medicine.[20]

---

appears in Nicolaos of Damascus, *FGrH* 90 F 66, 43–44. But this is not necessarily correct. Hamilton (1969: liii, 191) believes Ctesias is the source of Plutarch's *Alexander* 69.1.

[13] For a high opinion of Ctesias' account of the revolt of Inaros see the references in Bigwood 1976: 1 n. 2. Cf. Cawkwell 1972: 39–40. For Ctesias as basically trustworthy on the tyrannical and capricious ruthlessness of rulers see Lewis 1977: 29. See also Stevenson 1997: 72 ("basic honesty in the description of contemporary events in which he was not personally involved"), 75, 81; Murray 2001: 42 n. 57; Dalley 2003: 182; Lenfant 2004: CXXIII; Llewellyn-Jones/Robson 2010: 53; Stronk 2010: 54. For a view that sees Ctesias as faithfully transmitting local traditions see Momigliano 1931; cf. Lenfant 1996.

[14] Brown 1978: 10: between 440 and 435.

[15] See Nutton 2004: 69–70.

[16] There is clearly some corruption of the name in the MSS tradition. Ctesias' father was apparently also a physician (cf. F 68), and the family regarded itself as Asclepiad (T4: ἦν Ἀσκληπιάδης τὸ γένος). Ctesias was contemporary to Hippocrates; cf. Lenfant, 2004: VIII, and is described as one of his relatives (συγγενὴς αὐτοῦ [*scil.* Ἱπποκράτους]). Cf. F 67.

[17] It is clear that the second version Plutarch cites at 21.4, and according to which the physician is said to insert a section into Conon's letter, suggesting that Ctesias would be sent to assist the Athenian admiral, does not come from another author (*contra* Haug 1854: 98; Smith 1881: 4; Mantey 1888: 17; Brown 1978: 17; Stevenson 1997: 117–118 and Binder 2008: 284) but from Ctesias himself as a tale illustrating an instance of heroic trickery, modeled on Odysseus and others.

[18] As Lenfant (2004: xxii–xix) points out, the trial mentioned (καὶ κρίσις πρὸς τοὺς Λακεδαιμονίων ἀγγέλους ἐν Ῥόδωι, καὶ ἄφεσις: at Rhodes there was a trial concerning the Spartan envoys followed by an acquittal) is in fact not of Ctesias, but of the Spartan delegates, *contra* Jacoby 1922: 2036; Brown 1978: 18; Eck 1990: 423–424. Cf. Llewellyn-Jones/Robson 2010: 17.

[19] Sparta: cf. Lenfant 2004: XX–XIX; Cnidus: Brown 1978: 18; Lenfant 2004: XXIII.

[20] Brown 1978: 19.

Ctesias' account, however, is problematic, as the circumstances of his captivity are not clear[21] and the story of his escape bears a striking resemblance to the tale of Democedes, who escaped to Croton after a period of medical service in the court of Darius the Great (Hdt 3.129–137).[22] The MSS of Diodorus state that Ctesias spent seventeen years (ἑπτακαίαδεκα) in Persia. This figure appears also in Tzetzes (*Chil.* 1.85–89 [= 82–86 Kiessling] = T1b) and should not be considered a scribal error, but the correct form inserted by either Ctesias himself or a later reader. Since it is known that the year of Ctesias' departure from Persia is the year 398/397,[23] it would seem that Ctesias' medical services began with Darius II in 415/414 BCE, even though this is not corroborated.[24] It might be the case that the number of years was fabricated by the physician, presumably just as the whole story of the way in which he arrived at Persia might have been falsified.[25] Some scholars suppose that Ctesias was not captured, but actually invited to the king's court because of his medical skills.[26] In fact, it might be that Ctesias never claimed to have been captured: no story of such an event exists in ancient summaries of his work, and one would assume it should be found in some form had the physician dwelled on these circumstances. It is not entirely unlikely that some later reader inserted this depiction to the introduction, in an error stemming from a conflation of the story of Democedes with that of Ctesias. Another option would thus be to discard the number "seventeen," like some scholars who emend the text to "seven years" (ἑπτὰ ἔτη), corresponding to the date of Artaxerxes' rise to power (405/404).[27] The emendation might be in place.[28] It might be that some confusion entered Ctesias' MSS, presumably the introduction to his renowned work, the *Persica* (see below). It would seem that the physician referred to himself as working in the service of Artaxerxes II. Since he left Persia in the year 398/397 (and apparently finished the story recounted in the work at this dramatic date), he seems to have written only on the first seven years of the Persian monarch (405/404–398/397 BCE). A conclusion of one reader was apparently that Ctesias spent seven years in court, a detail which he inserted. Although this comment found its way into the text of Ctesias, it does not prove that it is precise; nothing in fact prevent Ctesias from coming to the Achaemenid court later than 405/404 and for a shorter period than seven years. All the events in which he describes his own personal presence in Persia are between 401 and 398/397 BCE. To solve some discrepancy which another reader found

---

[21]   See the suggestion of Brown (1978: 7–10) to the effect that Ctesias was captured during Pissouthnes' revolt (414 BCE). Cf. Stronk (2004/2005: 102–104) on the proposal that it was during the revolt of Amorges, followed by Llewellyn-Jones/Robson (2010: 14). See the equally unconvincing attempt of Stevenson (1997: 4–6) stressing Lysander's role.

[22]   On the resemblance, see Griffiths 1987: 48, who also proposes that Ctesias borrowed from Herodotus the story of the circumstances that brought his predecessor to Persia, in order to justify his own employment at the court of the foreign king. Lenfant (2004: X–XI n. 19) rejects the comparison.

[23]   F 30.72–74; cf. Plut. *Art.* 21.4 and Diodorus 14.46.6.

[24]   See Bigwood 1978: 20 n. 3.

[25]   See Jacoby 1922: 2033 (allegedly to be superior to any other predecessor). Cf. Bigwood 1964: 177.

[26]   Cf. Briant 2002: 264, who assumes Ctesias was contracted.

[27]   Following Müller 1844: 2. See Drews 1973: 103; Bigwood 1978: 19.

[28]   Note that even those who accept the figure of "seventeen" propose that Ctesias began his actual royal service in 404 BCE, spending previous years at the service of the satrap Tissaphernes. Cf. Brown 1978: 8–10; Eck 1990: 431–432.

in the work (seemingly what he construed as evidence for Ctesias' presence in court during Darius II's reign),[29] in a second interference with the text, the figure was manifestly and erroneously hyper-corrected to "seventeen." It would seem that the ancients were not sure about the period of Ctesias' stay in Persia, a perplexity which is also relevant to the date of composition of his most important book (below).

The first certain event related to Ctesias is his medical assistance to the king during the battle of Cunaxa and his treatment of his flesh wound (Plut. *Art.* 11.3) in 401 BCE.[30] Treatment of the king was presumably not the main reason for Ctesias' presence at court. Ctesias' narrative also portrays him as the personal physician of the queen mother Parysatis and the Great King's wife and children (Plut. *Art.* 1.4).[31] As we mostly hear of Greek physicians treating Persian royal women (Democedes and Atossa: Hdt. 3.133–134; Apollonides of Cos and Amytis: F 14.44), one might presume that Ctesias was largely employed (or even contracted) to attend to the court women, especially Parysatis.[32] It may be that Ctesias' service was called for as he happened to be at the scene of battle, probably escorting the royal entourage.[33] For his service to the king he received royal gifts; he reports that once he was given two swords (F 45.9), one from the king and the other from the king's mother Parysatis. The occasion could well be the aftermath of Cunaxa (Plut. *Art.* 14.1).[34]

Apart from attending to the royal family, Ctesias maintained that he had participated in various activities. He claimed to have negotiated with Cyrus' Greek soldiers immediately after the battle of Cunaxa, as part of a delegation which included a person loyal to Tissaphernes, namely Phalinus (Plut. *Art.* 13.5–6). This service might have been asked of him since as a Greek on the spot he was most suited to conversing with the mercenaries. This does not necessarily mean that Ctesias was loyal to Tissaphernes, but quite the con-

---

[29] Cf. an interesting inference of Syme (1988: 139) to the effect that Ctesias already attended upon Darius II in 405 and accompanied him during the campaign of northern Media (see Xen. *Hell.* 2.1.12). But cf. Bigwood 1978: 20 n. 3 and Llewellyn-Jones/Robson 2010: 13 on the relatively short treatment of Darius II in the *Persica*.

[30] Cf. Diodorus' depiction of Cunaxa (14.23.6). Cf. Plut. *Art.* 14.1 on the award given to Ctesias after the battle. It does not seem probable that Ctesias was captured during the battle of Cunaxa, as mentioned by Bähr (1824: 13–15) and König (1972: 1 n. 17); cf. Jacoby 1922: 2033–2035, but it may be that the king's wound provided him with the first opportunity to be of service to the king. If this interpretation is true, it corresponds exactly to the story of Democedes, who treated Darius the Great's sprained ankle. Cf. Bigwood (1983: 348) on the possibility that this assistance was exaggerated by Ctesias. Cf. the latter's description of the injury incurred by Cyrus the Great in his battle against the Derbikes (F 9.7: πίπτει καὶ αὐτὸς Κῦρος ἐκ τοῦ ἵππου... ἐξ οὗ καὶ τελευτᾶι. τότε δὲ ζῶντα ἀνελόμενοι αὐτὸν οἱ οἰκεῖοι ἐπὶ τὸ στρατόπεδον ᾔεσαν; Cyrus fell off his horse... as a consequence Cyrus died... however, Cyrus was taken up before dying and brought back to camp by his servants). Though carried out of the battle, Cyrus' life could not be saved by his men (as opposed to Ctesias' own achievement).

[31] On the role of the physician in the Achaemenid court, see Briant 2002: 264–266; Llewellyn-Jones/Robson 2010: 15. Ctesias mentions another Greek doctor at court (Apollonides of Cos: F 14.34, 44, who treated Megabyzus and Amytis, Artaxerxes I's daughter. Other physicians were Egyptians (cf. Hdt. 3.129).

[32] All the doctors reported to have saved a male noble (Diorous I: Hdt. 3.132 and Megabyzus: F 14.34, respectively) and later to be employed in the service of women. On Ctesias' contemporary Greek gynecological knowledge and practice, found in the Hippocratic texts, see Hanson 1991 and King 1998.

[33] On the manner royal women travelled with the court during military campaigns or the seasonal migration of the king see Brosius 1996: 84, 87, 90–93. Cf. Curtius Rufus, 3.3.22–25; Plut. *Alex.* 43.2.

[34] See Bigwood 1995: 137.

trary, that the king wanted another Greek in the delegation, to balance the person loyal to his dubious satrap. Ctesias helped Clearchus, Cyrus the Younger's Spartan general, while waiting for his execution, by handing him a comb and providing for a meal to be sent to him (Plut. *Art.* 18.1–4). He claimed to have done so on behalf of the queen mother Parysatis (F 27.69: καὶ θεραπείαν δι' αὐτῆς ἔπραξε; cf. Plut. *Art.* 18.3: καὶ ταῦτα μὲν ὑπουργῆσαι καὶ παρασχεῖν χάριτι καὶ γνώμηι τῆς Παρυσάτιδος), which might be true, as only through a Greek messenger could Parysatis actively reward a soldier who was essentially employed against the king.[35] Presumably, this service was rendered in 400 BCE. Ctesias also came to admire the general (*Art.* 13.7). In return, Clearchos gave Ctesias his signet ring. As mentioned, Ctesias also functioned in various diplomatic activities with Evagoras on behalf of the Great King: once by receiving envoys in order to obtain letters from Aboulites [the secretary?] (F 30.72) and once by delivering a letter from Artaxerxes to Conon (Plut. *Art.* 21.1–4).[36] We learn that Ctesias attained this position when the letters failed to go through the hands of another court physician, Polycrites, who was presumably associated with another person in court. Since the purpose of the deal forming between Evagoras and Artaxerxes was to weaken Spartan power in the eastern Aegean and in Cyprus, Ctesias, a native of Cnidus, a pro-Spartan city (yet one that was a member of the Athenian confederacy between 479–412 BCE),[37] was in a perfect position to serve as a mediator, and to be employed in negotiations with the Spartans designed to deceive them.[38] The central place given to Ctesias in these negotiations also spells the reconciliation of the king and his mother, if it is true that after the murder of Stateira, Parysatis was banished to Babylon (Plut. *Art.* 19.10).[39] All or some of these accounts seemed suspect to ancient readers[40] and still are to modern ones. Dorati (1995) in fact goes on to propose that Ctesias was never really present at the court of Artaxerxes II, and that he concocted this story in order to be in a better position to refute Herodotus. However, outright rejection of Ctesias is not needed,[41] and there may be a grain of truth to his tales.[42]

Ctesias' most celebrated work was the lost *Persica*, which must have been impressive, narrating, in 23 books, the history of the East, from the legendary King Ninos (F 1 = Diod. 2.1.4–2.7.1) to the days of Artaxerxes II, down to the year 398/397 BCE.

---

[35]   Accepting this story are: Stevenson 1997: 73; Briant 2002: 238, 265; Lenfant 2004: XII–XIII.

[36]   The letter finds its parallel in the summary of Photius (F 30.74), where Conon is mentioned as sending a letter to the king and Ctesias.

[37]   And a pro-Spartan himself, as evidenced by his account of Spartan valour and enhanced importance during the wars with Persia. Cf. Plutarch's description of him as φιλολάκων (*Art.* 13.7). But cf. Eck 1990: 416–417.

[38]   See Brown 1978: 18 n. 83.

[39]   This "Babylonian exile" of Parysatis presumably also restricted her close physician, and might explain a period of about two years in which Ctesias was not employed in any diplomatic mission and did not have any knowledge of current affairs.

[40]   Isoc. *Evag.* 55–56 omits Ctesias' role altogether; cf. *Philip* 62. Cf. Diodorus 14.39.

[41]   Cf. an attempt to counter this theory by Lenfant (1996: 353 n. 14). Some of Dorati's arguments can be easily contested: e.g. for other historians we sometimes lack external evidence that they were historical agents – for instance, Diodorus never mentions Xenophon as such. The fact that Xenophon does not mention Ctesias may be done with other purposes in mind (see below) and does not necessarily disprove the physician's account.

[42]   Cf. Stevenson 1997: 116, who believes Ctesias on the last diplomatic mission ("…no obvious reason to exaggerate his role"). Cf. 140.

It would seem that at some point the work was divided into two parts.[43] Though widely read and popular, it is probably because of the various summaries made of this immense work that it has disappeared from sight.[44] Books 1–6, dealing with pre-Persian history and sometimes called *Assyriaca*, are largely known to us via Diodorus (= F 1–8) and the fragments of Nicolaus of Damascus.[45] The books were separated into three volumes of Assyrian history and three of Median history.[46] The story begins with the Assyrian king Ninus, who established an empire (through wars in Babylonia, Armenia and Media), and after campaigning in Bactria returned to found a new city (which he named after himself). Ninus conquered Bactra, with the machination of his wife Semiramis. The latter succeeded Ninus, to become a great queen and heroine of the first books. Semiramis founded the city of Babylon, and expanded the empire to the Indus. From Ninyas, her son and heir, and onward, Ctesias apparently derogatively portrayed Assyrian luxury and decadence. The last Assyrian king, Sardanapallus, was defeated by the Medes and commited suicide. Diodorus (F 5) provides a brief outline of the Median section, and especially omits the popular romance story between the Saka queen Zarinaia and the Mede Stryangeos (F 7–8). Ctesias did not have Cyrus the Great as a relative of the last Median king Astyages, but as his cupbearer, who gradually obtained power and eventually revolted.[47]

Books 7–23 of the *Persica* were summarized by the Byzantine patriarch and humanist scholar Photius (820–c. 892 CE) in his *Bibliotheca*.[48] This *oeuvre* consists of 279 chapters (codices), not uniform in length or quality, which serve to abridge the content of 386 works that its dedicatee (Photius' brother) manifestly did not read.[49] Most of the cited works are lost, including Ctesias' works (Codex 72). Book 7 of the *Persica* began with Cyrus the Great after he assumed power; his campaigns (Ecbatana, Bactria, Saka, Lydia and the Derbikkes) are related in Books 7–11 (F 9).[50] It may be the case that Book 10 was devoted to the ethnographic and geographical description of central Asia.[51] One might think of a parallel in Book 2 of Herodotus' *Histories*, dedicated to Egypt. After Cyrus' death from a fatal wound, the account moved to that of his successor, Cambyses, at the beginning of Book 12 (F 13). This book included a depiction of Cambyses' Egyptian campaign, his death and the familiar tale of the ururper-Magus ousted by the Seven conspirators, headed by Darius (cf. Hdt. 3.61–80 and DB. 26–71). Presumably Book 12

---

[43]   Broadly speaking, *Persica* is the name of the entire work, cf. T8, T9, F1h, F1n. But in a narrow sense, it is the title of only the second part, see Lenfant 2004: XXXIX. Cf. Strabo (14.2.15), who mentions two titles. See Jacoby 1922: 2040.

[44]   See in general Mendels 2004: 19–21.

[45]   It is thanks to Lenfant (2004) that some fragments of Nicolaus, disregarded by Jacoby, are now included among the fragments of Ctesias (F 1pδ-ε, F 6b, F 8c, F 8d).

[46]   On Diodorus' adaptation of Ctesias, see: Bigwood 1980; Llewellyn-Jones/Robson 2010: 38–40; Sulimani 2011. Cf. Comploi 2002, for a theory that Diodorus' version of Semiramis' story should not be regarded as a mere summary of Ctesias.

[47]   Yet Lenfant (2004: 93) puts Cyrus' ascent in Book 7.

[48]   For the date of this work, see: Mango 1975: 38, 40–42; Wilson 1983: 85, 93–94; Lemerle 1986: 38.

[49]   On some occasions, Photius is even known to repeat himself, see Llewellyn-Jones/Robson 2010: 43–44. In others still, he is seen to be inaccurate, see Wilson 1994: 5.

[50]   It could be that Photius intentionally disregarded books 1–6, see Stronk 2010: 14, 141ff; but it is more likely that these were not in his possession.

[51]   See Nichols 2008: 26.

continued with the reign of Darius I, and dwelled on his two Scythian campaigns (the first lead by Ariaramnes). Book 13 would then have been devoted to Xerxes' rule and the Greco-Persian War (F 13.24–32). After Xerxes' assassination and upheaval in court, Artaxerxes I assumed power, and his reign apparently began in Book 14. This part of the *Persica* is marked by the intricate relations of the courtier and satrap Megabyzus with the king and court, and the revolt of Inaros the Lybian. It also contains one of three dominant women of the *Persica*, namely Amestris, the widow of Xerxes and the king's mother (F 14.34, 39, 42–46). Her death as well as that of Artaxerxes I come at the end of Book 17. The next book is devoted to Darius II Ochus, the violent way he gained power and the suppression of internal revolts (Arsites, Artyphios, Pisuthnes, the eunuch Artoxares and the king's son-in-law Terituchmes). It also introduces the last powerful woman of the work, Parysatis (first mentioned at F 15.48). The last books, from 19 and onward, relate the reign of Artaxerxes II; Photius' epitome here can be compared with Plutarch's adaptation in the biography *Artaxerxes*.[52] The contents of Books 19 and 20 are Cyrus the Younger's rebellion, its aftermath and court intrigues which saw Parysatis' systematic efforts to remove the men responsible for Cyrus' death and desecration of his body. Book 21 had the imprisoned Clearchus as its focus; the general was executed, presumably at the request of Queen Stateira. This book (or probably Book 22) contained the assassination of the latter. The last book reported Ctesias' last diplomatic mission, though Photius' summary is garbled and probably indicates his weariness of the lengthy account.

In the same codex (72), Photius also abridges another lost work of the physician, a monograph on India called *Indica*.[53] In this composition Ctesias apparently included ethnographic, geographical, botanical and zoological descriptions of India (F 45–52), or properly speaking only of the Indus valley and its north-western geographical part. Placed within the genre of marvel or paradoxical descriptions, it was notorious for its colorful tall stories,[54] especially about dog-headed people (Κυνοκέφαλοι: F 45.37) or unicorns (F 45.45, cf. F 45q), or miraculous springs (e.g. F 45.6, 20, 31, 49).[55] The people described are said to be very just (F 45.16, 20, 30; cf. 23, 37, 43). Yet, these fantasies were not completely figments of Greek or Ctesias' own imagination, as the portrayals at times correspond with local pictures or traditions.[56] Some creatures described might be real, like the elephant (F 45.7, 15) or the parrot (F 45.8).[57] Ctesias apparently included more factual ethnographic material than the extant text reveals, but it seems that this was of less interest to Photius or any other excerptor.[58]

---

[52] On which see Almagor, forthcoming (b).

[53] Or λόγοι Ἰνδικοὶ (F 46a).

[54] Of immensely tall creatures (F 45.7–8) or incredible people, like the Enotokoitai, who have ears big enough to cover their arms as far as the elbow and their entire back (F 45.50).

[55] On the character of the *Indica*, see Stevenson 1997: 7–8; Lenfant 2004: CXXXVII–CLVI; and Nichols 2011: 18–21. For real animals that can be Ctesias' "wild horned asses" see Shepard 1930: 26–33.

[56] For instance, the long-eared people are found in the *Mahābhārata* (2.28.44; 6.47.13): the *Karnaprāvarana* meaning "the people who cover themselves with their ears." See Kirtley (1963).

[57] See Bigwood 1993a and 1993b. See Karttunen 1997: 635 n. 2.

[58] Cf. F 45.16, 30; Nichols 2011: 105–106.

Unfortunately, Photius' methods in his epitomes are not entirely clear,[59] and this fact hinders a true appreciation of such lost works as that of Ctesias.[60] Yet, compared with Plutarch's account, his sections pertaining to the period of Artaxerxes II seem extremely succinct.[61] This conclusion becomes apparent when one bears in mind the notoriously lengthy nature of Ctesias' descriptions (cf. below). There are signs that original speeches and whole conversations were removed by Photius, or reduced by him to indirect speech (cf. F 16.67 and Plut. *Art.* 15.1–7).[62] Some details are missing. For instance, in Photius' summary of the account of the battle of Cunaxa, Tissaphernes, the Persian Satrap does not appear, yet his role seems to have importance in the narrative, judged by other passages (cf. F 24, 27.68) and from the rewards he is known to have received (Diod. Sic. 14.26.4); it is more probable that Photius shortened the original version.[63] Out of carelessness, apparently, the patriarch refers only to an anonymous person who picked up the blood-soaked saddlecloth of Cyrus the Younger after he was hit (F 16.67: Ἀρτοξέρξης δῶρα ἔδωκε τῶι ἐνέγκαντι τὸν Κύρου πῖλον), and not to the fact that it was an attendant of Mithridates (Plut. *Art.* 11.6), who is later to play a significant role in the next scenes, as can be inferred from Plutarch (*Art.* 11.5, 14.5, 15–16) and from Photius' subsequent reading (Ἀρτοξέρξης παρέδωκεν αἰτησαμένηι Μιτραδάτην Παρυσάτιδι, ἐπὶ τραπέζης μεγαλαυχήσαντα ἀποκτεῖναι Κῦρον...).[64] A summary written in haste is also Photius' brief note that the Carian, the other person who fatally injured Cyrus the Younger, is tortured by Parysatis, allegedly of her own accord (F 16.67), a statement which is seen not to be accurate by comparison to Plutarch (*Art.* 14.10).[65] Photius is not quick to correct himself, after he had a mistake; at one point he believes that the king himself severed the head of Cyrus the Younger (F 16.64: καὶ αἰκισμὸς τοῦ σώματος Κύρου ὑπὸ τἀδελφοῦ Ἀρτοξέρξου· τήν τε γὰρ κεφαλὴν καὶ τὴν χεῖρα, μεθ' ἧς τὸν Ἀρτοξέρξην ἔβαλλεν, αὐτὸς ἀπέτεμε, καὶ ἐθριάμβευσεν), but afterwards wrote as if it was another person (F 16.67: ...Βαγαπάτου τοῦ ἀποτεμόντος προστάξει βασιλέως τὴν κεφαλὴν ἀπὸ τοῦ σώματος Κύρου; corresponding to Plut. *Art.* 17). Another inference from this comparison to Plutarch is that Photius' summary appears erroneous and even self-contradictory

---

[59]   On different conjectures with regard to his methods see: Wilson 1968; 1983: 95 [on writing from memory]; Lemerle 1986: 39–40, 223–224; Hägg 1973: 213–218 [on diverse methods]. Regarding Photius' reliability, see Goossens 1950 (esp. 519 on his reading of Ctesias). On the manner in which Photius adapted his original, see Hägg 1973: 97–116.

[60]   On Photius' summary of Ctesias, see Bigwood 1976: 2–5; Stronk 2010: 34–35, 141–146, who does not exclude the possibility that Photius used an altered copy of the work, perhaps even an *epitome* of the *Persica*, and one made by Pamphila of Epidaurus (1st century CE). Yet, the mistakes Photius makes (below) seem to reflect a reading of the original.

[61]   See Bigwood (1989: 308) on the *Indica*. In comparison with another work, it appears that Photius' version at a certain point is less than a fifth of the original account.

[62]   See Gera 1993: 207–208. Photius was interested only in the content of the descriptions and less in their structure or form; cf. Bigwood 1989: 311.

[63]   See Bigwood 1983: 355 n. 64. Plutarch also seems to minimize this satrap's role. See Wylie 1992: 128.

[64]   The conclusion of Binder (2008: 233–234) that a different source is used by Plutarch is not needed.

[65]   It seems inconceivable that Parysatis had the authority to execute the Carian herself; indeed immediately afterwards (F 16.67), Photius himself remarks that Parysatis requested Mithridates of the king. There is no reason to infer conclusions based on this careless summary. Cf. Brosius 1996: 114 n. 76. Cf. Bigwood 1976: 4 n.13, who claims that "Photius has perhaps been led astray by the fate of the Carian eunuch [*sic!*], which he described in the preceding sentence."

at times (cf. Plut. *Art.* 14–17 and 14.10). The names given in Photius' MSS are occasionally different from those of Plutarch (cf. Plut. *Art.* 1.4, 17.1), and this variance may stem from textual corruption during the copying of either Ctesias' work or the *Bibliotheca*.[66]

The possibility that Ctesias' sojourn in Persia lasted seven and not seventeen years has been proposed above. This figure might already have been found interpolated in the introduction to the *Persica*. The work's date of publication is hard to ascertain, but a remark found in Photius' summary is usually employed to shed light on the date. According to this account, palm trees grew on the grave of Clearchus the Spartan, after he was executed by the king (cf. Plut. *Art.* 18.8). Photius claims that this spectacle was seen eight years after Clearchus' death (F 27.71: καὶ τὸ χῶμα δὲ τοῦ Κλεάρχου δι' ἐτῶν ὀκτὼ μεστὸν ἐφάνη φοινίκων, οὓς ἦν κρύφα Παρύσατις, καθ' ὃν καιρὸν ἐκεῖνος ἐτελεύτησε, διὰ εὐνούχων καταχώσασα). Since the event took place in c. 401/400 BCE, the year 393/392 BC is usually given as the *terminus post quem* for the work.[67] This interpretation might not be necessary, if the figure of "eight" comes not from Ctesias, but from Photius' misunderstanding of the "seven years" mentioned at the beginning of the work. If Ctesias' version had καὶ νῦν at this point,[68] it is easy to comprehend the divergence between Plutarch's phrase "shortly afterwards" (φοινίκων δέ τινων διασπαρέντων, ὀλίγῳ χρόνῳ θαυμαστὸν ἄλσος ἀναφῦναι) as his own interpretation, and Photius' "in the eighth year," as two attempts to clarify the date.[69] The two descriptions are hardly compatible with each other, and this fact seems to suggest that the original indication of time was not sufficiently clear. The "eight years" of Photius seem to be his own phrasing, based on the understanding that the work was written in the eighth year of Artaxerxes II.[70] If this constraint is removed, the work could just as well have been written even later than the 390s BCE.

Related to this question is the issue of the location where Ctesias' works were published. It does not seem obligatory for Ctesias to be present in Persia at the time of composition.[71] Yet, sometimes we do find in antiquity the view that he wrote his works while serving the monarch. See Lucian's opinion (*Hist. Conscr.* 39 = T11hδ): "The one duty of the historian is to relate how things happened. He [Ctesias] would not be able to do this as long as he was either afraid of Artaxerxes, whom he served as physician, or hoped to receive a purple garment or a horse from Nisaeon as payment for praising

---

[66]   The differences between Plutarch and Photius probably stem from copyists' errors. On other instances in other sections of the *Bibliotheca*, see Bigwood 1976: 6–9; 1978: 27 n. 30. For convincing arguments in favor of the Plutarchan variant, see Lenfant 2004: 272 n. 608; 274 n. 629; Schmitt 2006: 75–77, 177.

[67]   See Brown 1978: 6; Eck 1990: 433–434; Stevenson 1997: 6; Lenfant 2004: VIII, XXIV n. 72; 159 n. 728.

[68]   It must be remembered that Ctesias does not profess to have seen it. See Stevenson 1997: 4 and Lenfant 2004: 159 n. 728. Cf. the far-fetched assumption of König (1972: 26 nn. 13, 29) that the physician returned to Persia, rightly rejected by Lenfant 2004: XXII. Cf. the equally implausible suggestion of Rettig (1827), that Ctesias did not leave Persia before 394–393.

[69]   Palm trees (*Phoenix dactylifera*) bear fruit four to eight years after planting. Therefore, Jacoby's two attempts to emend the text as an attempt to reconcile Plutarch and Photius are clearly wrong and not needed: the first (1922: 2034) was to propose "during two years" and the second (1958: 481) was διὰ μηνῶν ὀκτώ (eight months).

[70]   Cf. the question of Brown (1978 n. 23): "Can he be counting the eight years from 398 instead of 400 BC?".

[71]   Cf. Jacoby 1922: 2046–2047.

the king in his writing."[72] In this image, Ctesias was apparently cautious and managed to maintain a neutral position in the conflicts at court. But his *Persica* appears more of an open and outspoken work, which did not present Artaxerxes II (or any Persian king) in an entirely favorable light.[73] Following this logic, the *Persica* was probably written in a Greek country, outside of the monarch's reach,[74] and the *Indica*, which has far more nuances and innuendos, should have been composed in Persia.[75] For some of these innuendos, it is possible to compare some scenes in Plutarch's *Artaxerxes*, adapted from the *Persica*, or some scenes from the later books summarized by Photius, and observe that the *Indica* fragments allude to them.[76] If the *Indica* was composed earlier and insinuated actual contemporary scenes at court, it would be probable to assume that it was written during Ctesias' presumed stay in Babylon (400–398 BCE). There are, in fact, several hints pointing to this venue: the *Matrichora*'s description (below) evokes the Dragon of Marduk shown on the Gate of Ishtar at Babylon;[77] Ctesias claims to have seen an elephant uproot a date-palm in Babylon (F 45bα); there is a comparison of the palms in India to those in Babylon (F 45.29). In the *Persica* Ctesias seems to have reworked some themes from the earlier work, and to have now placed them in the right context.[78] One interesting passage is mentioned by Diodorus, to the effect that Semiramis heard stories about India, which convinced her to attack the country (F 1b.2.16.2–4):

> When she heard that the people of the Indians was the greatest in the world and that they had the largest and most beautiful land, she decided to campaign against India... India is a land of surpassing magnificence divided by many rivers... there is such a profusion of life's provisions that the natives are always supplied by abundant of pleasures. It is said that there has never been a famine or loss of crops in this country because of its good climate. It has an unbelievable number of elephants beyond those in Libya... there is also an inconceivable source of gold, silver, iron and bronze, and moreover, there are precious stones of all sorts and everything which relates to luxury and wealth.[79]

---

[72] Τοῦ δὴ συγγραφέως ἔργον ἕν – ὡς ἐπράχθη εἰπεῖν. τοῦτο δ' οὐκ ἂν δύναιτο ἄχρι ἂν ἢ φοβῆται Ἀρταξέρξην ἰατρὸς αὐτοῦ ὢν ἢ ἐλπίζῃ κάνδυν πορφυροῦν καὶ στρεπτὸν χρυσοῦν καὶ ἵππον τῶν Νισαίων λήψεσθαι μισθὸν τῶν ἐν τῇ γραφῇ ἐπαίνων.

[73] Cf. Stronk (2010: 51) who claims that Lucian's jeer against Ctesias is unjust.

[74] See Lenfant 2004: XVII, XXIII.

[75] Cf. Stronk (2010: 34), who maintains that Ctesias began writing or at least taking notes with the intention of writing a book.

[76] For instance, *Art*. 19.4, taken from the *Persica*, relates a small bird called *rhyntakes* which has no excrement (γίνεται δὲ μικρὸν ἐν Πέρσαις ὀρνίθιον, ὧι περιττώματος οὐδέν ἐστιν), and is the size of an egg (F 27.70), used as an instrument in the assassination of Stateira. This description parallels the elements found in one depiction of the *Indica* (F 45.34). It describes a small bird called *dikairon* the size of a partridge egg, which buries its excrement so it cannot be found (καὶ ὄρνεόν φησιν ἐπικαλούμενον δίκαιρον... τὸ μέγεθος ὅσον πέρδικος ὠιόν. τοῦτο τὸν ἀπόπατον κατορύσσει, ἵνα μὴ εὑρεθῆι). Cf. Ael. *NA* 4.41.

[77] See Nichols 2011: 105.

[78] Another case can be made between, on the one hand, a reference to a drink that works like wine in disclosing the truth (F 45.31), used by the Great King and on the other, the unfortunate story of Mihtridates, who caused the death of Cyrus the Younger and having revealed this fact while intoxicated at a banquet, brought about his own painful end (*Art*. 11, 15–16).

[79] πυνθανομένη δὲ τὸ τῶν Ἰνδῶν ἔθνος μέγιστον εἶναι τῶν κατὰ τὴν οἰκουμένην καὶ πλείστην τε καὶ καλλίστην χώραν νέμεσθαι, διενοεῖτο στρατεύειν εἰς τὴν Ἰνδικήν... ἡ γὰρ Ἰνδικὴ χώρα διάφορος οὖσα τῷ κάλλει καὶ πολλοῖς διειλημμένη ποταμοῖς ἀρδεύεταί τε πολλαχοῦ καὶ διττοὺς καθ' ἕκαστον ἐνιαυτὸν ἐκφέρει καρπούς· διὸ καὶ τῶν πρὸς τὸ ζῆν ἐπιτηδείων τοσοῦτον ἔχει πλῆθος ὥστε διὰ παντὸς ἄφθονον ἀπόλαυσιν τοῖς ἐγχωρίοις παρέχεσθαι. λέγεται δὲ μηδέποτε κατ' αὐτὴν γεγονέναι σιτοδείαν ἢ φθορὰν

If Diodorus does in fact give a short version of Ctesias here, there are two possible conclusions to be drawn: the parallel themes and verbal echoes of this passage and the fragments of the *Indica* lead one to speculate that the *Persica* at this point intentionally alluded to Ctesias' earlier work. A different interesting conclusion would be to propose that the *Indica* is none other than this very digression itself, along the lines of Herodotus' Book 2. This assumption is hampered by the fact that the *Indica* as Photius relates it apparently included references to Ctesias as a historical agent (receiving swords from royal family members) or as an investigator, commenting on animals and sites he had seen. We do not know whether Ctesias inserted himself so early in the *Persica* and alluded to Artaxerxes and Parysatis, who were to appear much later in the work. We should not rule out the possibility that this section, probably written before the *Persica* to form a seemingly single work, was later separated from the rest of the work.

Two other works attributed to Ctesias are the Περὶ τῶν κατὰ τὴν Ἀσίαν φόρων (F 53, 54), whose content was presumably a catalogue of goods that were transferred to the royal house,[80] and the Περίοδος or Περίπλων: F 55–60, containing three books.[81] All have been lost, and there are not enough fragments to construct their content. In the cases of these obscure works, once again, we might suggest that certain sections of the *Persica* could have been taken out and presented as stand-alone works. It is especially hard to imagine a colorful author such as Ctesias composing volumes made up entirely of pedestrian lists. Either these items were falsely identified with Ctesias,[82] because of his renown as a writer describing Persia setting the standard for the following works on the area, just like the spurious works on mountains and rivers (F 73–74),[83] or otherwise (more probably) they were taken out of context from his works to form the relevant books.[84] The same goes for the account of the number of stages, days and parasangs in the Achaemenid Empire, that was ostensibly to be found in the last part of Ctesias' work and that Photius read in his copy (F 33).[85] This section seems to have been a later interpolation in the *Persica*, together with the list of kings "from Ninus and Semiramis to Artaxerxes II," just like a parallel list at the end of Xenophon's *Anabasis* (7.8.26).[86]

καρπῶν διὰ τὴν εὐκρασίαν τῶντόπων. ἔχει δὲ καὶ τῶν ἐλεφάντων ἄπιστον πλῆθος, οἳ ταῖς τε ἀλκαῖς καὶ ταῖς τοῦ σώματος ῥώμαιςπολὺ προέχουσι τῶν ἐν τῇ Λιβύῃ γινομένων, ὁμοίως δὲ χρυσόν, ἄργυρον, σίδηρον, χαλκόν· πρὸς δὲ τούτοις λίθων παντοίων καὶ πολυτελῶν ἔστιν ἐν αὐτῇ πλῆθος, ἔτι δὲ τῶν ἄλλων ἁπάντων σχεδὸν τῶν πρὸς τρυφὴν καὶ πλοῦτον διατεινόντων. ὑπὲρ ὧντὰ κατὰ μέρος ἡ Σεμίραμις ἀκούσασα προήχθη μηδὲν προαδικηθεῖσα τὸν πρὸς Ἰνδοὺς ἐξενεγκεῖν πόλεμον.

[80]   See Lenfant 2007: 205.

[81]   See Stevenson 1997: 143.

[82]   Especially disconcerting is the reference to a region in Italy (F 59). Most of the areas mentioned are in the Black Sea region.

[83]   The work Περὶ τῶν κατὰ τὴν Ἀσίαν φόρων could be identified with the lost work of another *Persica* author, Heracleides of Cumae, termed Παρασκευαστικοί (scil. Βίβλοι) (*FGrH* 689 F 2, 4), which recorded Persian particularities (such as the king's dinner) in five books.

[84]   In fact, Gilmore (1888: 3) has suggested that the minor works of Ctesias were portions of the *Persica*. Cf. Stronk (2010: 12) for a contrary position. Yet, this view may also be correct for the works on mountains and rivers, discussing natural medicinal cures. Similarly, the allegedly medical treatises (F 67–68), in which he criticizes Hippocrates could be derived from the *Persica* or the *Indica*.

[85]   ἀπὸ Ἐφέσου μέχρι Βάκτρων καὶ Ἰνδικῆς ἀριθμὸς σταθμῶν, ἡμερῶν, παρασαγγῶν. κατάλογος βασιλέων ἀπὸ Νίνου καὶ Σεμιράμεως μέχρι Ἀρτοξέρξου. ἐν οἷς καὶ τὸ τέλος.

[86]   See Almagor, forthcoming (a).

Among his sources, Ctesias apparently mentioned royal documents (βασιλικαῖς ἀναγραφαῖς: Diodorus 2.22.5, or βασιλικῶν διφθερῶν: Diod. 2.32.4), which presumably listed or narrated court events.[87] There were also oral traditions, one would imagine, of the distant past, so that Ctesias could have echoed Persian and Near-Eastern folktales, which can be traced in material as early as Mesopotamian myths and prayers and as late as the medieval Epos of Ferdowsi, the *Shahnameh* (the book of kings).[88] It appears that Ctesias gained the trust of the highest-ranking persons at court and was privy to the most intimate secrets of the royal family. For instance, his knowledge of Artaxerxes' original nickname (Ἀρσάκαν: F 15.51; Plut. *Art*. 1.4: Ἀρσίκας), which is different from the official Ar-shu.[89] The version that Ctesias mentions is most probably a name based on the hypocoristic suffix *-ka-*,[90] and he may have learnt of this from Parysatis herself.[91]

Ctesias also claims autopsy (F 8, 15.51, 45.24, 45g),[92] even of phantastical creatures (F 45.15, 45dβ, 45dγ: the *Matrichora*[93]), but he appears to derive most of his facts from informants (soldiers, merchants, officials, courtiers).[94] Although Ctesias mentions the Behistun monument (F1b.2.13.1: πρὸς ὄρος τὸ καλούμενον Βαγίστανον), it should be questioned whether he had actually seen it. Firstly, he attributes its erection to Semiramis and not to Darius I, which cannot be expected. Secondly, although Ctesias' story of Cambyses' assassination of his brother and the tale of the Magus imposter who succeeded to the throne (F 9.8, 13.13) are in some respects closer to the version of the Behistun Inscription (DB 1.26–71) than to that of Herodotus (3.61–80),[95] and although he mentioned the seven Persian nobles led by Darius to oust the pretender, Ctesias' list of the conspirators (F 13.16: Onophas, Idernes, Narondabates, Mardonius, Barisses, Ataphernes, and Darius) disagrees with that of Herodotus (3.70), who is closer to the one in the Behistun inscription (DB 4.80–86).[96] One would assume that almost all of his informants

---

[87] Jacoby (1922: 2047) denies the existence of these written documents, with no good reason. Cf. Briant 2002: 889. Yet see Esther, 2.23, 6.1, 10.2 with Llewellyn-Jones/Robson 2010: 61–64 and Stronk 2010: 15–21, who suggests documents written on perishable material, such as hides or papyri, and in Imperial Aramaic.

[88] Llewellyn-Jones/Robson 2010: 64–65; Stronk 2010: 27–30.

[89] Sachs-Hunger 1988, e.g. 381, 382, close to the Greek Ἄρσης, and apparently derived from the Persian *Rŝa*, stemming from *rŝan-* (= "hero"). This goes against suggestions that take Deinon's version as mentioned by Plutarch (*Art*. 1.4), namely, Ὀάρσης, and reconstruct its original Persian form as derived from the prefix "hu" (= "good"); see Stevenson, 1997: 76–77; cf. Justi 1895: 231; Hintz 1975: 131.

[90] See Kent 1953: 55 § 164; Schmitt 2006: 76.

[91] See Lenfant 2004: 275 n. 632. See the piece of information on Cyrus' name (see below): ...καί φησιν ὁ συγγραφεὺς αὐτὸς παρ' αὐτῆς ἐκείνης τῆς Παρυσάτιδος ταῦτα ἀκοῦσαι... (F 15.51).

[92] F 8: φησὶ δὲ αὐτὸν τῶν πλειόνων ἅ ἱστορεῖ αὐτόπτην γενόμενον ἢ παρ' αὐτῶν Περσῶν, ἔνθα τὸ ὁρᾶν μὴ ἐνεχώρει, αὐτήκοον καταστάντα, οὕτω τὴν ἱστορίαν συγγράψαι. See Marincola 1997, 87, 107. Cf. Bichler 2007.

[93] A name probably deriving from Old Persian *martiya-* ("man") and *khordeh* ("eating"); cf. McCrindle 1881: 298 n. 25. In Modern Persian *mard-kwār* signifies a tiger. It could be that the physician referred to this animal as well. Ctesias' source could have been either Persian or Indian. Cf. Karttunen 1991: 79; cf. also Lenfant 2004: 302 n. 810.

[94] Cf. Drews 1973: 107.

[95] In placing the death of Tanyoxarkes before Cambyses' Egyptian campaign (F 13.12) and in suggesting that the Magus had a different name than the legitimate royal heir (Ctesias: Sphendadates; Behistun: Gaumata; Herodotus: Smerdis). Cf. Bickerman/Tadmor 1978.

[96] Herodotus' Seven are Otanes, Intaphernes, Gobryas, Megabyzus, Hydarnes, Aspathines and Darius (3.70). The Behistun Inscription (DB 68) has Utāna, Vidafarnah, Gaubaruva, Bagabuxša, Vidarna, Ardumaniš

spoke Greek at some level, or at least through Greek interpreters;[97] Ctesias' knowledge of Persian or even Elamite is hardly likely to have been great.[98] A comparison between Plutarch and Photius reveals that, in some instances, Ctesias mentioned the significance of words or names in Persian, for example the fact that Cyrus' name comes from the Persian for "sun": F 15.51 (τίκτει δὲ αὐτῶι ἕτερον υἱὸν βασιλεύουσα, καὶ τίθεται τὸ ὄνομα αὐτοῦ ἀπὸ τοῦ ἡλίου Κῦρον) and Plut. *Art.* 1.3 (μὲν οὖν Κῦρος ἀπὸ Κύρου τοῦ παλαιοῦ τοὔνομα ἔσχεν, ἐκείνῳ δὲ ἀπὸ τοῦ ἡλίου γενέσθαι φασί).[99] Other cases for Persian phrases are Photius' mention of the word for leper, πισάγας (F 14.43, from the Old Persian *paesa, pīs* apparently used for lepers,[100] ἀζαβαρίτης (F 15.49, from Old Persian *hazarapatiš*, "commander of one thousand" (= chiliarch), κίταρις (F 15.50, probably a semitic loanword to denote a crown that entered Old Persian).[101] Another instance still would be Plutarch's 'Ἐξίστασθε, πενιχροί.' τοῦτο δὲ περσιστὶ πολλάκις αὐτοῦ βοῶντος (11.4; cf. Xen. *Anab.* 1.8.26).[102] For the *Indica* passages, Ctesias had Indian informants (F 45.8, 18, 45bα). If Ctesias could speak one of the Imperial languages, it would be best to consider Aramaic the official *lingua franca*.[103] It is interesting to note that some of Ctesias' informants may have spoken in Aramaic, for instance, if the name of "Cunaxa" is indeed a distortion of the Aramaic form Kenishta, namely, (Jewish) synagogue.[104]

Ctesias was well versed in Greek literary sources, for example Herodotus, whom he clearly used,[105] and also deliberately attempted to correct (T 8a, 13, F 9, 13.26, 16.62, cf.

---

and Darius – thus only one name (Aspathines vs. Ardumaniš) does not coincide. Cf. Lenfant 1996: 373–379; 2004: LXXVII–LXXX on the variances. Ctesias' Idernes is apparently the only name corresponding to the Behistun list and Herodotus. Concerning Ctesias' Onophas, note that Herodotus (7.62) has Anaphes as the son of Otanes. cf. Briant 2002: 135, and note that Diodorus (31.19.1) mentions Anaphas as one of the Seven. Similarly, Ctesias' Mardonius could be Gobryas' son. Cf. Lenfant 2004: 262 n. 484. Ctesias thus seems to be based on somewhat misinterpreted oral traditions.

[97] One of them could have been Clearchus, one of Cyrus the Younger's mercenary generals. See Stevenson 1997: 7. Cf. Plut. *Art.* 13.7 on his depiction as Lover of Clearchus (φιλοκλέαρχος).

[98] In general, Greeks had no knowledge of Persian, see Miller 1997: 131–133. Cf. Llewellyn-Jones/ Robson (2010: 55–56) and Stronk (2010: 21–22) for the opinion that Ctesias could understand the language.

[99] Cf. Hesychius, s.v. "Κῦρος"; linguistically, it is hard to base the name *Kurush* on OP **hwar* (= sun; MP *Khwur* or *Hur*). Indeed, this etymological explanation is rejected by Weissbach 1924 and Schmitt 2002: 59–60; 2006: 104. This fact shows perhaps that Ctesias' knowledge of Persian was not profound. Cf. Lenfant 2004: 274 n. 630, who rightly proposes that this piece of information was given to the physician by Parysatis.

[100] Cf. König 1972: 78.

[101] See Ritter (1965: 170–172); Calmeyer (1977: 182–185). Cf. Nicolaus, *FGrH* 90 F 66.45. Cf. the Hebrew "כתר" ("Keter", crown).

[102] Cf. Llewellyn-Jones/Robson 2010: 56. Persian would have been used only sparingly by Ctesias if at all.

[103] Notice the point indicated by Stronk (2010: 22) based on a remark of Diodorus (2.22.5), which he makes into a new fragment (F.*0b); Ctesias depended on hearsay for the use of royal archives in earlier periods.

[104] Obermeyer 1929: 73 n. 1, 249. The Jewish community is probably that of "Kenishta de Safyatib," built, according to Jewish tradition, from stones of the temple in Jerusalem; cf. *Megilah Tractate* 29a. See Barnett 1963: 16–17; Lendle 1986: 198 n. 10; Gasche 1995: 201 n. 1. If this assumption is true, then there is a great probability that Ctesias' informants were familiar with the place and presumably inhabited it.

[105] Compare one obvious borrowing: Herodotus (4.195) mentions an autopsy of a sight in Zakynthos: "even in Zakynthos I saw myself pitch brought up out of a pool of water" (καὶ ἐν Ζακύνθῳ ἐκ λίμνης καὶ ὕδατος πίσσαν ἀναφερομένην αὐτὸς ἐγὼ ὥρων), which is repeated in Ctesias' *Indica* (F 45.20): "In Zacyn-

F 37).[106] Ctesias' familiarity with Attic literature and drama is evidenced, for instance, in his adaptation of Euripides' *Medea*'s phrase and alliteration (v. 476: ἔσωσά σ', ὡς ἴσασιν Ἑλλήνων ὅσοι; I saved your life – as witness all the Greeks who [went on board the Argo with you]; Cf. 515) into ἐγὼ μὲν σὲ ἔσωσα, καὶ σὺ μὲν δι' ἐμὲ ἐσώθης, ἐγὼ δὲ διὰ σὲ ἀπωλόμην ("I saved you and because of me you are still alive, but now I am ruined because of you;" F 8b = Demetr. *De eloc.* 213; cf. 8b* = *P. Ox.* 2330), uttered by Strangeos in a love letter to Zarinaia (on whom see above). One toponym may be specifically derived from an Aeschylan line; the Egyptian (and not Phoenician) town Byblos (F 14.37) evokes the Bybline mountains (*PV* 811) "from which the Nile sends forth his stream" (Βυβλίνων ὀρῶν ἄπο ‖ ἵησι σεπτὸν Νεῖλος εὔποτον ῥέος).[107] The famous (or notorious) dog-heads of India (F 45.37–43; cf. Gell. *NA* 9.4.9; F45oβ; F45pα; F45pβ), that is, the group of people with canine heads who apparently howl like dogs, dwell in caves, wear thin strips of leather, sleep on mattresses of straw and live for 170 (or 200) years, were already seen previously in Herodotus, yet located in the west, in northern Africa (4.191). They even seem to have been mentioned earlier, in Aeschylus (Κυνοκεφάλους) if Strabo (1.2.35) is reliable in his reference. Cf. Hesiod (Ἡμίκυνας: also from Strabo) for an earlier instance.[108] When Ctesias appeared to be writing from his imagination, it seems to be have been fashioned by his reading and from images he was familiar with.[109]

On Ctesias' style and presentation we are not in a position to comment with certainty. His works are completely lost.[110] Yet, ever since the publication of the papyrus *P. Ox.* 2330 (second century CE), there is a consensus among scholars that it reflects the *ipsissima verba* of the physician/historian and that we therefore have at least 29 fragmentary lines of his work.[111] Yet there may be some reasons to believe that the papyrus may be some reworking of Ctesias or even the context of the celebrated line used to establish the

---

thus, there is a spring filled with fish from which pitch is drawn" (καὶ ἐν Ζακύνθωι κρηνῆδας ἰχθυοφόρους εἶναι, ἐξ ὧν αἴρεται πίσσα).

[106] See Bichler 2004: 506; cf. Bigwood 1964: 76, 95–96. Contrary to Herodotus (1.193, 2.150), Nineveh is set on the Euphrates (F 1b.2.3.2). Cf. Lenfant 2004: 235 n. 107. Ctesias also presumably placed the battle of Plataea before that of Salamis (F 13.28–29). Cf. the reference of Dio Chrysostom (11.145) to a historian who altered the order of events; however, the (presumably tongue in cheek) presentation could have been set in a geographical and not chronological order. See the inference of Bigwood (1976: 4; 1978: 19). Ctesias reversed the order of Cyrus the Great's campaigns (F 9.1) from the Herodotean one (1.153) of Lydians before Bactrians and the Saka. Drews (1973: 106) terms this practice "a woeful correction of Herodotus."

[107] See Bigwood 1976: 23–24.

[108] This image was popular afterwards: Scylax, author of the *Periplus* (cf. *FGrH* 688 F 51b; Tzetzes seems to imply, on the contrary, that this was the Scylax the elder) and Artemidorus (Str. 16.4.14). Cf. also Karttunen 1989: 181–182. There have been attempts in research to identify this people or to connect this description to folkloristic traditions. See Lassen 1874: 659–661; Fischer/Wecker 1924: 26; Shafer 1964; Lindegger 1982: 55–62; Karttunen 1989: 183; White 1991: 28–29, 48–50, 71.

[109] See Bigwood 1978: 23.

[110] Cf. the conclusion of Gilmore (1888: 2): "scarcely a sentence of [Ctesias'] text has come down to us verbatim" before the fragment *P. Ox.* 2330 was discovered (= F 8b*). There are also some words or phrases in Photius' epitome which might be regarded as verbatim (e.g. F 13.13: "τοῦτον", ἔφη "νομίζετε Τανυοξάρκην;" ὁ δὲ Λάβυξος θαυμάσας "καὶ τίνα ἄλλον" ἔφη "νομιοῦμεν;").

[111] See Biltciffe 1969; Bigwood 1986: 406 ("There is in fact no linguistic feature, just as... there was no stylistic consideration, which gives us reason to deny attribution of the fragment to Ctesias"); Stronk 2007; 2010: 2–3.

attribution (see above).[112] If *P. Ox.* 2330 can be relied upon, Ctesias apparently wrote in the Attic dialect, or to be precise in a less rigorous or a modified Ionic with Attic forms.[113] This was perhaps not accidental, as the time of writing coincided with Athenian new marine ascendancy (post Cnidus, 394 BCE). Ctesias employed forms of Ionicism in his work, as Photius claims (T 10, 13), probably corresponding to Ionic historiographic writing, and this can occasionally be seen in the patriarch's epitome (F 16.67: δοκέοντα).[114] Photius claims that Ctesias employed Ionisms more frequently in the *Indica* (T 10).[115] Another feature is the use of simple grammatical structures and repetitions. Common to both passages cited above on Cyrus' name, one can easily spot one apparent characteristic of Ctesias' style, namely, the hiatus (ἀπὸ τοῦ ἡλίου).[116]

We are not sure whether Ctesias referred to himself in the third or rather first person,[117] and what was the earliest point in the narrative where he mentioned himself. It seems that the *Persica* was built as a series of episodes (cf. T 13: διηγημάτων),[118] a structure which is clearly reflected in Photius' summary and in Plutarch's presentation. These episodes, however, obviously did not strike the reader as digressions from the main narrative, if Photius' impression is any guide (T 13: οὐδὲ πρὸς ἐκτροπὰς δέ τινας ἀκαίρους, ὥσπερ ἐκεῖνος, ἀπάγει τὸν λόγον). Another feature discernible in his work is the practice of echoing backwards, making earlier episodes in his history duplicate circumstances in his own lifetime,[119] or, on the other hand, hinting forward to future events. For instance, Ctesias (ap. Plut. *Art.* 14.2) narrated the case of Arbaces, a Mede who, in the battle of Cunaxa, had run away to Cyrus, and, when Cyrus fell, had changed back again to Artaxerxes. Previously in his *Persica*, he mentioned another Median Arbaces who revolted from Sardanapallus the Assyrian (F 1b.2.1.24–28, cf. F1pδ- ε, F 5.2.32.5–6, F 6b, F 8d.1, 12). Cf. also the case of persons called Bagapates (F 16.66 ~ F 13.9, 13, 15–16, 23) or Artasyras (Plut. *Art.* 12.1 ~ F 13.9, 13, 15–16, 23). Or see the case of Cyrus the Great, who, before dying, appointed Cambyses as his successor on the throne and gave his other son Tanyoxarkes authority on a territory in central Asia (F 9.8) – a description which pre-

---

[112]   See the arguments of Giangrande 1976: 31–41.

[113]   See Del Corno 1962: 128; Bigwood 1976: 400–406. Cf. Stevenson 1997: 8.

[114]   Cf. Arrian. *Ind.* 3.6, which has the form Κτησίης in a reference to the *Indica*. But cf. the spelling in Arr. *An.* 5.4.2 (= T11gα); cf. Lenfant 2004: 11 n. 39.

[115]   If the possibility that the Indica was originally part of the Persica, and later circulated separately, is correct, one would have to conclude that Photius had a separate copy of the Indica, with a different tradition of transmission, one which kept many of the original Ionisms, as opposed to the *Persica*, which was reworked till it reached the patriarch's hands.

[116]   Cf. Bigwood 1986: 398. On Plutarch's avoidance of hiatus see Ziegler 1951: 932–935; Russell 1973: 18–41. On the *Artaxerxes* see Schottin 1865: 14–16. Cf. σὲ ἔσωσα above.

[117]   Cf. Marincola 1997: 185 and n. 56, relating to F 68, our only evidence for the latter choice; cf. 134; Llewellyn-Jones/Robson 2010: 8. Cf. Dorati 1995: 37, 41, who is convinced of a first-person narrative. Stronk, 2010: 2 admirably tries to reconstruct Ctesias' proem in the first person, but in comparison with those of Herodotus and Thucydides, and in view of Xenophon' depiction of himself in the third person (*Anab.* 3.1.4), we perhaps should consider the other possibility.

[118]   See Gera 1993: 209 on the *Persica*: "a chain of novellas arranged in chronological order and interspersed into descriptions of lands, customs, battles and the concrete achievements of each noteworthy monarch."

[119]   Cf. Jacoby 1922: 2049. Bigwood (1976: 19–20) perhaps presses too far the case of court intrigues.

ceded the arrangement made at Darius II's death bed, between Artaxerxes II and Cyrus the Younger (Plut. *Art.* 2.6).

The Greek traits of his narration are visible. A cursory reading of Photius' summary, as well as Plutarch's rendition and other authors preserving fragments, reveals several recurrent themes and images in Ctesias' *Persica*: for instance, his fondness for single duels of the Greek epic type (Megabyzus and Inaros: F 14.37, Megabyzus and Ousiris: F 14.40, Udiastes and Terituchmes: F 15.54). From Photius' epitome, it can be gathered that Ctesias portrayed his royal figures (e.g. Cyrus the Great: F 9.6, Artaxerxes I: F 14.39, 43, 44; Darius II: 15.50, 52, 54, 56) as controlled by the court women, and as being unable to restrain their anger, employing various cruel methods of torture as a result (cf. Artaxerxes I: F 14.34; Artaxerxes II: Plut. *Art.* 16). Ctesias follows and develops the image of Persians as not free, slaves either to the king or to their passions, with the portrayal of the Persian court as a scene of decadence, harem intrigues, corruption, arbitrary decisions, hypocrisy, betrayal of trust and brutality.[120] In accordance with the prevailing orientalist image of the Eastern Empire,[121] men are depicted as effeminate and women as dominant. Persia is seen as a place which breeds creatures on the fringes of human society, such as strong eunuchs (e.g. F 9.6, 13.9, 13, 15–16, 24, 31, 33, 14.33, 42–43, 15.48, 51, 54, 16.66).[122] With Parysatis at the end of the work calling to mind the strong female character of Semiramis at its beginning,[123] there is a sense of a recurrent motif in the *Persica*.

Among the ancient readers who liked Ctesias' writing are Dionysius of Halicarnassus (T 12) – for its pleasing style, although lacking in beauty (ἡδέως μὲν ὡς ἔνι μάλιστα, οὐ μὴν καλῶς γ' ἐφ' ὅσον ἔδει) – and Photius (T 13), for its clear and simple style, interwoven with pleasure, although it sometimes contains vulgar speech (σαφής τε καὶ ἀφελὴς λίαν, διὸ καὶ ἡδονῆι αὐτῶι σύγκρατός ἐστιν ὁ λόγος... καὶ εἰς ἰδιωτισμὸν ἐκπίπτειν). Photius claims that Ctesias' narrative is full of emotion and the unexpected (τὸ παθητικὸν καὶ ἀπροσδόκητον ἐχούσηι πολὺ). The *De elocutione* attributed to Demetrius of Phaleron attests to the impression Ctesias' lengthy style made on ancient readers (T 14 = *De eloc.* 212, 214, 216; F 24): the charge that he is garrulous because of his repetition is perhaps justified (ὡς ἀδολεσχοτέρωι διὰ τὰς διλογίας, πολλαχῆ μὲν ἴσως ἐγκαλοῦσιν ὀρθῶς; cf. Plut. *Art.* 11.11), yet Ctesias' depiction has liveliness (ἐναργεία), or the emotion of liveliness (τὸ ἐκ τῆς ἐναργείας πάθος), and necessitates repetitiveness. Demetrius praises Ctesias' measured and prolonged description, leaving the listener in suspense as well as portraying a character (...κατὰ μικρόν, κρεμῶντα τὸν ἀκροατὴν καὶ ἀναγκάζοντα συναγωνιᾶν... μάλα ἠθικῶς καὶ ἐναργῶς... ἐμφήνας).

Ctesias' impact on subsequent generations was immense.[124] Suffice it here to mention some of his fourth century BCE readers. The earliest evident one was another Greek

---

[120]	Cf. Kuhrt 2007: 563.

[121]	See Sancisi-Weerdenburg 1987: 43–44, who claims that Ctesias introduced the concept of *Orient* for the first time in European historiography.

[122]	See Sancisi-Weerdenburg 1987; Nippel 2001: 290. On eunuchs see Guyot 1980: 181ff.; Briant 2002: 268–272.

[123]	Rightly pointed out by Llewellyn-Jones/Robson 2010: 76. One should also add the character of Amestris, who anticipates Parysatis.

[124]	See Llewellyn-Jones/Robson 2010: 53–55.

participant in the battle of Cunaxa, but one who came from the opposite side of the conflict, being a mercenary soldier from Athens in the service of Prince Cyrus the Younger, namely Xenophon, son of Gryllus. The significance of the writings of Ctesias for the understanding of some of Xenophon's literary accounts – e.g. in the *Cyropaedia* – is now acknowledged.[125] Llewellyn-Jones/Robson (2010: 69–70) point out Ctesias' influence on Xenophon in terms of the novella form, in particular the four episodes interwoven within the main historical narrative: (a) Panthea the Lady of Susa (*Cyr.* 5.1.1–30; 6.1.30–55; 6.4.1–20; 7.3.3–17), (b) King Croesus (*Cyr.* 7.2.1–29), (c) Prince Gobryas (*Cyr.* 4.6.1– 12; 5.2.1–14; 5.4.41–51), and (d) Gadatas the chieftain (*Cyr.* 5.3.15–4.51). Among the features Llewellyn-Jones/Robson (2010) indicate as characteristic of these stories are: (1) episodic presentation, (2) a link with the work's main narrative framework, not as digressions, (3) scenes of emotional intensity, (4) dialogues. These characteristics can all be traced back to Ctesias' writing, whose stories can be seen as novellas.[126] In what amounts to the reception of the *Persica* in the first generation after its publication, Xenophon used his precursor's descriptions of the military encounter, its background and its immediate aftermath in his own work the *Anabasis*.[127] (See more in the Appendix below.)

Another fourth-century reader of Ctesias was the obscure historian Deinon, about whose lost writings little is known – and even less of his life.[128] He may have been a native of Colophon and the father of the popular historian Cleitarchus, if indeed this is the same person Pliny refers to in his *Historia Naturalis* (1.10: *Dione Colophonio*).[129] This information, however, does not help us determine the dates of Deinon's life, as we cannot be certain of the date of Cleitarchus' writing. The prevailing view is that he lived at the end of the fourth century,[130] and hence Deinon presumably lived a genera-

---

[125] See Gera 1993: 115–118, 199–215, 240–241. Cf. Jacoby 1922: 2067.

[126] Llewellyn-Jones/Robson (2010: 71) claim that "There can be little doubt that Xenophon drew on Ctesias' *Persica* as a source of inspiration for his novellas." Xenophon's Panthea especially evokes Ctesias' Semiramis; in both stories there is a motif of a love triangle or the suicide of the loving spouse.

[127] That Xenophon used Ctesias for the *Anabasis* was suggested by Reuss (1887: 3–5), and Neuhaus (1901: 279), dealing mainly with small sections, sometimes reaching wrong conclusions, and not tracing the intricate modes of dependence and rejection the Athenian historian displayed towards his predecessor. Neuhaus in particular seems off the mark in believing Xenophon's comments on the Phocaean woman (= Aspasia; *Anab.* 1.10.2) to be derived from Ctesias. Jacoby (1922: 2067), does not discard this view but is more cautious. Bigwood (1983: 347 n. 33) also acknowledges the possibility of Xenophon's employment of the *Persica*, but only for two details (the arrest and release of Cyrus and the death of Artagerses). Her claim that "some use" was made of Ctesias (342 n. 10) definitely needs to be revisited. Cf. the statement of Momigliano 1971: 57 that "[i]n the matter of military campaigns Xenophon has learned something from Thucydides and perhaps also from Ctesias."

[128] There are two forms of his name in Greek: Δείνων, which appears in this biography and in *Them.* 27.1 and Δίνων in some MSS of *Alex.* 36.4. On both forms see Schwartz 1905, who prefers the second one.

[129] Cf. *HN* 10.136. Some of the fragments of Deinon have the form "Dio" (e.g. *FGrH* 690 F 6 = DL 9.50; F 18 = Nep. *Con.* 5.4; F 20 = Luc. *Macrob.* 15). This form might explain why in the Suda, under one heading (Delta, 1239: Δίων), some features of Deinon are attributed to Cassius Dio: ἔγραψε ʻΡωμαϊκὴν ἱστορίαν ἐν βιβλίοις π'... Περσικά, Γετικά... (He wrote a Roman History in 80 books. Persika, Getika...).

[130] See Hamilton 1961: 448–449; Badian 1965: 5–6; Bosworth 1980: 30 n. 52. The only reference to Cleitarchus as a contemporary of Alexander is based on an understanding of Diodorus, 2.7.3 = *FGrH* 137 T 5: ὡς δὲ Κλείταρχος καὶ τῶν ὕστερον μετ' Ἀλεξάνδρουδιαβάντων εἰς τὴν Ἀσίαν τινὲς ἀνέγραψαν. Cf. Jacoby 1921: 622–624. There is a Cleitarchus mentioned with Stilpo the sophist, i.e., circa 307 BCE (DL 2.113), but we cannot be certain whether it is the same person. Some scholars therefore favor a date after 280 BCE:

tion before.[131] The work of Deinon, which also dealt with Persia and was also termed *Persica*, was divided into three series (συντάξεις: *FGrH* 690 F 1–3), each containing several books; they were probably published separately.[132] Deinon followed the genre, subject matter and style of Ctesias, thus expanding it further to the second half of the fourth century BCE.[133] Moreover, when a comparison with his predecessor's version is possible, it appears that Deinon not only appropriated significant scenes but also did not diverge much in terms of detail.[134] One case in point is the story of the murder of Queen Stateira during dinner through poison smeared on a certain bird. There are variances in detail between Ctesias and Deinon (Plut. *Art.* 19), but the main scene is adopted and its outline repeated.[135] The fact that Deinon seems to have placed this scene before the death of Cyrus (Plut. *Art.* 6.9) could merely point to the fact that Deinon's arrangement of episodes was not chronological but thematic, and built as a series of digressions. Scholars usually consider Deinon a fabricator of facts and denigrate his stories as either adapting Ctesias' accounts or echoing the official court version.[136] Yet, disregarding their Hellenic coloring and dramatic flavor, Deinon's stories seem to convey fairly reliable details of Persian life.[137] In this respect, they can be considered true successors to Ctesias' tales.

It should never be forgotten that Ctesias was a Greek author, writing in Greek to a Greek audience. While conveying local Eastern traditions, his work is set in an entirely Hellenic context. The *Persica* plays with known images and genres, maintaining some key features while subverting others, for instance setting India and the East as the "other"

---

see Pearson 1960: 226–227. Note Pliny's claim (*HN* 3.57) that Cleitarchus described Romans as reaching Alexander in Asia, a reference that seems far too early for an author of the fourth century – but this could be a later interpolation in his text.

[131]   According to Jacoby (1921: 622–624) Deinon was contemporaneous with Alexander, since in his opinion, the *Persica* genre died out after that period. Yet, the argument clearly begs the question.

[132]   The earliest known event of Deinon's *Persica* mentions Queen Semiramis (F 7); its latest is Artaxerxes III Ochus' conquest of Egypt in 343/342 BCE (*FGrH* 690 F 21).

[133]   Cf. Stevenson 1997: 15, 66–67, 70, 80; Llewellyn-Jones/Robson, 2010: 53–55. Deinon seems to repeat stories found in Herodotus as well (*FGrH* 690 F 11 = Hdt. 3.2.1: Cambyses in Egypt). It is known that the fifth book of the first series mentioned Amytis, Xerxes' sister [presumably an error for Artaxerxes I] (*FGrH* 690 F 21); that would make the second and third series include the period till Artaxerxes III, eighty years in all, unless the reference to Amytis comes in a flashforward (*prolepsis*) which anticipates future events.

[134]   *Contra* Drews 1973: 117 ("Dinon corrected Ctesias just as often as Ctesias corrected Herodotus, but since Ctesias' subject matter was inconsequential, Dinon's 'corrections' seem less grotesque"). The version brought in Chapter 10 of the *Artaxerxes* concerning Cyrus' the Younger's death does not come from Deinon in its entirety, but is actually a combination of two sources (Deinon and Ctesias) by Plutarch, *contra* Jacoby (*FGrH* 690 F 17). Also, the second version in Chapter 21 of the biography does not derive from Deinon (*contra* Dorati 1995: 45; Stevenson 1997: 25, 118). See Almagor, forthcoming (b).

[135]   In Ctesias' account, the one who administered the poison was called Belitaras; Deinon names him Melantas (19.2) and has him cutting the bird with the poisoned knife (19.6). Ctesias claims that Parysatis is the one who sliced the bird. Ctesias seems to implicate the queen mother in the murder, while Deinon appears to exonerate her from the charges. See Stevenson 1997: 71–72.

[136]   Fabrication and adaptation: Drews 1973: 117–118; Stevenson 1987: 29; 1997: 42–43, 49, 63–67, 80 (alongside an appreciation of Deinon as a serious historian), 94–100. Cf. Schottin 1865: 6–7. Official version: Kaemmel 1875: 681; Stevenson 1997: 29; Bassett 1999: 475.

[137]   Even Nepos explicitly praises his trustworthiness (*Con.* 5.4). Increasingly popular in late republican and early imperial Rome, Deinon was used by Cicero (*De div.* 1.46) and probably by Nepos in *Datames* and *De regibus*, by Pompeius Trogus (cf. *Prol.* 10; Justin, 10.1–2) and by Diodorus in books 15–16. Plutarch draws on him extensively in the *Artaxerxes* and also mentions him in *Themistocles* (27.1) and *Alexander* (36.4).

country to balance Hecataeus' and Herodotus' Egypt (Hdt. 2 & 2.143) or transposing images from the African to the Indian edge of the world (the *Cynocephaloi*). While Ctesias engages in telling stories from the Persian side, this is not entirely a "Persian Version" of the events, for instance of the Greco-Persian Wars.[138] One theme that Ctesias was able to develop, by means of focalization on the Persian monarchy, was that of imperial fortunes, which was a predominant concern of Greek authors from Herodotus onwards, all throughout the fourth century. Ctesias developed the idea of a series of world empires (which would later assume the form of *translatio imperii*).[139] It was already seen in Herodotus (1.95; 1.130), but Ctesias developed it as a model with three items (Assyria-Media-Persia),[140] while inventing an extended and significant Median Empire.[141] Ctesias' concern, as made clear by the structure of the work, tightly linking all episodes of the *Persica* together, together with the closure between Semiramis and Parysatis mentioned above, is the theme of the rise of empires and the lapse into decadence and demise (cf. Xen. *Cyr.* 8.8). The notion of transition of imperial power was not restricted to struggles between East and West, but also to conflicts within the Greek world. While the work of Herodotus was composed before the Athenian empire crumbled and Persian involvement in the Greek world prevailed, Ctesias' *Persica* was already written after Sparta lost its naval supremacy, Athens was on the rise again and the Persian presence as a major player in the Hellenic sphere was a basic fact of Greek politics. The question which the *Persica* presumably posed to its readers was whether this situation might change yet again.

Appendix: Xenophon's *Anabasis* and Ctesias' *Persica*

Xenophon's version of the events surrounding the clash of Cyrus the Younger and Artaxerxes II was written perhaps in the late 380s or early 370s BC;[142] there are some who would push the date even further in time, to the 360s.[143] Since the *Anabasis* was composed subsequent to the publication of other reports,[144] it has been suggested that one of these earlier descriptions of the war of Cyrus and Artaxerxes was that of Sophaenetus of Stymphalus, a commander of one thousand of Cyrus' mercenaries (*Anab.* 1.1.11, 1.2.3), and the eldest chief officer of the Greeks on their retreat from Persia (cf. *Anab.* 5.3.1;

---

[138] *Pace* Llewellyn-Jones/Robson 2010: 30, 33, 52, 57–58, 81.

[139] See Le Goff 1964, Ch. VI.

[140] A scheme of four empires appears in the OT book of Daniel (2: 1–40; cf. 7: 2–3), variously interpreted, and one of five successive kingdoms is found in authors from the Roman period. See Mendels 1981, Wiesehöfer 2003, and Almagor 2011: 3 n. 9 with references.

[141] See Sancisi-Weerdenburg (1988).

[142] MacLaren 1934: 244–247; Delebecque 1957: 199–206; Breitenbach 1967: 1641–1642; Perlman 1976/1977: 245 n. 10; Wylie 1992: 131; Stevenson 1997: 8 n. 11.

[143] See Körte 1922: 16; Dillery 1995: 59, 94; Cawkwell 1972: 16; 2004: 48. Cf. Stylianou 2004: 72 n. 13. But see Rood 2004: 307.

[144] Very much like Xenophon's *Apology*, which was admittedly written after accounts of the trial of Socrates had already been circulating (*Apol.*, 1: γεγράφασι μὲν οὖν περὶ τούτου καὶ ἄλλοι καὶ πάντες ἔτυχον τῆς μεγαληγορίας αὐτοῦ) which may be seen as a possible allusion to Plato's *Apology*. On the relation of Xenophon to the latter see Mitscherling 1982; Vander Waerdt 1993, especially p. 14–15; Waterfield 2004: 93.

6.5.12). Sophaenetus is thought to have written about the march, the battle and the return of the soldiers, as well as to have influenced the account of Diodorus (Ephorus), who mentions the elder general (14.19, 14.27–29, 14.31), but barely refers to Xenophon (not until 14.37.1).[145] Yet the evidence for the existence of an *Anabasis* by Sophaenetus is scanty. The only mention of a work called Κύρου Ἀνάβασις by Sophaenetus is in an abridged version of Stephanus Byzantinus' *Ethnica* from the sixth century CE (the fragments are gathered under *FGrH* 109). The four references to this work cite names of places and nations in Asia, all on the route of the Ten Thousand. It is hardly probable that this work was forgotten, and only surfaced hundreds of years later.[146] One may even question whether such a work existed at all, as the four references could easily derive from Xenophon's account.[147]

It is much more probable that Ctesias' *Persica* was the earlier report which Xenophon knew. It is not that the latter wrote in response to Ctesias or that the reason for composing the *Anabasis* was to correct his predecessor's account, but Xenophon's report is linked in a special way to the *Persica*. Xenophon had to take into consideration the stories he found there.[148] Xenophon's stance towards his forerunner appears to blend attitudes of appreciation and disapproval. On the one hand, he does not seem to value the physician's work or judgments very highly, yet on the other hand he is influenced by Ctesias and relies on his reports.

Although he was present at the combat zone (*Anab.* 1.8.15ff.), in Proxenus' battalion[149] and was an eye-witness for some of the occurrences, there are many details that Xenophon simply did not know, and whose absence is conspicuous in the *Anabasis*.[150]

---

[145] See Tarn 1927: 8 n. 2; Barber 1935: 126–127; Manfredi 1978: 63; 2004: 322; Dillery 1995: 59. Cawkwell (1972: 17–21; 2004: 50, 60–62) even believes that Xenophon wrote his *Anabasis* in response to the report of Sophaenetus, which provoked him to set down his own account.

[146] Cf. Anderson 1974: 81–82; Stylianou 2004: 70; *contra* Cawkwell 2004: 61.

[147] Χαρμάνδη is in *Anab.* 1.5.10, the Φύσκος river is in *Anab.* 2.4.25, the Καρδοῦχοι are in *Anab.* 3.5.15–17, 4.1.4, 4.1.8–11, 5.5.17, 7.8.25. While the Τάοι appear in *Anab.* 4.4.18, 4.6.5, 4.7.1, 5.5.17 but as Τάοζοι. Bux 1927: 1012–1013, probably builds too much on the latter variation. The difference may stem from a copier's mistake. Cf. von Mess 1906: 362, 372 and n. 3. Indeed, rather than assume that oral narratives gave rise to a mistaken belief that there was an actual account by Sophaenetus (Stylianou 2004: 74) or that the work was a late forgery (Jacoby 1930: 349; Westlake 1987: 269), it may be suggested that the very name Sophaenetus as the author of a work called Κύρου Ἀναβάσι is the result of some later corruption and a hyper-correction of "Xenophon". It is quite possible that the name of the Athenian historian was somehow miswritten in an epitome of his work, and there are several known mistaken versions of his name in late antiquity. Compare the attribution of the mention of Aspasia (cf. *Anab.* 1.10.2) to one "Zenophanes" (Ζηνοφάνης) in what appears to be a Byzantine interpolation into Athenaeus' text (13.576d). Cf. also Ath. 10.424c. The suggestion is that there were several corrupt varieties of the name Xenophon, and that one was eventually hyper-corrected into the intelligible form Σοφαίνετος (perhaps via Ζοφάνης/Σοφάνης, a shorter form of Ζηνοφάνης). In addition, Diodorus' (or Ephorus') version may be the outcome of a conscious downplaying of Xenophon's role and need not come from another source (see Stylianou 2004 for the reliance of Diodorus/Ephorus on Xenophon in this narrative). See Bigwood (1983: 343 n. 14), on the possibility that these authors adapted their sources.

[148] Nothing precluded Xenophon from being acquainted with the text of Ctesias, composed approximately two decades previously. The historian himself testifies to the circulation of book rolls in the Greek world, and their transportation across the sea in cargos of ships (*Anab.* 7.5.14). Cf. Turner 1952: 19–21.

[149] See Lendle 1986: 435.

[150] Such as the role of the non-Greek force in Cyrus' army, especially in its left wing, and the composition of the king's army. Xenophon mistakes Tissaphernes' position and function, as well as the length of the

All things considered, the battle picture in his work gives the impression of a reconstruction done years after the event, comprising memories of a youthful mercenary and
information he acquired later,[151] presumably from Ctesias. An instance of a detail that
Xenophon may have found in the *Persica* and could not possibly have remembered is
the impressive scene in which the head of the king's advance guard, Artagerses, clashed
with Cyrus and was slain by him. This episode is elaborately related in the biography
of Plutarch (*Art.* 9), who also indicates that the scene was described by almost every
author writing on Cunaxa (9.4), that is from Ctesias onwards. Xenophon mentions the
end of Artagerses – presumably because it highlights the fighting qualities of Cyrus – in
a brief but heroic passage (*Anab.* 1.8.24): καὶ ἐμβαλὼν σὺν τοῖς ἑξακοσίοις νικᾷ τοὺς
πρὸ βασιλέως τεταγμένους καὶ εἰς φυγὴν ἔτρεψε τοὺς ἑξακισχιλίους, καὶ ἀποκτεῖναι
λέγεται αὐτὸς τῇ ἑαυτοῦ χειρὶ Ἀρταγέρσην τὸν ἄρχοντα αὐτῶν. (and, attacking with
his six hundred, he was victorious over the forces stationed in front of the king and put
to flight the six thousand, slaying with his own hand, it is said, their commander Artagerses). One should note the λέγεται ("it is said" here, which may reasonably refer to
Ctesias' account.[152]

Tissaphernes' slanderous accusation against Cyrus, which was brought before the
king and almost precipitated the prince's execution, may be another case in point. Both
Xenophon (*Anab.* 1.1.3) and Photius (F 16.59) mention this episode, but it is elaborated
in our extant texts only in Plutarch' biography (*Art.* 3.2–4). According to this tale, Cyrus
was allegedly plotting against his brother in a temple, where he was supposed to lie in
wait during the investiture ceremony of the new monarch. It was a priest and former
teacher of Cyrus in the wisdom of the Magi, allegedly privy to the scheme, who reported
it and was instrumental in convincing Artaxerxes. Xenophon's report seems secondary
and derivative, as it merely mentions an accusation, but does not provide its substance. It
is much more feasible to assume that Xenophon willfully omitted a number of elements
than speculate that these items were only later added to the story in the *Anabasis* and
were not known to him. As Photius informs us that the story already appeared in Ctesias'
Persica, it is hard to imagine, given the physician's predilection for tall tales and lengthy
accounts (T 8, T 14a), that he would not have elaborated on the details of the accusation
of conspiracy and on Cyrus' arrest, but would have settled for a short version instead.
Ctesias' stories abound in false allegations[153] and the involvement of priests in conspira-
cies and plots[154] of exactly the sort that we find in Tissaphernes' case, and these details
may be considered some of the typical characteristics of his court stories.

Moreover, the consequences of this affair in the accounts of Xenophon and Ctesias
are amazingly similar. What is striking when comparing the two reports is the crucial
part assigned to Parysatis by the two authors in saving her son from the death sentence

---

enemy's front line. See Tarn 1927: 8; Bigwood 1983: 341–343; Wylie 1992: 126–127, 129, 132. He does not
even give the name of the battle site (Plut. *Art.* 8.2).

[151] Cf. Wylie 1992: 132. This conclusion is made without entering the question of whether Xenophon the
soldier kept a diary or not. See Cawkwell 2004: 54–59 and Stylianou 2004: 75–77.

[152] See Lenfant 2004: 147 n. 680. Notwithstanding the fact, rightly pointed out by Jacoby (1922: 2067),
that not every λέγεται in Xenophon's account necessarily refers to Ctesias.

[153] E.g. F 13.11–12, 14.32–33, 16.60.

[154] E.g. F 13.11, 19.

and in installing him back in his province. While Xenophon claims that the queen mother pleaded for him, and had him sent back to his region (1.1.3: ἡ δὲ μήτηρ ἐξαιτησαμένη αὐτὸν ἀποπέμπει πάλιν ἐπὶ τὴν ἀρχήν), Photius has Cyrus running to Parysatis, by whose intervention he was cleared of the charge and returned to his satrapy (F 16.59: καταφεύγει Παρυσάτιδι τῆι μητρί, καὶ ἀπολύεται τῆς διαβολῆς. ἀπελαύνει Κῦρος ἠτιμωμένος παρὰ τοῦ ἀδελφοῦ πρὸς τὴν οἰκείαν σατραπείαν, καὶ μελετᾶι ἐπανάστασιν). In both reports, Cyrus appears as a prince whose royal ambition is fuelled by his mother's aspirations.[155] The humiliation and disgrace inflicted upon Cyrus are considered by both Ctesias and Xenophon the key factors in his decision to begin preparations for a revolt.[156] The similarities in the storylines of Ctesias and Xenophon are so astonishing that they seem to betray the dependence of Xenophon on his predecessor's account.

Xenophon thus appears to be particularly dependent on Ctesias in making use of those portions of the *Persica*'s narrative that offer the background to Cyrus' revolt.[157] Furthermore, Xenophon apparently could not have witnessed Cyrus' manner of death and discovered it only later. There is a high degree of probability that he learned the specific details from Ctesias' *Persica*. According to the physician's narrative, the prince was first hit by a spear near the eye, by a young Persian named Mithridates, who did this unconscious of his victim's identity (Plut. *Art.* 11.5). After Cyrus fell to the ground and was slowly recovering from the blow, another person – a Carian slave – stabbed him from behind, in the back of the leg, again ignorant of the identity of his prey. This last injury caused Cyrus' death by making him strike his temple against a stone (Plut. *Art.* 11.9–10) in the very same place he had already been wounded. Accidents and coincidences feature strongly in this incredible tale. Mithridates and the Carian would prove significant to the rest of Ctesias' story. As they would later contradict the official royal version, which had Artaxerxes as the sole killer of Cyrus, they would be put to death (Plut. *Art.* 14.8–10, 16.1–7; F 16.67). Xenophon's narrative looks like a concise summary of this story, since it lacks many elements. The Athenian historian accepts that Cyrus was injured near or below the eye[158] and merely mentions that "someone" threw his lance at Cyrus (ἀκοντίζει τις παλτῷ: *Anab.* 1.8.27), thereby demeaning the thrower and his act. The prince is even made to look more heroic by the portrayal of his injury as occurring at the precise moment that he strikes the king. Cyrus dies instantaneously, and not, as in Ctesias' account, only after a while. The brief version of the *Anabasis* may be construed

---

[155] Cf. *Anab.* 1.1.4: Παρύσατις μὲν δὴ ἡ μήτηρ ὑπῆρχε τῷ Κύρῳ, φιλοῦσα αὐτὸν μᾶλλον ἢ τὸν βασιλεύοντα Ἀρταξέρξην. But cf. Manfredini/Orsi/Antelami 1987/1996²: 270.

[156] Cf. F 16.59 and *Anab.* 1.1.4. Here, Plutarch's similar assertion (*Art.* 3.6) may be taken from Ctesias as much as it can be an adaptation of Xenophon. Hence, it cannot be considered conclusive evidence.

[157] Cf. Stronk 2007: 26.

[158] I would not ascribe a great deal of importance to the different prepositions used in Xenophon's version (*Anab.* 1.8.27: ὑπὸ τὸν ὀφθαλμὸν) or in that of Plutarch (παρὰ τὸν ὀφθαλμόν: *Art.* 11.5), although Bassett (1999) does. After all, we do not have Ctesias' report and must allow the possibility that either Xenophon or Plutarch amended the original expression to suit their needs. The fact that Cyrus' eye is mentioned in both cases makes the accounts very similar indeed. I would also not go along with supposing that the difference is significant in expressing Xenophon's belief that Cyrus wore a helmet when he was struck (Bassett 1999: 476–477). Had the historian wished to convey this opinion, I believe he would have stated it clearly, and not leave his readers guessing as to his intent. The impression one derives from the *Anabasis* passage is that Cyrus was without headgear.

as one that follows the story of Ctesias, but not slavishly, and is pointedly opposed to the unbelievable elements in it, such as the coincidences of Cyrus' injuries and the figure of a Carian stabbing the prince.

Admittedly, one could say that Xenophon got this specific detail elsewhere. As a puzzled young soldier, he was surely curious to know how his leader had died and sought information without delay. Some rumors circulating in the field undoubtedly filled that void.[159] Yet it may be entirely plausible that Xenophon was not aware of the exact manner of Cyrus' death until Ctesias published his version. It is hard to imagine that any of Xenophon's colleagues could have had any knowledge of so precise a detail as a wound near Cyrus' eye. The Greeks were not close by (*Anab.* 1.8.19–20, 1.10.4), and there was no one to inform them. It is also not probable that this detail was to be found in some written account of the event other than the *Persica*, if such existed at all prior to the *Anabasis*. The exact location of Cyrus' wound would be very appropriate in the text of a physician, and indeed this accurate physical description may be thought of as one of the characteristic features of Ctesias' writing.[160]

It would also seem that Ctesias' presence as a historical figure was removed by Xenophon. As mentioned above, we can gather that Ctesias apparently presented himself in his work as an important agent in three decisive events during the battle and immediately afterwards – that is, in the medical treatment of the Great King, in a delegation headed by Phalinus that was dispatched to negotiate with the Greek mercenaries, and in the care given to the imprisoned Clearchus after he was taken captive to Babylon. Xenophon says nothing about Ctesias being involved in any of these activities. And yet he acknowledges that Cyrus did injure his brother, that Clearchus was indeed imprisoned and that there was a delegation to the Greeks. Of these three events, Xenophon could have witnessed only one, the diplomatic mission to the Greek generals. Here he merely states (*Anab.* 2.1.7–23) that on the morning following the battle heralds from the king and Tissaphernes arrived, and that these were barbarians, with the exception of Phalinus. The latter is presented as the one who in fact demanded that the mercenaries surrender their arms. Xenophon's insistence that there was only a single Greek delegate (*Anab.* 2.1.7: οἱ μὲν ἄλλοι βάρβαροι, ἦν δ' αὐτῶν Φαλῖνος εἷς Ἕλλην) looks like an oblique polemic directed against Ctesias' contention that he was a member of this group.[161] In the *Life* of Artaxerxes, Plutarch concludes from Xenophon's ignorance of the presence of Ctesias that the physician is lying (13.6). This inference, however, is unnecessary. Xenophon may have chosen to remove Ctesias from his depiction of the embassy for his own reasons or for the sake of literary arrangement.

So far we have seen the manner in which Xenophon both borrows details from Ctesias and implicitly argues against the account of the *Persica*, while being cautious not to

---

[159] The possibility of eyewitnesses' accounts of Persian soldiers or oral tales heard after the battle is certainly to be taken into consideration (cf. Cawkwell 2004: 51), yet one should remember the communication problems, noted by Wylie 1992: 132. None of the Greeks spoke Persian (except some of the generals, perhaps). Very few Persians spoke Greek.

[160] See Stevenson 1997: 29; Bassett 1999: 476 n. 10. Cf. Bigwood 1983: 348; Tuplin 2004a: 336.

[161] See Lendle 1995: 92–93; Dorati 1995: 39–40; Cawkwell 2004: 50 n. 7.

mention his precursor. Such conduct is also typical of Xenophon with relation to Plato.[162] As must be admitted, there are two utterances in the *Anabasis* which specifically refer to Ctesias as a source and seem to present him as citing Ctesias, therefore apparently contradicting this picture. However, they may not be authentic. The first (*Anab.* 1.8.26) addresses the injury inflicted by Cyrus on Artaxerxes and the healing of it by the physician. It comes immediately after the description of Cyrus' headlong rush against his brother and the blow he delivers to the king. Disrupting the dramatic scene almost like an intermission, the following note appears: καὶ τιτρώσκει διὰ τοῦ θώρακος, ὥς φησι Κτησίας ὁ ἰατρός, καὶ ἰᾶσθαι αὐτὸς τὸ τραῦμά φησι (…and he wounded him through the corselet, according to the statement of Ctesias, and he states that he himself healed the wound). The narrator then returns to Cyrus, who is dramatically depicted as being struck at the very moment he is delivering the blow (παίοντα δ' αὐτὸν...). The second mention of Ctesias appears almost instantly, following the report on the ensuing struggle between the entourages of Cyrus and Artaxerxes.[163] It states that Ctesias provided the number of slain on the king's side (*Anab.* 1.8.27) – but oddly enough, no figure is specified: ὁπόσοι μὲν τῶν ἀμφὶ βασιλέα ἀπέθνῃσκον Κτησίας λέγει: παρ' ἐκείνῳ γὰρ ἦν (how many of the king's side died is stated by Ctesias, for he was with him). Following this note is a portrayal of Cyrus' fall together with eight of his bravest companions.

More than a hundred years ago, a proposition was put forward by the scholar Dürrbach (1893: 363 n. 1). His proposal was that these two references to Ctesias are in fact the result of a later intervention in the text of the *Anabasis* and are not Xenophon's own comments. Dürrbach's arguments are three and, slightly modified, they are as follows: (1) The allusions are very awkwardly inserted in the story and seem alien to it; (2) As a rule Xenophon never refers to his sources,[164] and there is no apparent reason why he should do so – twice – in this particular place; (3) The reference pertaining to the Great King's wound contradicts the ensuing description in Xenophon's account, according to which Artaxerxes is very active in the subsequent encounter: at the head of his men, he pursues and falls upon Cyrus' camp, plunders it (*Anab.* 1.10.1, 2, 4), masses his troops and lines up against the Greeks (*Anab.* 1.10.5); he then advances to their rear (*Anab.* 1.10.6) and joins forces with Tissaphernes and his division (*Anab.* 1.10.6, 8).

---

[162] As elaborately shown by the late Prof. Michael Stokes in his paper at the Xenophon conference in Liverpool (2009): "Xenophon's *Apology*, Xenophon's *Memorabilia* and Plato's *Apology*: some Comparisons."

[163] This report is also suspect of being not authentic, given its grammatically incoherent structure: καὶ ἐνταῦθα μαχόμενοι καὶ βασιλεὺς καὶ Κῦρος καὶ οἱ ἀμφ' αὐτοὺς ὑπὲρ ἑκατέρου. The description is certainly understandable without these thirteen words. Moreover, this report appears as an unclear retrospective synopsis of the battle scene. This sentence, like the second reference to Ctesias, may have been a marginal gloss, influenced by Ctesias' account of the clash of the supporters of the two brothers, but inserted in the wrong place within the text of the *Anabasis*, since that fight preceded Cyrus' wound, and did not follow it. Finally, by excising this item, Xenophon's account would be more coherent, in that Cyrus' injury would debilitate him and cause his immediate death. The removal of this sentence would also make the picture more dramatic, in that the prince's moment of death would be clearer.

[164] Cf. Marincola 1997: 227.

Dürrbach's suggestion has not been widely accepted by the scholarly community, and the two references are still considered by many a scholar as genuine.[165] Yet it seems there has been no real attempt to consider Dürrbach's arguments directly or in detail.[166] The main contention that could be brought against his case is Plutarch's claim in the *Life of Artaxerxes* (13.6), that Xenophon is quoting from Ctesias' work.[167] Anticipating this line of reasoning, Dürrbach argues that Xenophon's MSS had already incurred an interpolation at some stage before Plutarch read the work for his biography, that is, sometime between the end of the fourth century BC and the first century AD. In disagreement with Dürrbach, the curious references to Ctesias in the *Anabasis* have been variously defended by scholars as authentic, once with the argument that Xenophon is indeed quoting his predecessor only to express doubt concerning the physician's descriptions,[168] and once with the contention that Xenophon referred to Ctesias in order to support his own depiction.[169] But one has to seriously question both lines of argument. The case for the demonstration of Xenophon's disbelief is not convincing. Each of the two references to Ctesias comprises two claims, with the second one serving to support the first and lend it credibility. In the first reference we have the fact of healing performed by the physician as an occurrence which guarantees the reality of the wound; in the second, the claim "for he was at his side" is meant to back up the assertion regarding the casualties of the Great King's army. It is utterly unclear why Xenophon would put much effort in establishing claims which he himself regards as dubious.

The other argument, to the effect that the references to Ctesias are there because Xenophon needed them to vouch for his portrayal of the scene, fares none the better. In the second case, that is, the mention of Ctesias on the number of fallen soldiers, it is absolutely perplexing why the physician's report should be alluded to if the actual figures are not given. Even the rhetorical purpose of this allusion is not clear bearing in mind the absence of any number, and compared with the definite figure of eight followers dying on the corpse of Cyrus, which immediately ensues.[170] In the first reference to Ctesias, it is not at all clear what mention should be made of his account if it is so out of harmony with the rest of the narrative of the *Anabasis*. Some would say, perhaps, that the mention of the physician healing the king would explain Artaxerxes' activity later on.[171] But this rationalization does not really account for the indication of the wound: why mention a minor flesh wound (judging by the monarch's rapid recovery) in the first place if it is to be disregarded as quickly as it is brought in? Xenophon's report is perfectly consistent without it. His whole point is that Cyrus was hit while throwing his spear. Why should he obscure this detail with a vanishing wound?

---

[165]   See Jacoby 1922: 2067 ("natürlich sind das keine Interpolationen"). Cf. Cawkwell 1972: 17; Bigwood 1983: 347; Wylie 1992: 132; Stronk 2010: 185, 368–369.

[166]   See Bassett 1999: 475 n. 6; Lenfant 2004: 226 n. 12.

[167]   μέμνηται γὰρ αὐτοῦ καί τοῖς βιβλίοις τούτοις ἐντετυχηκὼς δῆλός ἐστιν (He [Xenophon] makes mention of him and had evidently read his works).

[168]   See Bigwood 1983: 348 and n. 39. Cf. Dorati 1995: 38.

[169]   See Gray 2003: 119 (= 2010: 565). Cf. Tuplin 2004b: 155.

[170]   This vague statement on the fallen royal soldiers also blurs the impact of the description of Cyrus' death.

[171]   Xenophon's insistence on the activity of the king may go back to his recollection of Tissaphernes' words (*Anab.* 2.3.19), which probably influenced him. I owe this observation to C. Tuplin.

It is unacceptable that these citations of Ctesias should be considered authentic. Firstly, this assumption contradicts Xenophon's reluctance to mention his forerunner, even in a situation where he has to address him. Secondly, the mention of Ctesias as a reliable witness for the king's wound and for the fact that there were casualties in the royal army necessitates an acceptance of many other items related to the physician and cannot possibly end in adopting these elements only. It would necessitate as true that Ctesias was in the king's service and did heal the monarch, that Artaxerxes was incapacitated and could not continue to participate in the battle and that there is a grain of truth for the physician's other figures. Ultimately, given Xenophon's general skepticism regarding Ctesias, it might cast doubt upon his own account. Hence, it is hardly believable that Xenophon would have endangered his reliability in this manner. Thirdly, there is scarcely any ancient author who treated Ctesias as a historical agent without reservations. Why would Xenophon do it, twice, within a space of a few lines? Fourthly, the assumption that the references are genuine (especially the second) would entail that Xenophon relied on his readers' acquaintance with Ctesias' *Persica* in order to understand the allusion, yet this is entirely at variance with his practice not to mention other written works (notable in the case of Plato).[172] A reference of the sort that compels the reader to look for the exact number of casualties according to Ctesias in another work would suit a note made by a later librarian, not by the author Xenophon.

Dürrbach's hypothesis, against which there is no strong argument, should be endorsed.[173] It may even be elaborated by suggesting that the text of the *Anabasis* has undergone several interpolations at different stages. Given the uncomfortable grammatical structure and stylistic peculiarity of the first reference to Ctesias, it would seem that the initial intervention noted the wounding of the king through his armour. The following one presumably referred to the healing by Ctesias, added as a gloss to the previous annotation. And the third was presumably influenced by the previous mention of Ctesias. It also includes the superfluous παρ' ἐκείνῳ γὰρ ἦν, perhaps indicating another hand. At some point, these notes probably drifted from the margins of the text to its main body. After this stage the particle μέν was added in order to make the second reference cohere with the rest of the sentence. If this interpretation is correct, these glosses were made during the four hundred years that separate the writing of the *Anabasis* from Plutarch's time, when definite evidence for interpolation emerges.[174] The position presented here, to the effect that Xenophon borrowed some elements from Ctesias' story but did not mention him at all, is consistent, coherent and typical of his writing. The other view, which regards the references to Ctesias as authentic yet denies that Xenophon used any other item from the *Persica*, is incomprehensible, self-contradictory and goes beyond what is known of Xenophon's practices.

Of the two authors' works, it was the fate of Xenophon's to survive. Conceivably, this was not by chance, for besides the merits of his storytelling ability and the superiority

---

[172]   He does not even mention himself as an author when treating his own *Anabasis*. Cf. *Hell.* 3.1.2.

[173]   This approach has no bearing on Dürrbach's other suggestion that the *Anabasis* was written as an *apologia* or defense of Xenophon's conduct.

[174]   An undeniable fact is that the text of the *Anabasis* suffers from multiple interpolations and external interventions and this case is no exception. The notable ones are at 1.8.6; 2.2.6, as well as the passages at the beginning of books 2, 3, 4, 5 and 7 and at 6.2.1.

of his account compared with some of the questionable pictures found in the *Persica*, Xenophon did borrow parts of his predecessor's composition, in the process making Ctesias' account of Cunaxa seem redundant,[175] on top of being fanciful. Today, students and scholars read the *Anabasis* first, before they ever get to see the fragments of the *Persica*; but we must not forget that the real relationship between the two works was the reverse, and this fact should guide our reading of Xenophon's depiction of those historical events.

BIBLIOGRAPHY

Almagor, E. (2011): Plutarch on the End of the Persian Empire, *Graeco-Latina Brunensia* 16: 3–16.

Almagor, E., Forthcoming (a): The King's Road in Greek Sources, in: J. Ma/C.J. Tuplin (eds.), *Arshama and Egypt – The World of Achamenid Satrape* (Oxford: OUP).

Almagor, E., Forthcoming (b): *Plutarch and the Persica* (Edinburgh: EUP).

Alonso-Núñez, J.-M. (1996): Ctésias, Historien Grec du Monde Perse, in: P. Carlier (ed.), *Le IVe siècle av. J.-C.*, Nancy: 325–333.

Anderson, J.K. (1974): *Xenophon*, London.

Auberger, J. (1991): *Ctesias. Histoires de l'Orient*, Paris.

Badian, E. (1965): The Date of Cleitarchus, *PACA*: 5–11.

Bähr, J.C.F. (1824): *Fragmente des Ktesias von Knidos*, Frankfurt.

Barber, G.L. (1935): *The Historian Ephorus*, Cambridge.

Barnett, R.D. (1963): Xenophon and the Wall of Media, *JHS* 83: 1–26.

Bassett, S.R. (1999): The Death of Cyrus the Younger, *CQ n.s.* 49: 473–483.

Bichler, R. (2004): Some Observations on the Image of the Assyrian and Babylonian Kingdoms with the Greek Tradition, in: R. Rollinger, C. Ulf (eds.), *Commerce and Monetary Systems in the Ancient World. Means of Transition and Cultural Interaction*, Wiesbaden: 499–518.

Bichler, R. (2007): Ktesias 'korrigiert' Herodot, in: R. Bichler, *Historiographie – Ethnographie – Utopie. Gesammelte Schriften*, Teil 1: *Studien zu Herodots Kunst der Historie*, Wiesbaden: 229–245.

Bickerman, E.J., Tadmor, H. (1978): Darius I, Pseudo-Smerdis, and the Magi, *Athenaeum*, n.s. 56: 239–261.

Bigwood, J.M. (1964): *Ctesias of Cnidus*, Diss. Harvard University.

Bigwood, J.M. (1965): Ctesias of Cnidus, *HSPh* 70: 263–265.

Bigwood, J.M. (1976): Ctesias' Account of the Revolt of Inaros, *Phoenix* 30: 1–25.

Bigwood, J.M. (1978): Ctesias as Historian of the Persian Wars, *Phoenix* 32: 19–41.

Bigwood, J.M. (1980): Diodorus and Ctesias, *Phoenix* 34: 195–207.

Bigwood, J.M. (1983): The Ancient Accounts of the Battle of Cunaxa, *AJP* 104: 340–357.

Bigwood, J.M. (1986): P. Oxy. 2330 and Ctesias, *Phoenix* 40: 393–406.

Bigwood, J.M. (1989): Ctesias' *Indica* and Photius, *Phoenix* 43: 302–316.

Bigwood, J.M. (1993a): Aristotle and the Elephant Again, *AJP* 114: 537–555.

Bigwood, J.M. (1993b): Ctesias' Parrot, *CQ* 43: 321–327.

Bigwood, J.M. (1995): Ctesias, His Royal Patrons and Indian Swords, *JHS* 115: 135–140.

Biltcliffe, A.W. (1969): P. Oxy. N° 2330 and its Importance for the Study of Nicolaus of Damascus, *RhM* 112: 85–93.

---

[175] Even Plutarch has to apologize for relying on Ctesias for the account of the battle and not on Xenophon (*Art.* 9.4).

Binder, C. (2008): *Plutarchs Vita des Artaxerxes. Ein historischer Kommentar*, Berlin.

Bosworth, A.B. (1980): Alexander and the Iranians, *JHS* 100: 1–21.

Braun, T. (2004): Xenophon's Dangerous Liaisons, in: R. Lane Fox (ed.), *The Long March. Xenophon and the Ten Thousand*, New Haven, CT–London: 96–130.

Breitenbach, H.R. (1967): Xenophon, *RE* IX A: 1567–2052.

Briant, P. (ed.) (1995): *Dans les pas des Dix-Mille*, Toulouse.

Briant, P. (2002): *From Cyrus to Alexander*, Winona Lake, IN (translation of *Histoire de l'empire perse: De Cyrus à Alexandre*, 1996, Paris).

Brosius, M. (1996): *Women in Ancient Persia (559-331 B.C.)*, Oxford.

Brown, T.S. (1978): Suggestions for a Vita of Ctesias of Cnidus, *Historia* 27: 1–19.

Burn, A.R. (1962): *Persia and the Greeks*, London.

Bux, E. (1927): Sophainetos, *RE* IIIA: 1008–1013.

Calmeyer, P. (1977): Vom Reisehut zur Kaiserkrone: b. Stand der archaeologischen Forschung zu den Iranischen Kronen, *AMI* 9: 168–190.

Cawkwell, G.L. (1972): Introduction, in: R. Warner (tr.), *Xenophon. The Persian Expedition*, London.

Cawkwell, G.L. (2004): When, How and Why did Xenophon Write the *Anabasis*, in: R. Lane Fox (ed.), *The Long March. Xenophon and the Ten Thousand*, New Haven, CT–London: 47–67.

Cizek, A. (1975): From the Historical Truth to the Literary Convention. The Life of Cyrus the Great viewed by Herodotus, Ctesias and Xenophon, *AC* 44: 531–552.

Comploi, S. (2002): Die Darstellung der Semiramis bei Diodorus Siculus, in: R. Rollinger, C. Ulf (eds.), *Geschlechterrollen und Frauenbild in der Persektive antiken Autoren*, Wiesbaden: 223–271.

Cook, J.M. (1983): *The Persian Empire*, London–New York.

Dalley, S. (2003): Why did Herodotus not mention the Hanging Gardens of Babylon?, in: P. Derow, R. Parker (eds.), *Herodotus and his World*, Oxford: 171–189.

Del Corno, D. (1962): La lingua di Ctesia (POx. 2330), *Athenaeum* 40: 126–141.

Delebecque, E. (1957): *Essai sur la vie de Xénophon*, Paris.

Dillery, J. (1995): *Xenophon and the History of His Times*, London–New York.

Dorati, M. (1995): Ctesia falsario?, *Quaderni di storia* 41: 33–52.

Drews, R. (1973): *The Greek Accounts of Eastern History*, Cambridge, MA.

Dürrbach, F. (1893): L'apologie de Xénophon dans l'Anabase, *REG* 6: 343–386.

Eck, B. (1990): Sur la vie de Ctésias, *REG* 103: 409–434.

Evans, J.A.S. (1968): Father of History or Father of Lies. The Reputation of Herodotus, *CJ* 64: 11–17.

Fehling, D. (1989): *Herodotus and his "Sources"* (trans. J.G. Howie), Leeds.

Fischer, C.T., Wecker, O. (1924): *Kynokephaloi*, *RE* XII: 24–26.

Gasche, H. (1995): Autour des Dix-Mille. Vestiges archéologiques dans les environs du 'Mur de Medie', in: Briant 1995: 201–216.

Gera, D.L. (1993): *Xenophon's Cyropaedia. Style. Genre and Literary Technique*, Oxford.

Giangrande, G. (1976): On an alleged fragment of Ctesias, *QUCC* 23: 31–46.

Gilmore, J. (1888): *The Fragments of the* Persika *of Ktesias*, London.

Goossens, G. (1950): Le sommaire des Persica de Ctésias par Photius, *Revue Belge de philologie et d'histoire* 28: 513–521.

Gray, V.J. (2003): Interventions and citations in Xenophon, *Hellenica* and *Anabasis*, *CQ* n.s. 53: 111–123 (= V.J. Gray (ed.) (2010): *Xenophon. Oxford Readings in Classical Studies*, Oxford: 558–570).

Griffiths, A. (1987): Democedes of Croton. A Greek Doctor at Darius' Court, *Achaemenid History* 2: 35–71.

Guyot, P. (1980): *Eunuchen als Sklaven und Freigelassenen in der griechisch-roemischen Antike*, Stuttgart.

Hägg, T. (1973): Photius at Work. Evidence from the Text of the *Bibliotheca*, *GRBS* 14: 213–222.

Hanson, A.E. (1991): Continuity and Change. Three Case Studies in Hippocratic Gynecological Therapy and Theory, in: S.B. Pomeroy (ed.), *Women's History and Ancient History*, Chappel Hill, North Carolina: 73–110.

Hamilton, J.R. (1961): Cleitarchus and Aristobulus, *Historia* 10: 448–458.

Hamilton, J.R. (1969): *Plutarch, Alexander. A Commentary*, Oxford.

Haug, M. (1854), *Die Quellen Plutarchs in den Lebensbeschreibungen der Griechen*, Tübingen.

Henry, R. (1947): *Ctésias, la Perse, l'Inde, les sommaires de Photius*, Brussels.

Henry, R. (1959): *Photius. La Bibliothéque*, Paris.

Hintz, W. (1975): *Altiranisches Sprachgut der Nebenüberliefrungen*, Wiesbaden.

Jacoby, F. (1921): Kleitarchos (2), *RE* XI: 622–654.

Jacoby, F. (1922): Ktesias, *RE* XI: 2032–2073.

Jacoby, F. (1930): *Die Fragmente der griechischen Historiker*, vol. IId, Berlin.

Jacoby, F. (1958): *Die Fragmente der griechischen Historiker*, vol. IIIc, Leiden.

Justi, F. (1895): *Iranisches Namenbuch*, Marburg.

Kaemmel, O. (1875): Die Berichte über die Schlacht von Kunaxa und den Fall des Kyros am 3 September 401 vor Chr., *Philologus* 34: 515–538, 665–696.

Karttunen, K. (1980): The Reliability of the *Indika* of Ctesias, *Studia Orientalia* 50: 105–107.

Karttunen, K. (1989): *India in Early Greek Literature*, Helsinki.

Karttunen, K. (1991): The *Indica* of Ctesias and its Criticism, in: *Graeco-Indica, India's Cultural Contects [sic] with the Greek World: in Memory of Demetrius Galanos (1760–1833), a Greek Sanskritist of Benares*, New Dehli: 74–85.

Karttunen, K. (1997): Greeks and Indian Wisdom, in: E. Franco, K. Preisendanz (eds.), *Beyond Orientalism. The Work of Wilhelm Halbfass and its Impact on Indian and Cross-Cultural Studies*, Amsterdam: 117–122.

Kent, R.G. (1953): *Old Persian Grammar Texts Lexicon*, New Haven, CT.

King, H. (1998): *Hippocrates' Woman. Reading the Female Body in Ancient Greece*, London.

Kirtley, B.F. (1963): The Ear Sleepers. Some Permutations of a Traveler's Tale, *Journal of American Folklore* 76: 119–130.

König, F.W. (1972): *Die Persika des Ktesias von Knidos*, Graz.

Körte, A. (1922): Die Tendenz von Xenophons *Anabasis*, *NJbb* 49: 15–24.

Kuhrt, A. (2007): *The Persian Empire*, 2 vols., London.

Lassen, C. (1874): *Indische Alterumskunde*, Leipzig.

Le Goff, J. (1964): *La civilisation de l'Occident medieval*, Paris.

Lemerle, P. (1986): *Byzantine Humanism* (trans. H. Lindsay & A. Moffat), Canberra.

Lendle, O. (1986): Xenophon in Babylonien. Die Märsche der Kyreer von Pylai bis Opis, *RhM* 129: 193–222.

Lendle, O. (1995): *Kommentar zu Xenophons Anabasis*, Darmstadt.

Lenfant, D. (1996): Ctésias et Hérodote, ou les réécritures de l'histoire dans la Perse achéménide, *REG* 109: 348–380.

Lenfant, D. (1999): Monsters in Greek Ethnography and Society in the Fifth and Fourth Centuries BCE, in: R. Buxton (ed.), *From Myth to Reason? Studies in the Development of Greek Thought*, Oxford: 197–214.

Lenfant, D. (2004): *Ctésias de Cnide. La Perse, L'Inde, Autres Fragments*, Paris.

Lenfant, D. (2007): Greek Historians of Persia, in: J. Marincola (ed.), *A Companion to Greek and Roman Historiography*, vol. 1, Oxford: 201–209.

Lenfant, D. (2009): *Les Histoires perses de Dinon et d'Héraclide*. Fragments édités, traduits et commentés, Paris.

Lewis, D.M. (1977): *Sparta and Persia*, Leiden.

Lindegger, P. (1982): *Griechische und römische Quellen zum peripheren Tibet*, Teil II: *Überlieferungen von Herodot bis zu den Alexanderhistorikern (Die nordösten Grenzregionen Indiens)*, Zurich.

Llewellyn-Jones, L., Robson J. (2010): *Ctesias' History of Persia. Tales of the Orient*, London.

MacGinnis, J.D.A. (1988): Ctesias and the Fall of Nineveh, *ICS* 13: 37–43.

MacLaren, M. (1934): Xenophon and Themistogenes, *TAPA* 15: 240–247.

Manfredi, V. (1978): Proposte per una revisione itineraria e per un commento topografico dell'Anabasi di Senofonte, *Aevum* 52: 62–67.

Manfredi, V. (2004): The Identification of Mount Thekes in the Hincrary of the Ten Thousand: A New Hypothesis, in: C. Tuplin (ed.), *Xenophon and this World: Papers from a Conference held in Liverpool in July 1999*, Stuttgart: 319–324.

Manfredini, M., Orsi, D.P., Antelami, V. (1987; 1996[2]): *Plutarcho, Le Vite di Arato et di Artaserse*, Roma.

Mango, C. (1975): The Availablity of Books in the Byzantine Empire, A.D. 750–850, in: C. Mango, I. Ševčenko (eds.), *Byzantine Books and Bookmen. A Dumbarton Oaks Colloquium*, Washington, DC–New York: 29–45.

Mantey, O.A. (1888): *Welchen Quellen folgte Plutarch in seinem Leben des Artaxerxes*, Greifenberg in Pommern.

Marincola, J. (1997): *Authority and Tradition in Ancient Historiography*, Cambridge.

McCrindle, J.W. (1881): *Ancient India as Described by Ktesias the Knidian*, Calcutta–Bombay.

Mendels, D. (1981): The Five Empires. A Note on a Propagandistic Topos, *AJPh* 102: 330–337.

Mendels, D. (2004): *Memory in Jewish, Pagan and Christian Societies of the Graeco-Roman World*, London–New York.

Mess, A. von (1906): Untersuchenen über Ephoros, *RhM* 61: 360–407.

Miller, M. (1997): *Athens and Persia in the Fifth Century BC. A Study in Cultural Receptivity*, Cambridge.

Mitscherling, J. (1982): Xenophon and Plato, *CQ* n.s. 32: 468–469.

Momigliano, A. (1931): Tradizione e invenzione in Ctesia, *Atena e Roma* n.s. 12: 15–44.

Momigliano, A. (1958): The Place of Herodotus in the History of Historiography, *History* 43: 1–13.

Momigliano, A. (1971): *The Development of Greek Biography*, Cambridge, MA–London.

Momigliano, A. (1975): *Alien Wisdom. The Limits of Hellenization*, Cambridge.

Müller, C. (1844): *Ctesiae Cnidii et Chronographorum Castoris, Eratosthenes, etc. Fragmenta*, Paris.

Murray, O. (2001): Herodotus and Oral History, in: N. Luraghi (ed.), *The Historian's Craft in the Age of Herodotus*, Oxford: 16–44.

Neuhaus, O. (1901): Die Überlieferung über Aspasia von Phokaia, *RhM* 56: 272–283.

Nichols, A. (2008): *The Complete Fragments of Ctesias of Cnidus. Translation and Commentary with an Introduction*, PhD diss., University of Florida.

Nichols, A. (2011): *Ctesias on India*, London.

Nippel, W. (2001): The Construction of the 'Other,' (trans. A. Nevill), in: T. Harrison (ed.), *Greeks and Barbarians*, Edinburgh: 278–310.

Nutton, V. (2004): *Ancient Medicine*, London–New York.

Obermeyer, J. (1929): *Die Landschaft Babylonien in Zeitalter des Talmuds und des Gaonats*, Frankfurt am Main.

Pearson, L. (1960): *The Lost Histories of Alexander the Great*, New York.

Perlman, S. (1976/1977): The Ten Thousand. A Chapter in the Military, Social and Economic History of the Forth Century. *RSA* 6/7: 241–284.

Pritchett, W.K. (1993): *The Liar School of Herodotus*, Amsterdam.

Rettig, H.C.M. (1827): *Ctesiae Cnidii vita cum appendice de libris quos Ctesias composuisse fertur*, Hannover.

Reuss, E. (1887): *Kritische und exegetische Bemerkungen zu Xenophons Anabasis*, Wetzlar.

Ritter, H.W. (1965): *Diadem und Königsherrschaft*, München.

Rood, T. (2004): Panhellenism and Self-presentation. Xenophon's Speeches, in: R. Lane Fox (ed.), *The Long March: Xenophon and the Ten Thousand*, New Haven, CT–London: 305–329.

Russell, D.A. (1973): *Plutarch*, London.

Sachs, A.J., Hunger, H. (1988): *Astronomical Diaries and Related Texts from Babylonia*, vol. 1: *Diaries from 652 B.C. to 262 B.C.*, Wien.

Sancisi-Weerdenburg, H. (1983): Exit Atossa, in: A. Cameron, A. Kuhrt (eds.), *Images of Women in Antiquity*, London: 20–33.

Sancisi-Weerdenburg, H. (1987): Decadence in the Empire or Decadence in the Sources? From Source to Synthesis: Ctesias, *Achaemenid History* 1: 33–46.

Sancisi-Weerdenburg, H. (1988): Was there Ever a *Median* Empire?, *Achaemenid History* 3: 197–212.

Schmitt, R., (2002): *Die Iranischen und Iranier-Namen in den Schriften Xenophons*, Vienna.

Schmitt, R. (2006): *Iranische Anthroponyme in den Erhaltenen Resten von Ktesias' Werk*, Vienna.

Schottin, (1865): *Observationes de Plutarchi Vita Artaxerxeis*, Budissin.

Schwartz, E. (1905): Dinon (2), *RE* V: 654.

Shafer, R. (1964): Unmasking Ktesias' Dogheaded People, *Historia* 13: 499–503.

Shepard, O. (1930): *The Lore of the Unicorn*, London.

Smith, C.F. (1881): *A Study of Plutarch's Life of Artarxerxes*, Leipzig, PhD diss.

Stadter, P.A. (1965): *Plutarch's Historical Methods*, Cambridge, MA.

Stevenson, R.B. (1997): *Persica*, Edinburgh.

Stronk, J. (2004/2005): Ctesias of Cnidus. From Physician to Author, *Talanta* 36–37: 101–122.

Stronk, J. (2007): Ctesias of Cindus. A Reappraisal, *Mnemosyne* 60: 25–58.

Stronk, J. (2010): *Ctesias of Cnidus' Persica*. Editio Minor with Introduction, Text, Translation and Historical Commentary, vol. 1, Düsseldorf.

Stylianou, P.J. (2004): One *Anabasis* or two?, in: R. Lane Fox (ed.), *The Long March. Xenophon and the Ten Thousand*, New Haven, CT–London: 68–96.

Sulimani, I. (2011): *Diodorus' Mythistory and the Pagan Mission. Historiography and Culture-Heroes in the First Pentad of the Bibliotheke*, Leiden.

Syme, R. (1988): The Cadusii in History and in Fiction, *JHS* 108: 137–150.

Tarn, W.W. (1927): Persia. From Xerxes to Alexander, *CAH* VI[1]: 1–24.

Tuplin, C.J. (2004a): Doctoring the Persians. Ctesias of Cnidus, Physician and Historian, *Klio* 86: 305–347.

Tuplin, C.J. (2004b): The Persian Empire, in: R. Lane Fox (ed.), *The Long March. Xenophon and the Ten Thousand*, New Haven, CT–London: 154–183.

Turner, E.G. (1952): *Athenian Books in Fifth and Fourth Centuries B.C.*, London.

Vander Waerdt, P.A. (1993): Socratic Justice and Self-sufficiency. The Story of the Delphic Oracle in Xenophon's Apology, *OSAPh* 11: 1–48.

Waterfield, R. (2004): Xenophon's Socratic Mission, in: C.J. Tuplin (ed.), *Xenophon and his World*, Stuttgart: 79–114.

Weissbach, F.H. (1922): Kounaxa, *RE* XI: 2193–2194.

Westlake, H.D. (1987): Diodorus and the Expedition of Cyrus, *Phoenix* 41: 241–254.

White, D. (1991): *Myths of the Dog-man*, Chicago.

Whitmarsh, T. (2008): Introduction, in: T. Whitmarsh (ed.), *The Greek and Roman Novel*, Cambridge: 1–14.

Wiesehöfer, J. (2003): The Medes and the Idea of the Succession of Empires in Antiquity, in: G.B. Lanfranchi, M. Roaf, R. Rollinger (eds.), *Continuity of Empire (?) Assyria, Media, Persia*, Padova: 391–396.

Wiesehöfer, J., Lanfranchi, G., Rollinger, R. (eds.) (2011): *Die Welt des Ktesias von Knidos*, Stuttgart.

Wilson, N.G. (1968): The Composition of Photius' *Bibliotheca*, *GRBS* 9: 451–455.

Wilson, N.G. (1983): *Scholars of Byzantium*, London.

Wilson, N.G. (ed.) (1994): *Photius, The Bibliotheca*, London.

Wylie, G. (1992): Cunaxa and Xenophon, *AC* 61: 119–134.

Ziegler, K. (1951): *Plutarchos*, Stuttgart.

ELECTRUM * Vol. 19 (2012): 41–60
doi: 10.4467/20843909EL.12.002.0743

THESSALY AND MACEDON AT DELPHI

Emma M.M. Aston

Abstract: The Daochos Monument at Delphi has received some scholarly attention from an art-historical and archaeological perspective; this article, however, examines it rather as a reflection of contemporary Thessalian history and discourse, an aspect which has been almost entirely neglected. Through its visual imagery and its inscriptions, the monument adopts and adapts long-standing Thessalian themes of governance and identity, and achieves a delicate balance with Macedonian concerns to forge a symbolic rapprochement between powers and cultures in the Greek north. Its dedicator, Daochos, emerges as far more than just the puppet of Philip II of Macedon. This hostile and largely Demosthenic characterisation, which remains influential even in modern historiography, is far from adequate in allowing for an understanding of the relationship between Thessalian and Macedonian motivations at this time, or of the importance of Delphi as the pan-Hellenic setting of their interaction. Looking closely at the Daochos Monument allows for a rare glimpse into the Thessalian perspective in all its complexity.

Keywords: Daochos, Philip II of Macedon, the Daochos Monument, Delphi, Thessaly.

Introduction

Reconstructing Thessaly's early involvement in Delphi and its Amphiktyony draws the scholar towards the shimmering mirage of Archaic Thessalian history. Like all mirages, it is alluring, and represents something which the viewer wishes keenly to find: in this case an ambitious, powerful, energetic Thessaly extending its influence outside its own borders and claiming a stake in wider Greek affairs.[1] Also in the nature of mirages, when grasped it proves insubstantial. It is made, in large part, of legend – figures such as Aleuas and Skopas, who plainly were important historical figures but whose deeds are

---

[1] See for example Larsen 1968: 13. Here the strong and ambitious Thessaly of the Archaic period is described as 'the original Thessaly' – the 'weakened Thessaly' of the fifth and fourth centuries is seen as degenerate successor to this powerful state. Sordi places the Thessalian heyday later, at the end of the sixth century and the opening years of the fifth: it is in this period that she locates the activities of Skopas and Aleuas, who establish control over Thessaly and its *perioikis*; Delphic involvement, in her view, follows as a secondary stage. For critical discussion of her views, see Helly 1995: 134–137.

overlaid by the fantastic[2] and are in any case hard to tether to specific times. More notably still, with very few exceptions the ancient testimonies on which the reconstruction of early Thessaly and Delphi rests derive from the fourth century BC or later. The First Sacred War is the perfect encapsulation of this situation. It *may* represent Thessalian control of one of the crucial early phases of the Delphic Amphiktyony's development in the early sixth century, but the episode is hopelessly hard to reconstruct convincingly;[3] more specifically, the role of the Thessalian Eurylochos as the commander of the forces against Krisa is only detailed explicitly by Pindaric *scholia*, although it is likely that these drew on the fourth century *Register of Pythian Victors* compiled apparently by Aristotle and Kallisthenes.[4] Aristotle was also responsible for the *Constitution of the Thessalians* to which we are indebted for our (very limited) knowledge of Aleuas and his reforms.[5] A direct link between Aleuas and Delphi has to wait as late as Plutarch.[6]

The date of the earliest mentions of Aleuas alerts us to something which is either frustrating or significant, depending on one's point of view: the extreme importance of the fourth century BC as a time when Thessalian history was being written about. This is frustrating if one is trying to recover sixth century events: every lead one follows abruptly deposits one two centuries later. But if one is prepared to relinquish the mirage of the Archaic Thessalian heyday the fourth century can in fact provide fruitful territory for the reconstruction of various Thessalian ambitions and preoccupations, in which Delphi has an undeniably important role to play.

That said, the fourth century presents a new factor which may appear to muddy the waters: the involvement of Macedon. From the moment when Philip II becomes involved at Delphi, Thessalian activity in the sanctuary has Macedonian 'fingerprints' all over it, and it becomes distinctly difficult to disentangle the agendas of the two northern powers. The Thessalian Amphiktyons, for all their sudden gratifying visibility in the epigraphic record, can start to seem mere puppets, worked by strong Macedonian hands. It is easy for the historian of Thessaly to deplore this situation, concerned as he or she naturally is with lifting Thessalians out of their perennial obscurity. However, it is dangerous to become too preoccupied with sole agency, especially at Delphi, a place where interaction was paramount. In this article, I shall argue for the value of seeing the sanctuary in

---

[2] Especially Aleuas: according to the Hellenistic author Hegemon (*FGrH* 110 F 1 = Ael. *De Nat. An.* 8.11) he inspired erotic affection in a serpent. Helly obviates the implications of such tales by positing two figures called Aleuas: a purely legendary one, and a historical leader of the sixth century responsible for political reform (Helly 1995: 118–124). I should rather suggest that by the time of Hegemon's writing – and possibly earlier – it was amply possible to endow the historical Aleuas with mythical qualities and deeds. The far more famous example of Alexander the Great shows how an undoubtedly real person may become embellished with elements of the legendary and the fabulous almost as soon as he has perished.

[3] For an argument of extreme scepticism, see Robertson 1978, who claims that the war was wholly and entirely a fourth century invention designed to legitimise Macedonian involvement at Delphi. For a less stark discussion of the historical uncertainties and their implications, see Hall 2007: 276–283.

[4] What remains of the *Register* is Aristotle frs. 615–617 Rose. We also have an inscription (*SIG*³ 275) recording formal Amphiktyonic praise of Aristotle and Kallisthenes for their work. For discussion of the text of the inscription, see Rhodes/Osborne 2003: 392–395. For the influence of the *Register* on the Pindaric *scholia*, see Robertson 1978: 54–60.

[5] Aristotle frs. 497–498 Rose.

[6] Plut. *De Frat. Am.* 21.

the fourth century as a place where Thessalians and Macedonians could stage a delicate symbolic interaction founded on shared northern culture, myth and religion.

The main example used to demonstrate this will be Daochos of Pharsalos and his Monument, the first actual building commissioned by a Thessalian at Delphi, which housed a series of statues of Daochos and his family, each accompanied by an inscription detailing the person's activities and virtues. The dating of the Monument is uncertain (the controversy is discussed in detail below), but the most probable theories place it between 337 and 332 BC – that is, either in the last two years of Philip II's life or in the first four years of the reign of Alexander. Considerable archaeological and art-historical attention has been granted to the Daochos Monument in recent decades, and the present article does not attempt to add to that sphere of work; it will not, for example, reflect at length on the stylistic features of the structure or of the statues within it. On the other hand, there has never yet been a detailed discussion of its expressive power set in proper context – that of recent Thessalian history and the Thessaly/Macedon relationship. It has tended to be read simply as an advertisement of lineage, but as this article will show it bears a great deal more significance than that.

1. Some historical background

The strong and abiding links between Thessaly and the Argead kings of Macedon have recently started to achieve more recognition from scholars working on northern Greek culture.[7] Throughout the Classical period we receive sporadic glimpses of a relationship between the Argeads and the Larisaian Aleuadai,[8] which Graninger is surely right to identify as a case of *xenia* between families;[9] certainly it has not the consistency of a formal alliance, for it seems flexible enough to survive some serious temporary deviations such as Amyntas III's alliance with Jason of Pherai in 371 BC.[10] The Macedon/Pherai rapprochement, however, died with Jason; thereafter on a number of occasions the Macedonian kings sent aid to the Aleuadai against the rulers of Pherai, and it is this emerging pattern which provides the backdrop for Philip II's Thessalian connections, connections which were of the greatest possible importance in furthering his southward ambitions.[11] Philip was called in by the Aleuadai to aid them against Lykophron of Pherai in around 353; his subsequent defeat of Lykophron allowed him to accomplish an ideo-

---

[7] For example, the recent *Blackwell Companion to Ancient Macedonia* contains an article on Macedon and Thessaly (Graninger 2010). Earlier extensive discussion of political and cultural overlap between Macedon and Thessaly may be found in Hatzopoulos 1994.

[8] For example, when the Spartan general Brasidas marches north through Thessaly in 424, he is aided by one Nikonidas of Larisa, a friend of the Macedonian king Perdikkas: Thuc. 4.78.2. At the end of the fifth century, Archelaos appears to have become deeply involved in Larisaian politics; Thrasymachos' fragmentary *On Behalf of the Larisaians* bewails the 'enslavement' of the Larisaians to the Macedonian king, but the precise details of the king's intervention are unknown; it is likely that he provided support for the ruling oligarchic faction.

[9] Graninger 2010: 310.

[10] Diod. 15.60.2.

[11] For detailed analysis of Philip's relations with Thessaly, see Sprawski 2005.

logically powerful 'freeing' of Pherai and a settlement of the whole of Thessaly, obscure in its details but no doubt highly advantageous to his interests.[12] Philip gained immense influence in Thessaly, which he cemented in his own typical style with two strategic marriages, with Philinna of Larisa and with Nikesipolis of Pherai. These marriages illustrate the way in which Philip, ever adroit, balanced inherited Larisaian connections with other, newer ties.

Thessaly was for Philip a gateway to Delphi, geographically and metaphorically. At the Thessalians' invitation he led their forces in the Third Sacred War which was waged against the Phokians and their allies (including Athens and Sparta) from c. 354 to 346 BC.[13] When the Phokians, defeated, were stripped of their two votes in the Amphiktyonic council, these votes were awarded to Philip instead. Thus, overall, we can see that the relationship between Thessaly and Macedon in the Delphic sanctuary was no superficial or short-term phenomenon, but rather is one of the many instances of Philip exploiting long-standing arrangements, with a generous admixture of luck, to manoeuvre himself into positions of the greatest influence.

Alexander the Great largely continued his father's relationship with Thessaly and certainly inherited his recognition of the region's usefulness. In the wake of Philip's assassination, the region joined in to some extent with the surge of anti-Macedonian feeling in Greece, but briefly and without success:[14] Alexander overcame resistance at Tempe, and, marching south through Thessaly on the way to quash southern insurrection, was ratified as the leader of the Thessalian *koinon*.[15] Thessalians – both individuals[16] and the famous cavalry[17] – contributed significantly to his campaigns. And though himself far distant from Greece, Alexander continued Macedon's Amphiktyonic representation, his representatives rubbing shoulders with those of Thessaly.[18]

Exactly what reorganisation Philip imposed on Thessaly's political structure is not entirely clear. Demosthenes tells us that Philip set up *tetrarchiai* in Thessaly;[19] his reference to Philip enslaving the Thessalians 'by tribe' indicates that the institution of *tetrarchiai* should probably be read as a recycling of the long-standing division of the region into the four cantons of Thessaliotis, Phthiotis, Pelasgiotis and Hestiaiotis. Philip presumably increased their functional importance as administrative units, each controlled by a *tetrarchos*. (One of these *tetrarchoi* was the chief subject of this article, Daochos of Pharsalos.)

---

[12] Diod. 16.38.1.

[13] On Thessaly and Macedon in the context of the Third Sacred War, see Buckler 1989: 58–81.

[14] Polyain. 4.3.23.

[15] Just. *Epit.*11.3.

[16] Not surprisingly given the region's reputation for gluttony, it was a Thessalian, Medeios, who persuaded Alexander to rejoin the party which may have contributed to his ill-health and eventual demise! (Arr. *Anab.* 7.25.) On Thessalians as gluttonous in ancient perception, see Bakola 2005: 611–612; Pownall 2009.

[17] Thessalian excellence at the battle of Gaugamela: Diod. 17.21.4.

[18] Stamatopoulou 2007: 222 notes the high degree of continuity in the Thessalian presence at Delphi between the reigns of Philip and Alexander, especially the prominence of Pharsalians. On the Delphic involvement of Philip and Alexander, see Miller 2000: 267–274.

[19] Demosth. 9.26: ἀλλὰ Θετταλία πῶς ἔχει; οὐχὶ τὰς πολιτείας καὶ τὰς πόλεις αὐτῶν παρῄρηται καὶ τετραρχίας κατέστησεν, ἵνα μὴ μόνον κατὰ πόλεις ἀλλὰ καὶ κατ᾽ ἔθνη δουλεύωσιν.

Considerable doubt and controversy attend the question of whether Philip's settlement of Thessaly included his own election as Archon of the Thessalian league.[20] Probably influenced by Demosthenes' rhetoric of enslavement, past scholarship has tended to assume so, and to interpret certain literary sources accordingly.[21] However, a challenge to this perspective comes from Sprawski (2003), who makes the attractive suggestion that Philip's position in Thessaly should be considered in terms of influence rather than a fixed constitutional command, with a close parallel being identified in the case of the Theban Pelopidas. The analogy is a strong one: Pelopidas, like Philip, combined political reshaping[22] with military involvement; Pelopidas, like Philip, adroitly espoused the cause of Thessalian freedom and won considerable Thessalian support – and all this without an official title such as Archon or Tagos. This picture of the situation does not, however, lessen the extent to which Philip was able to steer Thessalian affairs; his leadership in the Third Sacred War and his control of customs and revenues (strongly linked with control of the *perioikis*)[23] gave him unsurpassed influence in the region, and his relationship with individuals such as Daochos also reveals the power of his backing: having Philip on one's side was plainly very useful to an ambitious local figure keen to further his own standing.

2. Daochos and Macedon

Daochos is a prime example of Philip's particularly assiduous cultivation of Pharsalian connections. Pharsalos had a greater record of Delphic involvement than the traditional Macedonian ally, Larisa, at least if the dedications are anything to go by,[24] and this fact would surely have been an ingredient in their usefulness to Philip. From what we can see, Philip conferred on Daochos a position of great power within Thessaly, or at least ratified and enhanced his existing status,[25] though the precise nature of the arrangements is unclear. In the inscription attached to his statue (see below), Daochos refers to himself as '*tetrarchos* of the Thessalians,' and, as has been said, Philip set up a system of *tetrarchiai* in Thessaly;[26] it therefore seems likely that Philip used his influence to install Daochos as a *tetrarchos* or ruler of one of the four parts, presumably Phthiotis, the part

---

[20]　It should be noted that the very nature of centralised power in Thessaly is fraught with difficulties of interpretation and reconstruction. The fullest – and at the same time the most contentious – discussion of the subject is that of Helly 1995, which builds on (and substantially disagrees with) Sordi 1958 and Larsen 1968. For useful briefer summaries of the evidence and interpretations, however, see Sprawski 1999: 18–20, and Graninger 2011: 7–23. Some of the pivotal evidence is collated by Rhodes 1986: 182–185.

[21]　The key texts in this matter are Diod. 17.4.1 and Just. *Epit.* 11.3.1–2, both of which speak of Alexander the Great taking over his father's position in Thessaly.

[22]　Diod. 15.67; Plut. *Pelop.* 26 (relating to 369/368 BC).

[23]　Customs and revenues: Demosth. 1.22; the *perioikis*: Philochoros *FGrH* 328 F 56; Sprawski 2003: 60.

[24]　Earlier Pharsalian dedications: Paus. 10.13.5 (statue-group of mounted Achilles with Patroklos); *SEG* 1.210 (statue of a horse). See Stamatopoulou 2007: 339–340.

[25]　Helly 1995: 51 argues that Daochos was already ruler before Philip's domination, and was simply confirmed in his position; this is plausible, as we cannot rightly imagine Philip producing him out of nowhere and imposing him on the Pharsalians without some track record of political command.

[26]　Demosth. 9.26.

in which Pharsalos lay. The importance of Demosthenes as a source of information in this matter is inescapable but also deeply regrettable, since he pursued a strong rhetorical line which consisted of depicting the Thessalians as betrayed by their own countrymen, Daochos prominent among them.[27]

οἵ, ὅτ' ἦν ἀσθενῆ τὰ Φιλίππου πράγματα καὶ κομιδῇ μικρά, πολλάκις προλεγόντων ἡμῶν καὶ παρακαλούντων καὶ διδασκόντων τὰ βέλτιστα, τῆς ἰδίας ἕνεκ' αἰσχροκερδίας τὰ κοινῇ συμφέροντα προΐεντο, τοὺς ὑπάρχοντας ἕκαστοι πολίτας ἐξαπατῶντες καὶ διαφθείροντες, ἕως δούλους ἐποίησαν, Θετταλοὺς Δάοχος, Κινέας, Θρασύδαος·

At a time when Philip's resources were weak and entirely small, when I was frequently warning and exhorting and instructing for the best, these men flung away shared advantage for the sake of personal gain; they cajoled and corrupted all the citizens within their grasp, until they had made them into slaves. So the Thessalians were treated by Daochos, Kineas, Thrasydaos…

Demosth. 18.295

The quotation comes from Demosthenes' *On the Crown*, delivered in 330 BC, in which he defends his associate Ktesiphon against Aischines' charge of having illegally proposed honours for Demosthenes to the Assembly. Much of his rhetorical energy, however, is expended in defence of his own conduct in opposition to Philip. Here he attempts to deflect Aischines' various accusations by listing men in several Greek states who, he says, in contrast to his own irreproachable behaviour, have betrayed their communities to the Macedonian.

Daochos and Thrasydaios (or Thrasydaos as Demosthenes spells it[28]) in particular tend to appear together in the few scattered references which exist in the literature of the time, and they are always presented as working on Philip's behalf,[29] though not always with as much vitriol as Demosthenes deploys on them.[30] Despite the very transparent oratorical purpose of Demosthenes' accusation, modern scholars have not really tried to look beyond the characterisation of Daochos as Philip's instrument, and it has certainly coloured readings of their role in Delphic inscriptions. A good example is *FD* 3.5: 47 (*CID* 2.74). This is an Amphiktyonic decree of c. 339/338, concerning the regulation of financial contributions to the sanctuary. Daochos and Thrasydaios are not the Thessalian hieromnemones in that year (Kottyphos and Kolosimmos are clearly named in that role in line 31);[31] but they head the inscription in the genitive, plainly responsible in some capacity for the stipulations it contains. This much is clear. But Bourguet's assertion that their function is just that of Philip's agents, pushing through measures *he* desired en-

---

²⁷ On the depiction of southern Greek presentations of Thessaly-Philip relations at this time, see Sprawski 2003: 55–59; Aston (forthcoming).

²⁸ Because the form Thrasydaios is the one used in Amphiktyonic inscriptions, it is preferred in this article.

²⁹ See e.g. Plut. *Demosth.* 18, citing Marsyas of Pella: Philip sends Daochos and Thrasydaios as envoys to persuade the Thebans not to oppose Macedon (whereas Demosthenes urges them to join with Athens against Macedon).

³⁰ For another scathing treatment, however, this time of Thrasydaios alone, see Theopompos, *FGrH* 115 F 209: 'Philip set up Thrasydaios the Thessalian as tyrant of his countrymen. He was an intellectual pigmy but a gigantic flatterer.'

³¹ On Thessalian – primarily Pharsalian – hieromnemones in the age of Philip and Alexander, see Stamatopoulou 2007: 222.

acted, is taking a large step into unsupported conjecture. This is just one example of the way in which the Demosthenic perspective has encouraged certain interpretations of the epigraphic material, and certain assumptions with regard to Daochos and Thrasydaios and their relationship with Philip.

It is certainly true that Daochos and Thrasydaios are exceptionally conspicuous in the Delphic inscriptions, all the more so because of the frequent use of the formula ἱερομνημονούντων τῶμ μετὰ Δαόχου καὶ Θρασυδαίου in lieu of the traditional Amphiktyonic list in which the representatives of all twelve *ethnê* are given. The Thessalians clearly held the presidency of the Amphiktyony while Daochos and Thrasydaios were in post, and it is also probable that they owed this special distinction to Philip, though we are once again reliant on Demosthenes for the theory that Philip gave (or gave back[32]) the Amphiktyonic presidency to the Thessalians, and the precise historical circumstances are very unclear.[33] Though it is with Philip that – thanks to Demosthenes – we primarily associate Daochos and his colleague, it must be noted that they continue to be listed as Amphiktyons on Delphic inscriptions after his death, when the formula introducing Macedonian delegates has changed from παρὰ Φιλίππου to παρ' Ἀλεχάνδρου.

But even if it is true that Daochos and Thrasydaios owed their positions of influence, at Delphi and in Thessaly, to Philip, it does not entitle us to see them as nothing more than shadow-men, following Philip's orders (and later his son's), and forming a useful cloak for the exercise of Macedonian control at Delphi.[34] They would have had their own concerns and ambitions. Those of Thrasydaios are entirely beyond discovery, but Daochos holds out more hope: his Monument allows us to catch at least a glimpse of how he wished himself to be perceived by those who came to Delphi: fellow Thessalians, Macedonians, the representatives of other Greek states.

3. The Daochos Monument and questions of dating

The Daochos Monument was, as one of its inscriptions makes clear, a gift to Apollo, and by no means the first which Thessalians had consecrated in the sanctuary.[35] However, it

---

[32] This frequent interpretation rests on the assumption, impossible to verify, that the Thessalians had held the presidency at some earlier time, and subsequently lost it.

[33] Demosth. 5.23, 6.22, 10.67.

[34] The extent to which Philip obscures his own involvement in the Amphiktyonic inscriptions should not be overstated: if the Thessalian Amphiktyons are a cover for his own power, it is not being used very intensively. Philip's own name is not hidden in the list of representatives, but tends to take second position after the Thessalians. An example in good condition is *FD* 3.5: 14 (*CID* 2:36), in which the standardised formula τῶμ παρὰ Φιλίππου on line 23 immediately follows the names of the Thessalian hieromnemones at the time (somewhere between 343 and 340 BC), Kottyphos and Kolosimmos.

[35] Known earlier Thessalian dedications include: a statue of Apollo, 'the earliest,' dedicated by Echekratidas of Larisa (Paus. 10.16.8); a statue of a horse, dedicated by the Thessalians in 457 after the battle of Tanagra (*SEG* 17.243; see Daux 1958); a statue of riders, dedicated by Pherai some time after 457 in celebration of victory over Athenian cavalry (Paus. 10.15.4); a statue of Achilles and Patroklos, dedicated by Pharsalos in the second half of the fifth century BC (Paus. 10.13.5); a statue of a horse, also dedicated by Pharsalos some time during the fifth or fourth centuries BC (*SEG* 1.210); a statue of Pelopidas, dedicated by the Thessalians in 369 BC (*SEG* 22.460).

marked a departure from the previous Thessalian tradition of statue dedication in its size, scale and structure: not one statue but at least nine, and housed in a building which may even, according to one recent reconstruction, have been roofed over.[36] It appears to have had at least a partial counterpart set up in the dedicator's homeland: a bronze statue of Hagias by the famous artist Lysippos, accompanied by an inscription identical with that of the Hagias statue in the Monument.[37] It is possible that bronze versions of all the statues in the Monument were dedicated in Pharsalos, making it clear that Daochos wished his fellow-countrymen, as well as travellers to Delphi, to be aware of his *grande geste*.

But which Daochos? It is time to acknowledge a lingering controversy as to the identity of the dedicator and the date of the Monument's creation. Jacquemin and Laroche, the scholars who have performed the most recent and most meticulous analysis of the archaeological material, adhere unswervingly to the longstanding identification of the dedicator as the Daochos known from Demosthenes and the epigraphy to have been Philip's associate. There is, however, a lone voice raised in opposition: that of Geominy, who argues that the structure was in fact consecrated by the grandson of Philip's Daochos in the early third century.[38] This Hellenistic Daochos is depicted in the second statue labelled with that name, and the first, rather than being a fifth century figure, is in fact Philip's Daochos. Geominy posits a very different political context for the dedication, in which the Hellenistic Daochos is '[taking] advantage of the short Macedonian power vacuum in 288–278 B.C.E. to demonstrate the key ancestral role the Thessalians had played at Delphi.'[39]

It is true that, as Geominy points out, one would be unwise to place excessive reliance on the somewhat slippery Lysippan statue which supposedly constituted an exact Pharsalian counterpart to the effigy of Hagias at Delphi; the inscription, seemingly identical in wording to the Delphic one, is now unfortunately lost, and the Lysippan authorship of the statue, and its date, are not wholly secure. However, a re-identification of the two Daochoi as being a generation later is itself more problematic. In the first place, no Hellenistic Daochos appears in the surviving epigraphic record, either of Delphi or of Thessaly, a fact which does not marry comfortably with the idea of an ambitious, self-promoting hieromnemon. In the second, if the elder Daochos were taken as the mid fourth century figure, this would surely not be compatible with the claim in the inscriptions that he 'ruled all Thessaly' (for the inscriptions, see below). The extent of his rule is most likely to have been a single canton, Phthia; it would surely have been exceptionally difficult for the Hellenistic Daochos to claim his grandfather as a pan-Thessalian leader other than by the most bare-faced fiction-writing. Such adjustment of history is perhaps imaginable if the Hellenistic Daochos were, as Geominy argues, trying to assert Delphic predominance at the expense of Macedonian interests, but, as will now be shown, the Daochos Monument has certain features which suggest that it was intended to express a cultural rapprochement between Thessaly and Macedon, rather than competition and separation.

---

[36]　Jacquemin/Laroche 2001.

[37]　The inscription: *IG* IX² 249; Decourt 1995: 73–75, no. 57. Discussion: Preuner 1900; Maass 1993: 206; Jacquemin/Laroche 2001: 125.

[38]　Geominy 2007.

[39]　Geominy 2007: 85.

4. Position: an *espace thessalien?*

The Daochos Monument would have been recognised as a significant departure from previous Thessalian dedicatory practices in the sanctuary, through its size and function. In common with other Amphiktyonic communities, the Thessalians had not previously inclined towards monumental dedication, instead preferring to give statues and statue-groups. Daochos' decision to house his statues within a substantial built structure, possibly roofed although this remains uncertain, is therefore all the more striking. However, at Delphi sheer size is not the only way of making an impression.

It hardly needs stating that, when it came to adding a monument or other dedication to the crowded built environment of the Apollo sanctuary, positioning was of paramount importance. Daochos was plainly aware of this, and did not shrink from claiming a spot of the greatest visibility and prominence, near the entrance to the Temple and at the culmination of the Sacred Way. In addition, a key ingredient of position is juxtaposition, and it is important to examine whether by placing his Monument where he did Daochos was establishing any significant connections with existing structures and objects. It has in fact been claimed that the Monument occupied a place within what has been termed an *espace thessalien*, a zone with particularly strong Thessalian associations.[40] If true, this would have some important implications. Daochos would be consolidating an assertion of special Thessalian identity rather than just the credentials of his own family.

The theory of the *espace thessalien* rests chiefly on the Daochos Monument's immediate neighbour to the north-east: the shrine of Neoptolemos. There is absolutely no doubt that this shrine and the Daochos Monument were intended to be viewed together and to strike the viewer with their visual and spatial correspondence. So similar are the two structures in design and execution that it has been plausibly argued that the creation of the Daochos Monument included, at the same time, a Thessalian restoration of the Neoptolemos shrine, and in particular the creation of a new *peribolos*.[41] So to look for some kind of thematic and symbolic relationship between Daochos and the figure of Neoptolemos is quite justifiable. However, caution must be applied as to how exactly that relationship is defined. In particular, problems occur when one tries to argue that what Daochos was associating himself with was a hero – and a hero-cult – of predominantly Thessalian identity and character. This supposition underpins the idea of a Thessalian zone, but requires closer examination.

There is absolutely no evidence for special Thessalian involvement in the cult of Neoptolemos at Delphi before the construction of the Daochos Monument.[42] The details of the cult are hard to reconstruct, but we have evidence of one important regular ritual, the *theoxenia*, at which Apollo entertained a number of heroes at a ritual meal whose chief element was the symbolic distribution of shares of meat among the human participants.[43] Neoptolemos seems to have had a privileged role in this ritual, presiding over the distribution of the meat as guarantor of good order. This benevolent role forms

---

[40]   Jacquemin 1999: 52, reasserting the suggestion of Pouilloux/Roux 1963: 144–145.

[41]   Homolle 1899: 424–425; Jacquemin/Laroche 2001: 308.

[42]   This despite the attempt by Sordi 1979 to argue that the cult of Neoptolemos was a mainstay of the Delphic propaganda campaign of Aleuas the Red in the late sixth century and early fifth.

[43]   Rutherford 2001: 310–315.

an inverted counterpart of his depiction in myth, specifically the stories concerning his death, in which he is killed during a rather shabby quarrel over the distribution of sacrificial carcasses.[44]

There are some suggestions from the evidence that the cult of Neoptolemos was, so to speak, *about* Thessaly, that it reflected in the conjoined languages of ritual and myth upon the role of Thessaly at Delphi.[45] But who took part in the *theoxenia*, and would it have involved Thessalians? Pindar's sixth *Paian* says that the sacrifice is made 'on behalf of illustrious Panhellas',[46] but this does reveal the extent of actual participation, let alone giving detail of constituent groups. Epigraphic evidence reveals a link between Delphi and the island of Skiathos, and the inscription in question does make mention of the *theoxenia*, suggesting that a group on the periphery of Thessaly's orbit was involved in some capacity.[47]

However, from Pindar's seventh *Nemean* and sixth *Paian*, the Aiginetans are the group which emerge as the most energetic in their participation. The two poems by themselves are clear evidence of great interest in Neoptolemos by Aiginetans, and indeed Aiakid references abound in Pindar's Aiginetan odes; but there seems to have been a basis of ritual reality as well. Both Rutherford and Currie argue for a regular *theoria* from Aigina to Delphi for the *theoxenia*, and though the reconstruction of this event involves some conjecture from scanty evidence it is plausible on the basis of known religious links between the two places.[48] Aigina claimed to be the birthplace of Aiakos, the offspring of Zeus and the nymph Aigina,[49] and thus to have produced the whole Aiakid line. The interest in Neoptolemos is therefore part of this wider pattern of Aiginetan self-representation, and they certainly seem to have been the group most actively involved in his Delphic cult, though there is faint evidence also of Molossian interest,[50] which tallies with the claims to descent from Neoptolemos made by the Molossian royal family.[51] The

---

[44] For enumeration and analysis of all the variants of the myth of Neoptolemos' death, see Fontenrose 1960: 191–266; Suárez de la Torre 1997: 154–155. For a sophisticated reading of both myth and cult within the framework of the characterisation of the Homeric hero, see Nagy 1979: 118–141.

[45] The fullest and most recent exposition of this view is that of Kowalzig 2007: 198–199, who argues that the myths of Neoptolemos' death at Delphi were developed as a reflection of, and on, the fraught circumstances in and following the First Sacred War which led to the establishment of Amphiktyonic power at Delphi, with Thessaly in the dominant role. For an earlier political reading of Neoptolemos's cult and mythology, see Woodbury 1979.

[46] Pind. *Pai.* 6.61.

[47] Sokolowski 1962: no. 41; Amandry 1939 and 1944–1945.

[48] Rutherford 2001: 331; Currie 2005: 331–343; see also Walter-Karydi 2000. For a somewhat different view, see Figueira 1981: 314–321; he argues that the Aiginetan cult of Apollo Pythiaieus, a key component of their Delphic connections, was in fact strongly oriented as much towards the Peloponnese as towards Delphi.

[49] Among the earliest sources for this genealogy (apart from several references in Pindar): Hes. *Cat.* fr. 53 M-W = schol. Pind. *Nem.* 3.21; Bacchyl. frs. 9 and 13 Snell-Maehler; Corinna fr. 654 Page.

[50] Molossian interest in the depiction of Neoptolemos is discernible in Pind. *Nem.* 7.64–67, though this does not provide secure evidence of Molossian involvement in the Delphic cult.

[51] Molossian claims to Aiakid origins go back to the Epic Cycle, to the *Nostoi* (in the summary provided by Proklos in his *Chrestomathia*), which describes Neoptolemos as returning from Troy after its fall, in which he has been savagely instrumental; he briefly meets Odysseus in Thrace, and comes to Molossia where he is greeted by Peleus.

Aiakid stemma serves as a strong link between Molossian and Thessalian mythology;[52] however, Thessalian involvement in the Delphic cult of Neoptolemos is simply not discernible.

This does not, of course, mean that Daochos was not trying to assert the Thessalianity (to coin a word) of Neoptolemos by aligning his ancestors with the hero; it just means that we cannot see his dedication as exploiting an existing association between the hero and Thessaly which viewers would have recognised and mentally referred to. Instead, he must be viewed as an innovator in this regard, and a slightly audacious one, given how very un-Thessalian Neoptolemos actually was. True, his father Achilles was born and raised in Thessaly, in Phthia no less, on Daochos' very doorstep, and there is some evidence of religious interest in Neoptolemos' mother Thetis in Pharsalos and its environs;[53] but Neoptolemos himself was born on Skyros, and even his movements as an adult – Troy, Molossia, Delphi – generally do not include Thessaly.[54] Thessaly does not have an automatic claim on Neoptolemos, and if Daochos was intending to establish a Thessalian zone around his shrine the hero would not have provided an uncontroversial basis for it.

There is, however, another way of reading the significance of Neoptolemos in this situation: to see it as expressing, not simply a bold Thessalian claim of ownership, but rather a combination of Thessalian and Macedonian interests. In 357 BC Philip of Macedon married Olympias, a Molossian princess, who brought with her into the Macedonian court some discernible elements of her native culture, not least a fervent identification with the Aiakids of myth. It is probable that by the time the Daochos Monument was erected Olympias had become alienated from Philip; 337 BC saw Philip's marriage to his last wife, and the famous symposium at which Alexander perceived his own status to have been slighted by the girl's father Attalos, and responded by taking his mother back to Molossia and himself to Illyria.[55] However, this estrangement did not terminate Philip's Molossian connections; far from it. He adroitly ensured that the important connection was not severed, by marrying his daughter Kleopatra to Alexandros of Epeiros, whom he had installed as king in 342;[56] and we know that Alexander the Great cherished

---

[52]   The Molossians seem sometimes to have exploited this connection: Paus. 1.13.2–3 relates how, in the third century, the Molossian Pyrrhos, having defeated Antigonos Gonatas in battle, dedicates some of the spoils in the federal Thessalian sanctuary of Athena Itonia, with an inscription referring to himself as an Aiakid.

[53]   Thetis appears to have had a cult in the area of Pharsalos, and perhaps also in the city itself, though the evidence is not unproblematic. References to a Thetideion (or a place called Thetideion) near Pharsalos suggest cult: see e.g. Plut. *Pelop.* 32.1; Polyb. 18.20.6. Euripides (*Andr.* 20) and Strabo (9.431) indicate a cult within the city, but the corroboration of this which has been thought to be provided by an inscription (*SEG* 45.637) is in fact insubstantial because the restoration of the text which includes Thetis' name and details of cult practice is almost certainly faulty. For the older, more optimistic reading see Arvanitopoulos 1911; for a more recent and more sceptical interpretation, see Decourt 1995: 97–99, no. 77. My own inspection of the stone has led me to believe that scepticism is unfortunately warranted.

[54]   Homer's *Odyssey* (3.188–189) has Neoptolemos bring the Myrmidons back to their home in Phthia; likewise Euripides in the *Andromache* makes Neoptolemos come to Thessaly. This has led some to suggest a Thessalian performance-context for the play, and Thessalian concerns shaping its plot: see e.g. Taplin 1999: 44–48. Other versions tend to exclude Thessaly entirely from Neoptolemos' route.

[55]   Plut. *Alex.* 9.

[56]   Just. *Epit.* 8.6.4–5 – though the author characteristically lards his account with sexual scandal, the basic events are likely to be correct.

52 Emma M.M. Aston

a strong identification with Achilles, partly inherited, partly personal.[57] So, whether one thinks that the Daochos Monument was built in Philip's time or during the reign of his son, it is extremely plausible to suggest that its connection with the Neoptolemos shrine would have chimed resoundingly with Macedonian interests, beliefs and self-perception.

I would argue that this is not accidental: that Daochos was deliberately choosing to locate his Monument where he did in order to assert common mythical material linking Thessaly and Macedon. This reading is, if anything, strengthened if we imagine that Alexander was king at the time, in light of Justin's assertion that Alexander himself, at the beginning of his reign, referred to shared Aiakid associations as a way of appealing for Thessalian loyalty and support.[58] Diodoros makes him cite Herakles as common ancestor instead;[59] this is his paternal rather than maternal heritage, and reveals how much common mythology northern states and regions could indeed draw upon when desired, especially once the arrival of Olympias into the Macedonian royal family had added Aiakid strands to existing Heraklid ones.[60] If Alexander was on the Macedonian throne when the Daochos Monument was commissioned and constructed, it is very plausible to see it as a gesture by Daochos towards this shared mythology which Alexander himself had previously cited before a Thessalian audience, this time intended to reassure the king of Daochos' loyalty.

In addition, it should be remembered that in all their various manifestations the Aiakidai are far better suited to the expression of inclusion than of exclusive ownership, and are used accordingly by communities and individuals. Through motifs of travel and genealogy, they serve to link places and peoples, and even the most energetic claims on association with them do not attempt to work against this. The case of the Aiginetan Aiakid-myths is a good illustration of this. Developing the story that she produced Aiakos himself gave Aigina a special position, and indeed claims of primacy are a common tool,[61] but she did not use this position to cut her off from other regions. Her claim was not to the detriment of the other places involved. It did not deprive Thessaly, or Molossia, of their respective shares in the Aiakidai. In the realm of the pan-Hellenic (pan-Hellenic epic stories, pan-Hellenic gatherings and events), status derives from *connection*, from involvement in something broader than the boundaries of an individual place or community. In keeping with this, the Daochos Monument's location would have been

---

[57] For a collection and discussion of the sources relating to Olympias' and Alexander's interest in Achilles and the Aiakids, see Carney 2006: 5–6.

[58] Just. *Epit.* 11.3.

[59] Diod. 17.4.1. It should be noted that mythological links between Molossia and Thessaly predated Philip by a considerable time, and were not limited to the Aiakid connection; for example, in the early fifth century, we hear of a Molossian ruler called Admetos (Thuc. 1.136), a name with Pheraian associations. It is probable, therefore, that Olympias' introduction into the Macedonian court brought with it a stronger sense of legendary connection with Thessaly than Philip and his son would otherwise have felt.

[60] Within Thessaly, the group who laid the most energetic claim on Heraklid ancestry was the Aleuadai of Larisa, who also had traditional ties with the Argeads, as discussed above. The opening lines of Pindar's *Pythian* 10, commissioned by an Aleuad, emphasises this ancestry.

[61] It is worth noting the opposite device, the claim of being last, exercised by the Molossians – at Eur. *Andr.* 1246–1247 the child of Andromache and Neoptolemos, the forefather of the Molossian royalty, is described as the last of the Aiakid line. In this way, the Molossian kings gained a form of uniqueness on the grounds that they alone perpetuated a dynasty otherwise confined to the distant past.

calling upon Neoptolemos' power to forge connections, with Macedon certainly being an intended target.

Its position was not the only feature of the Daochos Monument which can plausibly be read as expressing Thessaly/Macedon connections. For one thing, it has long been recognised that it bears a physical similarity with the Philippeion at Olympia, another family statue group set up either by Philip or by Alexander,[62] and it may well have been influenced by that structure; festival-goers attending both the Pythian and the Olympic games may have noticed the correspondence. Moreover, it has been argued that the cloak worn by the statue of Daochos I is of a distinctively Macedonian type.[63] Claims regarding the precise development of the Macedonian garment are open to various criticisms, but one thing is clear and interesting; short cloaks associated with horse-riding and the cavalry were connected in antiquity *both* with Macedon *and* with Thessaly.[64] Thus the striking use of the garment in the Daochos Monument may have been intended to reinforce the sense of a shared northern identity common to both Thessaly and Macedon.

The inscriptions, however, which accompany the statues in the Monument give a rather different impression. They do not make any mention of shared epic past or of the contemporary reality of the rapprochement between Daochos and the Macedonian throne. Instead they refer to specifically Thessalian history (with an admixture of legend, perhaps). And it is in the inscriptions that a visitor able to read would have found messages detaching Daochos and his family from the ambit of Macedon, and asserting their own independent credentials.

5. The inscriptions: sole rule and just rule

For the sake of completeness, I provide in table form all the inscriptions accompanying the eight statues contained within the Monument; however, the discussion will focus on three, which are highlighted in bold text.

Previous scholarly interest has been focused chiefly on the three brothers distinguished by their athletic accomplishments, Hagias, Telemachos and Agelaos,[65] and Aknonios and the two Daochoi have been comparatively neglected. But in fact the inscriptions accompanying the statues of Aknonios and Daochos I constitute a far more intricate reflection on the dedicator's own position than has previously been recognised, and their full implications cannot be understood without reference to important aspects of recent and contemporary Thessalian history. The most obvious contemporary ref-

---

[62] For the Philippeion and its artistic and architectural parallels, see Schulz 2009. Whether one regards it as having been set up by Philip or his successor depends on how one reads the dative case in Pausanias' comment, φιλίππῳ δέ ἐποιήθη (Paus. 5.20.10): does this mean 'it was made by Philip' or 'it was made *for* Philip'? For discussion, see Schulz 2009: 128–131, who argues that in any case the monument was constructed according to Philip's plan.

[63] Lattimore 1975.

[64] Cloaks of a distinctively Thessalian style: Bacchyl. 18.54; Philostr. *Vit. Ap. Ty.* 4.16 and *Her.* 10.5. It has been argued that the Macedonian version was very similar but with rounded corners; see e.g. Saatsoglou-Paliadeli 1993: 143–145.

[65] See e.g. Ebert 1972, esp. 137–145.

Personage	Inscription	Translation
Aknonios, son of Aparos	Ἀκνόνιος Ἀπάρου τέτραρχος Θεσσαλῶν.	**Aknonios son of Aparos, tetrarch of the Thessalians.**
Hagias, son of Aknonios	πρῶτος Ὀλύμπια παγκράτιον, Φαρσάλιε, νικᾶις, Ἁγία Ἀκνονίου, γῆς ἀπὸ Θεσσαλίας, πεντάκις ἐν Νεμέαι, τρὶς Πύθια, πεντάκις Ἰσθμοῖ· καὶ σῶν οὐδείς πω στῆσε τροπαῖα χερῶν.	You, Pharsalian, Hagias son of Aknonios, won the Pankration at Olympia, the first to do so from the land of Thessaly; five times you won at Nemea, thrice at Pythia, five times at the Isthmos. And no-one ever set up trophies of victory from your hands.
Telemachos, son of Aknonios	κἀγὼ τοῦδε ὁμάδελ[φος ἔ]φυν, ἀριθμὸν δὲ τὸν αὐτὸν ἤμασι τοῖς αὐτοῖς [ἐχφέρ]ομαι στεφάνων, νικῶν μουνοπά[λης], Τ[. .]σηνῶν δὲ ἄνδρα κράτιστον κτεῖνα, ἔθελοντό [γε δ' οὔ]· Τηλέμαχος δ' ὄνομα.	I was born own brother to this man, and I bear away the same number of victory-garlands on the same days, winning as a wrestler; I killed the best man of the …ians, though I did not will it. My name is Telemachos.
Agelaos, son of Aknonios	οἵδε μὲν ἀθλοφόρου ῥώμης ἴσον ἔσχον, ἐγὼδὲ σύγγονος ἀμφοτέρων τῶνδε Ἀγέλαος ἔφυν· νικῶ δὲ στάδιον τούτοις ἅμα Πύθια παῖδας· μοῦνοι δὲ θνητῶν τούσδ' ἔχομεν στεφάνους.	These men had equal shares of prize-winning strength, and I Agelaos was born the sibling of them both. I won the stade-race for boys at the Pythian games alongside them; we alone of mortals have these victory-garlands.
Daochos I, son of Hagias	**Δάοχος Ἁγία εἰμί, πατρὶς Φάρσαλος, ἁπάσης Θεσσαλίας ἄρξας vac. οὐ βίαι ἀλλὰ νόμωι, ἑπτὰ καὶ εἴκοσι ἔτη, πολλῆι δὲ καὶ ἀγλαοκάρπωι εἰρήνηι πλούτωι τε ἔβρυε Θεσσαλία.**	**I am Daochos son of Hagias. My homeland was Pharsalos; I ruled all of Thessaly, not with force but with law, for twenty-seven years, and Thessaly burgeoned with great and fruitful peace, and with wealth.**
Sisyphos I, son of Daochos	οὐκ ἔψευσέσε Παλλὰς ἐν ὕπνωι, Δαόχου υἱὲ Σίσυφε, ἃδ' εἶπε σαφῆ θῆκεν ὑποσχεσίαν· ἐξ οὗ γὰρ τὸ πρῶτον ἔδυς περὶ τεύχεα χρωτί, οὔτ' ἔφυγες δήϊους οὔτε τι τραῦμ' ἔλαβες.	Pallas did not deceive you in a dream, Sisyphos son of Daochos, and the clear things which she told you she set down as a promise. For from the moment you first clothed your skin with armour, you never fled your foes nor received a single wound.
Daochos II, the dedicant, presumably son of Sisyphos I	**αὔξων οἰκείων προγόνων ἀρετὰς τάδε δῶρα στῆσεμ Φοίβωι ἄνακτι, γένος καὶ πατρίδα τιμῶν, Δάοχος εὐδόξωι χρώμενος εὐλογίαι, τέτραρχος Θεσσαλῶν ἱερομνήμων Ἀμφικτυόνων.**	**Increasing the virtues of my family's ancestors, I set up these gifts to lord Phoibos, honouring my people and my homeland – I, Daochos, possessed of glorious praise, tetrarch of the Thessalians, hieromnemon of the Amphiktyons.**
Sisyphos II, son of Daochos II	Σίσυφος Δαόχου.	Sisyphos son of Daochos

erence has already been mentioned: Daochos held the position of *tetrarchos*, and the verbal echo of the phrase *tetrarchos Thessalôn* between the Aknonios inscription and that of Daochos II[66] reinforces the sense that the ancestral figure of Aknonios provides a precedent for his scion's position. This precedence simply cannot be verified historically; scholarly reconstructions of the career of Daochos I tend to rely exclusively on the Daochos Monument's inscriptions, an arrangement of hideous circularity. But claiming an ancestor whose existence is somewhat mythical is of course a common strategy in ancient power-display.

The Daochos I inscription is longer and even more ambitious than that of Aknonios. It lays claim not to the rule of a tetrad, but to pan-Thessalian rule. This appears to present Daochos the dedicator in a very different light to that of Demosthenes' obsequious lackey – as the name-sharing successor of a man who occupied that most contested of positions, ruler of all of Thessaly. Should this be interpreted as a *rebuttal* of the hostile characterisation, and as a claim on political legitimacy through inheritance? Would the rule of Daochos I have served to validate the more limited[67] sway of his grandson in the face of swirling accusations of treachery?

In favour of such an interpretation is the fact that the fourth century saw other cases of Thessalians with ambitions to rule developing ancestral figures as a way of reinforcing their claims. As has been mentioned, the figure of Aleuas, legendary ruler of all Thessaly, is certainly shaped and burnished – of not actually invented – in the fourth century. One of the two precious surviving fragments of Aristotle's *Constitution of the Thessalians* in fact names the legendary Aleuas the Red as the originator of the tetradic division of Thessaly.[68] It is impossible to ascertain where and from which group(s) Aristotle derived his material about Aleuas' tetradic organisation, but the appearance of his head on Larisaian coins[69] testifies to the interest felt by the leading men of that city in asserting their ownership of the eponym and his achievements. Pharsalian Daochos lays claim far more directly by naming his ancestor *tetrarchos* on the Delphic stage where the gesture would have been seen by Macedonians and southern Greeks.[70]

---

[66] Though it should be noted that in the Daochos II inscription the phrase is extra-metrical: this, however, gives it more prominence if anything, and a certain quality of the bluntly factual quite different from the idealising language which otherwise prevails.

[67] That said, the formula *tetrarchos Thessalôn* does seem designed to convey a pan-Thessalian impression.

[68] Harpokration s.v. *Tetrarchia*: τεττάρων μερῶν ὄντων τῆς Θετταλίας ἕκαστον μέρος τετρὰς ἐκαλεῖτο, καθά φησιν Ἑλλάνικος ἐν τοῖς Θετταλικοῖς. ὄνομα δέ φησιν εἶναι ταῖς τετράσι Θεσσαλιῶτιν Φθιῶτιν Πελασγιῶτιν Ἑστιαιῶτιν. καὶ Ἀριστοτέλης δὲ ἐν τῇ κοινῇ Θετταλῶν πολιτείᾳ ἐπὶ Ἀλεύα τοῦ Πυρροῦ διῃρῆσθαί φησιν εἰς δ μοίρας τὴν Θετταλίαν. ('Thessaly was divided into four parts, each of which was called a tetrad, as Hellanikos says in his *Thessalian History* [*FGrH* 4 F 52]: he says the names of the tetrads were Thessaliotis, Phthiotis, Pelasgiotis and Hestiaiotis. Aristotle in his *Thessalian Constitution* [fr. 497 Rose] says that the Thessalians were divided into four sections at the time of Aleuas the Red.')

[69] See e.g. BMC *Thessaly* pl. 5, no. 12.

[70] It is worth contemplating the possibility of Larisaian agency behind the story told by Plutarch, of how Aleuas' rule of all of Thessaly was ratified by the Pythia: see Plut. *de Frat. Amor.* 21. If this story was generated by the Aleuadai in the fourth century it would constitute an intriguing challenge to the Pharsalian domination of Thessalian activity in the sanctuary as well as to the history of tetrarchic power.

Pherai, the most ambitious Thessalian community of the century, would not have benefited from a connection with Aleuas,[71] but it does appear that Jason may have found a satisfactory alternative as ancestral precedent for his appropriation of tribute from the *perioikoi* – the figure of Skopas, whose historicity is as nebulous as that of Aleuas. According to Xenophon, Jason προεῖπε δὲ τοῖς περιοίκοις πᾶσι καὶ τὸν φόρον ὥσπερ ἐπὶ Σκόπα τεταγμένος ἦν φέρειν ('ordered all the *perioikoi* to bring the tribute as had been organised in the time of Skopas').[72] This appears to be another example of a powerful Thessalian making reference to historical precedent to enhance the legitimacy of his actions. The fourth century was a time of great innovation in Thessaly's power structures, and for this very reason generated a surge in the development and adaptation of traditions. Daochos' emphasis on a regional ruler in his family tree should be viewed as part of this wider tendency of the age.

However, on the other side of the scale there are reasons why this strategy would not have been straightforwardly effective. First, it should be borne in mind that there was no strong tradition of *hereditary* sole rule of Thessaly, and therefore heredity itself was not an established and accepted criterion of command. In fact, one of the few things which may be said with certainty about the mysterious institution of the Thessalian *koinon* is that its leader, when there was one, was certainly appointed rather than ruling by right of birth – or else he pushed his way to power through military might and force of character. For this reason, Daochos' conspicuous identification of an Archon among his ancestors does not automatically gild his own status as *tetrarchos*. However, in the fourth century the waters had been muddied, in this regard, by Pherai, many of whose leading men strove for, and at times achieved, pan-Thessalian rule: this rule did have a strongly dynastic dimension. Jason, the most successful such figure, is the only one for whom we have a reasonable amount of information;[73] he may well have been the son of Lykophron, with whom Pherai's ambitions to more than local rule essentially began. When Jason was assassinated in 370 BC, various close male relatives took over his position: first his brothers Polydoros and Polyphron, and later his nephew Alexandros. The successors of Jason were hardly unopposed in their assumption of power – in fact it was opposition to Alexandros which eventually brought about Philip's involvement in Thessalian affairs. But their example showed that in the fourth century attempts were made to base pan-Thessalian rule on heredity.

And yet, a further problem for Daochos would have been the tarnished credentials of other figures who had recently vied for pan-Thessalian control. Indeed, at the time of his Delphic activities Pheraian affairs would have made inherited sole rule a *controversial* topic from a Thessalian perspective, rather than something to be accepted and taken for granted. It is also probable that the career of Jason would have left an especially strong aura of discomfort at Delphi. According to Xenophon, whose account – while it is certainly marked by a strong authorial interest in exploring the character of Jason – is not to be dismissed as fictional, Jason's ambitions extended beyond the unification of Thessaly

---

[71]   *Pace* Wade-Gery 1924: 61–64, who argues that the Aleuas coins of Larisa were in fact minted by Jason once he controlled the city, in a bid to claim that heritage for his own purposes. However, the impossibility of accurately dating the coins makes this pure speculation, and it does not convince.

[72]   Xen. *Hell.* 6.1.19.

[73]   See the extensive study of this figure by Sprawski 1999.

under his rule: at the time of his assassination, he was planning to stage a dramatic take-over of the presidency of the Pythian Games.[74] This bid for Amphiktyonic supremacy would, he intended, follow on from an extraordinary *grande geste*: his arrival in the sanctuary with a cavalcade of thousands of sacrificial beasts garnered, symbolically, from all parts of his subordinated homeland. None of this came to pass, in the event, but if Xenophon is correct its imminence caused waves of anxiety in the southern states,[75] and this must have been especially so in Delphi itself, where there is said to have been fear lest Jason try to appropriate the sacred treasures.[76] Some three decades later, Daochos and his fellow Thessalians at Delphi must still have been living down this dangerous example of northern involvement.

For this reason, and because mere heredity by itself was not enough to confer legitimacy of status, the inscriptions of the Monument serve another important function: to define rule, within the family, as *just* rule. In particular the phrase ἄρξας οὐ βίαι ἀλλὰ νόμωι is, for all its apparent simplicity, laden with contemporary and contextual significance. It has been argued that ruling with *nomos* is an especially northern – particularly Macedonian and Thessalian – ideal. This argument rests on the notion that *nomoi* – interpreted as unwritten ancestral customs – were all that northern communities had by way of law, all that held *bia* at bay, in the absence of constitutional government.[77] Were this so the implications would be important: we could read ἄρξας οὐ βίαι ἀλλὰ νόμωι as a verbal gesture on Daochos' part towards the northern culture he and Philip shared. However, the theory is made vulnerable by the difficulty of proving that *nomoi*, and rule according to *nomos*, held any special and exclusive significance in Thessaly and Macedon. To see the primacy of unwritten ancestral custom as limited to the north is unrealistic in view of the fact that *nomoi* all over Greece carried this meaning, and that almost no Greek state in the classical period had a written and undeviating constitution. *Nomoi* were no less important as guarantors of good social and political conduct in the south as in the north, and the rhetoric of ruling according to *nomoi* cannot with any security be classed as a uniquely northern one.

That does not, however, rob the phrase of all its special implications with regard to a Thessalian ruler. When in 498 BC Pindar wished to commend the rule of the Aleuad Thorax, who had commissioned his *Tenth* Pythian, good governance (referring specifically to the *nomos Thessalôn*) is one of the motifs used. This was a common enough ingredient of praise, but one which in the next century took on a special urgency. When other Greeks in the fourth century wish to criticise Thessalians or the Thessalian character (which they do with increasing frequency), *anomia* and closely related concepts, such as *ataxia* and *akolasia*, feature prominently among the terms used. This is especially so among philosophical texts, in which Thessaly appears as a paradigm of poor governance; the most famous example of this occurs in Plato's *Crito*, where the personified Laws of Athens say of Thessaly ἐκεῖ γὰρ δὴ πλείστη ἀταξία καὶ ἀκολασία ('There disorder

---

74 Xen. *Hell.* 6.4.29–30; Sprawski 1999: 118–127.

75 Xen. *Hell.* 6.4.32. The claim that Jason intended to seize general control of Greece is also made by Diodoros: 15.60.1.

76 Xen. *Hell.* 6.4.30.

77 Mooren 1983.

and ill-discipline abound'),[78] and the motif also appears in Xenophon.[79] However, the theme of Thessalian lawlessness is not limited to philosophy; according to Theopompos, their undisciplined nature was what gave the Thessalians a natural affinity with Philip.[80] Although it cannot be proved that Daochos was aware of such criticisms against his homeland, it is likely – given his considerable contact with the delegates of other Greek states – that he was, and the Daochos I inscription should be read as a brief but direct refutation of the stereotype.

We may also interpret it as a renewed claim, at a time when such a claim was especially necessary, on the virtues which Pindar accorded to Thorax and his family. That the inscriptions of the Daochos monument contains some strikingly Pindaric qualities has already been demonstrated by Cummins, who discusses the presentation of family relationships in both works;[81] to this broad theme we may add specific verbal echoes of *Pythian* 10 in the Daochos II inscription. In addition to the use of *nomos* mentioned above, the first word of the inscription, *auxôn*, recalls *auxontes* in line 71 of *Pythian* 10 (referring to the governance of Thorax and his brothers). There is also a strong emphasis on heredity in the Ode: the phrase πατρώϊαι κεδναὶ πολίων κυβερνάσιες – 'trusty ancestral governance of cites' – ties good governance and patrilineal succession together, and the Daochos Monument, with its combination of visual imagery and inscriptions, achieves the same juxtaposition.

It seems very likely that Pindar's ode entered the canon of Thessalian self-representation. Even though Thorax and Daochos were primarily associated with different cities, this is not really an impediment to the idea, given the strong interconnections between Thessalian ruling families; there could even have been a competitive edge to the process: Pharsalian Daochos in the fourth century appropriating ideology cherished by the Aleuadai in the early fifth. Though set upon a pan-Hellenic stage, the Monument represents a continuation and development of established internal Thessalian discourses on power, on who wields it and how.

Conclusions

What has previously been lacking from discussion of the Daochos Monument is discussion of its dedicator *as a Thessalian*, with a Thessalian's background, memory and preoccupations. This article has put forward a portrait of Daochos as the product of his homeland and its history. It is especially in the inscriptions that this character emerges; that of a man striving for connection with the ideals of the past, and separation from the negative associations of the fourth century.

---

[78]   Plat. *Crito* 53d-e. it should also be noted that Plato's *Meno* presents its Pharsalian subject, Menon, as someone whose idea of the good life is the imposition of one's will on others – essentially, the application of *bia*.

[79]   Xen. *Mem.* 1.2.24: Thessaly is characterised as a place whose inhabitants live in a state of *anomia* rather than *dikaiosunê*. For more detailed discussion of this stereotype, see Pownall 2009; Aston (forthcoming, 2013).

[80]   *FGrH* 115 F 162.

[81]   Cummins 2009.

Thessalian Daochos was not, however, operating in a vacuum. In addition to positioning his monument within the richly crowded built landscape of the Apollo sanctuary, he was managing a delicate political relationship with Macedon, first with Philip and then with Alexander. The alignment of the Daochos Monument with the renovated shrine of Neoptolemos expresses, not unique Thessalian religious associations, but rather – via the pan-Hellenic figure of the hero – the inclusion of Thessalians within a wider mythical picture. More specifically, Macedonian interest in the Aiakidai under Philip and Alexander strongly suggest that by positioning his dedication where he did Daochos was making reference to the shared Aiakid associations of his own homeland and the royal family of Macedon. The rhetoric of Demosthenes in the face of Philip's rise to power relied on a simple dichotomy of treachery and loyalty. The Daochos Monument reveals what one could in any case suspect: that the complexities of Daochos' position and self-perception cannot be encompassed within such a basic model.

BIBLIOGRAPHY

Amandry, P. (1939): Convention religieuse conclue entre Delphes et Skiathos, *BCH* 43: 183–219.

Amandry, P. (1944–1945): Note sur la convention Delphes–Sciathos, *BCH* 68–69: 411–416.

Aston, E.M.M. (2013): Friends in High Places: the Stereotype of Dangerous Thessalian Hospitality in the Later Classical Period, *Phoenix*, in press.

Bakola, E. (2005): A Missed Joke in Aristophanes' Wasps, *CQ* 55: 609–613.

Buckler, J. (1989): *Philip II and the Sacred War*, Leiden.

Carney, E. (2006): *Olympias, Mother of Alexander the Great*, London–New York.

Cummins, M.F. (2009): The Praise of Victorious Brothers in Pindar's *Nemean* Six and on the Monument of Daochus at Delphi, *CQ* 59: 317–334.

Currie, B. (2005): *Pindar and the Cult of Heroes*, Oxford.

Daux, G. (1958): Dédicace thessalienne d'une cheval à Delphes, *BCH* 82: 329–334.

Decourt, J.-C. (1995): *Inscriptions de Thessalie I. Les cités de la vallée de l'Énipeus*, Athens.

Ebert, J. (1972): *Griechische Epigramme auf Sieger an gymnischen und hippischen Agonen*, Berlin.

Figueira, T.J. (1981): *Aegina. Society and Politics*, New York.

Fontenrose, J. (1960): *The Cult and Myth of Pyrrhos at Delphi*, Berkeley.

Geominy, W. (2007): The Daochos Monument at Delphi. The Style and Setting of a Family Portrait in Historic Dress, in: P. Schultz, R. von den Hoff (eds.), *Early Hellenistic Portraiture. Image, Style, Context*, Cambridge: 84–98.

Graninger, D. (2010): Macedonia and Thessaly, in: J. Roisman, I. Worthington (eds.), *Blackwell Companion to Ancient Macedonia*, Malden, MA–Oxford: 306–325.

Graninger, D. (2011): *Cult and Koinon in Hellenistic Thessaly*, Leiden.

Hall, J. (2007): *A History of the Archaic Greek World, ca. 1200–479 BCE*, Malden, MA–Oxford.

Helly, B. (1995): *L'État thessalien. Aleuas le Roux, les tétrades et les tagoi*, Lyon.

Homolle, Th. (1899): Lysippe et l'ex-voto de Daochos, *BCH* 23: 421–485.

Jacquemin, A. (1999): *Offrandes monumentales à Delphes*, Paris.

Jacquemin, A., Laroche, D. (2001): Le monument de Daochos ou le trésor des Thessaliens, *BCH* 125: 305–332.

Kowalzig, B. (2007): *Singing for the Gods*, Oxford.

Larsen, J.A.O. (1968): *Greek Federal States. Their Institutions and History*, Oxford.

Lattimore, S. (1975): The Chlamys of Daochus I, *AJA* 79: 87–88.

Maass, M. (1993): *Das antike Delphi. Orakel, Schätze und Monumente*, Darmstadt.

Miller, S.G. (2000): Macedonians at Delphi, in: A. Jacquemin (ed.), *Delphes. Cent ans après la grande fouille*, (*BCH* Suppl. 36), Paris: 263–281.

Mooren, L. (1983): The nature of the Hellenistic monarchy, in: E. Van 't Dack, P. Van Dessel, W. Van Gucht (eds.), *Egypt and the Hellenistic World*, Leuven: 206–240.

Nagy, G. (1979): *The Best of Achaeans. Concepts of the Hero in Archaic Greek Poetry*, Baltimore, MD.

Pouilloux, J., Roux, G. (1963): *Énigmes à Delphes*, Paris.

Pownall, F. (2009): The Decadence of the Thessalians. A Topos in the Greek Intellectual Tradition from Critias to the Time of Alexander, in: P. Wheatley, R. Hannah (eds.), *Alexander and his Successors. Essays from the Antipodes*, Claremont, CA: 237–260.

Preuner, H.E. (1900): *Ein delphisches Weihgeschenk*, (Inaugural Dissertation), Strassburg.

Robertson, N. (1978): The Myth of the First Sacred War, *CQ* 28: 38–73.

Rhodes, P.J. (1986): *The Greek City States. A Sourcebook*, Cambridge.

Rhodes, P.J., Osborne, R. (2003): *Greek Historical Inscriptions, 404–323 B.C.*, Oxford.

Rutherford, I.C. (2001): *Pindar's Paeans. A Reading of the Fragments with a Survey of the Genre*, Oxford.

Saatsoglou-Paliadeli, C. (1993): Some Aspects of Macedonian Clothing, *JHS* 113: 122–147.

Schultz, P. (2009): Divine Images and Royal Iconography in the Philippeion at Olympia, in: J. Jensen *et al.* (eds.), *Aspects of Ancient Greek Cult. Context, Ritual and Iconography*, Aarhus: 125–194.

Sokolowski, F. (1962): *Lois sacrées des cités grecques. Supplément*, Paris.

Sordi, M. (1958): *La lega tessala fino ad Alessandro Magno*, Rome.

Sprawski, S. (1999): *Jason of Pherae*, (*Electrum* 3), Kraków.

Sprawski, S. (2003): Philip II and the Freedom of the Thessalians, *Electrum* 9: 56–66.

Sprawski, S. (2005): All the King's Men. Thessalians and Philip II's Designs on Greece, in: D. Musiał (ed.), *Society and Religions. Studies in Greek and Roman History,* Toruń: 31–49.

Stamatopoulou, M. (2007): Thessalians Abroad, the Case of Pharsalos, *Mediterranean Historical Review* 22: 211–236.

Suárez de la Torre, E. (1997): Neoptolemos at Delphi, *Kernos* 10: 153–176.

Taplin, O. (1999): Spreading the Word through Performance, in: S. Goldhill, R. Osborne (eds.), *Performance Culture and Athenian Democracy*, Cambridge: 33–57.

Wade-Gery, H.T. (1924): Jason of Pherae and Aleuas the Red, *JHS* 44: 55–64.

Walter-Karydi, E. (2000): Égine et Delphes, in: A. Jacquemin (ed.), *Delphes. Cent ans après la grande fouille*, (*BCH* Suppl. 36), Paris: 87–98.

Woodbury, L. (1979): Neoptolemos at Delphi. Pindar, *Nem.* 7.30ff., *Phoenix* 33: 95–133.

ELECTRUM * Vol. 19 (2012): 61–81
doi:10.4467/20843909EL.12.003.0744

THE IMPORTANCE OF THE HOPLITE ARMY IN AENEAS TACTICUS' *POLIS*[1]

Bogdan Burliga

Abstract: The identification of Aeneas Tacticus has always been a matter of dispute. Most often he is supposed to have been a mercenary officer, probably from Stymphalus, to whom Xenophon makes reference in *Hellenica*, 7.3.1. Accordingly, one may find the views that in Aeneas' treatise a mercenary perspective is adopted, a claim also supported by the observation that the author records the phenomenon of the ubiquitous popularity of paid soldiers in the Greek warfare system of the fourth century BC. In this paper it is argued that Aeneas' outlook in fact had little in common with mercenary ethics; instead, it is the writer's deep commitment to civic values (explicitly stated in the *Preface*) that is stressed. Especially worth pointing out remains Aeneas' belief that during siege civic patriotism still matters. It is a value on which success in overwhelming the invaders depends: all the steps and preventive actions of the city's dwellers leading to a successful defense of a native *polis* must be rooted – according to him – in the conviction that *polis* in its material (territory, estates, shrines, temples, walls) and spiritual dimension (religion, gods, respect for the parents) constitutes the best framework for life. By the same token, a relatively high importance is given by Aeneas to hoplite troops, usually consisting of yeomen and farmers who were the owners of land. In the author's conviction they could provide the best possible protection to a *polis*. Looking from a purely military point of view, hoplite forces – together with auxiliary troops (the light-armed and cavalry, if possible) – were also useful at the time when the enemy entered the city's territory and ravaged it before attempting a direct assault on the walls.

Keywords: Aeneas Tacticus, the hoplites, the Greek warfare.

1. Manuscript, as usual

As every reader of Aeneas' treatise knows, the text of his work has been preserved in a very bad condition (cf. Hunter/Handford 1927: xl). There is practically no sentence which has not been corrupted in some way. In this respect the case of Chapter XV § 5 remains interesting but on the opposite basis: this time the meaning of the sentence is clear enough, but one word has been replaced by the modern editor. When describ-

---

[1] This article is an extended version of a paper delivered at a conference held in Gregynog, Wales, and organized by Dr. Maria Pretzler (Swansea University), September, 2–4, 2010. I thank Dr. Pretzler for inviting me to participate in the conference as well as for her great hospitality; I am also grateful to Dr. Philip de Souza for his valuable comments. All the remaining faults are my own.

ing how the defenders' land forces sent against an enemy plundering their own territory should proceed (cf. Best 1969: 120; Lazenby 1994: 4), the writer advises that the cavalry (if available, cf. also Aeneas, 6.6; 26.4; cf. Arist., *Polit.* 1321a, 8–12) and the light-armed troops must first conduct a reconnaissance (cf. Galitzin 1874: 145; Ober 1995: 45; Trundle 2004: 51). Then, and only then, could hoplite troops ("the mainstay in Greek armies in Xenophon's time"[2]) track with caution: Πρὸ δὲ αὐτῶν δεῖ πρώτους τοὺς ὑπάρχοντας ἱππέας καὶ κούφους ἐξιέναι, μηδὲ τούτους <ἀτάκτους>, προεξερευνῶντάς τε καὶ προκαταλαμβάνοντας τὰ ὑψηλὰ τῶν χωρίων, ἵν' ὡς ἐκ πλείστου προειδῶσιν οἱ ὁπλῖται τὰ τῶν πολεμίων καὶ μηδὲν ἐξαίφνης αὐτοῖς προσπέσῃ.[3]

However, it is worth stressing that in the famous MS Medicus-Laurentianus LV. 4 the noun ὁπλῖται is not found in the text, nor does it appear in the copies descending from it. In the relevant place an anonymous Byzantine scholar wrote: ΠΟΛΙΤΑΙ. Accordingly, working on one of the copies of MS LV. 4, the great Casaubon (1670: 1664) retained the MS reading, translating it in the following way: *omnia diligenter explorantes* (sc. *equites et levis armatura*), *& loca edita occupantes ut quam primum resciscant* **cives**, *quid hostes agant, aut ubi sint.* The first editor who decided to change the MS reading into ΟΠΛΙΤΑΙ was Hermann Köchly (in Köchly/Rüstow 1853: 40–41), and his emendation was accepted by later editors and translators, including Hercher (1870: 32), Hug (1874: 32), Oldfather (2001: 76–79), Hunter/Handford (1927: 30), and Schoene (1911: 31). Recently this conjecture also won the favor of Whitehead (1990: 60) and Vela Tejada (1991: 64, n. 79).

The emendation begs the question as to why the great German authority failed to explain his reasons for replacement of *politai* by *hoplitai*.[4] The obvious answer is that it was simply logic which led him to do so. Köchly might have found supporting evidence in Chapter XVI, called ἄλλη βοήθεια ("another method of relief;" here and elsewhere the translation of D. Whitehead 1990), where Aeneas tackles a similar problem, namely, when a city tries to organize defensive operations while the enemy is already engaged in plundering the countryside, hoplites – especially if the terrain is rough – must go out in a compact array – τοὺς δ' ὁπλίτας ἀθρόους ἐν τάξει ("the heavy infantry in formation;" cf. also Xen., *Oec.* 8.4; *Vect.* 2.2; Arist., *Polit.* 1297b, 20–21). At both 15.5 and 16.7, then, the order of dispatching a relief as proposed by Aeneas remains essentially the same: *hippeis* and light infantry should march in advance, and their task is eventually to enter a preliminary skirmish with the enemy troops. The fact that the hoplites usually went at the end of the whole expeditionary force during such an operation was a practice also proved by Aeneas' contemporary, Xenophon, in his *Education of Cyrus* (*Cyr.* 4.2.24 and 5.3.56; cf. Vela Tejada 1991: 64, n. 79), as heavy infantry usually had difficulties with quick maneuvering (cf. Diodorus, 15.44.2: δυσκινήτων ὄντων). Given all this, when one comes back to Köchly's emendation, the connection between hoplites and citizens seems to be quite obvious and understandable (see also Ridley 2007: 157). Additionally, by way of comparison we may adduce other cases where the ancients identified the two terms. The first external evidence comes again from Xenophon, this time from *Resp. Lac.* 11.4, where the MS Vatic. Gr. 1335 reads: ἑκάστη δὲ τῶν πολιτικῶν

---

[2]   Lee 2009: 391; also Hunt 2007: 108–109; cf. Krasilnikoff 1992: 27; Spence 2002: 166.

[3]   Dain/Bon 1967.

[4]   The MS version was not changed by Haase (1835: 95–97) in his list of the proposed conjectures.

μορῶν χει πολέμαρχον ἕνα ("each citizen regiment;" trans. E.C. Marchant, Loeb; cf. Lipka 2002: 194; Gray 2007: 173; emphasis mine – B.B.), but in the copy at the disposal of Johannes Stobaeus in the fifth century AD (*Floril.* 4.3.23), in the quotation of the same sentence from *Resp. Lac.* in the version ὁπλιτικῶν μορῶν appears. Xenophon's case was preceded by the passage in Old Oligarch's *Resp. Ath.* 1.2. In this famous pamphlet the editors read today οἱ ὁπλῖται καὶ οἱ γενναῖοι καὶ οἱ χρηστοί, yet, as G.W. Bowersock reminds us, the noun ὁπλῖται is also an emendation made by Krüger, whereas the principal manuscripts (ABCM) contain the version *politai*.[5]

It is clear, then, that according to the commonly held opinion the two terms simply overlapped – it was mainly the *politai* which served as a city militia and wore heavy equipment (Sekunda 2000: 4). This identification is seen perfectly, among others, in Xenophon's *Hell.* 4.4.19 and 5.3.25, where a careful distinction is made between the citizen army and allied forces (cf. Underhill 1900: 140 and 143).[6] In the first case the Spartan king Agesilaus seized the Corinthian walls that had been restored by the Athenians. On this occasion the reader is told that καὶ τότε μὲν ταῦτα πράξας ὁ Ἀγησίλαος τό τε τῶν συμμάχων στράτευμα διῆκε καὶ τὸ πολιτικὸν οἴκαδε ἀπήγαγεν; in the second instance, the same ruler intervened in the internal affairs of the citizens of Phlius who had surrendered to the Spartans: here one hears of the same phrase, namely that ταῦτα δὲ ποιήσας τοὺς μὲν συμμάχους ἀφῆκε, τὸ δὲ πολιτικὸν οἴκαδε ἀπήγαγε; earlier on, it was Aristophanes who in the *Knights* identified the citizens as *hoplitai* enrolled according to the muster lists, *katalogoi* (*Eq.*1369: Ἔπειθ' ὁπλίτης ἐντεθεὶς ἐν καταλόγῳ; cf. *Pax*, 1180–1181; also Thuc. 6.31; see Andrewes 1981: 1; Christ 2001: 399). A further example is provided by the Aristotelian *The Athenian Constitution*, 42.4, when reporting that the Athenian ephebes serving in border forts reviewed ἀσπίδα καὶ δόρυ παρὰ τῆς πόλεως ("a shield and a spear from the state" (trans. P.J. Rhodes); cf. Rhodes 1993: 508).

2. The problem

Given all this, one fundamental objection may certainly be raised against the remarks expressed above: whatever version we adopt in Aeneas 15.5, the final interpretation leads essentially to the same conclusion. Without doubt, Aeneas' *politai*, being well-to-do enough to afford arms, were mainly hoplites,[7] so – one would argue – there is practically no difference in evaluating of his military advice; in effect, the problem becomes quite secondary.

Yet if I mentioned this somewhat minor textual dilemma in Aeneas, I did so purportedly in the conviction that the MS lesson should be restored as it stood just for this fundamental reason:[8] there is the Medicus–Laurentianus LV.4 (otherwise, *codice M mendoso et lacunoso* – Schoene 1911: xii) no trace of a corruption. Nor do we have any remark from a Byzantine scholar who in copying Aeneas' text was always careful in putting in

---

[5] Bowersock 2000: 474. See Marr/Rhodes 2008: 63–64.
[6] Cf. Bettalli 1990: 26–27.
[7] See Raaflaub (1997): "The hoplite farmers were *the* essential group among the citizens."
[8] I therefore translated it accordingly: Burliga 2007: 86.

marginal glosses which clearly indicate his doubts. Behind this, lies, however, a more general problem.

If, regarding the military aspect at least, it really does not matter whether at 15.5 we follow the MS or not, retaining the *politai*-lesson may carry some consequences, I would suggest, for reinterpreting the two problems in Aeneas. The first is the importance of the citizen hoplite force during siege and it may be formulated as follows: although in his *poliorketike biblos* the writer does not seem to be especially interested in the mechanics of hoplite battle or a detailed *Schlachtordnung* as such (small wonder – I will return to this topic below),[9] he nevertheless sees the presence of the hoplites as necessary in defending the invaded territory as it is the infantry militia which provides the most effective military protection of the countryside (Hunt 2007: 109; cf. Lissarague 1989: 43; Winterling 1991: 207; Chandezon 1999: 202; Rzepka 2011: 84). The second problem concerns Aeneas' social standpoint and his *Persönlichkeit*: since at that time the majority of hoplite infantrymen were citizens, he sees in them the (relatively) most loyal element among the city's inhabitants (Xen., *Oec.* 6.9–10; Ps. Arist., *Oec.* 1343b, 2–7); accordingly, for a would-be-commander they constitute the most valuable group of the defenders. If this point is valid, it allows us to look at the author himself from a slightly different angle.

As everyone agrees, a striking feature and novelty of Aeneas' handbook is its openly didactic and (sophistically) neutral manner which the writer adopts in instructing his audience (the rhetorical use of historical examples, the language imitating "military" commands; Burliga 2008). In this respect Aeneas was rightly regarded as a true literary pioneer. Bearing in mind that the book was written "in a curiously impersonal way" (Hunter/Handford 1927: xviii), one may feel justified in arguing that Aeneas addressed his works to a wider audience than did Xenophon in his two short military treatises on cavalry (Whitehead 1990: 39–40; Hornblower 2007: 51), so in this sense he may be labeled "objective" or (in a somewhat ahistorical manner) a "scientific" observer. As a consequence, a similar interpretation of the alleged political dimension of the treatise itself follows. It is suggested that Aeneas' work differs conspicuously from Xenophon's, whose aristocratic claims (or prejudices) were expressed so openly that they became something obvious (e.g. Lehmann 1980: 76). On this occasion, I also fully agree with Professor Whitehead's statement (1990: 32) that Aeneas' "socio-political vocabulary" differs from that of the political philosophers or, especially, the Old Oligarch, and in consequence, to quote another of Whitehead's perceptive remarks (1990: 31), the author's "political *Tendenz* is in fact indeterminable."[10] Indeed, through his written poliorcetic *apodexis* the author purportedly *seems* to have avoided expressing of his political sympathies or bias (but see e.g. Chapter 14) – in short, he appears not to be engaged in the disputes which he is actually describing.

To some modern scholars this observation led to the conviction that Aeneas must have belonged to an increasing group of military instructors, former commanders or, at least, itinerant mercenary officers (the writer knows distant regions of Greece and

---

9   Or, as Whitehead (1990: 24) called him, "no prisoner of the pitched-battle mentality;" see, however, Aeneas' enthusiastic opinion on the victory the Abderites won over the Triballians (15.3), and his remarks on *parataxis*, 1.2.

10   Cf. already Bengtson (1962: 461) *contra* Lehmann (1980: 77). See Urban 1986: 1000.

is familiar with its northern areas, Peloponnese or the western coast of Asia Minor; cf. Spaulding 1937: 53; Bon 1967: ix–x), who were a common phenomenon in the military landscape of fourth-century Greece (McKechnie 1989: Chapter 4). If we connect this supposition with further attempts at identifying him with Aeneas of Stymphalus, a *strategos* of the Arcadians who liberated Sicyon (mentioned by Xen., *Hell.* 7.3.1; Hug 1877: 29–30; Whitehead 1990: 12: "probably"), a relatively clear portrait of the author seems to emerge. In this way, it is believed, the picture of a half-cosmopolitan figure – an officer spiritually closer to the mercenary soldiers of the Hellenistic era, and a man of great military experience and knowledge – agrees with his approach towards military matters: "cold," methodical, and analytical, rather than ideologically biased or colored.

In what follows, I would like to make a small amendment to this well established portrait. Generally, it is not my goal to deny the above interpretation: whether Aeneas was a hired *strategos* or not cannot be decided with certainty. But even if one assumes that he really belonged to a group of professional mercenaries, must it automatically lead to the conclusion that he had no personal observations, remarks or sympathies, even though they cannot be attributed to any particular political faction or constitution? The answer is: he certainly had these, and the case of *politai/hoplitai* at 15.5 may be taken as a point of departure in seeking "other" Aeneas: a personality deeply addicted to such social values as loyalty, friendship or even, I daresay, patriotism.[11] I see him neither as an adventurous swashbuckler nor a totally indifferent, "scientific" or cynical observer. Consequently, it will be argued that his character was not that of *il condottiero*, according to the later, popular stereotype attributed to this term and associated with the chiefs of medieval companies (Mallett 1974: 79–80; Burliga 2007: 81, n. 149, *ad* 12.4). Although he served as a mercenary,[12] he was no type of ancient "Hawkwood," like for instance Charidemus of Oreos (cf. Aen. Tact. 24.3–12; Pritchett 1974: 85–89; McKechnie 1989: 86), but a citizen-soldier whose political and military thinking was connected with the old civic *ethos* deeper than we care to admit; parochial in its essence, rather than worldly. If it is appropriate to make any sensible comparison, it could be said that with his cool mentality and realistic outlook Aeneas resembles Thucydides, rather than Xenophon: although well acknowledged with the sophistic methods of teaching and writing, a man of a highly conservative mind. To sum up: such a portrait of Aeneas – as far as the treatise permits to see it – fits well his remarks on the tasks and operations the hoplite army takes in the times of danger.

3. The hoplite ideal in fourth-century Greece

Modern discussions about hoplite warfare and the place (or: evolution) of the infantry troops in the *polis* system of the fourth century BC inevitably remain under the strong influence of the famous statement formulated by Demosthenes around 340 in the third

---

[11]   On this see generally Baker 1999: 249.

[12]   Or whether he was "a man possessing sagacity and a range of experience which could only be gained by a career of travel and adventure such as fell to the captains of the fourth century" – Hunter/Handford 1927: xxxii.

speech against Philip of Macedon (*or.* 9; cf. Burckhardt 1996: 212–213). The passage became notorious as it contrasted the "old" way of fighting (§ 48) with the new methods introduced by the brute Macedonian conqueror (§ 49–50; cf. also Polyb. 13.3.1–8[13]). Leaving aside the question of how much the orator exaggerated the differences between them, let us recall the characteristics of classical (here: Spartan[14]) *polis* warfare (cf. Herod. 7.9β. 2; Hall 2007: 155). First, according to the statesman, it was based on seasonal campaigns (Λακεδαιμονίους τότε καὶ πάντας τοὺς ἄλλους, τέτταρας μῆνας ἢ πέντε, τὴν ὡραίαν αὐτήν);[15] the invaders ravaged the enemy land with hoplites and civic armies (ἐμβαλόντας ἂν καὶ κακώσαντας τὴν χώραν ὁπλίταις καὶ πολιτικοῖς στρατεύμασιν) and then returned home (ἀναχωρεῖν ἐπ' οἴκου πάλιν). In preferring this kind of war their behavior was "old-fashioned," chivalrous (οὕτω δ' ἀρχαίως εἶχον) and "civic" (μᾶλλον δὲ πολιτικῶς), that is conducted by rules and openly (εἶναι νόμιμόν τινα καὶ προφανῆ τὸν πόλεμον). He goes on to suggest that it was battles that decided the earlier wars whilst "now" (νυνὶ), under Philip, they did not (οὐδὲν δ' ἐκ παρατάξεως οὐδὲ μάχης γιγνόμενον; § 49). This was possible because the *polis* army was a hoplite phalanx, consisting of citizens (τῷ φάλαγγ' ὁπλιτῶν) – again in sharp contrast to the practices of King Philip, whose troops consisted of light-armed, cavalry, archers, hired soldiers (τῷ ψιλούς, ἱππέας, τοξότας, ξένους). Later on (§ 51), the "old" kind of land warfare is even called "a simplicity" by the speaker (τὴν εὐήθειαν τὴν τοῦ τότε πρὸς Λακεδαιμονίους πολέμου; cf. Meissner 2010: 280).[16]

Demosthenes' views may be supported by recalling the congruent conservatism or civic chauvinism of Xenophon, voiced in the *Oec.* 4.2–3; 8.6 (cf. Hanson 1999: 317), who assumed that the best hoplites were farmers, and in *Ways and Means*, 2.3–4 conceded that the Athenian army "now" relied on foreigners, i.e. metics (Lydians, Phrygians, Syrians), instead of recruiting citizens to serve in the infantry (cf. Gauthier 1976: 63–64; Foxhall 1993: 142; Hunt 1998: 191). The same sentiment may be found in Isocrates, *On Peace* (or. 8.48, about 355 BC), revealing a longing for a "pure," civic army:

ὅτε μὲν εἰ τριήρεις πληροῖεν, τοὺς μὲν ξένους καὶ τοὺς δούλους ναύτας εἰσεβίβαζον, τοὺς δὲ πολίτας μεθ' ὅπλων ἐξέπεμπον· νῦν δὲ τοῖς μὲν ξένοις ὁπλίταις χρώμεθα, τοὺς δὲ πολίτας ἐλαύνειν ἀναγκάζομεν, ὥσθ' ὁπόταν ἀποβαίνωσιν εἰς τὴν τῶν πολεμίων, οἱ μὲν ἄρχειν τῶν Ἑλλήνων ἀξιοῦντες ὑπηρέσιον ἔχοντες ἐκβαίνουσιν, οἱ δέ, τοιοῦτοι τὰς φύσεις ὄντες οἵους ὀλίγῳ πρότερον διῆλθον, μεθ' ὅπλων κινδυνεύουσιν

---

[13]   With the notes of Walbank 1967: 416–417. As Walbank remarks, "P.'s discussion is clearly linked with the reference to the Lelantine War in Strabo, x. 448," but as Wheeler (1987) has convincingly shown, the inscription quoted by Strabo from Ephorus and concerning an alleged treaty between Chalcis and Eretria is a forgery.

[14]   However, Ellen Millender (2006: 245) has clearly proved that even Sparta relied heavily on mercenaries: she even speaks of a "mercenary industry in the 390s;" no different was the situation in Athens – see Bugh 2011: 74; cf. below note 15.

[15]   Butcher 1903.

[16]   Likewise, in the First Phillipic (*or.* 4) written about 351 BC and calling for a retaliatory expedition against Macedonian territory after Phillip's unsuccessful 352 attempt at invading central Greece through Thermopylae pass (cf. Wooten 2008: 5; Trevett 2011: 68–71), Demosthenes advises relying *also* on a civic army. He deplores the situation (4.23) when "now" it is mercenaries who defend the city instead of the citizens; cf. Bugh 2011: 74.

In those days, when they manned their triremes, they put on boards crews of foreigners and slaves but sent our citizens to fight under heavy arms. Now, however, we use mercenaries as heavy armed troops but compel citizens to row ships, with the result that when they land in hostile territory these men, who claim the right to rule over the Hellenes, disembark with their cushions under their arms, while men who are of the character which I have just described take the field with shield and spear![17]

No different was Aristotle's theoretical analysis presented in the *Nicomachean Ethics*, 1116a, 15–19. Considering the nature of bravery, the philosopher maintains that it is a civic value (Ἔστι μὲν οὖν ἡ ἀνδρεία τοιοῦτόν τι [...] πρῶτον μὲν ἡ πολιτική; cf. Herod. 7.103.3),[18] since it is the citizens alone who possess courage (δοκοῦσι γὰρ ὑπομένειν τοὺς κινδύνους οἱ πολῖται διὰ τὰ ἐκ τῶν νόμων ἐπιτίμια καὶ τὰ ὀνείδη καὶ διὰ τὰς τιμάς). Inevitably (1116a, 27–29), civic courage means virtue – it is based on honor and a sense of pride (δι' ἀρετὴν γίνεται· δι' αἰδῶ γὰρ καὶ διὰ καλοῦ ὄρεξιν (τιμῆς γάρ)). Such a conviction agrees with the critique of the mercenaries (ἐν τοῖς πολεμικοῖς δ' οἱ στρατιῶται) at 1116b, 5–1116b, 23. Here the argument runs as follows: being experienced in the war (δοκεῖ γὰρ εἶναι πολλὰ κενὰ τοῦ πολέμου), they are cowards, in fact (οἱ στρατιῶται δὲ δειλοὶ γίνονται), and if confronted with an enemy who is more numerous and better equipped (ὅταν ὑπερτείνῃ ὁ κίνδυνος καὶ λείπωνται τοῖς πλήθεσι καὶ ταῖς παρασκευαῖς), they just run away (πρῶτοι γὰρ φεύγουσι). Conversely, a man who participates in the government dies bravely (τὰ δὲ πολιτικὰ μένοντα ἀποθνήσκει; cf. Eurypides, *Rhes.* 510–511). The citizen's ethos is then glorified again: as the escape is a shame for him, death is preferred, not safety (τοῖς μὲν γὰρ αἰσχρὸν τὸ φεύγειν καὶ ὁ θάνατος τῆς τοιαύτης σωτηρίας αἱρετώτερος).[19] Hired men are audacious, to be sure, but, Aristotle continues, they are deprived of the sense of honor, so in the face of death they simply flee (φεύγουσι, τὸν θάνατον μᾶλλον τοῦ αἰσχροῦ φοβούμενοι; cf. Demosthenes, 4.47). Someone who is really a brave man acts differently (ὁ δ' ἀνδρεῖος οὐ τοιοῦτος; cf. Vernant 1988: 48; Bryant 1990: 501–505).[20]

Such and similar voices reflect a strong belief in the superiority of the citizens fighting together in the ranks of the infantry (cf. Lysias, 14.6 and 11; Cartledge 2001: 161; van Wees 2004: 116). The sentiments are, of course, moral in their tone, and the phenomenon has of late rightly been called "hoplite ideology" (Connor 1988: 17; Hanson 1996: 295; 2000: 117–118; Prost 1999: 73ff).[21] Its beginning may be found even in ancient times, with Homeric poetry (cf. *Il.* 2.198–199; cf. van Wees 2004: 195) or, later,

---

[17]	Mathieu 1942; trans. G. Norlin, Loeb.

[18]	Bywater 1894.

[19]	Such sentiments were anticipated as early as the fifth century, especially in the speeches of Pericles as recorded by Thucydides; cf. Lengauer 1979: 25–26, who adduces relevant passages; cf. Cartledge 2001: 161.

[20]	See Dover's (1974: 229–234) discussion on *philotimia*: he quotes on this occasion several sources, e.g. Lycurgus, *Leocr.* 15; cf. Bassi 2003: 32–37. According to the Xenophontic definition of glory, it relies essentially on bravery (*Resp. Lac.* 9.2: δῆλον δὲ ὅτι καὶ εὔκλεια μάλιστα ἕπεται τῇ ἀρετῇ; ed. E.C. Marchant).

[21]	Cf. Thucydides, 7.77.4; 8.83; 8.97.1, with the comment of Hornblower (2008: 1034): "hoplite constitution;" Aristotle, *Polit.* 1297b, 1–2. At Thucydides, 6.21.1, Nicias gives advice that the Athenians must take not only a fleet and less worthy crews but a large body of infantry, especially if they want to do something worthy of their plans (οὐ ναυτικῆς καὶ φαύλου στρατιᾶς μόνον δεῖ, ἀλλὰ καὶ πεζὸν πολὺν ξυμπλεῖν, εἴπερ βουλόμεθα ἄξιον τῆς διανοίας δρᾶν).

with Tyrtaeus,[22] Aeschylus (*Persae*, 240),[23] and many others.[24] The same conviction was proudly manifested in Greek art (vase painting or sculpture – e.g. the friezes of the Lycian Nereid Monument from Xanthus; cf. Hölscher 1998: 155;[25] Childs/Demargne 1989: pl. 20 [BM 859], 54 [BM 875], 55 [BM 871L]). It is therefore claimed nowadays that the nostalgic voices heard from ancient elite writers prove, at best, their strong pretentions to cultural dominance in a *polis* society (Snodgrass 1999: 77). This hoplite ideology, it is additionally argued, was thus a social phenomenon at its roots; its goal was to create a strong sense of identity (Ober 1996: 60). It expressed civic ethics, the communal values of *polis* citizenry, where honor and courage were praised and highlighted not as abstract ideals but as true virtues of the *politai* who, serving in amateur armies, defended their possessions (Raaflaub 1999: 137) and thus proved a deep "commitment to their native city" (Krasilnikoff 1992: 28, n. 16; cf. Mitchell 1996: 98). The glorifying of the hoplites was made, of course, at the expense of "the others," less well-to-do groups participating in war: either non-elite city-dwellers who could not afford heavy armor and fought as light infantry (cf. Thuc. 4.80.5; 4.90.1; 7.57–58.3; 8.25; cf. van Wees 1995: 162–164; Raaflaub 2007: 132; Krentz 2010: 44–45), served as naval crews, or the slaves who were the attendants (*skeuophoroi*) – in a word, all those who were ideologically excluded and their role either diminished or simply omitted (Anderson 1970: Chapter 7; Loraux 1986: 162; Osborne 1987: 140–141; 2000: 28ff.; Strauss 1996: 313–314; Hunt 1998: 190–191; van Wees 2004: 61–76; Miller 2010: 331–332).

When dealing with the socio-political conditions in the fourth century BC especially, it has often been pointed out of late that this phenomenon still remains particularly visible, but the military reality was different (Xen., *Hell.* 4.3.15). Rather, Delbrück's (1900: 115) famous old verdict may here be quoted as representative for such an interpretation: he spoke of "Der allmählige Übergang vom Bürger-Kriegerthum zum Sold-Kriegerthum," and in this view, it is further claimed, the voices of the ancient observers like Demostenes and others were highly distorted. Around the middle of the fourth century warfare certainly become more complicated, for, as Sekunda (1994: 192) put it aptly, "Hoplite infantry ceased to be the queen of the battlefield" – already the famous bloodbath which the Athenian light-armed troops under Iphicrates (cf. Aeneas, 24.16; Sage 1996: 144) managed to inflict on the Spartan *mora* at Lechaeum in 390 BC may be recalled as a representative example of this process (Xen., *Hell.* 4.5.10–17).[26] In effect,

---

[22]   Tyrtaeus, fr. 11, 4 West; cf. Ducrey 1986: 61.

[23]   Bovon 1963: 580–584, figs. 1–4 and 7; 589, fig. 13; Hodkinson 1983: 256; Lissarague 1990: 13ff. and Lissarrague 2002: 113ff.

[24]   Ps.-Hesiod. *Scut.* 139ff. (ed. F. Solmsen); Callinus, fr. 1, 10 West, *IEG*; Euripides, *Her.* 157–164; Plut., *Lac. Apopht.* = *Mor.* 220A; *Inst. Lac.* 34 = *Mor.* 239B; also Horace, *Carm.* 2.7.10 and Valerius Maximus, 6.3.1. The opposite – abandoning the arms – meant cowardice: Archilochus, fr. 5 West; Alcaeus, fr. 357, 15 Lobel & Page; Anacreon, fr. 381b Page, *PMG*; Theophrastus, *Char.* 25.3–6.

[25]   Hölscher's analysis pertains to Athens, but his observation in fact remains valid when one regards manifestations of hoplite values.

[26]   There were other famous precedents in the fifth century BC, reported by Thucydides (cf. Best 1969: 17–18). Here I omit the problem of what hoplite fighting really looked like in the archaic age (cf. Schwartz 2009: 102–105). Opinions vary. In his study, P. Krentz (2000: 183–199) gives an extremely useful and suggestive list of cases of deception in Greek warfare: it seems as if less honest means of conducting the wars were always accepted and employed by the Greeks (cf. Polyb. 9.12.1–5). It is also clear that there was quite

what we should bear in mind is a gap between the literary or pictorial representation and the less obvious importance (not to speak of dominance) of the heavy infantrymen in warfare in the times of Demostenes (and Aeneas).

Additionally, the problem is complicated by the question of whether communal values prove the existence of "a middle class,"[27] as Aristotle suggested in *Politics* (1297b, 16; with Robinson 1995: 109–111; cf. Andrewes 1974: 34; see *Hell. Oxyrh.* 6.3, cf. McKechnie/Kern 1988: 133).[28] Were the hoplites a relatively homogenous political group (*mesoi*, farmers; Lazenby 1989: 78; Ober 1996: 60; Raaflaub 1999: 135), bound by sharing the same values,[29] or was the structure of heavy infantry forces in a *city* hierarchical by its nature (van Wees 2004: Chapter 4; but see Schwartz 2009: 175), consisting of men of different social statuses and backgrounds,[30] who strove (see Plato, *Resp.* 556c–d; van Wees 2002: 70 ff.), if opportunity permitted (Burliga 2012), for personal glory and excellence, often in the mode of Homeric heroes?

Aeneas' handbook is an interesting piece of evidence in this respect.

4. Old veteran's testimony

If we had to answer the last question, it should be stated that the author suggests the latter be true, rather than the former – as far as the situation in the mid-fourth century BC is at stake (cf. 10.20; 14.1). No honest hoplite ideal of "arms and valor" (ὅπλα καὶ ἀρετή – Xen., *Anab.* 2.1.12; trans. C.L. Brownson, Loeb) is praised by him in an open way. It was always a striking feature of Aeneas' work that his view is that of the soldier and pragmatist: first of all, the only thing he believes in without any restrictions is careful preparation (*praef.* 3: παρασκευῆς); the second is the fundamental rule of "trusting no one" (1.3; 22.7). As a result, as has been mentioned above, at first glance he stands above the "ideological" prejudices and the diseases of factionalism of his day (cf. 11.7–11.10: the episode at Argos). But even if Aeneas was a careful disciple of the sophists and their ways of teaching, it would be naive to assume that he was totally indifferent to what he was analyzing. If anything, the gloomy social reality in a fourth-century *polis* provides a true basis for his book (see e.g. Chapter 10), so everything he advises is inevitably based on the presumption that *polis* society is deeply divided and civil strife always remains an potential and imminent danger (cf. also *Hell. Oxyrh.* 17.1). Since the lack of agreement among the citizens is an established fact and the mutual distrust remains a common, daily matter, these factors must have been taken into account by any com-

---

a wide spectrum of hoplite activities "beyond phalanx" (in L. Rawling's phrase 2000: 234) in which hoplites were useful (cf. also especially Ober 1994: 174–190; see too Anderson 1970: 138–140).

[27] Or, taken in more general terms, beginning already in the archaic epoch, with a "middling tradition," as some scholars maintain (Morris 1996: 28, term; at p. 35). Morris maintains that phalanx "became the standard image for citizen solidarity").

[28] Regarding Athens, cf. *Resp. Ath.* 7.4.

[29] See the discussion by Hall 2007: 162.

[30] As it is assumed today that not every infantryman in a phalanx wore a full hoplite panoply; see the discussion in Krentz 2010: 40–44. If the depository at Olimpia can be a guide, breastplates were the rarest type of armor.

mander of a city under attack. In this way, it is obvious, social circumstances determined military steps: the latter are undertaken in a response to the actual, political situation. Where, then, according to Aeneas, should the remedy be sought?

My answer to this question is less obvious than those given in many excellent books and commentaries on this author. Although far from any open enthusiasm for hoplite bravery and manliness (ἀνδρεῖα), honor (τιμή) or shame (αἰδώς), Aeneas saw the best solution in relative terms to the problem in appealing to and relying on the "old" civic ideology. It is communal values (see Thuc., 2.42.2; cf. note 43, below) that are praised, and in fact, in his view the whole idea of defending the city is embedded in this.[31] It is plain, then, that such ideology could not have been exposed by an experienced soldier without illusions in an ostentatious way, and that in this respect the author's language is far more reserved than it was in the case of the other members of the literate elite. Nevertheless, it is present in Aenas' *poliorketike biblos*, and this is less surprising than one might expect from an experienced mercenary captain.[32]

How is it possible to detect traces of this traditional hoplite rhetoric in Aeneas' booklet? In two ways, I think.

The first is relatively clear to acknowledge. The civic ideology may easily seen by reminding ourselves of Aeneas' judgment of the "others" in a *polis*. Generally, the others are for him foreigners, dangerous especially, if comprising a military force (Bengtson 1962: 467; Aymard 1967: 303–304). One might say that in his military calculations, they are certainly Aeneas' obsession[33] – it would be appropriate here to invoke the famous phrase of Thucydides (3.109.5): when the historian describes hired men in the army of Amprakiots battling the Athenians and Acarnanians in 426 BC, he uses a derogatory tone: τὸν μισθοφόρον ὄχλον [τὸν ξενικόν] ("mercenary followers;" trans. R. Warner; cf. also Aeneas, 8.25).[34] It was no different (not surprisingly) with Aeneas. From his perspective, as he just suggests it, the best solution would be to avoid the presence of the others inside the walls, but this is of course a dream (cf. 24.1), so military employment of the *xenoi* must be done with utmost caution (13.1: Ἂν δὲ δέῃ ξενοτροφεῖν, ὧδε ἂν ἀσφαλέστατα γίγνοιτο; see Ducrey 1986: 133–134). Paid soldiers are constantly contrasted by Aeneas with city dwellers (cf. also Demosthenes, 4.25), hence Aeneas' great emphasis on the walls (cf. McK Camp II 2000: 47). At 3.3 and 22.29 he narrates the cases when the walls of the *polis* are guarded by the allied forces: φρουρίου ὑπὸ συμμάχων φρουρουμένου. No doubt, according to the author, such a solution creates a highly dangerous situation, as in the opinion of the writer they provide "a potential source of trouble" (Whitehead 1990: 104). Likewise, at 22.19 he advises keeping the ways up to the wall kept closed. Of exceptional importance is the famous chapter concerning the proclamation of the "An-

---

[31] On this cf. Wheeler 2007: lxi; see Moggi 2002: 205.

[32] H. van Wees (2004: 76) rightly reminds us that the ideal of the hoplite citizen was still alive at the end of the fourth century; in fact, hoplite sentiments were strong in the Hellenistic epoch – as Chaniotis (2005: 21, 79) points out, the epigraphical data prove that the rise of professional armies did not mean an end to the citizen militias: "in many, if not most, Hellenistic cities, citizen armies survived and were an important element of local pride;" see also Ma 2000.

[33] As Trundle (2004: 30) has observed, it is ironic that "the Greek mercenaries who served outside the Greek mainland were themselves hoplites," whereas those "who fought for the Greek cities themselves did so with servile and non-Greek weapons;" cf. especially Roy 2004: 270.

[34] See Bettalli 1995: 132–133.

nouncements" (Κηρύγματα). On the eve of the enemy approaching the walls (9.1: Ἂν δὲ θρασύνεσθαί τι ἐπιχειρῶσιν οἱ ἐπιόντες πρὸς σέ), severe restrictions against the mercenary forces standing in the city must be issued: so, at 10.7 every citizen is forbidden Στρατιώτας μὴ μισθοῦσθαι μηδὲ ἑαυτὸν μισθοῦν ἄνευ τῶν ἀρχόντων (to "hire soldiers, or to serve as a soldier for hire, without permission of the authorities"), whilst at 10.9 "foreigners arriving must carry their weapons openly and ready to hand" (Ξένους τοὺς ἀφικνουμένους τὰ ὅπλα ἐμφανῆ καὶ πρόχειρα φέρειν). Special proclamations (10.18– 19) must be issued to the mercenary troops (ξενικῷ στρατοπέδῳ). Most of all, such an army cannot be numerically superior to citizen troops; if it is, the community inevitably falls under the mercenaries' control (ἀεὶ χρὴ ὑπερέχειν πλήθει καὶ δυνάμει τοὺς ἐπαγομένους πολίτας τῶν ξένων· εἰ δὲ μή, ἐπ' ἐκείνοις γίγνονται αὐτοί τε καὶ ἡ πόλις). The same remains true of a piece of advice sounding like a proverb (12.4; cf. also 12.3) that Δεῖ οὖν μήποτε εἰς πόλιν οἰκείαν μείζω δύναμιν ἐπακτὸν δέχεσθαι τῆς ὑπαρχούσης τοῖς πολίταις, ξένοις τε χρωμένην ἀεὶ δεῖ τὴν πόλιν πολλῷ ὑπερέχειν τῆς τῶν ξένων δυνάμεως· οὐ γὰρ ἀσφαλὲς ξενοκρατεῖσθαι καὶ ἐπὶ μισθοφόροις γίγνεσθαι. Especially striking is Aeneas' warning that mercenaries (ξενικὸν: 23.11) are generally the *a priori* hostile element not only in a city but near it, if they are at the disposal of an enemy who aims at seizing a *polis* (11.8 – the case of Argos; 18.13 – the case of Teos; 24.6: ξένους τεθωρακισμένους under Charidemus; 28.5 – the case of Clazomenae). One of the most emotionally passages certainly remains that at 24.8, where the author ends the story of Charidemus by writing that when his mercenary force entered the city (Ὅπου δὴ εὐθὺς οἱ εἰσελθόντες), it "got to work (ἔργου εἴχοντο), killing the gatekeeper (τόν τε πυλωρὸν ἀποκτείναντες) and generally behaving as mercenaries do" (καὶ εἰς ἄλλας ξένας πράξεις ὁρμήσαντες) – again, the last remark is close to the opinions expressed by such keen observers as Thucydides, 7.28–30 (on the Thracian mercenaries and their annihilation of the Boeotian city of Mycalessus; cf. Hornblower 2008: 599), Polyb. 13.6.4 (on the mercenaries of Nabis; cf. Walbank 1967: 420, referring to Theopompus, *FGrH* 115, F 225), or Polyaenus, 2.30.1 (Clearchus' hired troops).[35]

All these passages leave no doubt that Aeneas' attitude towards the ubiquitous phenomenon of the mercenary service is characterized by great dislike (cf. Best 1969: 126– 127, who speaks of "gangs of mercenaries;" also Bettalli 1990: 26–27). The difficulty with the author's attitude, supposing that he was a hired soldier, is hard to explain unless we assume that his condemnation of mercenary military garrisons stationing in the cities (not to speak of the mercenary army awaiting outside the walls; cf. Isocr. 5.120–121; cf. Bugh 2011: 74) was based on grounds different than military ones:[36] it must indicate that there were other reasons for doing so. Be that as it may, this does not mean that

---

[35] See Isocrates' *Evagoras* (9.8–10) and *Philip* (5.96, with Landucci Gattinoni 2001: 74). A more positive picture of mercenaries and their milieu is given by Menander (see Bugh 2011: 73–74), although his perspective is that of a playwright.

[36] Trundle (1999: 30) thinks the picture of a well-disciplined mercenary army of Jason of Pherae in Xenophon, *Hell.* 6.1.4–7 is positive. This is true, as it highlights the professionalism of the mercenaries and relates to Jason's military regime, which was in fact clearly different from the world of the Greek *polis* communities (cf. Sprawski 1999: 111). Like Xenophon (cf. *Hiero*, 10.6–8, with Gray 2007: 141; *Equit. mag.* 9.3–4; *Hell.* 4.4.16: the Arcadian hoplites avoided a pitched battle with the peltasts under Iphicrates; on the other hand, the same peltasts feared the Lacedaemonian heavy infantry); Aeneas was also very much aware that the amateur army (6.2: οἱ ἄπειροι τάξεων καὶ πολέμου) might be less effective than the troops of the

by the same token the citizen-militias (1.1: τῶν σωμάτων σύνταξιν; 1.5: σώματα; 2.1: σωμάτων; 3.1: τοὺς πολίτας; cf. Raaflaub 1999: 137) were an ideal solution to the difficulties an ordinary city met in the face of siege. Yet in such circumstances as he witnessed them, civic militiamen appeared in the eyes of a conservative observer to be the only remaining remedy.

A constant factor in Aeneas' thinking is that a city under siege may be captured not only by an assault carried by an invading enemy force (16.1: τοὺς ἐμβεβληκότας; 23.6: οἱ δὲ καὶ ἔξωθεν; 29.2: ἔξωθέν τι φοβερὸν), even if it is great (8.1), but by the treason of its inhabitants, as there are many plotters inside the city (1.6: τοῖς ἐναντία θέλουσιν ἐν τῇ πόλει; 10.3: τῶν ἐπιβουλευόντων; 10.14: τινὰ ἐπιβουλεύοντα τῇ πόλει; 14.1; 23.6: οἱ μὲν ἔσω τῆς πόλεως; 29.2: ἔσωθεν φοβερὸν).[37] Unanimity (10.20;[38] 14.1) is thus a condition much desired by the city-commander, and it sometimes happens (22.21; cf. Gehrke 1985: 357–358, n. 11). But most often it happened that the opposite was true (17.1). From the point of view of a *strategos*, the majority of his efforts must have concerned the establishment of a firm group of supporters (1.5; 1.6): their help is compared by the author to the role of a citadel in a city (ἀντ᾽ ἀκροπόλεως); they must be τῶν πολιτῶν τοὺς πιστοτάτους ("the most trustworthy citizens;" see 1.4; cf. also Onesander, *Strat.* 2.2–3: τοὺς εὐνουστάτους τῇ πατρίδι, πιστοτάτους, εὐρωστοτάτους), satisfied with the actual government (1.6: εὔνους τε καὶ τοῖς καθεστηκόσι πράγμασιν); elsewhere, at 9.3, their presence is also taken for granted by Aeneas (τοῖς μὲν φιλίοις θάρσος ἐμποιήσεις).

Having discussed the author's bias against the others, we may pass to the second argument and adduce the evidence that shows how important (and crucial, in fact) the loyalty of the citizens was for him; by the same token this latter case will show how indispensable the same citizens were in exercising their military functions – as χάλκεοι ἄνδρες, "the men of bronze" (to recall Herodotus' famous phrase, 2.152.3) serving in phalanx for the defense of the city under siege and therefore proving that in the author's days they still mattered and by no means constituted "dinosaurs" (to quote Professor Hanson's famous comparison).[39]

To begin with, we must recall something obvious and trivial. It is worth remembering that Aeneas understands "siege" – to follow Korus (1969: 511) and Whitehead (1990: 20) – in the broadest possible sense (cf. 10.20: ἐν πολιορκίᾳ; see also 10.23); the term encompasses the time when peace still holds (Chapters 1–14; cf. 22.26: Ἐν δὲ τοῖς ἀκινδυνοτέροις; ἀκινδύνων δὲ καὶ εἰρηναίων) and when the enemy is approaching and the invasion of "our" territory becomes a fact (4.1; 4.5; 7.1; 10.23; Chapters 15–30; cf. 23.1: τοῖς προσκαθημένοις πολεμίοις; 32.1: Πρὸς δὲ τὰς τῶν ἐναντίων προσαγωγὰς σώμασιν). Such a broad understanding of the term "siege" has important consequences for the author's whole line of argument, since the bulk of military actions on the part of the defenders is undertaken outside the walls, in the hinterland – the city's countryside (cf. Xen., *Mem.* 3.5.27; cf. Burford Cooper 1973: 162); as a consequence, a relevant

---

trained mercenaries (cf. Parke 1933: 20–22). However, in the situation that is the subject matter of his handbook, there is no choice – loyalty is a much more important value (cf. 1.4; 1.6; 10.11).

[37] See Bryant (1996: 244–245), who speaks of "the decomposition of the Polis-citizen bond."

[38] A famous chapter which is used as a source of information on the social conditions in a fourth-century *polis*.

[39] Hanson 1999: 321–349.

(quite large) part of the treatise deals by necessity with the question of sending sorties and regular army in order to prevent any land assault (1.2: Τοὺς μὲν γὰρ ἐκπορευομένους; 1.5: εἴς τε τὰς ἐξόδους; 4.5: τὰ ἀποστελλόμενα ἐκ τῆς πόλεως) and field operations (4.5: ἐπί τινα πρᾶξιν) – otherwise an old form of warfare, as Thucydides has already noted (1.15.2).

All such advice is firmly based on a broader, fundamental conviction that the survival of a *polis* is crucial for the citizens' identity (cf. Whitehead 1991: 144; Foxhall 1993: 143). It is striking to observe how grand, if not bombastic vocabulary is used on this occasion by the old-fashioned mercenary soldier. Suffice it to say that in one place he calls such a possibility a misery (18.2: κακουργεῖται). Such "civic" philosophy resembles not only the famous remarks Aristotle presented in his *Politics*, according to whom *polis* constituted the framework of a civic life, but – above all (and unsurprisingly) – the political "philosophy" recorded by Thucydides in the second half of the fifth century (Lengauer 1974: 24; 1979: 25).[40] The loss of a *polis* is viewed as a potential catastrophe, so in the solemn language in which *the Preface* is composed, the native territory is contrasted by Aeneas to a life abroad, spent in the mode of exiles (*praef.* 1; cf. Kulesza 1998: 110 quoting Tyrtaeus, fr. 10 West). The existence of the "native soil and state and fatherland" (οἰκεία τε χώρα καὶ πόλις καὶ πατρίς) is thus essential for being a Greek and human likewise (cf. Ostwald 2000: 50);[41] equally, saving the ἱερῶν καὶ πατρίδος καὶ γονέων καὶ τέκνων ("shrines and fatherland and parents and childrens": *praef.* 2) is included by Aeneas in "the fundamentals" (τῶν μεγίστων; *praef.* § 3: ὑπὲρ τοσούτων καὶ τοιούτων; cf. Garlan 1974: 20; Hansen 2004: 49–52) and his civic rhetoric may be compared to the values defended by the Athenians in the times of the Persian wars (Herodotus, 8.144.2); nothing, in fact, the author argues, can be compared to the doom of the *polis* when a siege will appear successful – there will be οὐδεμία ἐλπὶς σωτηρίας ὑπάρξει ("no hope of salvation;" Bettalli 1990: 212; Foxhall 1993: 143; Kulesza 1998: 112).[42] There is little doubt that Aeneas would agree with an anonymous writer that *polis*, i.e. *oikiai*, *chora* and *ktemata* (possessions), enable a good life (*pros to eu dzen*; Ps.- Aristotle, *Oec.* 1343a,10).

These appeals to communal, civic values are relatively clear in Aeneas' work, although no open hoplite chauvinism or snobbery, even less any Xenophontic aesthetic delight of the visual beauty of hoplite ranks, can be detected. On the contrary, generally this is far from the case. Nevertheless, bearing in mind that there is no rule without an exception, occasionally the author departs from his usually cold approach. There are four places in his handbook where he formulates something more than a mere appreciation of hoplite troops, thus bringing him nearer to the civic sentiments held by Isocrates or voices expressed by Demosthenes.

---

[40] Pointed out especially in Thucydides' version of the speech of Nicias at 7.61.1; 7.64.2; 7.69.2; cf. 7.75.5 (on the retreat of the Athenian army during the war against Syracuse): οὐδὲν γὰρ ἄλλο ἢ πόλει ἐκπεπολιορκημένη ἐῴκεσαν ὑποφευγούσῃ.

[41] It does not differ in tone from the famous oath of the Athenian ephebes (= Lycurg, *Leocr.* 77): ἀμυνῶ δὲ καὶ ὑπὲρ ἱερῶν καὶ ὁσίων καὶ ο<ὑ>κ ἐλάττω παραδώσω τὴν πατρίδα; cf. Tod 1948: 303, no. 204 = Rhodes/ Osborne 2003: no. 88; cf. also Xen., *Hiero*, 4.4.

[42] Recalling the later treatment of the Thebans by King Alexander after capturing the city in 335–334 BC; cf. also Thuc. 7.71.7 and especially 7.85–87.

The first of them appears at 15.8 and concerns the episode of the victory of the Abderites over the invading army of the Thracian Triballians; this was a typical victory of the defenders who fought after making "their dispositions for battle" (παράταξιν ποιησάμενοι; cf. note 8, above),[43] while the enemy, conversely, presented a "large and warlike horde" (πλῆθος πολὺ καὶ μάχιμον); the result was formulated by Aeneas in a more affectionless tone, recalling the language known from funerary orations: the former "won a fine victory" (κάλλιστον ἔργον εἰργάσαντο).

Of the second case, that of 16.4, mention was already made above: it narrates the organizing of ἄλλη βοήθεια, when the invaders ravage the defenders' land. Leaving aside the details of the operation, one meets the interesting phrase that the enemies "march from the outset with their strongest forces at the ready (τὸ ἰσχυρότατον αὐτῶν ἐν τάξει ἄγουσι), expecting an attack 'to be launched' against them and primed to repel it." Here some modern controversy arose as to what to do with the phrase τὸ ἰσχυρότατον ἐν τάξει. D. Whitehead (1990: 141) suspected peltasts here, on the grounds that they are described in the next § 5. Such an interpretation seems to be unconvincing, however: here τὸ ἰσχυρότατον must mean heavy infantry, rather than light-armed troops (cf. 16.7), as it is Aeneas himself who concedes that such a force looked forward to a pitched battle (προσδεχόμενοί τινας ἐφ' ἑαυτοὺς <ἰέναι> καὶ ἑτοίμως ἔχοντες ἀμύνεσθαι). For my purposes, the importance of the phrase again relies on the author's vocabulary, as he is simply thinking along traditional lines, regarding infantry militiamen as "the strongest" part of each army.

The third passage, at 16.11, is even more revealing. It concerns a case where the plundering of the territory is already advanced, and native forces have failed to prevent it. The writer advises managing a false pursuit of the retreating enemy, employing only small forces. The main task of recapturing booty from the plunderers who are withdrawing slowly and making dinner is put down on the ἄλλο δὲ πλῆθος ("the main body"). Here Aeneas is more precise: he adds that a section of this main army, reaching the borders along unknown roads, is ἀξιόχρεος δύναμις (μετὰ ἀξιοχρέου δυνάμεως). The passage is hardly easy to explain. It seems to be a rhetorical pleonasm, so Whitehead (1990: 63) renders it as "the main body – a considerable one;" earlier on, Hunter and Handford (1927: 35) understood it as "the main army, in full strength," while Oldfather (2001: 83) took it to signify the "army as a whole, in considerable strength." But what in this context does the Ionic adjective ἀξιόχρεος (Hunter/Handford 1927: lxiv) mean? As *LSJ*[9] (*s.v.*, 171) explains it, the primary meaning is "worthy" (Herodotus, 5.65: ἀξιόχρεα ἀπηγήσιος), "worthy of a thing," "noteworthy" – again as in Herodotus, 5.111 (ὑπὸ ἀξιοχρέου καὶ ἀποθανεῖν). It would be justified to say that Aeneas perhaps made an evaluation here, stressing that in the whole army *its* most valuable part should be excelled (cf. Beekes 2010: 111) – to be sure he stops to indicate what part was at stake, yet given the nature of the military operation and the author's other laudatory remarks in the treatise, there remains little room for doubt that hoplite forces were meant – what's more, it may also be supposed that ἄλλο δὲ πλῆθος was purportedly contrasted in this sentence to the best part of the army – ἀξιόχρεος δύναμις.[44]

---

[43]   Oldfather (2001) renders the phrase as: "formed in a battle array."

[44]   The sentiment connected with heavy armed infantrymen has left a clear mark in later military literature, the so-called *Tactica*. In the three standard treatises, by Asclepiodotus (*Tact.* 1.2), Aelian (*Tact.* 2.6), and Arrian (*Tact.* 3.1–2), the traditional division into hoplites, light-armed and peltasts is retained.

The last significant example of Aeneas' traditional outlook is found at 27.9. Here the soldiers in the army of the Spartan harmost Euphratas are called "more worthwhile men" (τῶν πουδαιοτέρων ἀνδρῶν) and "of the interior sort" (τῶν δὲ φαύλων).[45] Scholars speculate as to what the basis for such an evaluation was. Hunter and Handford (1927: 191) maintained that the Spartan hoplites experienced such a fear; Whitehead (1990: 176) cites the opinion of M. Cary, who believed they were mercenaries. Be that as it may, one thing cannot escape the notice of the modern reader: again Aeneas did not hesitate to employ a strong vocabulary, albeit it is not wholly clear if he was thinking in social or purely military terms (Whitehead 1990: 176). However, following Oldfather's interpretation (2001: 141: "more respectable soldiers – one of baser sort"), it would again be tempting to suppose that at the heart of such military contrast lay the author's civic sympathies.[46]

The last question is that of the writer's interest in the problems concerning the army itself. Since the subject-matter of Aeneas' handbook is siege, battles and tactics remain essentially beyond his interest (n. 8, above), although no one can arbitrarily reject the possibility that the theme was treated by him in full in the lost treatises on *Preparations* (ἐν δὲ τῷ Παρασκευαστικῷ: 21.1; cf. 8.5), or in the *Encampment* (ἐν τῇ Στρατοπεδευτικῇ βίβλῳ: 21.2). Relying, however, on what remained, one must concede that besides the case of *hoplitai/politai* at 15.5, D. Barends (1955: 98) quotes only three other places where the noun ὁπλῖται occurs in the text. If one realizes that the first cursorily refers to an old battlefield custom of the Cyreneaean citizens (16.15: *hoplitai en taksei genomenoi*), and the second (17.4) is Meineke's emendation ὁπλ<ί>των of MS' lesson τῶν προσαλισθέντων ὅπλων (not accepted by other scholars; cf. Barends 1955: 98; Bettalli 1990: 272), the last remaining instance is that from Chapter 16.7, where the MS reads τοὺς δ' ὁπλίτας ἀθρόους ἐν τάξει. There is also the participle ὁπλίζοντα (16.3), referring to a commander who must equip his men with "arms and armor" (Whitehead's 1990: 61–62 rendering; cf. Barends 1955: 98). A similar case constitutes the noun φάλαγξ, which is found in the text only one time (at 29.9: ὡς φάλαγξι γενομένου) in its technical sense of "battle formation" (see also Hunter/Handford 1927: 75). All the examples leave nothing but a plain impression: they are surprisingly few. But, as I have said above, although the theme of battle tactics is "essentially" absent from the book, only the above sketchy comments indicate that the theme was not omitted by the mercenary captain "totally." And it could not be, of course, as a crucial thing should be noted: although the presence of hoplites in a *polis* during a siege is by no means highlighted by Aeneas in a special way, reading the treatise shows that their usefulness still remained crucial in his days – in an objective sense, so to speak (Cartledge 1987: 43). Again, such a conviction comes from the fact that it was the hoplite "class,"[47] whose loyalty might guarantee a relative

---

[45]　Hunter/Handford 1927: 69: "best men" – "less valuable men."

[46]　An analogy might be a passage from Thuc. 3.98.4; narrating the Athenian loss at Aegition in Aetolia, he adds that among the casualties there were about 120 hoplites whom he calls "the best men" (βέλτιστοι δὴ ἄνδρες ἐν τῷ πολέμῳ τῷδε ἐκ τῆς Ἀθηναίων πόλεως διεφθάρησαν; cf. also 3.92.2; cf. generally Loraux 1975: 1 and 25); this term raises the controversy of who these men were (see Gomme 1956: 407–408). I believe the vocabulary is social, that is the main stress is laid on the fact that they were the citizens – the most valuable soldiers. The same way of thinking is in Aeneas. To put it briefly, he does not refer to the status of these men and in this sense his standpoint is "civic," so to speak.

[47]　A term used by Ober 1996 and Raaflaub 1999.

protection of *polis*, men ready to defend its property behind the walls (cf. esp. 7.1; see Ducrey 1986: 61).[48] By the way, remembering that "the pitched-battle mentality" (see n. 9, above) is difficult to find in Aeneas, it is not wholly true that Aeneas is uninterested in the problems of an army during a campaign. The most visible case for this is that coming from Chapter 6.2, where he does discuss the emotions of the average rank-and-file soldier after the loss of a battle (cf. Lysias 16.15). The picture is particularly vivid and proves him to be a keen and insightful observer. In the same vein, like a forerunner of the modern "face of battle" approach, at 26.7–8 Aeneas devotes some perceptive remarks to the lack of spirit and courage among the soldiers, whose army suffered from losses (cf. Salazar 2000: 7). By the same token, it is clear that the author's attention frequently focuses on the more substantial problems with a civic army and its lack of experience (6.2: *apeiroi takseon kai polemou*; see note 35, above),[49] so the result is a wearisome monotony in his constant advice to keep order, both among the citizens within a *polis* (1.4; 1.5; 3.1; 3.4) and among those who went on campaign (1.5–7; 15.2–3).

To sum up, the perspective adopted by Aeneas in his treatise is thoroughly that of a citizen. He introduces himself to the reader as militiaman, fully conscious of the difficulties related to the *polis* amateur army, raised up on the eve of emergency. Above all, he was a realist, knowing perfectly well what difficulties faced a community under siege. This sense of reality pervades the treatise itself, but it cannot be confined to military matters only. It is also visible in the author's open recognition of communal values. In other words, Aeneas seems to have stood far from sophistic, "anthropological" approaches toward society, and in this respect he was not a disciple of the sophists. As a consequence, one may also claim that by no means should he be called a man whose attitude denounced the more "cosmopolitan" attitudes of the world of the Hellenistic kingdoms. Conversely – he should rather be listed among the men whose mentality and way of reasoning was inseparable from that of the dwellers of a small city.

BIBLIOGRAPHY

Anderson, J.K. (1970): *Military Theory and Practice in the Age of Xenophon*, Berkeley–Los Angeles.
Andrewes, A. (1974): *The Greek Tyrants*, London.
Andrewes, A. (1981): The Hoplite Katalogos, in: G.S. Shrimpton, D.J. McCargar (eds.), *Classical Contributions. Studies in Honor of M.F. McGregor*, Locust Valley, NY: 1–3.
Aymard, A. (1967): Les étrangers dans les cités grecques aux temps classiques, in: A. Aymard, *Études d'histoire ancienne*, Paris: 300–313.

---

[48] It is striking that Aeneas has surprisingly little to say about the cavalry. He evidently presupposes that not every *polis* maintains cavalry troops; if so, its role is supporting: cf. 6.6; 8.4; 26.4; cf. Xen., *Equit. mag.* 4.7–11; see Ducrey 1986: 102. By the way, this brings to mind the relatively higher evaluation of the service in infantry troops than in cavalry, cf. Lysias, 14.11; see Liers 1895: 88–89.

[49] Sparta was an exception, see Xen., *Mem.* 3.9.2; Plut., *Pelop.* 23.4.

Baker, P. (1999): Les mercenaires, in: F. Prost (éd.), *Armées et sociétés de la Grèce classique. Aspects sociaux et politiques de la guerre aux Ve et IVe s. av. J.-C.*, Paris: 240–255.

Barends, D. (1955): *Lexicon Aeneium. A Lexicon and Index to Aeneas Tacticus' Military Manual "On the Defence of Fortified Positions"*, Assen.

Bassi, K. (2003): The Semantics of Manliness in Ancient Greece, in: R.M. Rosen, I. Sluite (eds.), *Andreia. Studies in Manliness and Courage in Classical Antiquity*, (*Mnemosyne* Suppl. 238), Leiden–Boston: 25–58.

Beekes, R. (2010): *Etymological Dictionary of Greek*, vol. I, Leiden–Boston.

Bengtson, H. (1962): Die griechische Polis bei Aeneas Tacticus, *Historia* 11: 458–468.

Best, J.G.P. (1969): *Thracian Peltasts and Their Influence on Greek Warfare*, Groningen.

Bettalli, M. (1990): *Enea Tattico, La difesa di una città assediata (Poliorketika)*, Pisa.

Bettalli, M. (1995): *I mercenari nel mondo greco I. Dalle origini alla fine del V sec. a. C.*, Pisa.

Bovon, A.M. (1963): La représentation des guerriers perses et la notion de barbare dans la 1re moitié du Ve siècle, *BCH* 87: 579–602.

Bowersock, G.W. (2000): Pseudo-Xenophon, Constitution of the Athenians, in: *Xenophon, Scripta Minora*, trans. E.G. Marchant, Cambridge (MA)–London: 460–507.

Bryant, J.M. (1990): Military Technology and Socio-cultural Change in the Ancient Greek City, *Sociological Review* 38: 484–516.

Bryant, J.M. (1996): *Moral Codes and Social Structure in Ancient Greece. A Sociology of Greek Ethics from Homer to the Epicureans and Stoics*, Albany, NY.

Bugh, G.R. (2011): Menander's Mercenaries, in: N.V. Sekunda, A. Noguera Borel (eds.), *Hellenistic Warfare 1*, Valencia: 73–88.

Burckhardt, L. (1996): *Bürger und Soldaten. Aspekte der politischen und militärischen Rolle athenaischer Bürger im Kriegswesen des 4. Jahrhunderts v. Chr.*, (*Historia Einzelschriften* 101), Stuttgart.

Burford Cooper, A. (1977): *The Family Farm in Greece, CJ* 73: 162–175.

Burliga, B. (2007): *Eneasz Taktyk. Obrona oblężonego miasta*, Warszawa.

Burliga, B. (2008): Aeneas Tacticus between History and Sophistry: The Emergence of the Military Handbook, in: J. Pigoń (ed.), *The Children of Herodotus. Greek and Roman Historiography and Related Genres*, Newcastle-upon-Tyne: 92–101.

Burliga, B. (2011): ἡ ἀσπὶς περιερρύη ἐς τὴν θάλασσαν: Homeric Glamour of Brasidas' Bravery in Thucydides, 4, 12, 1, in: J. Styka, S. Śnieżyński (eds.), *Studies of Greek and Roman Literature and Culture. Essays in Honour of Józef Korpanty*, (*Classica Cracoviensia* 14), Kraków: 95–112.

Butcher, S.H. (1903): *Demosthenis orationes* I, Oxford.

Bywater, I. (1894): *Aristotelis Ethica Nicomachea*, Oxford.

Cartledge, P. (1987): *Agesilaos and the Crisis of Sparta*, Baltimore–London.

Cartledge, P. (2001): The Birth of the Hoplite. Sparta's Contribution to Early Greek Military Organization, in: P. Cartledge, *Spartan Reflections*, Berkeley–Los Angeles: 153–166; 225–228.

Casaubon, I., Gronovius, J. (1670): *Polybii Historiarum quae supersunt*, tomus secundus, editio altera, Amstelodami.

Chandezon, Ch. (1999): L'économie rurale et la guerre, in: F. Prost (éd.), *Armées et sociétés de la Grèce classique. Aspects sociaux et politiques de la guerre aux Ve et IVe s. ac. J.-C.*, Paris: 195–208.

Chaniotis, A. (2005): *War in the Hellenistic World. A Social and Cultural History*, Oxford.

Childs, W.A.P., Demargne, P. (1989): *Le monument des Néréides. Le décor sculpté*, (*Fouilles de Xanthos* VIII), Paris.

Christ, M.R. (2001): Conscription of Hoplites in Classical Athens, *CQ* 51: 398–422.

Connor, W.R. (1988): Early Greek Land Warfare as a Symbolic Expression, *Past & Present* 19: 3–29.

Dain, A., Bon, A.-M. (1967): *Énée le Tacticien, Poliorcétique*, Paris.

Delbrück, H. (1900): *Geschichte der Kriegskunst im Rahmen der politischen Geschichte*, vol. I, Berlin.

Dover, K.J. (1974): *Greek Popular Morality in the Times of Plato and Aristotle*, Oxford.

Ducrey, P. (1986): *Warfare in Ancient Greece*, New York.

Foxhall, L. (1993): *Farming and Fighting in Ancient Greece*, in: J. Rich, G. Shipley (eds.), *War and Society in Ancient Greek World*, London–New York: 134–145.

Galitzin, N.S. Fürst (1874): *Allgemeine Kriegsgeschichte des Alterthums*, vol. I, Cassel.

Garlan, Y. (1974): *Recherches de poliorcétique grecque*, Paris.

Gauthier, P. (1976): *Un commentaire historique des Poroi de Xenophon*, Genève–Paris.

Gehrke, H.-J. (1985): *Stasis. Untersuchungen zu den inneren Kriegen in den griechischen Staaten des 5. und 4. Jahrhunderts v. Chr.*, (*Vestigia* 35), München.

Gomme, A.W. (1956): *A Historical Commentary on Thucydides*, vol. II, Oxford.

Gray, V. (2007): *Xenophon on Government*, Cambridge.

Haase, F. (1835): Über die griechischen und lateinischen Kriegsschriftsteller, *Neue Jahrbücher für Philologie und Pädagogik* 14: 88–118.

Hall, J.M. (2007): *A History of the Archaic Greek World ca. 1200–479 BCE*, Malden (MA)–Oxford.

Hansen, M.H. (2004): The Concept of *Patris*, in: M.H. Hansen, T. Heine Nielsen (eds.), *An Inventory of Archaic and Classical Poleis*, Oxford: 49–52.

Hanson, V.D. (1996): Hoplites into Democrats. The Changing Ideology of Athenian Infantry, in: J. Ober, Ch. Hedrick Jr. (eds.), *Demokratia. A Conversation on Democracies, Ancient and Modern*, Princeton: 289–312.

Hanson, V.D. (1999): *The Other Greeks. The Family Farm and the Agrarian Roots of Western Civilization*, 2nd ed., Berkeley–Los Angeles–London.

Hanson, V.D. (2000): The Classical Greek Warrior and the Egalitarian Military Ethos, *Ancient World* 31: 111–126.

Hercher, R. (1870): *Aeneae commentarius poliorceticus*, Berlin.

Hodkinson, S. (1983): Social Order and the Conflict of Values in Classical Sparta, *Chiron* 13: 239–281.

Hölscher, T. (1998): Images and Political Identity. The Case of Athens, in: D. Boedeker, K.A. Raaflaub (eds.), *Democracy, Empire, and the Arts in Fifth-Century Athens*, Cambridge (MA)–London: 153–184.

Hornblower, S. (2007): Warfare in Ancient Literature. The Paradox of War, in: P. Sabin, H. van Wees, M. Whitby (eds.), *The Cambridge History of Greek and Roman Warfare*, vol. I, Cambridge: 22–53.

Hornblower, S. (2008): *A Commentary on Thucydides*, vol. III, Oxford.

Hug, A. (1874): *Aeneae Commentarius poliorceticus*, Leipzig.

Hug, A. (1877): *Aeneas von Stymphalos. Ein arkadischer Schriftsteller aus Classischer Zeit*, Zürich.

Hunt, P. (1998): *Slaves, Warfare, and Ideology in the Greek Historians*, Cambridge.

Hunt, P. (2007): Military Forces, in: P. Sabin, H. van Wees & M. Whitby (eds.), *The Cambridge History of Greek and Roman Warfare*, vol. I: 108–146.

Hunter, L.W., Handford, S.A. (1927): *Aeneas on Siegecraft*, Oxford.

Köchly, H., Rüstow, W. (1853): *Griechische Kriegsschriftsteller*, Bd. I, Leipzig: 1–183.

Korus, K. (1969): Grecka samoobrona powszechna w epoce klasycznej wg Eneasza Taktyka, *Meander* 24: 507–520.

Krasilnikoff, J. (1992): Aegean Mercenaries in the Fifth to Second Centuries BC. A Study in Payment, Plunder and Logistics of Ancient Greek Armies, *Classica et Mediaevalia* 43: 23–36.

Krentz, P. (2000): Deception in Archaic and Classical Greek Warfare, in: H. van Wees (ed.), *War and Violence in Ancient Greece*, London: 167–200.

Krentz, P. (2010): *The Battle of Marathon*, New Haven–London.

Kulesza, R. (1998): *Polis apolis. Wysiedlenia, przesiedlenia i ucieczki ludności w świecie greckim w V i IV wieku p. n. e.*, Warszawa.

Landucci Gattinoni, F. (2001): I mercenari e l'ideologia della guerra, in: M. Sordi (ed.), *Il pensiero sulla guerra nel mondo antico*, Milano: 65–85.

Lazenby, J.F. (1989): Hoplite Warfare, in: General Sir J. Hackett (ed.), *Warfare in the Ancient World*, London: 54–81.

Lazenby, J.F. (1994): Logistics in Classical Greek Warfare, *War in History* 1: 3–18.

Lee, J.W.I. (2009): Land Warfare in Xenophon's Hellenika, in: R.B. Strassler (ed.), *The Landmark Xenophon's Hellenika*, New York: 371–394.

Lehmann, G.A. (1980): Krise und innere Bedrohung der hellenischen Polis bei Aeneas Tacticus, in: W. Eck, H. Galsterer, H. Wolff (eds.), *Studien zur antiken Sozialgeschichte. Festschrift F. Vittinghoff*, Köln–Wien: 71–86.

Lengauer, W. (1974): Żołnierz-obywatel i żołnierz-najemnik w Grecji klasycznej, *Meander* 29: 23–29.

Lengauer, W. (1979): *Greek Commanders in the 5th and 4th Centuries B.C. Politics and Ideology: A Study of Militarism*, Warszawa.

Liers, H. (1895): *Das Kriegswesen der Alten mit besondrer Berücksichtigung der Strategie*, Breslau.

Lipka, M. (2002): *Xenophon's Spartan Constitution*, Berlin–New York.

Lissarague, F. (1989): The World of Warrior, in: C. Berard *et al.* (eds.), *A City of Images. Iconography and Society in Ancient Greece*, Princeton: 39–52.

Lissarague, F. (1990): *L'autre guerrier. Archers, peltastes, cavaliers dans l'imagerie attique*, Paris–Rome.

Lissarague, F. (2002): The Athenian Image of the Foreigner, in: T. Harrison (ed.), *Greeks and Barbarians*, Edinburgh: 101–124.

Loraux, N. (1975): HEBE et ANDREIA: deux versions de la mort du combattant athenien, *Ancient Society* 6: 1–31.

Loraux, N. (1986): *The Invention of Athens. The Funeral Oration in the Classical City*, Cambridge (MA)–London 1986.

Ma, J. (2000): Fighting Poleis of the Hellenistic World, in: H. van Wees, P. Beston, S. Deacy (eds.), *War and Violence in Ancient Greece*, London: 337–376.

Mallet, M. (1974): *Mercenaries and Their Masters. Warfare in Renaissance Italy*, London–Sydney–Toronto.

Marr, J., Rhodes, P.J. (2008): *The "Old Oligarch". The Constitution of the Athenians Attributed to Xenophon*, Oxford.

Mathieu, G. (1942): *Isocrate, Discours* III, Paris.

McK Camp II, J. (2000): Walls and the *Polis*, in: P. Flensted-Jensen, T.H. Nielsen, L. Rubinstein (eds.), *Polis & Politics. Studies in Ancient Greek History Presented to Mogens Herman Hansen on His Sixtieth Birthday*, Copenhagen: 41–57.

McKechnie, P.R. (1989): *Outsiders in the Greek Cities in the Fourth. Century BC*, London–New York.

McKechnie, P.R., Kern, S.J. (1988): *Hellenica Oxyrhynchia*, Warminster.

Meissner, B. (2010): War as a Learning-Process. The Persian Wars and the Transformation of Fifth Century Greek Warfare, in: K. Buraselis, K. Meidani (eds.), Μαραθών: η μάχη και ο αρχαίος Δήμος /Marathon. The Battle and the Ancient Deme, Athens: 275–296.

Millender, E. (2006): The Politics of Spartan Mercenary Service, in: S. Hodkinson, A. Powell (eds.), *Sparta & War*, London: 235–266.

Miller, M.C. (2010): I Am Eurymedon. Tensions and Ambiguities in Athenian War Imagery, in: D.M. Pritchard (ed.), *War, Democracy and Culture in Classical Athens*, Cambridge: 304–338.

Mitchell, S. (1996): Hoplite Warfare in Ancient Greece, in: A.B. Lloyd (ed.), *Battle in Antiquity*, London: 87–107.

Moggi, M. (2002): L'oplita e l'arciere (ideologia e realtà tra guerra antica e guerra moderna), *Ktema* 27: 195–206.

Morris, I. (1996): The Strong Principle of Equality and the Archaic Origins of Greek Democracy, in: J. Ober, Ch. Hedrick Jr. (eds.), *Demokratia. A Conversation on Democracies, Ancient and Modern*, Princeton: 19–48.

Ober, J. (1994): Hoplites and Obstacles, in: V.D. Hanson (ed.), *Hoplites. The Classical Greek Battle Experience*, London–New York: 173–196.

Ober, J. (1995): Fortress Attika. Defense of the Athenian Land Frontier 404–322 B.C. (*Mnemosyne* Suppl. 84), Leiden.

Ober, J. (1996): The Rules of War in Classical Greece, in: J. Ober, *The Athenian Revolution. Essays on Ancient Greek Democracy and Political Theory*, Princeton: 53–71.

Oldfather, W.A. (2001): Aeneas Tacticus, in: *Aeneas Tacticus, Asclepiodotus, Onasander*, trans. The Illinois Greek Club, Cambridge (MA)–London (reprint).

Osborne, R. (1987): *Classical Landscape with Figures. The Ancient Greek City and Its Countryside*, London.

Osborne, R. (2000): An Other View: An Essay in Political History, in: B. Cohen (ed.), *Not the Classical Ideal. Athens and the Construction of the Other in Greek Art*, Leiden–Boston–Cologne: 21–42.

Ostwald, M. (2000): *Oligarchia. The Development of a Constitutional Form in Ancient Greece*, (*Historia Einzelschriften* 144), Stuttgart.

Parke, H.W. (1933): *Greek Mercenary Soldiers. From the Earliest Times to the Battle of Ipsos*, Oxford.

Pritchett, W.K. (1974): *The Greek State at War*, vol. II, Berkeley–Los Angeles.

Prost, F. (1999): Les combattants de Marathon. Idéologie et sociétés hoplitiques à Athenes au Ve s. av. J.- C., in: F. Prost, *Armées et sociétés de la Gréce classique. Aspects sociaux et politiques de la guerre aux Ve et IVe s. av. J.-C.*, Paris: 69–88.

Raaflaub, K.A. (1997): Soldiers, Citizens, and the Evolution of the Early Greek Polis, in: L.G. Mitchell, P.J. Rhodes (eds.), *The Development of the Polis in Archaic Greece*, London–New York: 49–59.

Raaflaub, K.A. (1999): Archaic and Classical Greece, in: K.A. Raaflaub, N. Rosenstein (eds.), *War and Society in the Ancient and Medieval Worlds. Asia, the Mediterranean, Europe, and Mesoamerica*, Cambridge (MA)–London: 129–161.

Raaflaub, K.A. (2007): The Breakthrough of Demokratia in Mid-Fifth-Century Athens, in: K.A. Raaflaub, J. Ober, R.W. Wallace (eds.), *Origins of Democracy in Ancient Greece*, Berkeley–Los Angeles–London: 105–154.

Rawlings, L. (2000): Alternative Agonies. Hoplite Martial and Combat Experiences beyond the Phalanx, in: H. van Wees (ed.), *War and Violence in Ancient Greece*, London: 233–259.

Rhodes, P.J. (1993): *A Commentary on the Aristotelian Athenaion Politeia*, 2nd ed., Oxford.

Rhodes, P.J., Osborne, R. (2003): *Greek Historical Inscriptions 404–323 BC*, Oxford.

Ridley, R.T. (2007): The Hoplite as Citizen: Athenian Military Institutions in Their Social Context, in: E.L. Wheeler (ed.), *The Armies of Classical Greece*, Aldershot: 153–193.

Robinson, R. (1995): *Aristotle, Politics. Books III and IV*, Oxford.

Roy, J. (2004): The Ambitions of a Mercenary, in: R. Lane Fox (ed.), *The Long March. Xenophon and the Ten Thousand*, New Haven–London: 264–288.

Rzepka, J. (2011): *Cheroneja*, Warszawa.

Sage, M.M. (1996): *Warfare in Ancient Greece. A Sourcebook*, London–New York.

Salazar, Ch.F. (2000): *The Treatment of War Wounds in Graeco-Roman Antiquity*, (*Studies in Ancient Medicine* 21), Leiden–Boston–Köln.

Schoene, R. (1911): *Aeneae Tactici de obsidione toleranda commentarius*, Leipzig.

Schwartz, A. (2009): *Reinstating the Hoplite. Arms, Armour and Phalanx Fighting in Archaic and Classical Greece*, (*Historia Einzelschriften* 207), Stuttgart.

Sekunda, N. (1994): Classical Warfare, *CAH²*. *Plates to Volumes V and VI. New Edition*, J. Boardman (ed.), Cambridge: 167–192.

Sekunda, N. (2000): *Greek Hoplite 480–323 BC*, Oxford.

Snodgrass, A.M. (1999): *Arms & Armor of the Greeks*, 2nd ed., Baltimore–London.

Spaulding, O.L. (1937): *Pen and Sword in Greece and Rome*, Princeton–London.

Spence, I.G. (2002): *Historical Dictionary of Ancient Greek Warfare*, Lanham (MD)–London.

Sprawski, S. (1999): Jason of Pherae. A Study on History of Thessaly in Years 431–370 BC (*Electrum* 3), Kraków.

Strauss, B.S. (1996): The Athenian Trireme, School of Democracy, in: J. Ober, Ch. Hedrick Jr. (eds.), *Demokratia. A Conversation on Democracies, Ancient and Modern*, Princeton: 313–325.

Tod, M.N. (1948): *A Selection of Greek Historical Inscriptions* II. *From 403 to 323 BC*, Oxford.

Trevett, J. (2011): *Demosthenes, Speeches 1–17*, Austin, Texas.

Trundle, M. (2004): *Greek Mercenaries. From the Late Archaic Period to Alexander*, London–New York.

Underhill, G.E. (1900): *A Commentary with Introduction and Appendix on the Hellenica of Xenophon*, Oxford.

Urban, R. (1986): Zur inneren und äusseren Gefährdung griechischer Städte bei Aeneas Tacticus, in: H. Kalcyk, B. Gullath, A. Graeber (eds.), *Studien zur Alten Geschichte S. Lauffer zum 70. Geburtstag* , vol. III, Rome: 991–1002.

Vela Tejada, J., García, F.M. (1991): *Eneas el Táctico, Poliorcética. Polieno, Estratagemas,* Madrid.

Vernant, J.-P. (1988): City-State Warfare, in: J.-P. Vernant, *Myth and Society in Ancient Greece*, New York–London: 29–53.

Walbank, F.W. (1967): *A Historical Commentary on Polybius*, vol. II, Oxford.

Wees, H. van (1995): Politics and the Battlefield. Ideology in Greek Warfare, in: A. Powell (ed.), *The Greek World*, London–New York: 153–178.

Wees, H. van (2002): Tyrants, Oligarchs and Citizen Militias, in: A. Chaniotis, P. Ducrey (eds.), *Army and Power in the Ancient World*, Stuttgart: 61–82.

Wees, H. van (2004): *Greek Warfare. Myths and Realities*, London.

Wheeler, E.L. (1987): Ephorus and the Prohibition of Missiles, *TAPA* 117: 157–182.

Wheeler, E.L. (2007): Introduction, in: E.L. Wheeler (ed.), *The Armies of Classical Greece*, Aldershot: xi–lxiv.

Whitehead, D. (1990): *Aineias the Tactician. How to Survive under Siege*, Oxford.

Whitehead, D. (1991): Norms of Citizenship in Ancient Greece, in: A. Molho, K. Raaflaub, J. Emlen (eds.), *City-States in Classical Antiquity and Medieval Italy*, Ann Arbor: 135–154.

Winterling, A. (1991): Polisbegriff und Stasistheorie des Aeneas Tacticus. Zur Frage der Grenzen der griechischen Polisgesellschaften im 4. Jahrhundert v. Chr., *Historia* 40: 193–229.

Wooten, C. (2008): *A Commentary on Demosthenes' Phillipic I*, Oxford.

ELECTRUM * Vol. 19 (2012): 83–97
doi:10.4467/20843909EL.12.004.0745

The Ptolemies versus the Achaean and Aetolian Leagues in the 250s–220s BC

Tomasz Grabowski

Abstract: In the 250s and 240s continental Greece found itself in a particularly complicated situation. The growth of the Aetolian and Achaean Leagues, as well as Sparta's awoken ambitions, presented the Ptolemies with favorable conditions to actively pursue efforts to weaken the Macedonian influence there. Initially, the partner of the Ptolemies became the Achaean League. In this way, the Ptolemaic fleet gained important footholds, including both Corinthian ports, Kenchreai in the Saronic Gulf and Lechaion in the Corinthian Gulf. This strengthened the position of the Lagids at sea, and it was the islands on the Aegean Sea and the coasts of Asia Minor that were in the centre of the Ptolemies' interest. However, the Aetolian League could continue to be seen as one of their possible partners in Greek politics. We should not exaggerate the Achaean-Aetolian conflict. After the death of Antigonus Gonatas in 239, the two conflicted federations were joined by an alliance. It cannot be excluded that Sparta also cooperated with the coalition, and the king of Egypt could have been a convenient link in this cooperation. There is no information whatsoever to suggest an Egyptian initiative to form the coalition. After the defeat of the Egyptian fleet at Andros in ca. 245, the position of the Lagids in the Aegean Sea was not as strong as it had once been. This was all the more reason for Ptolemies to closely observe the Aetolians' intense activity on the Aegean Sea. The Ptolemies and Aetolians concluded *symmachia*. Ultimately, however, alliances were reversed: Aratus pushed the Achaean League towards a coalition with Macedonia, but earlier, having learned about the Achaean-Macedonian negotiations, Ptolemy decided to cancel his financial support for the Achaeans and hand it over to Sparta. It is very likely that the situation in the whole Aegean region (especially the expedition of Antigonus Doson to Caria in 227) played a role in changing the Ptolemies' policy. The contacts which the Aetolian League established in the region were all the more reason for Ptolemy III to choose Cleomenes and the Aetolians at the expense of the Achaean League. At that time, the beginning of closer relations between the Aetolians and the Attalids could also be observed. It cannot be ruled out that the Ptolemaic diplomacy was a mediator, since up until then the Aetolians had no common interests with Pergamum. For the Lagids, on the other hand, the Attalids were a force worth supporting against the Seleucids, just as the Aetolians were a valuable partner in the rivalry against Macedonia.

Keywords: Aetolian League, Achaean League, Sparta, Athens, the Ptolemies.

In the 250s–240s[1] continental Greece found itself in a particularly complicated situation. The growth of the Aetolian and Achaean Leagues, as well as Sparta's awoken ambitions, presented the Ptolemies (the Antigonid dynasty's main rivals in Greece at the time) with favorable conditions for actively pursuing efforts to weaken the Macedonian influence there. The kings of Egypt, in turn, were able to seize the opportunity and go back to the policy which had already been conducted, with varying luck, at the end of the fourth century. As was the case before, the Peloponnese became the most important arena of political contest.

We may pinpoint the year 314 as the beginning of the Ptolemies' involvement in Greece, although at the time Ptolemy confined himself to declaring the freedom of the Greek *poleis*, like Polyperchon and Antigonus Monophthalmus.[2] This fact is often interpreted as an intention to counterbalance the policy of Antigonus and an attempt to neutralize his act related to the same issue. Certainly, this was the foremost reason behind using the popular slogan, but it can also be interpreted as an introduction to a much larger-scale Greek policy. His declaration, like that of Antigonus', was after all aimed against the interests of Ptolemy's ally at the time, Cassander, and at the same time could have opened much broader future prospects for the satrap of Egypt. As we know, Ptolemy's direct military involvement came about a few years later, in 308, and the expedition was preceded by diplomatic efforts and propaganda. It seems that the Lagid's main goal was to capture the Peloponnese, and it also cannot be excluded that he had plans to establish a *symmachia* of Peloponnesian *poleis* under Ptolemy's aegis. Ultimately, the campaign did not bring much success, but Sicyon and Corinth remained in the hands of the king of Egypt for several years, and his successors could refer to their predecessor's activity on the Aegean Sea in their policy.[3] In continental Greece, apart from Athens, it was the Peloponnese that became the Lagids' main object of interest. We may suppose that this was a deliberate political line of the dynasty, for which the Peloponnese had a significant strategic value in the face of competition in the Aegean and on Crete.

In the following period, the attention of Ptolemy I and his successor concentrated mainly on the Aegean Sea, where he steadily expanded his sphere of influence. However, he rarely became directly involved in the events occurring in Greece.[4] There, the first two Ptolemies mostly focused on Athens, with which they tried to keep close contacts and which they provided with money and grain.[5] The Lagids' activity in Greece increased

---

[1]   All dates in this paper are BC.

[2]   This probably took place in the winter of 314/313: Errington 1977: 497; Huss 2001: 150. An expedition led by Polykleitos was also sent to Greece, but he left Hellas very quickly (Diod. 19.62.5; 64.3–5), which confirms that at that time Ptolemy had little opportunity to act in the face of the threat posed by Antigonus Monophthalmus in Syria.

[3]   *IG* V.2.550; XI.2.161; *I. Délos* 296; 313; Diod. 19.62.5; 64.3–5; 20.19.4; 37.1–2; Plut., *Demetr.* 15.1.3; Paus. 6.3.1; 6.16.3; Polyaenus, *Strat.* 8.58.f; Suda s.v. Δημήτριος ὁ Ἀντιγόνου. On Ptolemaic policy in Greece in these years see Moser 1914: 29–61, 76–94; Seibert 1969: 176–189; Huss 2001: 173–179; Grabowski 2008. Loss of influence in Corinth and Sicyon: Diod. 20.102.2–4; 20.103.1–3; Plut., *Demetr.* 25.1; Polyaenus, *Strat.* 4.7.2; 4.7.8.

[4]   E.g. cooperation with Pyrrhus: Plut., *Pyrrh.* 5.1; 5. 10–11; Iust. 17.2.13–15, support for Athens against Demetrius Poliorcetes in 287: *SEG* XXVIII, 60; Plut., *Demetr.* 33–34. Cf. Habicht 1979: 45–67; Osborne 1979.

[5]   *IG* II, 650; 682; *SEG* XXVIII, 60, *l.*14–15.

in the 260s, when Ptolemy II started to forge an anti-Macedonian coalition, which ultimately led to the outbreak of the Chremonidean War. The dynamic Ptolemaic diplomatic campaign and propaganda covered, apart from the insular states of the Aegean Sea, mainly the *poleis* in southern Greece. Finally, the emerging coalition, whose most important element was the alliance between Sparta and Athens, mainly included Peloponnesian city-states: apart from Sparta, the *poleis* of Arcadia, Elis and Achaea.[6] The Chremonidean War, despite the defeat, did not mean a complete loss of influence in Greece by the Ptolemies, and it brought them some important acquisitions on the Aegean Sea.[7] Having bases on the Aegean Sea and in Methana/Arsinoe on the Peloponnese, as well as considerable financial resources, enabled the Lagids to continue their active policy in Greece. The policy of Antigonus Gonatas, who based his strategy in Greece on keeping garrisons and enforcing pro-Macedonian tyrannies and oligarchies, could not calm moods in Hellas.

The events in continental Greece after the Chremonidean War opened up new perspectives to the Ptolemies. This period saw, on the one hand, an expansion of the Aetolian League, and on the other, rapid growth of a new power on the Greek political scene – the Achaean League. The Aetolian *koinon* continued the process of subordinating successive states in central Greece.[8] As a consequence, at the end of the 250s the Aetolians already had nine votes in the Delphi Amphictyonic Council;[9] the increased significance and ambitions of the League were also reflected in the expansion of the *Soteria* festival at Delphi in the 240s, which commemorated saving the sanctuary during the Gallic invasion and the Aetolian contribution to this success.[10] The strengthened *koinon* decided to break the alliance with Acarnania and to divide its territory together with Epirus.[11] This period also saw the increased involvement of the Aetolians in the two regions which were particularly important for the Lagids: the Peloponnese and the Aegean Sea. On the Peloponnese, the Aetolians had closer relations particularly with the Eleans, who in turn sought expansion in Arcadia. Regardless of whether we consider the Aetolian interventions in Peloponnesian affairs to be a result of the League's activity or a more individual initiative of some Aetolians organizing pillaging raids, the facts remains that their interest in the region increased.[12] At an unspecified date, the Aetolians entered into an alliance

---

[6]　On the Chremonidean War see Heinen 1972: 97–213; Gabbert 1983; 1997: 45–53; Huss 2001: 271–281; O'Neil 2008.

[7]　Ptolemy took over or extended his control of e.g. Miletus, Ephesus, several cities on Crete, probably also Thera and Lesbos, and even on the Peloponnese (Methana, renamed Arsinoe): *I. Milet* 139; *I. Cret.* III.4; *IG* XII, 5.1061; cf. Bagnall 1976: 141–145; van't Dack 1988: 146; Brun 1991; Hölbl 2001: 42–43.

[8]　As regards the development of the Aetolian League see Larsen 1968: 195–215; Walbank 1984: 232–236; Grainger 1999: 29–129; Scholten 2000: 16–95; 2003: 141–144; cf. also Lefèvre 1995: 33–39.

[9]　*CID* 4.45–48.

[10]　*SIG*³ 402. At that time, the programme of the games was expanded and a four-year cycle of organization was introduced, which characterised the most important Pan-Hellenic games. The distribution of seats on the Amphictyonic Council: *CID* 4.45–48.

[11]　Schmitt 1969: no. 485. The alliance with the Acarnanians, formed earlier (Schmitt 1969: no. 480), was strictly instrumental and enabled the Aetolians to calm the situation on the western borders of the League, see Dany 1999: 69–97; Grainger 1999: 132–139; Scholten 2000: 77–93.

[12]　*SIG*³ 472; Polyb. 4.18.8–12; 4.34.9; 9.34.9–10; Plut., *Arat.* 31–32; *Cleom.* 10.11; 18.3; Paus. 5.6.1; Polyaenus, *Strat.* 8.59. Researchers vary in their evaluation of the nature of these operations; it cannot be excluded that some of them were private raids of individual Aetolian generals. The clearest case is that of an

with the Messenians.[13] After establishing close relations with Elis, the Aetolian League was elevated to the group of the most influential powers on the peninsula.

The Ptolemies' contacts with the Aetolian League had not been particularly close,[14] but there is an interesting document from the time of the Chremonidean War which confirms that the Delphi Amphictyonic Council welcomed the most important festival of the Lagid monarchy, the Alexandrian *Ptolemaia*, which thus gained the status of Pan-Hellenic games. This was reportedly in 262/261, i.e. when the war was coming to an end and the Macedonian victory was unquestionable.[15] As we can see, although the Aetolians could not be enlisted for the anti-Macedonian coalition during the war, Ptolemy II's intensive propaganda was not completely futile. Naturally, such a step could have been motivated solely by the opportunism of the Aetolians, who concluded that they should look for a counterbalance to the triumphant Antigonus Gonatas. However, we can also interpret this as a success of the Ptolemaic diplomacy, which gave Ptolemy a chance to play the Aetolian card in the future.[16] Recognizing the *Ptolemaia* festival was even more significant in view of the fact that the Amphictyonic Council was at the time dominated by Aetolians.

The antagonism between the Achaean and Aetolian Leagues (the two most promising partners in their anti-Macedonian policy in the middle of the second century) posed a significant problem for the Ptolemaic diplomacy. The Aetolians' expansion on the Peloponnese threatened the vested interest of the other federation. The rivalry between the Aetolians and the Achaeans reached its peak in 245, when the Achaean League backed the Boeotians in their war against the Aetolian League, which ended in the Boeotians' defeat at Chaeronea.[17]

It was easier for the Ptolemies to find common ground with the Achaean League, whose military operations had an anti-Macedonian slant almost from the start. Closer mutual relations were also facilitated by the League's contacts with Pyrrhus during his expedition to the Peloponnese in 272, since the Epirote's policy in Greece was also supported by the Lagids.[18] However, the main bridge between Egypt and the Achaean

---

intervention in Laconia around 240, which should be considered an official campaign of the League. For that topic see Flacelière 1937: 239–244; Will 1979: 329–333; Grainger 1999: 157–164; Scholten 2000: 116–130.

[13] Polyb. 4.39; 6.11. Most likely the treaty was concluded around 244, cf. Roebuck 1941: 67.

[14] Cf. Grabowski 2010: 192–205.

[15] *FD* III 4.357 = *CID* 4.40. This decision was made during Pleiston's archonate. Bousquet (1958: 77–82) dated this event to the year 269 or 265, but Pleiston was an archon in 262/261: Lefèvre 1995: 179. The Aetolians had the majority of votes on the council at the time. The Lagids' interest in Apollo's oracle can already be observed a few years before. In 279, Alexandria received the privilege of *promanteia*. The theory about a kinship of the Ptolemaic capital with Delphi was also propagated (*SIG*³ 404; Bousquet 1991: 172).

[16] Grainger (1999: 142) seems to underestimate this decision of the Amphictyonic Council, emphasizing that at the time it was tied by *proxenia* with Megara and Cassandrea, i.e. cities under Macedonian control. Considering their situation in Hellas after the Chremonidean War, the decree of 262/261 should, after all, be interpreted as an intention to establish closer relations with the Lagids, who were still the only power that counterbalanced Macedonia.

[17] Polyb. 20.4.4–5.2; Plut., *Arat.* 16. Cf. Urban 1979: 46–48; Grainger 1999: 150–152; Scholten 2000: 83–92, 258–259.

[18] Plut., *Pyrrh.* 5.1; 5. 10–11; Iust. 17.2.13–15. Livy's account (35.26.5) about the Achaeans seizing a Macedonian ship shows that they participated actively in these fights. Cf. Lévêque 1957: 287–288; Heinen 1972: 192–193; Urban 1979: 10–12.

League could have been Sparta – the Ptolemies' ally during the Chremonidean War. After all, the Achaeans also participated in the conflict, indeed as the Spartans' allies, although there is no source information about any specific military operations they conducted.[19] Starting from Aratus' journey to Egypt in the winter of 251/250, the cooperation between the Ptolemies and the Achaean League tightened, and subsequently the *koinon* were able to rely on the financial backing of the kings of Egypt.[20] The Lagids' choice seemed to be the right one, since the Achaeans, aptly led by Aratus, recorded a series of victories, including the crucial capture of Corinth.[21] In this way, the Ptolemaic fleet gained important footholds, including both Corinthian ports, Kenchreai in the Saronic Gulf and Lechaion in the Corinthian Gulf. Another important base of the Egyptian fleet was Arsinoe/Methana, held by the Ptolemies, whose convenient location in Argolis on the peninsula jutting out to sea gave control of the sea traffic in the Saronic Gulf.[22] Ptolemy III, maintaining correct relations with the Aetolians and supporting the Achaeans, had a right to think that he was close to seizing control over the Corinthian Gulf, which could have opened up completely new prospects in the context of the rivalry with the Antigonids in Greece, as well as strengthening the position of the Lagids at sea. From the perspective of the fundamentals of the Ptolemaic foreign policy, whose most important area of interest was the Aegean Sea, this second aspect could have played an even more important role in Ptolemy's eyes. The backing of the Achaean League was even more essential in view of the fact that Ptolemy's relations with Athens, which were dominated by the Antigonids until 229, became looser.[23]

Choosing the Achaean League as a partner was even more natural considering the fact that the Aetolians not only maintained proper relations with Antigonus Gonatas, but even enlisted his support. Polybius mentions an alliance between Gonatas and the Aetolian League, but he fails to provide any detailed information about the time when it was made.[24] It is valid to link the alliance with Aratus' seizure of Corinth, since at that

---

[19]	Schmitt 1969: no. 476, *ll*. 23–26, 38–40.

[20]	Plut., *Arat.* 9–15; 24.4; 34.5–6; 35.1–5; 41.5; *Cleom.* 19.4; Paus. 2.8.5.

[21]	Regarding the development of the Achaean League in this period see Walbank 1933: 29–49; Larsen 1968: 215–240; Urban 1979: 38–62; Polybius (2.43.7–8) clearly shows the overall aim of Aratos: μεγάλην δὲ προκοπὴν ποιήσας τῆς ἐπιβολῆς ἐν ὀλίγῳ χρόνῳ λοιπὸν ἤδη διετέλει προστατῶν μὲν τοῦ τῶν Ἀχαιῶν ἔθνους, πάσας δὲ τὰς ἐπιβολὰς καὶ πράξεις πρὸς ἓν τέλος ἀναφέρων: τοῦτο δ' ἦν τὸ Μακεδόνας μὲν ἐκβαλεῖν ἐκ Πελοποννήσου, τὰς δὲ μοναρχίας καταλῦσαι.

[22]	L. Robert (1960: 159) aptly compared Methana to Gibraltar. It is unclear since when it had been in Ptolemaic hands, most likely since the Chremonidean War. Cf. also Meyer 1935: 1375–1379; Bagnall 1976: 135–136; Cohen 1995: 124–126.

[23]	Even so, the symbol of continuing his father's Greek policy was Ptolemy III erecting a statue of Glaucon (an Athenian statesman, who together with his brother, Chremonides, found refuge in Egypt after the Chremonidean War): *SIG*[3] 462. Athens established close relations with Ptolemy soon after overthrowing the Macedonian domination in 229. On the place of Athens in Ptolemy III's policy see Habicht 1982: 105–117; 1997; 73–75; Beyer-Rotthoff 1993: 137–143.

[24]	Polyb. 2.43.9–10; 45.1. According to Polybius, Antigonus Gonatas and the Aetolians supposedly agreed as to the division of the territory of the Achaean League between them, but this seems quite unlikely. However, this information fits perfectly this historian's large picture of this period and his opinion of the Aetolians (cf. e.g. Polyb. 4.3.1–2). In Polybius' vision, the Aetolians brought chaos to Greece and thwarted the Achaeans' policy aimed at freeing the Greeks from Macedonian domination. The Aetolians' behavior also served Polybius as an argument to explain the later agreement between Aratus and Antigonus Doson.

critical moment it would have been natural for Antigonus to look for a strong partner, and the coalition with the Aetolians was most probably his idea.[25] The friendlier relations between Ptolemy III and the Achaean League were likely a reaction of the other side to the closeness between the Aetolians and the Macedonians.[26] However, there is much evidence to suggest that earlier, during the rebellion of Alexander (Gonatas' nephew), who governed Corinth and Euboea, the Aetolians backed the king of Macedonia.[27] It seems that two camps formed at the time: on the one hand Alexander, the Achaeans and the Boeotians; on the other, Antigonus and his allies, including the Aetolians. Sources do not point out clear connections between the conflicts taking place at the time, but the sheer size of the military forces at Aratus' disposal indicates that the ongoing strife between the Aetolians and the Boeotians, supported by the Achaeans, was not just a local one; on the contrary, it was part of a much larger conflict.[28] Eventually, around 245, Alexander's death and the subsequent marriage of his widow, Nicaea, to Antigonus' son, Demetrius, enabled the Macedonian king to recapture control of Corinth for two years.[29] Even so, the situation in Greece continued to give the Ptolemies opportunities to pursue their anti-Macedonian policy on the Peloponnese. We may presume that after Alexander was eliminated, the Ptolemies became an even more desirable partner for the Achaean League, which lost its most valuable ally in Alexander and which was threatened from almost all directions by Macedonia and the Aetolians. Antigonus' relations with the Achaean League remained strained. Although some researchers[30] have concluded, based on Plutarch's account (*Arat.* 15), that the relations between Antigonus and the Achaean League improved, the account (which, incidentally, is marked by a strong rhetoric) more likely refers to an earlier period.[31] In Alexandria, it was certainly realized that the cooperation between the Aetolians and Macedonia was short-term and could not exclude the possible future alliance between the Aetolians and the Egyptians.

The years following Alexander's rebellion brought a sharpening of Antigonus Gonatas' policy towards Greek states. The king of Macedonia pushed tyranny in the Greek *poleis* even more frequently than before.[32] Installing this unpopular form of government proved to be a mistake, as it increased the Greeks' dislike of Macedonia. This was the grist to Aratus' mill, and the capture of Acrocorinth in 243 and the resulting removal of an important link in the chain of "the shackles of Greece" opened up new perspectives for the Achaean League. Corinth applied to join the League, followed by Epidaurus,

---

[25] Tarn (1913: 400) assumes the Aetolians were the initiators of this alliance, but Polybius' account does not suggest this.

[26] Cf. also Flacelière 1937: 205; Schmitt 1969: no. 490. Scholten (2000: 93) doubts the conclusion of a formal treaty.

[27] Scholten 2000: 85–86. For Alexander's rebellion cf. Will 1979: 316–324; Buraselis 1982: 171–172; Walbank 1984: 246–250; Orsi 1987; Hammond/Walbank 1988: 297–303.

[28] According to Plutarch (*Arat.* 16.1), Aratus had 10,000 men during the campaign which ended in the battle of Chaeronea. This is probably an overestimated number (e.g. in comparison with the Achaean forces during the war against Cleomenes III), but it indicates that the scale of the conflict was larger.

[29] Plut., *Arat.* 17.1–5.

[30] Walbank 1933: 43, 178–179; Will 1979: 297; Erington 2008: 93.

[31] Urban 1979: 31, 47.

[32] Polyb. 2.41.10; 9.29.6. See Tarn 1913: 276–286; Walbank 1967: 233.

Megara and Troezen.[33] Additionally, the Achaeans also signed a treaty with Sparta at that time.[34] The cooperation between the Lagids and the Achaean League also flourished during this period. In 243, Ptolemy III Euergetes was elected hegemon of the League, which was not just an honorary function.[35] We should also not overestimate the significance of Antigonus Gonatas' cooperation with the Aetolian League, as despite the tactical alliance the interests of the two sides were essentially conflicting. Therefore, we should not necessarily look for the influence of the king of Macedonia in the actions of the Aetolians, although their activeness on the Peloponnese was naturally against the Achaean League, and thus threatened the Lagids' interests. However, we should not exaggerate the Achaean-Aetolian conflict. In 241, the Aetolians attacked the Peloponnese.[36] It has been rightly observed that there is much to suggest the campaign was more of a small raid and its aim was not to destroy the Achaean League.[37] In any case, Plutarch, describing the events, refers to the Aetolian campaign as an attack against the Peloponnese, not the Achaean League, which did not have to be synonymous.[38] In this light, the behavior of Aratus becomes more understandable – he initially asked the Spartans for help, but eventually gave up their support and sent Agis IV back to Sparta.[39] This decision of the League's *strategos* is often explained by fear of social unrest, which was caused in the Peloponnesian cities by the reforms carried out by Agis IV in Sparta, mainly the abolition of debts and a new partition of lands.[40] However, this opinion does not have a strong basis in source material. Plutarch writes about the strong impression that the Spartan army made on the residents of the Peloponnese – their discipline and order, as well as Agis' simplicity of clothes and manners. On the other hand, according to Plutarch, the rich were worried that the example of the Spartan king would agitate the population. However, the Spartan army marched mostly across terrains which were on the Aetolian, not the Achaean-Spartan side, which – considering what the army behavior was usually like when it moved across enemy territory – may indicate that this passage has a rhetorical character.[41] Interestingly, listing the motives which caused Aratus to give up Agis IV's help, Plutarch refers directly to the diary of the Achaean strategos and does not say a word about Aratus' fears related to Agis and his social reforms.[42] Indeed, Plutarch clearly states that Aratus wanted to explain and justify his decision in his diaries. Aratus' reasoning – as relayed by Plutarch – indicates that the Achaean strategos did not regard

---

[33] *IG* IV²,1 70; Polyb. 2.43. 5; Plut., *Arat.* 24.3; Paus. 2.8.5; cf. Schmitt 1969: no. 489.

[34] Plut., *Agis* 13. According to some researchers (Walbank 1933: 49; Will 1979: 302), it was only the enthronement of Agis IV in Sparta and his internal policy that made the Achaean-Spartan alliance possible, but it would be too hasty to reject the possibility of cooperation in different circumstances.

[35] Plutarch's account (*Arat.* 24.4) seems to suggest that Ptolemy's hegemony had a purely titular character, and many researchers accept this interpretation (e.g. Will 1979: 299; Green 1990: 153; Hölbl 2001: 51), but cf. Urban (1979: 53–54).

[36] Plut., *Agis* 13.5–15; *Arat.* 31–32.

[37] Scholten 2000: 124.

[38] Plut., *Agis* 13.6; *Arat.* 31.2.

[39] Plut., Agis 13.4–15.3.

[40] Plut., *Agis* 6–11. Regarding Agis IV's policy and his reform see Oliva 1971: 208–222; Shimron 1972: 14–27; Cartledge/Spawforth 1989: 35–43; Walbank 1984: 252–255.

[41] Urban 1979: 55 n. 255.

[42] Plut., *Agis* 15.2.

the Aetolian threat as a grave danger.[43] Additionally, Aratus supposedly gave up not only the Spartan support, but also the backing of the other allies, at least a considerable number of them.[44]

Generally speaking, in favorable conditions the Ptolemies could count on a further increase of their influences and the Aetolian League could continue to be seen as one of their possible partners in Greek politics. Such conditions occurred after the death of Antigonus Gonatas in 239. The two conflicted federations were joined by an alliance. It remains an unanswered question who the initiator of this coalition was. We look back at the events at the time mainly through the eyes of Polybius and Plutarch, both of whom presented the facts from the point of view of the Achaean League and therefore did not doubt that it was Aratus' plan.[45] It cannot be excluded, however, that it was the Aetolians who proposed a change of alliances. It was at that time that their good relations with Macedonia began to crumble, which was caused by disagreements related to Epirus, where after Alexander II's death there was a clash of conflicting Aetolian and Macedonian interests.[46] In any event, the situation was very favorable for both leagues, since they could exploit the temporary weakening of Macedonia, which was natural after the change on the throne. This also presented Ptolemy III with a dream opportunity: for the first time he was able to work together with both of the Antigonids' most dangerous opponents. It cannot be excluded that Sparta also cooperated with the coalition, and the king of Egypt could have been a convenient link in this cooperation. Even though sources are silent on the subject of Sparta's formal cooperation with Ptolemy under Agis IV's rule, it was very likely, considering Agis' alliance with the Achaeans and Cleomenes III's later position. It is unlikely that in the interim, despite Agis' demise, there was a complete turnaround in the Spartan policy. In any case, it follows from Polybius' account that the animosity between Cleomenes and the Achaeans only started in 229,[47] and later it was Cleomenes who was the stronghold of the Ptolemaic anti-Macedonian policy. Therefore, everything points to the fact that in 239 a particularly strong coalition was born, which gathered together the most important Greek states at the time. We may presume, however, that Ptolemy was more of a beneficiary of Aetolian and Achaean efforts, since there is no information whatsoever to suggest an Egyptian initiative to form the coalition. Undoubtedly, though, it was to the Lagid's content; for him the Aetolians were a valuable ally not only because of the situation in continental Greece but – even more importantly for the dynasty's interests – also on the Aegean Sea.[48]

---

[43]   The lack of the motive of fear of Agis IV in Aratus' explanation is all the more puzzling given the fact that after the statesman's experiences with the next king of Sparta, Cleomenes III, Aratus could have easily presented himself as a farsighted statesman who had seen a threat to the Achaean League in Agis: Urban 1979: 56.

[44]   Plut., *Agis* 15.5; *Arat.* 31.2.

[45]   Polyb. 2.44.1; Plut., *Arat.* 33.1.

[46]   Justin (28.1) links the outbreak of war with events in Epirus: Olympias, the widow of Alexander II, feeling threatened by the Aetolians in Epirot, part of Acarnania, married her daughter Phthia to Demetrius II. With regard to the causes of Achaean-Aetolian *symmachia*; cf. also Larsen 1975; Beyer-Rotthof 1993: 134; Scholten 2000: 132–137.

[47]   Polyb. 2.45.4.

[48]   The fact that the relations between the Aetolian League and Ptolemy continued to be good may perhaps be illustrated by the Delphic dedications of the Aetolians, although they were private ones, for Ptolemy

The islands on the Aegean Sea and the coasts of Asia Minor were in the center of the Ptolemies' interest. This region was key for their position in the contemporary world. A strong presence in the region allowed them not only to maintain the naval power of the dynasty, but also to participate in the great political game of the Hellenic powers. After the defeat of the Egyptian fleet at Andros in ca. 245, the position of the Lagids there was not as strong as it had been.[49] This was all the more reason for Alexandria to closely observe the Aetolians' intense activity on the Aegean Sea. In the 250s and 240s, a network of connections began to tie the Aetolian League to many communities on the islands on the Aegean Sea and on the coasts of Asia Minor, such as Chios, Delos, Tenos, Miletus, Smyrna and Abdera.[50] At the time, the waters of the Aegean Sea also witnessed many pirate raids carried out by Aetolian commanders on their own.[51] The unstable situation and constant rivalry between the Antigonids and the Lagids on these waters created favorable conditions for such escapades, for which the Aetolians were well-known in the Greek world. Some of the activities undertaken by the Aetolian League on the Peloponnese were, in fact, connected to the Aetolian operations on the Aegean Sea. This followed from the fact that there were sea routes connecting Aetolia with the Aegean Sea along the coast of this peninsula, which provided a good opportunity to extend one's influence in a similar way as on the Aegean Sea.[52] The most important interests of the Aetolian League were, naturally, related to the Peloponnese. It was from there that danger was likely to come, as illustrated e.g. by the case of the campaign of the Spartan king Areus in 281 under the slogan of sacred war.[53] The Aetolians' involvement in Peloponnesian matters was certainly also intended to protect them from this side. This is how the 240 intervention in Sparta can be interpreted.[54] The Aetolians, summoned by the supporters of the murdered Agis IV, did not reach their goal of imposing friendly authorities in Sparta. Eventually, the intervention ended in plundering Laconia, but at least this raid somewhat restored the Aetolians' prestige, damaged by the defeat at Pellene at Aratus' hands the previous year.

Sources contain no information as to Ptolemy's direct military involvement in the war against the new Macedonian king, Demetrius II, started by the coalition of both Leagues. They are even silent on any possible financial support. However, it is difficult to imagine that Ptolemy, who had generously backed the Achaeans thus far, would have stopped providing help at such an opportune moment. What is more contentious is the

---

and his family: IG IX, 1² 1.202; 203. However, perhaps they only date back to the 220s. Habicht (1982: 11 n. 148; 1997: 177) connect it with the year 228 or 224–221; similarly Hölbl 2001: 52 (228 BC); Hammond/ Walbank (1988: 325 n. 2; 340 n. 1) with the 220s.

[49] On the situation in the region see Buraselis 1982: 164–179; Hölbl 2001: 50–51.

[50] *IG* IX 1² 1.185; 1.191; *ISE* II 78; *FD* III 1.482; 1.483; Schmitt 1969: no. 564. The Aetolians even offered Chios one of the seats on the Delphi Amphictyonic Council.

[51] *SIG*³ 520; 521. Such raids were extremely profitable. In this period, there was an increase in the number of private dedications in Delphi, often very expensive and massive (*IG* IX 1² 1.181; 200; 202; 203; 185; *SIG*³ 514). One of the Aetolians, Nikolaos of Proscheion, even founded a festival bearing his name (*Nikolaeia*) at Delos, following in the footsteps of Macedonian and Egyptian kings, who had established their own festivals there (*IG* XI 2.287B, *ll.* 126–128).

[52] Scholten 2000: 129.

[53] Iust. 24.1.2–8.

[54] Polyb. 4.34.9, 9.34.9; Plut., *Cleom.* 10.11, 18.3; Scholten 2000: 128–129.

matter of such help for the Aetolians, and the key to answering this question is the dating of a statue of Ptolemy III and his family, erected by the Aetolians at Thermon.[55] Some phrases lead us to believe that the time in question is the period of war against Demetrius (239–229), rather than the clashes against Antigonus Doson in the 220s, as some researchers claim.[56] Moreover, it seems that erecting such a statue would be more advisable after a victorious war rather than one which was a failure, which the war against Antigonus Doson must have been from the viewpoint of the Aetolians, since they lost control over Thessaly as a result.

On the contrary, the Demetrian War brought considerable success to the coalition. The Aetolians took advantage of the end of the Aeacidae dynasty in Epirus and captured the southern part of this state; most importantly, immediately after Demetrius' death, they tore away part of Thessaly (crucial for the Antigonids) from Macedonia.[57] The Achaean League gained the support of one of Demetrius' most important followers, Lydiadas the tyrant of Megalopolis.[58] Following in Lydiadas' footsteps, other Arcadian *poleis* joined the Achaean federation. Aratus also managed to strengthen his League by including such important cities as Argos, Megara and Aegina.[59] In the unanimous opinion of Polybius and Plutarch, this was when both the Achaean and Aetolian Leagues reached the peak of their powers.[60] The hegemony of the Antigonids in Greece was crushed. As Plutarch's account shows, getting Megalopolis to join the League also had some negative consequences from the Ptolemies' point of view.[61] Lydiadas turned out to be a very ambitious politician, who subsequently competed against Aratus for the position of the League's strategos, which could have had consequences for the effectiveness and cohesion of the Achaean League's actions, particularly due to a difference of opinion between Aratus and Lydiadas with regard to political strategy. Aratus tried to keep peaceful relations with Sparta, undoubtedly encouraged to do so by the king of Egypt, who had a vested interest in this. Megalopolis' conflict with Sparta posed, in turn, the most danger for the Ptolemaic interests,[62] particularly since in the same year that Lydiadas

---

[55]   *IG* IX, 1² 1.56. Habicht (1982: 111 n. 148 and 1997: 177); Beyer-Rotthoff (1993: 166 n.143), and Hölbl (2001: 52) relate this inscription to the times of the war against Antigonus Doson, placing it between 228 and 221. Huss (1975) and Urban (1979: 64 n. 302) connect it with the war against Demetrius II. Volkmann (1959: 1673) opts for 225/224.

[56]   The ending of the inscription (ἀρετᾶς ἕνεκεν καὶ εὐεργεσίας τᾶς εἰς ἔθν[ος καὶ τοὺς ἄλλους Ἕλλανας) matches the events of the war against Demetrius, during which the strongest Greek states jointly opposed the Macedonian hegemony, cf. Huss 1975: 320.

[57]   Iust. 28.3.13–15. Part of Thessaly joined the Aetolian League (Scholten 2000: 165–170, *contra* Grainger 1999: 234–243). Scholten also suspects that the Thessalians and the Phthiotian Achaeans, who also joined the Aetolian League at the time, may have been inspired by Ptolemy. However, there is nothing to indicate that, and their actions may be explained by the opportune situation due to the great crisis in Macedonia. Cf. also Hammond/Walbank 1988: 338–339.

[58]   Polyb. 2.44.5; Plut., *Arat.* 30.1–2.

[59]   Polyb. 2.44; Plut., *Arat.* 34.5–35.5; Iust. 28.3.13–15; cf. Urban 1979: 63–96.

[60]   Polyb. 2.45.1; Plut., *Arat.* 34.7.

[61]   Plut., *Arat.* 30.3; *Cleom.* 4.1.

[62]   Megalopolis' enmity towards Sparta had its origin in the establishment of this *polis* (Diod. 15.72.4; Paus. 8.27.1–8). Megalopolis, established at the time the Arcadian League was formed and with the participation of the Boeotians, was supposed to play the role of a stronghold protecting Arcadia against the Spartans. On the situation in the Achaean League at that time, see Oliva 1984.

joined the Achaean League with his *polis*, Cleomenes III became the king of Sparta. Like Agis IV, he had ambitions of restoring the Spartan hegemony on the Peloponnese. The Achaean-Aetolian-Spartan bloc, which had required so much effort to form, might crumble. Nevertheless, for the time being the Ptolemaic diplomacy was enjoying great success, even more so when the Athenians overthrew the Macedonian rule in 229 – the same Athenians who, impressed by the fleeting Macedonian success on the Peloponnese, had given honorary citizenship to Bithys, a general in Demetrius II's service, just a few years earlier, in 233.[63] Considering the prestige of Athens in the Greek world, and the role it played in the Lagids' policy, this was an event of great propagandist significance. Even though the initiative came from the Athenians, undoubtedly Ptolemy supported their efforts, at least financially.[64]

Ptolemy III then supported the Aetolians during the war against Antigonus Doson, who, after taking over power following Demetrius' death, instantly attacked in order to regain control of the whole of Thessaly.[65] Despite Ptolemy's backing, which this time undoubtedly took the form of *symmachia*,[66] the Aetolians did not succeed in defending their position in this region, and even suffered Antigonus' invasion of Doris and Phocis.

What was a much more serious problem for the Ptolemaic policy was the growing antagonism between the Achaean and Aetolian Leagues. Combined with the ambitions of the Spartan king Cleomenes III, this eventually led to a "reverse of alliances" and a collapse of the anti-Macedonian coalition. Ancient authors blamed the outbreak of war against Cleomenes III on the politicians of the Achaean League, unfriendly to Sparta, on Cleomenes or on the Aetolians.[67] According to Polybius, the latter, together with Sparta, were plotting an alliance with Antigonus Doson, but were outsmarted by Aratus, who thwarted their intentions. However, there is nothing to suggest such a course of events, and one of the clues may be the fact that the Aetolian League and Sparta maintained close relations with Ptolemy III, who was in conflict with Antigonus. Moreover, during the Achaean League's war against Sparta, which soon followed, the Aetolians remained neutral. Polybius' account can most easily be explained by saying that he tried to justify the choices made by Aratus, whom he admired, or that he found such an explanation in

---

[63]　*IG* II² 808; cf. Osborne 1981–1983, I: 185–187, no. D 87; II: 172–177; Hammond/Walbank 1988: 331 n. 4–6; Green 1990: 253, *contra* Henry 1990: 179–189, who identifies Bithys as one of the Lysimachus' *philoi* in the 280s).

[64]　Possibly through Aratus, who handed over 20 or 25 talents to Athens (Plut., *Arat.* 34.6; Paus. 2.8.6), *contra* Habicht 1997: 174. In any case, Athens' relations with the Lagids quickly became close, cf. n. 78.

[65]　Iust. 28.3.14.

[66]　*P. Haun* 1.6.18. Habicht (1980: 1–2) connected the account about the cooperation between Ptolemy and the Aetolians in this papyrus with the already mentioned statue of the Lagid king's family put up at Thermon, and so concluded that it was only in 229/228 that the two sides cooperated. However, there is no reason to discount the possibility that the statue and the papyrus are connected to two different events. On the other hand, Schwartz (1978: 98) arrives at the (not very valid) conclusion that Ptolemy supported the Aetolians only after the war finished. Possibly, it was at this time that the city of Ptolemais was established in Aetolia (*SIG*³ 545.6, cf. Cohen 1995: 118–119).

[67]　Polyb. 2.45; Plut., *Arat.* 30.5; *Cleom.* 3.6–4.1; cf. Urban 1979: 97–158; Beyer-Rotthoff 1993: 144–150.

Aratus' diaries.[68] Ultimately, the policy of the Achaean *strategos* led to signing an agreement with the king of Macedonia and to wasting the League's previous achievements.

In an atmosphere of growing tension between the hitherto allies, Ptolemy probably tried to mediate, although we have no source information on this subject. It is difficult to believe, however, that the Ptolemaic diplomacy did not try to save the anti-Macedonian coalition. After all, there are many indications that Aratus also tried to avoid an open conflict, at least to begin with. In the first phase of the Cleomenean War, the Achaean League continued its alliance with the Lagids. Ultimately, however, alliances were reversed: Aratus pushed his *koinon* towards a coalition with Macedonia, but earlier, having learned about the Achaean-Macedonian negotiations, Ptolemy decided to cancel his financial support for the Achaeans and hand it over to Cleomenes.[69] Euergetes' decision is usually explained either by his discovery of the talks between Aratus and Antigonus, or by the general line of Ptolemaic policy in Greece, which involved supporting anti-Macedonian forces. As Polybius himself admits, there is no doubt that Alexandria recognized Cleomenes as a much more effective partner than the Achaean League.[70] It is very likely, however, that the situation in the whole Aegean region also played a role. It was this region that attracted the most attention of the Ptolemies, and the worrying events happening there at the time must have been noticed in Alexandria. In 227, Antigonus Doson organized an expedition to Caria, which was an important link in the chain of Ptolemaic properties in the region. He managed to obtain several footholds there (such as Mylasa, Alinda and Priene in Ionia).[71] The contacts which the Aetolian League established in the region were all the more reason for Ptolemy to choose Cleomenes and the Aetolians at the expense of the Achaean League.[72] The Aetolians also signed a treaty with Knossos,[73] and Crete also occupied an important spot in the Lagids' policy, both due to the possibility of recruiting excellent mercenaries and as a foothold for the fleet operating on the Aegean Sea.[74] At that time, the beginning of closer relations between the Aetolians and the Attalids could also be observed.[75] It cannot be excluded that the Ptolemaic diplomacy was a mediator, since up until then the Aetolians had no common interests with Pergamum.[76] For the Lagids, on the other hand, the Attalids were a force worth supporting

---

[68] Polybius (2.56.2) points to Aratus' *Diaries* as the main source which helped him to relay the course of the Cleomenean War.

[69] Polyb. 2.51.2–4; Plut., *Arat.* 38.9; *Cleom.* 22.4; Schmitt 1969: no. 505–506.

[70] Polyb. 2.51.2.

[71] *I. Labraunda* 1.4–7; Pomp. Trog., *prolog* 28. Bengtson (1971: 24–25) suggests that Doson and Attalos planned to divide Caria, but the cooperation of the king of Pergamum with the Aetolians, Doson's opponents, contradicts this theory.

[72] Naturally, we cannot speak of friendship between Sparta and the Aetolians, but at that time the Achaean *koinon* was the main rival of the Aetolian League.

[73] Polyb. 4.53.8; 55.5. Epigraphic sources indicate Aetolian increasing interest in Crete, cf. Scholten 2000: 193–194, 195–196.

[74] Ptolemy III's close contacts with Cretan cities are confirmed by many inscriptions, cf. Spyridakis 1970: 76–77; Bagnall 1976: 117, 121–122; Beyer-Rotthoff 1993: 219–220; Huss 2001: 360–362.

[75] Attalos founded the *stoa* in Delphi (*SIG*³ 523). Polybius (4.65.6) mentions that Attalos sponsored the fortification at Elaos in western Aetolia in 219. Considering the scale of these reinforcements mentioned by Polybius, their construction must have begun earlier.

[76] Scholten (2000:194) believes that the Aetolians and the Attalids became closer as a result of a sense of common threat from Macedonia, but Antigonus Doson's campaign to Caria was most likely not an act aimed against the Attalids. On the place of Pergamum in Ptolemy III's policy, see Beyer-Rotthoff 1993: 76–80.

against the Seleucids, just as the Aetolians were a valuable partner in the rivalry against Macedonia. In Greece, Ptolemy's response to the Achaean-Macedonian alliance was to tighten their relations with the Aetolian *koinon*[77] as well as Athens.[78] This was also natural from the Aetolians' point of view, especially in view of Doson forming the Hellenic League, gathering the majority of Greek states around him.[79] In this way, the position of the Aetolian League in central Greece came under threat.

In the end, it turned out that Cleomenes was unable to face the coalition built by Antigonus Doson. Even before the decisive battle of Sellasia, Ptolemy III decided to stop his financial support for the king of Sparta, which sealed the ambitious king's fate. It was probably understood in Alexandria that without direct military involvement it would be impossible to keep up Sparta's resistance. Such an intervention went beyond Ptolemy III's political strategy in Hellas up to this time. Besides, Euergetes' attention began to be drawn to the affairs of a land which was key to his dynasty – Coele-Syria, where the Seleucid threat was growing.[80] Cleomenes was the victim not only of a level-headed evaluation of the situation by the Lagid, but also of his agreement with Doson. In the face of an increasing Seleucid threat, the king of Sparta was worth sacrificing for the normalization of relations with Macedonia, also in the Aegean. One of the fundamentals of the Ptolemaic policy in the region was not to let the two greatest rivals, the Seleucids and Antigonids, cooperate. The experiences of the Second Syrian War proved that it was hard to find success fighting against the two states at once.

These events also brought an end to such an active anti-Macedonian policy of the Lagids in Greece. However, the Ptolemies still had good relations with Athens and the Aetolian League; maintaining the latter in particular was beneficial due to the situation in the Aegean and the value of Aetolian mercenaries.

BIBLIOGRAPHY

Bagnall, R.S. (1976): *Administration of the Ptolemaic Possessions outside Egypt*, Leiden.
Bengtson, H. (1971): *Die Inschriften von Labranda und die Politik des Antigonos Doson*, München.
Beyer-Rotthof, B. (1993): *Untersuchungen zur Aussenpolitik Ptolemaios' III*, Bonn.
Bousquet, J. (1958): Inscriptions de Delphes, *BCH* 82: 61–91.
Bousquet, J. (1991): Inscriptions de Delphes, *BCH* 115: 167–179.
Brun, P. (1991): Les Lagides à Lesbos. Essai de chronologie, *ZPE* 85: 99–113.
Buraselis, K. (1982): *Das hellenistische Makedonien und die Ägäis. Forschungen zur Politik des Kassandros und der drei ersten Antigoniden (Antigonas Monophthalmos, Demetrios Poliorketes und*

---

[77] *IG* IX, 1² 1.202–203; cf. also n. 48.

[78] In Athens, a new *phyle* of Ptolemais was created, as well as a *deme* called Berenicidae; the cult of Ptolemy and Berenice was established and the king's statue was erected on the Athenian agora and in Delphi; the king in turn financed the construction of a *gymnasion* called the Ptolemaion. Finally, from 224/223, the festival of *Ptolemaia* began to be held: *IG* II² 836; Paus. 1.5.5; 10.10.2; St. Byz., s.v. Βερενικίδαι.

[79] Polyb. 2.54.3; Schmitt 1969, no. 507.

[80] Polyb. 5.41.6–42.4; Walbank 1967: 572.

Antigonas Gonatos) im Ägäischen Meer und in Westkleinasien, (*Münchener Beiträge zur Papyrusforschung* 73), München.

Cartledge, P., Spawforth, A. (1989): *Hellenistic and Roman Sparta. A Tale of Two Cities*, London.

Cohen, G.M. (1995): *Hellenistic Settlements in Europe, the Islands and Asia Minor*, Berkeley–Los Angeles.

Dany, O. (1999): *Akarnanien in Hellenismus. Geschichte und Völkerrecht in Nordwestgriechenland*, München.

Errington, R.M. (1977): Diodorus Siculus and the Chronology of the Early Diadochoi, 320–311 B.C., *Hermes* 105: 478–504.

Errington, R.M. (2008): *A History of the Hellenistic World 323–30 BC*, Oxford.

Flacelière, R. (1937): *Les Aitoliens à Delphes. Contribution à l'histoire de la Grèce centrale au IIIe siècle av. J.- C.*, Paris.

Gabbert, J.J. (1983): The Grand Strategy of Antioch Gonatas and the Chremonidean War, *AncW* 8: 129–136.

Grabowski, T. (2008): Ptolemy's Military and Political Operations in Greece in 314–308 BC, *Electrum* 14: 33–46.

Grabowski, T. (2010): Związek Etolski w polityce greckiej pierwszych Ptolemeuszy, in: E. Dąbrowa et al. (eds.), *Hortus Historiae. Księga pamiątkowa ku czci Profesora Józefa Wolskiego w setną rocznicę urodzin*, Kraków: 191–218.

Grainger, J.D. (1999): *The League of the Aitolians*, Leiden.

Green, P. (1990): *Alexander to Actium*, Berkeley–Los Angeles.

Habicht, C. (1979): *Untersuchungen zur politischen Geschichte Athens im 3. Jh. v. Chr.*, München.

Habicht, C. (1980): Bemerkungen zum P. Haun 6, *ZPE* 39: 1–5.

Habicht, C. (1982): *Studien zur Geschichte Athens in hellenistischer Zeit*, Göttingen.

Habicht, C. (1997): *Athens from Alexander to Anthony*, Cambridge, Mass.

Hammond, N.G.L., Walbank, F.W. (1988): *A History of Macedonia*, vol. III: *336–167 B.C.*, Oxford.

Heinen, H. (1972): *Untersuchungen zur hellenistischen Geschichte des 3. Jahrhunderts v. Chr. Zur Geschichte der Zeit des Ptolemaios Keraunos und zum Chremonideischen Krieg*, (*Historia Einzelschriften* 20), Wiesbaden.

Henry, A. (1990): Bithys, Son of Kleon of Lysimacheia: Formal Dating Criteria and IG II^2 808, in: E.M. Craik (ed.), *Owls to Athens. Essays on Classical Subjects Presented to Sir Kenneth Dover*, Oxford: 179–189.

Hölbl, G. (2001): *A History of the Ptolemaic Empire*, London.

Huss, W. (1975): Die zu Ehren Ptolemaios' III und seiner Familie errichtete Statuengruppe von Thermos (IG IX, 1, 1^2 56), *CE* 50: 312–320.

Huss, W. (2001): *Ägypten in hellenistischer Zeit 332–30 v. Chr.*, München.

Larsen, J.A.O. (1968): *Greek Federal States. Their Institutions and History*, Oxford.

Larsen, J.A.O. (1975): The Aetolian-Achaean Alliance of ca. 238–220 B.C., *CPh* 70: 159–172.

Lévêque, P. (1957): *Pyrrhos*, Paris.

Lefèvre, F. (1995): La chronologie du IIIe siècle à Delphes, d'àpres les actes amphictioniques (280–200), *BCH* 119: 161–206.

Meyer, E. (1935): Methana, *RE* XV, 2: 1375–1379.

Moser, G. (1914): *Untersuchungen über die Politik Ptolemaeos I in Griechenland (323–285 a. Chr. n.). Mit einer Voruntersuchung über die Begründung der ptolemäischen Seeherrschaft und einem Anhang über König Philokles von Sidon*, Leipzig.

Noeske, H.-C. (2000): Zum numismatischen Nachweis hellenistischer Stiftungen am Beispiel ptolemäischer Geldgescheneke, in: K. Bringmann (ed.), *Geben und Nehmen. Monarchische Wohltätigkeit und Selbstdarstellung im Zeitalter des Hellenismus*, Berlin: 221–248.

Oliva, P. (1968): Die Auslandspolitik Kleomenes III, *AAntHung* 16: 179–185.

Oliva, P. (1971): *Sparta and Her Social Problems*, Amsterdam.

Oliva, P. (1984): Der achäische Bund zwischen Makedonien und Sparta, *Eirene* 21: 5–16.

O'Neil, J.L. (2008): A Re-examination of the Chremonidean War, in: P. McKechnie, P. Guillaume (eds.), *Ptolemy II Philadelphus and his World*, Leiden: 65–90.

Orsi, D.P. (1987): La rivolta di Alessandro, governatore di Corinto, *Sileno* 13: 103–122.

Osborne, M.J. (1979): Kallias, Phedros and the revolt of Athens in 287 BC, *ZPE* 35: 181–194.

Osborne, M.J. (1981–1983): *Naturalization in Athens*, vol. I–IV, Brussels.

Robert, L. (1960): Sur un décret des Korésiens au Musée de Smyrne, in: L. Robert, *Hellenica. Recueil d'épigraphie de numismatique et d'antiquités grecques*, vol. XI–XII, Paris: 132–176.

Roebuck, C.A. (1941): *A History of Messenia from 369 to 146 B.C.*, Chicago.

Schmitt, H.H. (1969): *Die Staatsverträge des Altertums III. Die Verträge der griechisch-römischen Welt von 338 bis 200 v. Chr.*, München.

Scholten, J.B. (2000): *Politics of Plunder. Aitolians and Their Koinon in the Early Hellenistic Era, 279–217 B.C.*, Berkeley–Los Angeles.

Scholten, J.B. (2003): Macedon and the Mainland, 280–221, in: A. Erskine (ed.), *A Companion to the Hellenistc World*, Oxford: 134–158.

Schwartz, J. (1978): Athènes et L'Etolie dans la politique lagide (à la lumière de P. Haun 6), *ZPE* 30: 95–100.

Seibert, J. (1969): *Untersuchungen zur Geschichte Ptolemiaos' I. (Münchener Beiträge zur Papyrusforschung und antiken Rechtsgeschichte* 56), München.

Shimron, B. (1972): *Late Sparta. The Spartan Revolution, 243–146 B.C.*, Buffalo.

Spyridakis, S. (1970): *Ptolemaic Itanos and Hellenistic Crete*, Berkeley–Los Angeles–London.

Tarn, W.W. (1913): *Antigonos Gonatas*, Oxford.

Urban, R. (1979): *Wachstum und Krise des Achäischen Bundes. Quellenstudien zur Entwicklung des Bundes von 280 bis 222 v. Chr.*, (*Historia Einzelschriften* 35), Wiesbaden.

van't Dack, E. (1988): Le problème des commandants de place lagides à Théra réexamine, in: E. van't Dack, *Ptolemaica Selecta*, (*Studia Hellenistica* 29), Lovanni: 146–156.

Volkmann, H. (1959): Ptolemaios, no. 21, *RE* XXIII, 2: 1667–1678.

Walbank, F.W. (1933): *Aratos of Sicyon*, Cambridge.

Walbank, F.W. (1967): *A Historical Commentary on Polybius*, vol. I, Oxford.

Walbank, F.W. (1984): Macedonia and Greece, *CAH²*, VII, 1: 221–256.

Will, E. (1979): *Histoire politique du monde hellénistique (323–30 av. J.- C.)*, vol. I: *De la mort d'Alexandre aux avènements d'Antiochos III et de Philippe V à la fin des Lagides*, Nancy.

ELECTRUM * Vol. 19 (2012): 99–110
doi:10.4467/20843909EL.12.005.0746

DOCUMENTARY CONTEXTS FOR THE 'PISTIROS INSCRIPTION'

Denver Graninger

Abstract: This preliminary study of the so-called 'Pistiros Inscription' challenges the dominant interpretation of the document that has crystallized in the years since its preliminary publication, namely, that the inscription somehow guarantees the rights of traders operating within Pistiros. A reexamination of the rhetorical structure of the inscription and a reconstruction of the inscription's relationship with preexisting documents on this subject, which are not extant, raises the possibility that the function of the inscription was somewhat different than the *communis opinio*: the 'Pistiros Inscription' appears to have supplemented earlier regulation concerning Pistiros and to have attempted to limit the authority of an official, possibly a Thracian royal, who exercised dramatic power within Pistiros.

Keywords: Pistiros, the 'Pistiros Inscription', the Odrysian kings, Kotys.

Introduction

In 1988 a program of systematic archaeological research began at a Classical and early Hellenistic site located at Adzhiyska Vodenitsa, near Vetren, Bulgaria, in the upper Maritsa (anc. Evros) valley, close to the western edge of the Thracian plain. This project, initially led by Mieczysław Domaradzki, the great Polish archaeologist and historian of ancient Thrace, brought together an international team of scholars.[1] Their excavations revealed a Classical and Hellenistic settlement that complicates traditional assumptions about the urban development of this area of the eastern Balkans and its associated econo-

---

[1] Mieczysław Domaradzki (1949–1998), born in Brzeg, Poland, studied archaeology at Jagiellonian University in Kraków and completed his Master's thesis there in 1972 under the direction of Prof. Dr. K. Godłowski on the topic of Celtic shields in central Europe. In 1973, he won a fellowship to conduct doctoral research at the Bulgarian Academy of Sciences (BAS), and in 1976 he completed a dissertation at BAS under the supervision of Prof. Dr. Ivan Venedikov on the subject of Thrace and the Celtic invasions. He would continue to work in Bulgaria for the next twenty-plus years. Among his many achievements are his leadership of the project 'Archaeological Map of Bulgaria,' an attempt to compile a map of every known archaeological site in Bulgaria, and his direction of numerous archaeological excavation and survey campaigns in Bulgaria, including in the upper Maritsa valley and the site of Pistiros. He remains a towering figure in Bulgarian archaeology. For a complete bibliography of Domaradzki's publications, see Bouzek/Domaradzka 2005: vi–xiii.

mies.[2] In 1990, soon after the excavations at Adzhiyiska Vodenitsa began, there was discovered a large, granite block with a lengthy, partially preserved inscription from the nearby site of Assar Dere, located some 2 km to the northeast of Adzhiyiska Vodenitsa. The inscription is dated on historical and palaiographic criteria by most scholars to the period ca. 359–339 BCE.[3] Assar Dere corresponds most probably with the late Roman road station of Lissae or Bona Mansio on the so-called 'via diagonalis' that led from Belgrade (anc. Singidunum) and points further north and west to Istanbul (anc. Constantinopolis). Given the chronological correspondence between the site at Adzhiyiska Vodenitsa and the inscription from Assar Dere, and the lack of other contemporary sites of sufficient magnitude in the vicinity of Assar Dere, it is assumed that the inscription had originally been published at Adzhiyiska Vodenitsa and was later reused in a building associated with the road station. The inscription, as preserved, falls into two distinct parts: the first consists of a series of imperative constructions that appear to regulate a broad range of judicial, military, and economic practices concerning a range of constituents. A vivid trade is imagined, with goods moving within an elaborate network of *emporia* and Greek *poleis*, many of which are specifically named – Maroneia, Pistiros, 'the emporia Belana of the Prase[no]n.' The second half of the inscription contains the text of an oath that would seem to refer at least partially to some of the activities regulated in the first half of the inscription, as well as to other guarantees offered to other constituents – Apollonians and Thasians at Pistiros – not mentioned in what is preserved of the first half of the inscription. The centrality of the place Pistiros in the inscription coupled with the close geographical relationship between the inscription's *Fundort* (at Assar Dere) and presumed *Standort* (at Adzhiyiska Vodenitsa) have lead some scholars to assume that archaeological site at Adzhiyiska Vodenitsa was in fact Pistiros, and, however problematized the identification may be, the 'Pistiros Inscription' is a generally recognized, if not always fully endorsed, title for the document.[4]

As even this most preliminary sketch of the monument's archaeological context and substantive content has revealed, there is little about the Pistiros inscription that can be considered certain or uncontroversial. Inquiry into the document has tended to fall along three separate but often implicated lines: topography and historical geography, namely, where were/are the locations mentioned in the inscription, above all Pistiros; political history, namely, within what macro-political context is this monument best understood; and, finally, economies and *emporia*, namely, how did these exchanges work on the ground in real time and, ultimately, what was the Pistiros described in the inscription.[5] The tentative answers offered to these questions have tended more often than not to re-

---

[2] For excavation publications, see Bouzek *et al.* 1996; Bouzek *et al.* 2002; Bouzek *et al.* 2007, and Bouzek *et al.* 2010. Although it does not reflect results from most recent campaigns, an excellent synoptic presentation of the site in archaeological and historical context is Archibald *et al.* 2002.

[3] That is, after the assassination of Kotys I and before Thrace fell under Macedonian hegemony in 340 or 339. For a synopsis of the arguments and reference to key bibliography, see Archibald 2004: 887.

[4] The identification of the archaeological site at Adzhiyiska Vodenitsa as Pistiros nevertheless remains extremely controversial. For recent assessment of the key issues, see Demetriou 2010. I do not take a position in this debate. For the title of the inscription, cf., e.g., Bravo/Chankowski 1999, who would seem to prefer 'Septemvri Museum inscription.'

[5] Cf. Domaradzki 2000, an important collection of essays that situates Pistiros within a broader framework of exchange in the north Aegean and eastern Balkans.

flect the individual assumptions of scholars and, indeed, given the exceptional character of the document, some such circularity is only to be expected until either new evidence comes to light that can further explicate the content of the inscription or existing evidence can be brought into a more productive relationship with it.

The Text

I offer now a text of the most recent critical edition[6] of the inscription, together with an English-language translation.[7] These are furnished solely *exempli gratia* and to provide a point of departure for the preliminary study that follows:

    [---- *ca* 20 ----] ΙΚΙ/
    [---- *ca* 12 ----] ΔΕΝΝΥ . . Η ει δὲ . .
    [. . . . ὀμνύτ]ω τὸν Διόνυσογ καὶ
4   [. . . .] ὀφειλέτω · ὅ τι ἂν δέ τις τῶν
    [ἐμπ]ορίτέων ἐπικαλῆι ὁ ἕτερος τ-
    [ῶι ἑ]τέρωι, κρίνεσθαι αὐτοὺς ἐπὶ τ-
    [οῖς] συγγενέσι καὶ ὅσα ὀφείλετα[ι]
8   τοῖς ἐμπορίταις παρὰ τοῖς Θραιξ-
    [ί]ν, τούτωγ χρεῶν ἀποκοπὰς μὴ
    ποιεῖγ · γῆγ καὶ βοσκὴν ὅσην ἔχουσ-
    ιν ἐμπορῖται, ταôτα μὴ ἀφαιρεῖ-
12 [σθ]αι · ἐπαυλιστὰς μὴ πέμπειν το-
    [ῖς] ἐμπορίταις · φρουρὴμ μηδεμίαν
    εἰς Πίστιρον καταστῆσαι μήτε α-
    [ὐτ]ὸμ μήτε ἄλλωι ἐπιτρέπειν ·
16 [κλ]ήρους *vel* [ὁμ]ήρους Πιστιρηνῶμ μὴ λαμ-
    [βάν]ειμ μηδὲ ἄλλωι ἐπιτρέπειν ·
    [τὰ *vel* γῆν] τῶν ἐμπορίτέωμ μὴ [ἀ]φαιρεῖ-
    [σθ]αι μήτε αὐτὸμ μήτ[ε το]ὺς ἐ-
20 [αυτ]οῦ · τέλεα κατὰ τὰς ὁδοὺς
    μὴ πρήσσειν, ὅσα εἰς Μαρώνεια[ν]
    [εἰσ]άγεται ἐκ Πιστίρου ἢ ἐκ τῶν ἐ-
    [μ]πορίων ἢ 'γ Μαρωνείης εἰς Πίστ-
24 [ιρ]ον ἢ τὰ ἐμπόρια Βελανα Πρασε-
    [. ω]ν, τοὺς ἐμπορίτας τὰς ΑΠΑΞ

---

[6] Chankowski/Domaradzka 1999. Cf. *SEG* XLIX, 911 (*editio princeps* – Velkov/Domaradzka 1994). I examined the inscription directly in the Septemvri Museum in May 2011 and again in May 2012 and have been able to improve on Chankowski and Domaradzka's text in some areas. I intend to present the results of this autopsy in a subsequent publication. I am grateful to S. Popova, Director of the Septemvri Museum, for facilitating this research.

[7] Velkov/Domaradzka 1996: 207, based on Velkov and Domaradzka's *editio princeps* (Velkov/Domaradzka 1994). I have endeavored to bring this translation into agreement with the revised edition of Chankowski/Domaradzka 1999.

[– 2-3 –] καὶ ἀνοίγειν καὶ κλείειν · ἅμα
[καθ]άπερ καὶ ἐπὶ Κοτυος (:) ἄνδρα Μ-
28 [αρω]νίτην οὐ δήσω οὐδὲ ἀποκτ-
[ενέω] οὐδὲ ἐφαιρήσομαι χρήμα-
[τα] οὔτε ζῶντος οὔτε ἀποθανόν-
[τος] οὔτε αὐτὸς οὔτε τῶν ἐμῶν
32 [οὐ]δείς · οὐδὲ Ἀπολλωνιητέων, οὐδ-
[ὲ Θ]ασίων, ὅσοι ἐμ Πιστίρωι εἰσί[ν],
[οὔ]τε ἀποκτενέω οὐδένα, οὔτε
[δήσω] οὔτε ἀφαιρήσομαι χρήμα-
36 [τα οὔ]τε ζῶντος οὔτε ἀποθανό-
[ντος οὔτε] αὐτὸς οὔτε τῶν ἐμῶν
[οὐδείς · εἰ δέ τις] τῶν οἰκητόρων
[---- *ca* 14–16 ----]των οὗ ὁ ἐμπορ-
40 [---- *ca* 14–16 ----]ον εἰσὶν ΑΙΜ-
[---- *ca* 14–16 ----]ν, ἐὰμ μὴ ΑΜ-
[---- *ca* 14–16 ---- τ]ις ἀδικῇι τὸ
[ν δεῖνα *vel* ὺς δεῖνας] τε ΕΨΩΑΛΛΑ
44 [ἀναδο- *vel* ἀποδο]χεὺς τὴν ἐπ-
[---- *ca* 5–6 ---- δι' ἑκάστ]ου ἐνιαυτοῦ
[--------]Α.

'(Let him swear by) Dionysus and [4] ... let him owe a due. If any of the *emporitai* has a cause to plead against another, they will be judged each among his own relatives, and with respect to such things as are owed [8] to the *emporitai* by the Thracians, no cancellation of debts is to be made. The land and pasture belonging to the *emporitai* shall not be taken from them. [12] The *epaulistai* shall not be sent to the *emporitai*. No garrison is to be placed at Pistiros, neither by him nor should (any) be handed over to another. [16] *Kleroi* (or hostages) of the inhabitants of Pistiros are not to be taken nor handed over to another. Neither shall the possessions of the emporitai be appropriated by him or by any of his people. [20] No dues shall be levied on the goods which are imported to Maroneia from Pistiros or from the emporia, or from Maroneia to [24] Pistiros and to the emporia Belana of the Prasenoi. The emporitai ... to open and close. At the same time valid is as in Kotys' time: I will not send over any citizen of Maroneia; nor will I [28] kill him, nor will I let his property be confiscated, neither during his lifetime nor after his death, neither I myself nor any of my people. [32] Nor (will I kill) any of the Apollonians, nor the Thasians who are at Pistiros, nor will I (imprison any of them) nor will I deprive any man of his property, [36] neither alive or dead, neither I myself nor any of my people...'

Interpretations

While there continues to be uncertainty about the constitution of the text and its interpretation in isolated passages, a scholarly consensus has coalesced about the overall function of the document. As D. Demetriou has recently observed: 'The treaty records the rights of the Greek resident traders in relation to other Greek traders and the Thracian natives and rulers, the rights of the Thracian authorities in relation to the resident Greeks in Thracian lands, and various economic provisions that describe the trade routes used and the inviolability in general granted to traveling merchants and those residing in Pistiros. It also guarantees the Greek resident traders of Pistiros the same privileges they had under Kotys I, Kersobleptes' father, who ruled the Odrysian kingdom from 383/382 to 359 BC.' While different scholars add different nuances[8] and describe the inscription differently in terms of genre,[9] the overall picture of Thracian royal authority guaranteeing rights of Greek traders at Pistiros has been remarkably stable since the publication of the *editio princeps*.

I aim in this modest contribution to complicate in some measure the interpretive framework within which this inscription has been considered. I attempt this not by introducing new or previously unconsidered evidence, but by returning, somewhat myopically, to the language and rhetoric of the inscription itself. Two central possibilities will be raised. First, the 'Pistiros Inscription' gives hints that it did not exist in a vacuum, but that it was part of a broader documentary ecosystem that can be somewhat speculatively reconstructed in general outline. Specifically, I will suggest that, rather simply reaffirming an earlier set of regulations concerning activity within Pistiros, the 'Pistiros Inscription' actually supplemented them.

The second central possibility that I wish to raise concerns the type of power on display in this inscription. Interpretations of the 'Pistiros Inscription' that emphasize the document as somehow guaranteeing Greek merchants' rights within Pistiros lay inappropriate emphasis on the idea of positive rights. For unambiguous examples of such positive rights, compare the so-called 'Prospectus of the Second Athenian League' (*IG* II² 43), dated to 378/377, where adherents to the prospective treaty are 'free and autonomous, governed under whatever form of government he wishes, neither receiving a garrison nor submitting to a governor nor paying tribute'.[10] Compare the corpus of proxeny decrees, now rapidly growing by the early fourth century, which offers examples of such positive rights at the level of the individual (including, but not limited to, *asylia* of person and property, including relatives and their property, etc.). Such rights are not on display in the 'Pistiros inscription'. What can be seen instead is an attempt by the issuing authority to limit the power of an individual who seems to have exercised some form of command over or within Pistiros. This is a dramatically different conception of power.

For the moment, these can only be possibilities, incapable of confirmation or refutation in the current state of evidence. My hope, nevertheless, is that by returning attention to the monument itself, away from assumptions rooted in what is thought to be known

---

[8] As, indeed, does Demetriou 2010: 77, n. 1: 'All scholars cited in this paper consider this a bilateral treaty between one of the Thracian dynasts and the Greeks of Pistiros, or between the three dynasts acting as a collective and the Greeks of Pistiros. I will argue below that this is a multilateral treaty among each of the three dynasts individually and the Greeks of Pistiros.'

[9] E.g., Picard 1999: 331: 'la « charte » de l'*emporion*'; Loukopoulou 1999: 362: 'la forme d'un traité'; Archibald 2000: 267: 'It is not a treaty between one community and another, but a royal edict concerning specific groups operating within his subject territories.'

[10] Trans. Rhodes-Osborne.

from the broader historical context, new and potentially more productive questions may be asked.

Building Documentary Context

In simplest terms, the preserved content of the 'Pistiros Inscription' falls into two distinct halves: the first, characterized by an asyndetic series of imperatival clauses of varying content and with varying subjects. I describe these clauses non-prejudicially as regulations, that is to say, the issuing authority, whoever or whatever it is, is presented within the rhetoric of the inscription as capable of regulating certain activities within a region that includes Pistiros and other *emporia* in the region; the second, following directly upon the first with no real transition expressed, is more fragmentary but is clearly marked by a shift to first-person singular, future tense verbs that are typical of an oath.

Before taking up these two sections, let us begin by focusing on what has functioned as the hinge of the inscription in most interpretations, a short phrase in ll. 26–27: ἅμα [καθ]άπερ καὶ ἐπὶ Κοτυος. Scholarly debate has tended to focus on which direction the phrase looks – to the immediately preceding regulation, or perhaps even the entire series, or to the following oath.[11] The absence of transition between regulations and oath has been perceived as abrasive, intolerably so, and this sense of the Greek has provided at least some partial motivation for interpretation of the phrase as introductory for the oath. But this may be a red herring. Such an abrupt transition finds a good parallel in a Tegean inscription published at Delphi probably in 324/323 concerning the return of exiles to Tegea. In addition to providing incomparable insight into the complexities of reintegrating a population within the social, political, economic, and cultic life of a polis, the process eventually implemented by the local authority, Tegea, seems to have emerged via possibly contentious negotiation with the regional hegemon, almost certainly Alexander the Great.[12] The passage in question reads: '...as for those who did not go into forced exile after <their marriage> and who are now creeping back on the present occasion, themselves or their children, they shall be examined, both themselves and their descendants, in respect of their paternal and their maternal possessions in accordance with the transcript. I swear by Zeus, Athena, Apollo, Poseidon, that I shall show good will to those who have returned whom the city resolved to receive back...' (ll. 53–59).[13] In this particular passage, a lengthy series of regulations concerning the return of Tegean exiles to their home city concludes and is followed immediately by the text of an oath,

---

[11]   For summary of the debate, see Demetriou 2010: 87, n. 62.

[12]   Trans. Rhodes-Osborne, *ll.* 0–4: '[---- With reference to the things about which the city sent the envoys and King Alex]ander sent back his judgment to us, the transcript shall be written according to the corrections made by the city of what was spoken against in the transcript.'

[13]   *IG* V, 2, p. xxxvi–xxxvii (trans. Rhodes-Osborne). Concerning the absence of transition, cf. Plassart 1914: 159: 'Avec un manque de liaison plus frappant encore que celui qu'on a remarqué, au passage d'un quelconque des autres articles au suivant, on trouve..., sans un mot d'introduction, la formule, à la première personne du singulier, du serment, par lequel les citoyens restés à Tégée s'engageront à l'égard des bannis rentrés d'exil.'

the contents of which indicate unambiguously that the oath-takers are current residents of Tegea who had not left the city as exiles.

With no need to affect a transition between regulations and oath, one may consider the other key piece of evidence concerning the phrase and its direction of reference. In their 1994 *editio princeps*, V. Velkov and L. Domaradzka noted in their epigraphic commentary the presence of an interpunct before ἅμα and a second one after Κοτυος. Neither interpunct was introduced into the formal text of their edition, however.[14] Such interpuncts could impact interpretation by marking the phrase as a heading of sorts for the following oath. In their 1999 re-edition, Chankowski and Domaradzka modify this position. The initial interpunct before ἅμα is no longer mentioned in the epigraphic commentary, while the second interpunct is printed as an editorial correction.[15] This presentation of the text would strongly suggest that the phrase belonged to the preceding regulations.

My autopsy of the stone revealed only a slight dimple on the surface of the stone before ἅμα. It is not of depth equivalent to other letter strokes and not obviously the product of a tool. What the editors regard as an interpunct after Κοτυος is more complex. There is certainly a gouge on the surface, as deep as the typical letter strokes on the stone, but it is impossible to determine whether it is the result of deliberate activity on the part of the cutter of the inscription in antiquity or of subsequent and accidental damage to the stone. If deliberate, it has either been clumsily executed, as have, indeed, many of the letter strokes on the stone, or the original clean borders of a punch into the surface of the stone have been worn down by subsequent weathering or damage and resulted in the small crater visible today. Rather more probative, in my opinion, is the spacing between the sigma of Κοτυος and the initial letter of the word that opens the oath.[16] Even taking into consideration the fact that spacing between individual letters varies broadly throughout this inscription, there is a noticeable gap between these two letters. Such a finding would add support to a construal of the phrase ἅμα [καθ]άπερ καὶ ἐπὶ Κοτυος with what precedes rather than what follows.

With the need to find a transition between the regulations and the oath assuaged and good evidence for a *vacat* and possible punctuation between the end of the ἅμα-clause and the beginning of the oath, there are good grounds for associating the ἅμα-clause with the series of regulations, before even considering what 'at the same time just as in the time of Kotys' might mean. I focus for the moment on an important implication of the expression of 'just as in the time of Kotys,' namely, that activity within Pistiros had previously, during the time of Kotys,[17] been subject to oversight by the issuing authority

---

[14] Velkov/Domaradzka 1994: 4, *ad ll.* 26–27.

[15] Chankowski/Domaradzka 1999.

[16] These observation substantially agree with Bravo/Chankowski 1999: 277–279, although they continue to argue in spite of this spatial arrangement that the ἅμα-clause introduces the oath.

[17] Who was this Kotys? The assumption driving much scholarship is that he is to be identified with the great Odrysian king who ruled much of Thrace ca. 383/382–359. Two important observations must be made at this point, though. First, the name Kotys was quite common in Thrace in the Hellenistic and Roman periods and not simply among Odrysian elites (cf. *LGPN* IV, s.v. Κότυς 24–82). The extent to which this represents fourth-century reality is unknowable. Such data would in any case encourage caution in identifying this Kotys with the great king on the basis of shared prosopography alone. It is not good method. Cf. the apposite comments of Picard, 1999: 339–340. But a circumstantial case can be built on the basis of broader

of the current inscription, in the form of a series of formal regulations. Presumably these regulations would have been inscribed and publicly displayed.[18] The current inscription must therefore be seen within this broader context.

This point, although relatively uncontroversial and implicit in the dominant interpretations of the inscription, nevertheless merits expansion. A fragmentary, Hellenistic inscription from Mesambria is particularly suggestive on the matter of this broader documentary context.[19] In a decree, the Mesambrians award Sadalas, a little known dynast, certainly Thracian and possibly Odrysian, and his descendants citizenship, proxeny, and associated honors, including the annual award of a crown of fifty staters to Sadalas. The arrangement may be essentially tributary. The occasion for the declaration of these honors was apparently connected with the conclusion of an oath and agreements between Sadalas and the Mesambrians, and indeed the beginning of the text of one of these agreements (concerning, it would appear, shipwrecks[20]) is contained on the same stele, located just beneath the honorary decree after a *vacat*. The publication clause of the introductory honorary decree is worth quoting in full:

> τὸν δὲ ταμίαν τὸν ὅρκον καὶ τὰς ὁμολογία[ς]
> 12 γράψαντα εἰς στάλαν λιθίναν κοῖλα γράμ-
> ματα ἀναθέμεν εἰς τὸ ἱερὸν τοῦ Ἀπόλ-
> λωνος παρὰ τὰς στάλας τῶμ προγόνων
> Μοψυηστιος καὶ Ταρουτινου καὶ Μηδιστα
> 16 καὶ Κοτυος.

'And let the treasurer, after inscribing[21] the oath and the agreements[22] on a stone stele in hollow letters[23], set the stele up in the sanctuary of Apollo beside the stelai of his forbears, Mopsyestis and Taroutinos and Medistas and Kotys.'

---

historical context, viz., the Odrysians are well-known to have had fiduciary interests in emporia in (coastal) Thrace; cf. Dem. 23, 110. Some royal suzerainty over a place like Pistiros would seem an easy bet and is assisted by the Naukratis paradigm where similar dynamics would seem to be on display (cf. Loukopoulou 1999: 366–368). There is little evidence, these assumptions about Kotys notwithstanding, for the date of the inscription beyond the *terminus post quem* offered by the foundation of the settlement at Pistiros. The letter forms, always unreliable in the absence of closely dated and sited *comparanda*, would nevertheless appear somewhat earlier (particularly the slanted-bar alphas, which have a distinctly Archaic or early Classical appearance, at least in an Aegean context). Second, the phrase ἐπὶ Κοτυος indicates time, not agency. The two may be closely related, of course.

[18]   This point is also emphasized at Archibald 2000: 266: 'The second half of the text incorporates what appears to be a citation from a similar set of injunctions, issued in the name of Kotys.' Archibald assumes here that the problematic ἅμα [καθ]άπερ καὶ ἐπὶ Κοτυος looks forward to the oath. Cf. Archibald 2004: 895.

[19]   *IGBulg* I², 307; cf. *IGBulg* V, 5086. There is considerable uncertainty about the date of the inscription. Mihailov, *ad loc.*, has argued plausibly for 281–277.

[20]   Cf. Mihailov, *ad loc.* The situation resembles in some measure that described at Xen. *An.* 7, 5, 12–14.

[21]   That is to say, the treasurer will arrange for payment for such an inscription; most likely he would not have done the actual inscribing.

[22]   'The oath and the agreements' would also well capture the content of the 'Pistiros Inscription'.

[23]   A curious phrase that presumably refers to a distinction between letters that are simply painted on a stele and those that are actually inscribed. Mihailov (*ad loc.*): 'non atramento picta, sed insculpta.'

The content of the stelai of Sadalas' *progonoi* is not mentioned, but it is probable that they too contained the text of honors awarded by the Mesambrians to them as well as oaths and agreements previously concluded between king and city. If such an assumption is correct, then there may have been a considerable corpus of inscriptions detailing the history of the relationship between Mesambria and these local dynasts, possibly extending for some decades into the past. It is unknown whether Sadalas' oath and agreements with the Mesambrians would have resembled substantially those of Kotys. Some aspects of the relationship may have been traditional and relatively fixed for this duration – the type of honors awarded to the dynast *du jour* by the Mesambrians, for example; others perhaps appeared, disappeared, or evolved in response to changing internal or external dynamics.

At this point, I would like to open an editorial parenthesis on the opening word of the phrase ἅμα [καθ]άπερ καὶ ἐπὶ Κοτυος. If 'just as in the time of Kotys' can be made into tolerable sense, the presence of the adverb ἅμα, 'at the same time,' complicates interpretation considerably. Some scholars ignore the word altogether.[24] Velkov and Domaradzka's English translation reads: 'At the same time valid is as in Kotys' time.' The suggestion is that the following oath, which is regarded here as an extract from an earlier oath dating to the time of Kotys, is valid 'at the same time' as, presumably, the preceding regulations. Having diminished the likelihood that the phrase applies to the oath, however, one must find a way to understand the phrase solely with the preceding regulations. Are these regulations to be regarded as valid 'at the same time, just as in the time of Kotys'? In such an interpretation, ἅμα would be superfluous and frankly jarring in so stylistically sparing an inscription. To insist upon the simultaneity of the validity of the regulations seems overdetermined, even anxious.[25]

An easy correction of ἅμα to ἄ<λλ>α removes some of these difficulties. Such an error would be easy to explain as a misreading of the exemplar, for example, or even a technical error on the part of the cutter. Autopsy of the stone moreover reveals that, while the lettering of the inscription as a whole is fairly erratic, this mu deviates even more fully from what is expected; it cannot be ruled out that two lambdas were in fact inscribed, but done so in a cramped manner.[26] There is occasionally visible elsewhere on the stone at the right edge a tendency to crowding letters. I would interpret ἄ<λλ>α adverbially and translate the phrase: 'in other respects, just as in the time of Kotys.' Such an interpretation would indicate that these regulations were somehow additions to or changes of an earlier set of regulations dated to the time of Kotys. There are good partial parallels in Aegean Greek epigraphy, especially from Attica, where riders to decrees are regularly introduced: τὰ μὲν ἄλλα κάθαπερ, 'In other respects, in accordance with,' usually followed either by the name of the initial proposer of the decree, or, in the case of proboulematic decrees, simply τῆι βουλῆι or the equivalent.[27] The scenario that I im-

---

[24]　E.g., Avram 1997: 45, who translates 'comme du temps de Kotys.'

[25]　One could entertain the possibility that the ἅμα, perhaps the entire ἅμα-clause, applies to the two infinitives preserved in the immediately preceding regulation, ἀνοίγειν and κλείειν, were it not the case that opening and closing are opposite actions typically incapable of being performed simultaneously.

[26]　The stone is damaged where the two middle strokes of the mu may have joined.

[27]　See the discussion at Rhodes 1997: 22. The greatest obstacle to such an emendation and the interpretation following from it – and it may militate decisively against it – is the absence of the definite article τά, which is invariably present in the Aegean evidence.

agine in the case of the 'Pistiros Inscription' is parallel to the paradigm of the amended decree in the sense that the phrase points out a modification to existing legislation and indicates that everything beyond what is mentioned is to remain the same as in that existing legislation. In the case of the Pistiros inscription, such a modification would only strengthen the observation made earlier, namely, that this document supplements some earlier set of regulations and was perhaps displayed alongside them, as was perhaps the case for Sadalas and his *progonoi* at Mesambria.

At this point, I would like to transition to a broader consideration of the regulations in the first half of the inscription and to consider the nature of the power displayed therein. The concerns of the first half of the inscription are quite disparate and their seriatim presentation does not give an impression of being a systematic restatement of a 'charter' for Pistiros. Rather, these regulations read more like *ad hoc* responses to discrete problems or reflections of changed social, political, and economic conditions. I emphasize in particular the series of prohibitions in ll. 7–21 that seem to be limiting the power of a specific individual or officer. The subject of these prohibitions is only vaguely and occasionally mentioned, a nameless 'him,' sometimes linked with his associates. 'He' is prohibited: from establishing a garrison in Pistiros or entrusting that right to any other (ll. 13–15); from seizing *kleroi* or hostages of the Pistirenes or entrusting that right to any other (ll. 16–17); and from confiscating the possessions of the *emporitai* (ll. 18–20).[28] There are several other prohibitions in this section of the inscription, in which there is no explicit mention of the subject: there is to be no cancellation of debts owed to the *emporitai* by the Thracians (ll. 7–10); land, arable and pasture, owned by the *emporitai* is not to be confiscated (ll. 10–12); *epaulistai* are not to be sent among the *emporitai* (ll. 12–13); and transit tax is not to be charged on goods moving by road[29] (ll. 20–22). Construing these clauses as essentially subjectless and directed towards a general audience[30] is implausible. In each of these four cases, it is likely that the same 'him' is to be understood as subject. 'He,' too, may be the subject of the third-person imperatives in ll. 3–4.[31]

---

[28]   The prohibition in this last case is extended to this individual's associates as well: μήτε αὐτὸμ μήτ[ε το]ὺς ἑ|[αυτ]οῦ.

[29]   With Avram 1997: 39–41, I regard τέλεα κατὰ τὰς ὁδοὺς | μὴ πρήσσειν (*ll.* 20–21) as a complete regulation; and the following relative clause (ὅσα ... Πρασε | [νω]ν: *ll.* 21–25) as dependent on the main clause that begins in *l.* 25 (τοὺς ἐμπορίτας ... κλείειν) and in effect beginning a new, distinct regulation. I understand the content of that regulation, however, differently from Avram.

[30]   As in the translation of Velkov and Domaradzka offered above.

[31]   Avram 1997: 42–44, followed by Domaradzka at Chankowski/Domaradzka 1999: 250, suggests that the entire string of infinitives in ll. 4–26 is dependent upon ὀφειλέτω in l. 4 in the sense of 's'engager à.' This is a clever reading that warrants serious consideration. Avram sees two merits in such an interpretation. First, it allows one to remove the inconcinnity of distinct imperatival constructions following one upon the other, viz., the third-person singular imperatives followed by accusative and infinitives. Second, it allows for a smoother transition between the two halves of the inscription. The subject of the third-person imperative ὀφειλέτω can now easily be the first-person subject of the oath of the second half of the inscription. As A. Chaniotis observes at *SEG* XLIX, 911: 'the use of the verb ὀφείλω in L. 7 in the sense "owe" makes this interpretation improbable.' Note also that parallels for the intermingling of third-person imperatives and accusative and imperatival infinitive constructions are not lacking. Although geographically and chronologically remote, if comparable in terms of its very liminality, column A of the curious *lex sacra* from Selinous displays similar mixing (ed. pr. Jameson *et al.* 1993; cf. *SEG* XLIII, 630 and *NGSL*[2] 27). A greater problem is that Avram understands the subject αὐτόμ of the infinitives to be identical with the subject of ὀφειλέτω, upon

Many scholars, building on the assumption that one of Kotys' successors is the issuing authority of the document, imply that this Thracian royal is essentially limiting his own powers in this passage and that this constitutes the guarantee of privileges for those conducting business at Pistiros. But, *prima facie*, this would be a very curious way for an Odrysian king to express himself. It is easier to imagine the issuing authority prohibiting a third party from this range of activities rather than limiting itself. Given the nature of the prohibitions, this third party would have been an individual of considerable power: presumably the sort of person, who would need to be prohibited from installing garrisons, imposing taxes, and the like, possessed the capability of doing precisely that. Indeed, if my general reconstruction is correct, one may suspect that this individual had acted abusively towards Pistiros and that his powers are here sharply restricted.

What was the identity of this individual? While the Odrysian state does not seem to have wielded a complex or highly developed bureaucracy on a par with the Seleucid or Ptolemaic kingdoms of the following centuries, it would be a mistake to think that there was no bureaucracy at all. All that can be stated with certainty, however, is that he was powerful and that he was not identical with the issuing authority.[32] It is worth noting in this connection that these prohibitions carry no apparent sanction in the event of non-compliance.[33] So, far from guaranteeing that the residents of Pistiros would be free from garrisons and the like, this document cannot even guarantee that an individual who contravenes these explicit prohibitions would be punished. The *emporitai* remain in a very tenuous position.

BIBLIOGRAPHY

Archibald, Z. (2000): The Odrysian River Port near Vetren, Bulgaria, and the Pistiros Inscription, *Talanta* 32–33: 253–275.

Archibald, Z. (2004): Inland Thrace, in: M.H. Hansen, T.H. Nielsen (eds.), *An Inventory of Archaic and Classical Poleis,* Oxford: 885–899.

Archibald, Z., *et al.* (2002): A River Port and Emporion in Central Bulgaria. An Interim Report on the British Project at Vetren, *ABSA* 97: 309–351.

---

which the infinitives depend. In that case, however, one might expect a nominative subject of the infinitives rather than an accusative.

[32] Two other regulations are well-preserved in the first half of the 'Pistiros Inscription' that do not have this hypothetical Odrysian official as subject: guidelines for the arbitration of inter-*emporitai* disputes and a lengthy and complex directive regarding the movement of goods between Maroneia on the one hand and Pistiros (and other *emporia*) on the other. The latter in particular would appear to reflect some formal treaty between the Odrysians and Maroneia. If true, this would add an additional layer of documentary context to the Pistiros inscription. In any case, enforcement of both of these regulations would seem to fall within the purview of the hypothetical Odrysian official who is subject of the prohibitions.

[33] It is possible that the subject of these prohibitions is identical with the subject of the third-person imperatives that open the inscription as we have it, but there is no clear connection between that act of owing and the prohibitions that follow.

Avram, A. (1997): Notes sur l'inscription de l'emporion de Pistiros en Thrace, *Mar Nero* 3: 37–46.

Bouzek, J., Domaradzka, L. (eds.) (2005): *The Culture of Thracians and Their Neighbours. Proceedings of the International Symposium in Memory of Prof. Mieczyslaw Domaradzki, with a Round Table "Archaeological Map of Bulgaria"*, (*BAR* International Series, 1350), Oxford.

Bouzek, J., Domaradzki, M., Archibald, Z.A. (eds.) (1996): *Pistiros I. Excavations and Studies*, Prague.

Bouzek, J., Domaradzka, L., Archibald, Z.A. (eds.) (2002): *Pistiros II. Excavations and Studies*, Prague.

Bouzek, J., Domaradzka, L., Archibald, Z.A. (eds.) (2007): *Pistiros III. Excavations and Studies*, Prague.

Bouzek, J., Domaradzka, L., Archibald, Z.A. (eds.) (2010): *Pistiros IV. Excavations and Studies*, Prague.

Bravo, B., Chankowski, V. (1999): Cités et *emporia* dans le commerce avec les barbares, à la lumière du document dit à tort « inscription de Pistiros », *BCH* 123: 275–317.

Chankowski, V., Domaradzka, L. (1999): Réédition de l'incription de Pistiros et problèmes d'interprétation, *BCH* 123: 247–258.

Demetriou, D. (2010): Pistiros and a North Aegean Trade Network, *L'Antiquité Classique* 79: 77–93.

Domaradzki, M. (ed.) (2000): *Pistiros et Thasos. Structures économiques dans la péninsule balkanique aix VIIe–Ve siècles avant J.-C.*, Opole.

Jameson, M.H., Jordan, D.R., Kotansky, R.H. (1993): *A Lex Sacra from Selinous*, (*Greek, Roman, and Byzantine Mongraphs* 11), Durham, N.C.

Loukopoulou, L. (1999): Sur le statut et l'importance de l'*emporion* de Pistiros, *BCH* 123: 359–371.

Picard, O. (1999): Le commerce de l'argent dans la charte de Pistiros, *BCH* 123: 331–346.

Plassart, A. (1914): Inscriptions de Delphes. Règlement tégéate concernant le retour des bannis à Tégée, en 324 av. J.-C., *BCH* 38: 101–188.

Rhodes, P.J. (1997): *The Decrees of the Greek States*, Oxford.

Velkov, V., Domaradzka, L. (1994): Kotys I (383/382–359 av. J.-C.) et l'emporion Pistiros de Thrace, *BCH* 118: 1–15.

Velkov, V., Domaradzka, L. (1996): Kotys I (383/359 B. C.) and *emporion Pistiros*, in: Bouzek/Domaradzki/Archibald (1996): 205–216.

ELECTRUM * Vol. 19 (2012): 111–129
doi:10.4467/20843909EL.12.006.0747

The Alleged Failure of Athens in the Fourth Century[1]

P.J. Rhodes

Abstract: The view that the successes of Macedon in the fourth century marked the failure, or the end, of the Greek *polis* is increasingly being abandoned, and some scholars are abandoning also the view that Athens was great and glorious in the fifth century but degenerate in the fourth. However, the successes of Macedon meant for Athens the loss of that ultimate freedom which it had aspired to and had often enjoyed between the early fifth century and the late fourth, freedom not merely from receiving orders from others but to give orders to others, and in this paper I explore the reasons for that change. Some scholars believe that fourth-century Athens was led astray by "the ghost of empire;" others believe that the Athenians were unwilling to pay for a response which could have defeated Philip; I argue that except in the years after Leuctra the ghost of empire did not have malign effects, and even with more expenditure Athens could not have defeated Philip. There was nothing fundamentally wrong with Athens in the fourth century, but Sparta's success in the Hellespont in 387 and the resulting King's Peace, the rule in Macedon of Philip II, who was too clever diplomatically and became too strong militarily for the Athenians, and Alexander's succession in 336 and his success and survival in his campaigns, placed Athens in situations which it could not overcome.

Keywords: Athens, Sparta, Macedon, Philip II of Macedon, Persia.

The view that the successes of Macedon in the fourth century marked the failure, or the end, of the Greek *polis* is increasingly and I think rightly being abandoned.[2] Similarly some scholars, though not all,[3] are abandoning the view (inherited from the fourth-century orators) that Athens was great and glorious in the fifth century but degenerate in the fourth. It is, however, true that the successes of Macedon meant for Athens the loss of that ultimate freedom which it had aspired to and had often enjoyed between the early fifth century and the late fourth, freedom not merely from receiving orders from others

---

[1]   This paper has been lightly revised and updated from my contribution, with the title "Athens in the Fourth Century: What – If Anything – Went Wrong?" to a conference at Sunium organised by Mr. A. L. Pierris in July 2006 on "Mind, Might, Money: The Secular Triad in Golden-Age Athens;" the conference proceedings have not yet been published. I thank Mr. Pierris and all those involved in the Sunium conference; and Prof. Sprawski for inviting me to contribute to this volume and accepting this paper.

[2]   For my views see Rhodes 1994 (written in 1981/1982): 589–591; Rhodes/Lewis 1997.

[3]   For recent expressions of the view that fourth-century Athens was degenerate see, e.g., Samons 2004; Romilly 2005.

but to give orders to others:[4] archein gave way to what could be seen by comparison as *douleuein*. In this paper I want to focus on the reasons for that change.

A quarter of a century ago G.L. Cawkwell wrote "Notes on the Failure of the Second Athenian Confederacy", concluding that at first the Second League was a success and Athens kept the promises made at its foundation; but that after the defeat of Sparta at Leuctra had ended for ever the threat which the League had been founded to counter Athens revived its old imperial ambitions and practices, bankrupting itself and alienating its allies, so that when the opportunity arose several allies fought their way out in the Social War, and what survived of the League after that was of no great significance.[5] More recently E. Badian has seen a far more pervasive influence of "The Ghost of Empire" in fourth-century Athenian foreign policy, claiming that again and again a success led to hopes of imperial power which in turn led to *nemesis*, with a downward spiral marked by increasingly lower peaks and deeper troughs.[6] First came the Corinthian War and the naval campaign of Thrasybulus; then the League, which Badian sees as an attempt to make Athens a great naval power again, even if at first the promises were kept; later the imperial policies embarked on after Leuctra, in particular the attempt to regain Amphipolis and the disastrous attempt to do a deal with Philip at the beginning of his reign. After the Social War Eubulus, with his turn from imperial adventures to financial recovery, is seen as "the first major politician in Athens who had personally exorcised the ghost".[7] After the middle of the century there were still ambitious decrees and campaigns by ambitious generals, but the citizens would no longer pay for them; there was Demosthenes' opposition to Philip, the "Periclean" policy of Lycurgus and Demades; and finally the ghost led Athens to the Lamian War and to "political and military destruction".

Other scholars have painted very different pictures. L.J. Samons, in a book whose overriding purpose is to suggest that what was great about classical Athens was not its democracy, condemns that concentration on financial prosperity which Badian sees as the dawning of realism. The democracy with its payments to citizens had been created in the fifth century when the payments could be funded by the Delian League; in the fourth century the funding had to come from taxes and the richer citizens, and the poor would not give up their subsidies and the rich would not pay the heavier taxes which (Samons thinks) would have made effective resistance to Philip possible. Samons also thinks that increasing risks of prosecution for failure deterred men of sufficient calibre from putting themselves forward as military and political leaders.[8]

For yet another view we may turn to P. Harding. He rejects the usual concentration on leading figures and what are believed to be their policies, and also the claim of H. Montgomery, echoing Demosthenes, that the Athenian democracy was structurally incapable of maintaining an effective foreign policy in the face of a ruler such as Philip.[9]

---

[4] For this view of the highest kind of freedom see Hdt. 1.210.2, 9.122.3, cf. 6.109.3; [Xen.] *Ath. Pol.* 1.8; Thuc. 1.76.1, 2.63.1, 3.45.6, 6.18.3, 87.2, 7.75.7, 8.68.4; cf. 5.9.9 on what was possible for lesser states; Pl. *Grg.* 452 d; Dem. 22. *Androt.* 68; Lycurg. *Leoc.* 42.

[5] Cawkwell 1981.

[6] Badian 1995.

[7] Ibidem: 101.

[8] Samons 2004: esp. 95–99, 143–162.

[9] Cf. Montgomery 1983. Demosthenes contrasting decision-making by Philip and by Athens: esp. 18. *Crown* 235–236, 19. *Embassy* 184–186. I agree with Hansen 2005 that in so far as this was a problem it was a problem for any constitutionally governed *polis*, not specifically a problem for a democratic *polis*.

Harding takes a "bottom up" view, and argues that "the overall direction of Athenian foreign policy was by the people in the Assembly," and that after the King's Peace Athens pursued a consistent and often though not always successful policy. This was a defensive policy which involved identifying and protecting Athens' vital interests as far as limited resources allowed; by 340 "the Athenians had been so successful in containing and frustrating Philip that he had lost the initiative;" he was forced to invade Greece and fight at Chaeronea, where he won – but he risked real disaster if he did not win. For Athens Chaeronea was not the end, but by the time of the Lamian War the balance of power had changed too much for the attempt to strike back to succeed.[10]

So here I wish to ask once more how successful or unsuccessful Athens was in the fourth-century world, and why.

* * *

The consequences for Athens of defeat in the Peloponnesian War were much less drastic than we might have expected. Plague and war casualties had at best halved the number of citizens, and in this respect there was to be little recovery.[11] The city was not destroyed as some of Sparta's allies would have liked, but it lost all its overseas possessions, the long walls and the Piraeus walls were demolished, the navy was reduced to twelve ships, Athens was made a subordinate ally of Sparta, and although there was probably no formal requirement of constitutional change in the peace treaty[12] the oligarchy of the Thirty was set up under pressure from Lysander. Yet after a year the restoration of the democracy was facilitated by Pausanias; there was probably little long-term damage to Athenian agriculture;[13] the 2% tax was collected on 1,650 talents' worth of trade in 402/401 and on over 1,800 talents' worth in 401/400.[14] As for foreign affairs, Athens dutifully assisted in Sparta's war against Elis *c.* 401, and sent oligarchically-minded cavalrymen to Asia Minor with Thibron in 400;[15] but before long there were the beginnings of a move away from Sparta. In 397 officers and weapons were sent to Conon for the fleet which he was assembling for Pharnabazus, and envoys were dispatched to the Persian King but caught by the Spartans;[16] in 396 reinforcements were not sent to Asia with Agesilaus, and Demaenetus set out with a trireme to join Conon, though when that became known there was a panic in Athens.[17] In 395 Athens was drawn fairly readily into joining Sparta's disaffected allies in the Corinthian War, and Xenophon represents the Thebans

---

[10]   Harding 1995: both quotations from p. 124.

[11]   See, e.g., Hansen 1988: 14–28 (*c.* 60,000 in 431); 1986 (*c.* 30,000 after the war).

[12]   Silence of Xen. *Hell.* 2.2.20; Diod. Sic. 13.107.4; Andoc. 3. *Peace* 11–12; Plut. *Lys.* 14.8; contr. *Ath. Pol.* 34.3; Diod. Sic. 14.3.2, 6; Just. 5.8.5: see Rhodes 1981: 427.

[13]   Hanson 1998 is not in this respect refuted by Thorne 2001. The territory of Attica was, of course, the same after the Peloponnesian War as before; there were only half as many citizens after the war as before to share it (cf. above with n. 11), but Athens had no overseas possessions immediately after the war and not many other than Imbros, Lemnos and Scyros at any time in the fourth century.

[14]   Andoc. 1. *Mysteries* 133–134. That these were very large figures for Athens just after the Peloponnesian War is stressed by Hansen 2006: 92.

[15]   Elis: Xen. *Hell.* 3.2.25; Thibron: Xen. *Hell.* 3.1.4.

[16]   *Hell. Oxy.* 10.1 Chambers.

[17]   Agesilaus: Paus. 3.9.2–3; Demaenetus: *Hell. Oxy.* 9 Chambers.

as saying, "We all know that you would like to recover the empire you had before."[18] We do not know how soon Athens started rebuilding its navy, but the rebuilding of the walls was already under way at the end of 395/394, before the battle of Cnidus,[19] the sanctuary of Apollo on Delos was in Athens' hands again by 393/392,[20] and the north-Aegean islands of Imbros, Lemnos and Scyros had been regained by 392/391.[21]

The *Hellenica Oxyrhynchia* is one of the few texts which suggest that the Athenians were divided on class lines, with the "many and democratic" soon inclined to war against Sparta while the "respectable and propertied" were in 396 content with the *status quo*. Thrasybulus was on the side of caution in 396,[22] but in 395 he was in favour of joining in the Corinthian War and himself commanded the Athenian forces in Boeotia.[23] It seems clear that within a few years majority opinion shifted from subservience to Sparta to opposition to Sparta, and the main distinction is simply that some men were quicker than others to change.

Relations with Persia were complicated. Sparta, to gain Persian support against Athens in the Peloponnesian War, had undertaken to return the Asiatic Greeks to Persia; but from 400 it was fighting for the Asiatic Greeks against Persia, though from time to time pausing to consider a compromise deal. Persia therefore supported Sparta's enemies in Greece: it was probably in 397 or 396 and by Pharnabazus, the satrap of Dascylium, that Timocrates of Rhodes was sent to Greece with Persian money.[24] In 398 Pharnabazus had obtained the King's permission to raise a fleet, which was commanded by the Athenian refugee Conon, with the support of Conon's and Athens' friend Evagoras of Salamis in Cyprus, and in 394 that fleet defeated the Spartans at Cnidus. This was a Persian victory over Greeks, but it suited Athens to represent it as a Greek victory over Spartan imperialism and to award extravagant honours to Conon and Evagoras; Spartan harmosts were driven out, and Phranabazus promised to leave the *akropoleis* unfortified and the cities autonomous.[25] The inscription on Conon's statue base claimed that "Conon freed the allies of Athens:" Seager cynically comments, "The unfortunate break in Athenian domination was now at an end and could henceforth be disregarded."[26]

But in 392, with Sparta making no progress either in Asia or in Greece, Antalcidas made his first attempt at securing a common peace treaty, by which Sparta would after all return the Asiatic Greeks to Persia in return for Persian support in Greece. That first attempt failed, and the King sent Struthas to continue the war; but in 392/391 Sparta had a second attempt, with concessions which Andocides and his fellow envoys were willing to accept, but the Athenian assembly on account of the proposed abandonment

---

[18] Xen. *Hell.* 3.5.10.

[19] *IG* II² 1656–7 = Rhodes/Osborne 2003: no. 9.

[20] *IG* II² 1634 = *I. Délos* 97; *contra I. Délos* 87 = Rhodes/Osborne 2003: no. 3, of 403 or shortly after.

[21] Andoc. 3. *Peace* 12, 14.

[22] *Hell. Oxy.* 9.2–3 Chambers; cf. Ar. *Eccl.* 197–198.

[23] In favour: Xen. *Hell.* 3.5.16; commanding: Plut. *Lys.* 29.1; Paus. 3.5.4.

[24] *Hell. Oxy.* 10.2, 5 Chambers; Polyaen. 1.48.3 contra Xen. *Hell.* 3.5.1; Plut. *Artox.* 20.4; Paus. 3.9.8. See, e.g., Krentz 1995: 195.

[25] Honours for Conon: Isoc. 9. *Evagoras* 56–57; Dem. 20. *Leptines* 68–70; Paus. 1.3.2; for Evagoras: Lewis/Stroud 1979 = Rhodes/Osborne 2003: no. 11; Isoc. 9. *Evagoras* 56, 68. Harmosts, Pharnabazus' promise: Xen. *Hell.* 4.8.1–2.

[26] Statue base: Dem. 20. *Leptines* 69; Seager 1997: 103.

of the Asiatic Greeks was not.[27] Athens was still opposed to Sparta but now not so well disposed towards Persia: Conon had been arrested by Antalcidas' friend Tiribazus in 392;[28] Evagoras, who had been increasing his power in Cyprus, was from 391 onwards perceived by the Persians as a rebel who had to be dealt with, and Athens sent support to him, *c.* 390, intercepted by Persia's enemy Sparta, and *c.* 388.[29] It is against this background that we must set Thrasybulus' campaign of *c.* 390: whatever may have been the case in 395, by the end of the 390's Athens was rebuilding its walls and its navy and had begun to recover old possessions and to hope to recover more,[30] and it no longer thought that to oppose Sparta it needed to be on good terms with Persia. There can be no doubt about Thrasybulus' imperial ambitions:[31] his campaign, ostensibly to support democrats against pro-Spartan oligarchs in Rhodes, took him from Thrace and Thasos, Byzantium and Calchedon in the north to Aspendus, well outside the Aegean, in the south, and involved the revival of Alcibiades' 10% Bosporus tax, a 5% tax in the Aegean, a claim by Athens to exile men from the territory of Athens and its allies, and a willingness to impose governors and garrisons.[32] Thrasybulus was killed. Some of his subordinates were recalled and prosecuted,[33] but this does not seem to indicate disapproval of the policy: the Athenians supported Evagoras, and in the months before the King's Peace they talked of "not giving up Erythrae to the barbarians," and for Clazomenae they insisted on Thrasybulus' 5% tax and considered but decided against sending a governor and garrison.[34]

What brought this to an end was not any change of heart in Athens or any fundamental weakness but the large result of a small but important episode: in 387 Antalcidas regained control of the Hellespont for Sparta;[35] Tiribazus was by then again satrap in Sardis, and they were in a strong enough position to obtain from the King and impose on the Greeks terms almost the same as those first attempted in 392 (apart from the concession of the three north-Aegean islands to Athens). The Asiatic Greeks were "given up to the barbarians," but Agesilaus notoriously proclaimed that Sparta was not Medising but Persia was Laconising: except in Persia's sphere and Athens' three islands, all cities and islands were to be autonomous, and Agesilaus insisted that this requirement entailed the dissolution of the Boeotian federation and of the union of Corinth and Argos.[36] This was followed by a Spartan war of revenge against Mantinea, which ended with Man-

---

27 I accept the use of Philoch, *FGrH* 328 F 149 to date Andoc. 3. *Peace*, with, e.g., Keen 1995, 1998, against, e.g., Badian 1991, and against the argument that Andoc. 3 is a later rhetorical exercise advanced by Harris 2000.

28 Xen. *Hell.* 4.8.16.

29 *C.* 390: Xen. *Hell.* 4.8.24; *c.* 388: Xen. *Hell.* 5.1.10–12. The chronology of Persia's war against Evagoras was settled by Spek 1998: 240–251.

30 Andoc. 3. *Peace* 15 suggests that by 392/391 there was talk of regaining the Chersonese and other places.

31 See Seager 1997; Cawkwell 1976.

32 10% tax: Dem. 20. *Leptines* 60; 5% tax: *IG* II² 24.*a*.5–6, 28 = Rhodes/Osborne 2003: no. 18.7–8; exile: *IG* II² 24.*b*.4–6; governors and garrisons: *IG* II² 28 = Rhodes/Osborne 2003: no. 18.13–17 with 22–5.

33 Lys. 28. *Ergocles*; 29. *Philocrates*.

34 Erythrae: *SEG* XXVI,1282 = Rhodes/Osborne 2003: no. 17.11–14; Clazomenae: *IG* II² 28 = Rhodes/Osborne 2003: no. 18.

35 Xen. *Hell.* 5.1.6–7, 25–28; for Athenian recriminations see *IG* II² 29 = Rhodes/Osborne 2003: no. 19.

36 Persia Laconising: Plut. *Ages.* 23.4; *Artox.* 22.4; *Apophth. Lac.* 213b; Boeotia and Corinth-and-Argos: Xen. *Hell.* 5.1.32–4.

tinea's being split into its component villages, probably by a perverse application of the autonomy principle.[37]

The King's Peace was a new kind of treaty, with its stipulation about the Greek states in general, and what Athens could do and what Athens should do in this new world was not immediately clear. We have a fragmentary decree of 386/385 concerning land on Lemnos, one of Athens' three islands. In the same year Athens praised the Thracian ruler Hebryzelmis, and confirmed for him the honours voted to his forebears, but as Sinclair stressed the decree says nothing about an alliance.[38] In 384/383 a way forward was found in the alliance with Chios, perhaps on the initiative of Chios, which was a defensive alliance "on terms of freedom and autonomy, not contravening any of the things written on the *stelai* about the peace;" Methymna at least, and perhaps other states, also made an alliance with Athens.[39]

I am among those who believe that Lysias' (33) *Olympic Speech* is to be dated not to 388 but to 384, and that the disgraceful state of affairs of which he is complaining is that after the King's Peace:[40] as Gorgias had done already in the last years of the Peloponnesian War,[41] Lysias calls on the Greeks to stop fighting amongst themselves and unite against the barbarians, and in this new world and at a panhellenic gathering he regards the Spartans as the leaders of the Greeks.[42] Isocrates in his (4) *Panegyric* of *c.* 380 contrasts the disgrace of the King's Peace with the glories of the (actual or invented) mid-fifth-century Peace of Callias: at the beginning he says it is a commonplace of speakers that the Greeks ought not to fight against one another but to unite and fight against the Persians, and he goes on to say that this requires cooperation between Athens and Sparta – which turns out to mean that it requires acceptance by Sparta that Athens rather than Sparta deserves to be the leader of the Greeks. Much of the speech is then devoted to a defence of fifth-century Athens and the Delian League.[43]

Athens did not support Mantinea, but did take in refugees afterwards.[44] It sympathised with Olynthus when Sparta attacked it in 382, probably again with the ostensible intention of enforcing the autonomy clause of the King's Peace, but there is no good reason for dating the fragment of an inscribed alliance to this time.[45] It did, however, take

---

[37]   Note the Athenians' fear that if they supported Mantinea they might be in breach of the peace: Diod. Sic. 15.5.5.

[38]   Lemnos: *IG* II² 30; Hebryzelmis: *IG* II² 31 = Tod 117, with Sinclair 1978: 47–49.

[39]   Chios: *IG* II² 34 and 35 = Rhodes/Osborne 2003: no. 20; Methymna: *IG* II² 42 = Rhodes/Osborne 2003: no. 23.4–6.

[40]   388: Diod. Sic. 14.109.3; 384: Grote 1869/1884: ix. 291–292 n. 2; x. 312–313 n. 1 = 1888: viii. 72 n. 2; ix. 34–5 n. 1.

[41]   Gorgias, *Vorsokr.*⁶ 82A1.4 (*Olympic Speech*, to be dated 408 with Wilamowitz-Moellendorff 1893, I: 172–173 with n. 35), 1.5 (*Funeral Speech*, of unknown date).

[42]   Lys. 33. *Olymp.* 6.

[43]   King's Peace and Peace of Callias: Isoc. 4. *Panegyric* 115–121, cf. 175–180; commonplace: § 15; cooperation between Athens and Sparta: §§ 16–17; Athens ought to be leader: § 18 and much of speech, cf. 15. *Antidosis* 57–62.

[44]   *IG* II² 33.7–8.

[45]   Athens and Olynthus: Xen. *Hell.* 5.2.15; Sparta appealed to by Chalcidian cities: Xen. *Hell.* 5.2.11–23, by Macedon (which may also be true): Diod. Sic. 15.19.3; alliance: *IG* II² 36 = Tod 119, both dating it 384/383, 376/375, e.g. Lewis 1954: 33, and later dates have been considered (Zahrnt 1971: 124–127 favours the mid 370's but restores without an archon's name).

in refugees from Thebes when that city was occupied by Sparta.[46] That led to support for Thebes in 379/378 when some of the refugees set out from Athens and overthrew the pro-Spartan régime.[47] What changed everything was Sphodrias' raid on Attica, misplaced chronologically by Diodorus.[48] It was that which gave the Athenians the indignation and courage to declare that Sparta, while posing as the enforcer of the King's Peace, was itself in breach of the peace, and that they would head a new league to uphold the peace against the Spartans. The prospectus[49] shows two particular concerns: to spell out what was meant by the principle of autonomy, which Sparta had been exploiting since the peace was made; and to promise that Athens would not do various things for which it had been unpopular in the Delian League. What is surprising is that most of the states which joined the League in time to be included in its list of members (i.e., probably, by 375) were states of the Aegean and its Thracian coast, which as far as we can tell were not seriously threatened by Sparta after the King's Peace. However, the campaign of 376 was to show that, if Agesilaus was obsessed with Thebes, other Spartans had not given up on the Aegean;[50] and it may be that even before 376 the members recruited by Athens felt more vulnerable than our evidence allows us to see.

How lively was the ghost of empire? Isocrates provides evidence that some people were thinking of empire and of war against Persia; but Athens' practice since the King's Peace had been very cautious, and the Second League was founded not to fight Isocrates' war against Persia but to uphold the King's Peace against Sparta, and with promises that this league would not become an empire. In many respects the Athenians do seem to have behaved virtuously in the 370's, and it is striking that in spite of their past they were able to build up a sizeable league. Garrisons to protect Abdera against the Thracians, and in Cephallenia and perhaps elsewhere in the west, were contrary to the foundation promises, but probably in the particular situations in which they were installed they were welcomed – by most people in Abdera and by the supporters of Athens in the west.[51] Why additions to the list of members inscribed with the prospectus ceased after (probably) 375 remains a mystery, but the evidence suggests that, although that list omits Corcyra and contains only one city of Cephallenia, Corcyra and the whole of Cephallenia did eventually become members, and there is no need to rule out other additions.[52] *Stasis* in Paros was dealt with not by Athens but by the *synedrion* of the League, though

---

[46]   Xen. *Hell.* 5.2.31; Plut. *Pelop.* 6.3–5.

[47]   The support appears more official in Diod. Sic. 15.25.4–26.3, cf. Din. 1 *Demosthenes* 38–39, than in the different account of Xen. *Hell.* 5.4.9. Buck 1992, cf. 1994: 85–86 suggests that the Athenian generals were sent officially to the frontier region and on their own initiative went into Boeotia.

[48]   Diod. Sic. 15.28, 29.5–8. On the chronology I agree with, e.g., Rice 1975: 124–127 (but not with his putting even the expedition of 25.4–26.3 after Sphodrias' raid); Badian 1995: 89–90 n. 34, against, e.g., Cawkwell 1973: 51–56; Cargill 1981: 58–59, who defend Diodorus' placing of the foundation before Sphodrias' raid.

[49]   *IG* II² 43 = Rhodes/Osborne 2003: no. 22.

[50]   Xen. *Hell.* 5.4.58–61; Diod. Sic. 15.34.3–35.3.

[51]   Abdera: Diod. Sic. 15.36.4; Cephallenia etc.: *IG* II² 98 = *Agora* XVI: 46.16–17.

[52]   *IG* II² 96 = Rhodes/Osborne 2003: no. 24, 97 = Tod 127, 98 = *Agora* XVI: 43. See especially Tuplin 1984: 553–561, against Cargill 1981: 64–74, 109–111.

afterwards Paros was said to be a colony of Athens and was called on to send offerings to Athenian festivals.[53]

The promise that there would be no tribute is so emphatic that I think at the outset there can have been no compulsory levies of money under any name: a complaint in 375 that the Thebans were not contributing money towards the fleet in a campaign which they had instigated perhaps points to voluntary arrangements, but it may well have been assumed that in general each allied state would provide and fund its own forces. *Syntaxeis*, "contributions," were being collected in 373, and Timotheus' problems then in raising a fleet to go to Corcyra make that a likely time for the introduction of the new system.[54] Our little evidence for the *syntaxeis* suggests that they never yielded much money. The Athenians themselves reorganised the collection of *eisphora* from rich citizens and metics, grouping the payers in *symmoriai*, in 378/377.[55] In 374/373 the proceeds of the grain tax from the north-Aegean islands were ring-fenced for the stratiotic fund.[56] The Athenians' financial difficulties even in the early years of the League show that, whether their policies were altruistic or selfish, memories and/or hopes of naval power led them into campaigning beyond their financial means: to that extent at least the ghost was at work.

Leuctra and what followed in the next few years transformed the League and Athens' policy. Sparta was defeated in battle, it was deprived of Messenia, and a treaty involving Corinth and other states but not Sparta ended the Peloponnesian League – in each case not at the instance of Athens and its allies but of Thebes. As in the 390's, some Athenians made the change sooner and more readily than others, but in 369 Athens and Sparta became allies, and in 367 Thebes offered itself to Persia as the new agent of the King's Peace and started to indicate that Athens' naval power was its next target, so that Athens became less enthusiastic for the King's Peace. What was to become of a League which had been founded to oppose Sparta and to uphold the King's Peace? One might well ask. Mytilene did ask, and unfortunately there survives from Callistratus' response only the beginning, which justifies the anti-Spartan policy of the 370's, and what Callistratus went on to say about the new world after Leuctra has not survived.[57]

Immediately after Leuctra the Athenians had hoped that they could fill the power vacuum, and had themselves organised the common peace of autumn 371. I believe, first, that swearing "to abide by the treaty which the King sent down and by the decrees

---

[53] *SEG* XXXI, 67 = Rhodes/Osborne 2003: no. 29.

[54] Cf., e.g., Cawkwell 1963a: 91–93, contra, e.g., Badian 1995: 91–92 n. 37. Thebans: Xen. *Hell.* 6.2.1 with 5.4.62; *syntaxeis* in 373: [Dem.] 49. *Timotheus* 49; Timotheus' difficulties: Xen. *Hell.* 6.2.12–13; Diod. Sic. 15.47.2–3.

[55] Clidemus, *FGrH* 323 F 8.

[56] *SEG* XLVII, 96 = Rhodes/Osborne 2003: no. 26.51–5, the earliest surviving mention of this fund. In lines 55–61 other sums are directed εἰς τὴν διοίκησιν which I take to mean that they are to be part of the ordinary finances of the city, received by the *apodektai* and passed on to different spending authorities in the *merismos*.

[57] *IG* II² 107 = Rhodes/Osborne 2003: no. 31.35 sqq., of 369/368. It is interesting that in the prospectus of the League, *IG* II² 43 = Rhodes/Osborne 2003: no. 22, the pro-King's-Peace lines 12–15 were deleted but the anti-Spartan lines 9–12 were not: the talks in Persia in 367 and the willingness of one of the Athenian delegates to acquiesce provoked an angry reaction (Xen. *Hell.* 7.1.33–8; Plut. *Pelop.* 30; *Dem.* 19. *Embassy* 31, 137, 191), and I imagine that in that reaction the one clause was deleted and the thought that another clause also had become embarrassingly obsolete did not occur.

of Athens and the allies" means renewing the King's Peace and strengthening it with the interpretation of freedom and autonomy given in the League's prospectus and other documents, but not that the Persians were on this occasion directly involved or that the participants – including Sparta – were all enrolled in the League;[58] secondly, that later claims that the King and all the Greeks acknowledged Athens' right to Amphipolis and the Chersonese are Athenian interpretation of a clause in the treaty that the participants should ἔχειν τὰ ἑαυτῶν possess not just what they possessed at the time but what was theirs by right.[59]

In the middle of the fifth century, after Cimon's death, the Athenians (with or without a Peace of Callias) discontinued the Delian League's regular campaigning against Persia, but after a little uncertainty they kept the League in being as an Athenian empire.[60] In the same way after the unifying purpose of the Second League had disappeared the Athenians kept the League in being for their own purposes, and the 360's is the decade in which the ghost of empire walked most visibly. Athens began fighting for Amphipolis in 368, and in the Hellespont in 365; it had some successes as well as some failures, but did not succeed in gaining either Amphipolis or the Chersonese. On the west side of the Aegean Athens tangled with Macedon and Thessaly at the same time as Thebes: in Thessaly Thebes supported the *koinon* while Athens supported the tyrants of Pherae. On the east side, since Thebes was now the friend of the Persian King, Athens and Sparta supported the rebel satraps. In 366–365 Timotheus took Samos from the Persians (who under the terms of the King's Peace ought not to have had it) – but then it was not liberated but was taken over as an Athenian cleruchy.[61] In 364/363, when Timotheus had moved to the western Aegean, he captured Torone and Potidaea, and in 361, at the invitation of Athens' supporters there, cleruchs were sent to Potidaea too.[62] Samos and Potidaea were not members of the Second Athenian League, but all of this must still have seemed very alarming to the members.

In other ways Athens' actions did impinge directly on the members. On the island of Ceos there were four cities, and Athens preferred to deal with them as separate cities, but they or at any rate three of them preferred to function as a single federal state: this may lie behind the two stages of revolt in 363/362, after which all major lawsuits were to be transferred to Athenian courts.[63] In 361/360 Chares intervened in Corcyra, supporting an oligarchic revolt, "as a result of which the Athenian *demos* gained a bad reputation among the allies."[64] According to Aeneas Tacticus Chares was in Corcyra as

---

[58] Xen. *Hell.* 6.5.1–3, quoting § 2. Cf. Sordi 1951; Ryder 1965: 71–74, 131–133; *contra* Lewis 1997: 29–31.

[59] Cf. Jehne 1992; Rhodes 2008, and 2010: 233.

[60] I belong to the minority which does not believe in a Peace of Callias: see Rhodes 2010: 51–56.

[61] Capture: Dem. 15. *Freedom of Rhodians* 9; Isoc. 15. *Antidosis* 108, 111; cleruchy: Diod. Sic. 18.18.9, Str. 638/14.1.18; Arist. *Rhet.* 2.1384 b 32–35, cf. schol. Aeschin. 1. *Timarchus* 53 (121 Dilts).

[62] Capture: Diod. Sic. 15.81.6; Isoc. 15. *Antidosis* 108, 113; Polyaenus *Strat.* 3.10.15; cleruchy: *IG* II² 116 = Tod 147.

[63] *IG* II² 111 = Rhodes/Osborne 2003: no. 39; cf. decrees of separate cities *IG* II² 1128 = Rhodes/Osborne 2003: no. 40; stipulation that the Ceans were to be administered "by cities" *IG* II² 404.13 = *SEG* XXXIX, 73.14 (perhaps mid 350's, though at the *SEG* reference 363/362 is suggested). The city which tended not to join the others was Poeessa.

[64] Diod. Sic. 15.95.3 (quotation); Aen. Tact. 11.13–15.

a garrison commander. We certainly find garrisons in the 350's: in Andros during the Social War, paid for out of the *syntaxeis* with the approval of the *synedrion*; but in Arcesine on Amorgus probably before the outbreak of the Social War, and at the expense of the Arcesinians.[65]

Thebes and Athens began their rival involvement with Thessaly and Macedon in 369 and 368, and it was in 367 that the Thebans won the support of Persia and proposed common peace terms which would include the disbanding of the Athenian navy.[66] In 366 they exploited a dispute to take Oropus from Athens.[67] In the years that followed Epaminondas urged the Thebans to build dockyards and a hundred new triremes; he tried to win over members of the Athenian League, with a naval campaign to the eastern Aegean in 364 which scared off an Athenian squadron.[68] It may have been this challenge to Athens which encouraged the Ceans to revolt when they did. To increase Athens' problems, after the Thebans' defeat of Alexander of Pherae in 364 he turned against Athens, attacking Tenos in 362 and Peparethus and even the Piraeus in 361, in response to which the Athenians switched to a short-lived alliance with the Thessalian *koinon*.[69]

From the time of Timotheus' siege of Samos, winter 366/365, we have the beginning of a decree for Erythrae, on the mainland opposite Chios, connected in some way with him: the substance has been lost but Timotheus perhaps raised money there for the siege.[70] There are other signs that Athens continually had problems in funding its campaigns: Timotheus in the north-western Aegean issued bronze coins; Apollodorus reports a shortage of public money to pay ships' crews in 362–360.[71] There had been a shortfall in the payment of the property tax, *eisphora*. 364/363 sees the earliest mention of *proeisphora*, the liturgy through which the three richest members of each *symmoria* were required to advance the whole sum due from their *symmoria* and were left to recover the other members' share themselves.[72] In the early 350's there were 14 talents unpaid out of a total of about 300 talents – from 378/377 to perhaps the institution of *proeisphora* – and this was thought serious enough for Androtion to propose the creation of and himself to serve on a commission to collect the arrears (about half of the sum outstanding was collected).[73] The trierarchic system, under which originally one man had been given the

---

[65]   Andros: *IG* II² 123 = Rhodes/Osborne 2003: no. 52 (357/<u>356</u>); Arcesine: *IG* XII.vii 5 = Rhodes/Osborne 2003: no. 51 (Androtion praised perhaps 357/356 after a term of at least two years).

[66]   Xen. *Hell.* 7.1.36–7; Plut. *Pel.* 30, cf. Dem. 19. *Embassy* 31, 137, 191.

[67]   Xen. *Hell.* 7.4.1; Diod. Sic. 15.76.1; schol. Aeschin. 3. *Ctesiphon* 85 (186 Dilts); Agatharchides, *FGrH* 86 F 8 with Buckler 1977.

[68]   Diod. Sic. 15.78.4–79.1; Isoc. 5. *Philip* 53; Plut. *Philop.* 14.2–3. Epaminondas was made *proxenos* of Cnidus: *SEG* XLIV, 901; the Boeotians appointed a Byzantine *proxenos*: *SEG* XXXIV, 355 (neither inscription precisely dated). By the late 350's Byzantium had *synedroi* in what was probably a league of Thebes' allies: *IG* VII 2418 = Rhodes/Osborne 2003: no. 57.11, 24; cf. Lewis 1990; contr. Buckler 1980: 222–233, and 2000 = Bucker/Beck 2008: 165–179.

[69]   362: [Dem.] 50. *Polycles* 4; 361: Diod. Sic. 15.95.1–3; Polyaenus *Strat.* 6.2; Athens and *koinon*: *IG* II² 116 = Rhodes/Osborne 2003: no. 44 (361/360).

[70]   *IG* II² 108; generals raising money from Chios, Erythrae and wherever they could: Dem. 8. *Chersonese* 24–25.

[71]   Timotheus' bronze coinage: [Arist.] *Oec.* 2.1350a 23–9, cf. *CAH.*² plates v–vi no. 227; Apollodorus: [Dem.] 50. *Polycles*, e.g. 10–20.

[72]   *Proeisphora* mentioned 364/363: Isae. 6. *Philoctemon* 60; a date of 370–366 for the institution is suggested by Brun 1985.

[73]   Dem. 22. *Androtion* 42–46.

general and financial responsibility for a warship for a year, was under increasing strain: sharing the burden of one ship between two men had become common; in 358/357 a law of Periander organised the 1,200 hundred richest citizens in *symmoriai*, after which there were still trierarchs but some of each year's costs were shared among the whole body of 1,200; and in 354/353 Demosthenes unsuccessfully proposed changes in the new system.[74] Another source of emergency funding was an appeal for voluntary contributions, *epidoseis*: the word and lists of men who gave and men who promised but failed to give are attested for 394, but Demosthenes refers to what was in some sense the first appeal in 357.[75]

The 350's began with two protracted crises for Athens, of which one eventually turned out well but the other turned out badly. Late in 360 the Thracian king Cotys (whose sister Iphicrates had married) was murdered, and his son Cersebleptes was challenged by two other claimants, Amadocus and Berisades: it took Athens until the winter of 357/356 to achieve what was considered a satisfactory settlement, that for some purposes the three men were regarded as joint rulers but essentially Cersebleptes had the east, towards the Hellespont, Amadocus had the middle and Berisades had the west, and Greek cities on the coast had obligations both to Athens and its League and to the Thracian rulers.[76] In 359 Perdiccas of Macedon was killed in a battle against the Illyrians, and the throne passed not to his young son but to his brother Philip. Again there were rival claimants, and Athens backed one of them, Argaeus. To undermine Athens' support for Argaeus, Philip allowed the Athenians to think that he would let them regain Amphipolis, perhaps in exchange for Pydna, on the coast; in 357, once Argaeus had been defeated, he took Amphipolis for himself – and later Pydna, Potidaea (which he gave to Olynthus) and Methone.[77] Athens responded by declaring war on Philip, and, although other preoccupations prevented it from prosecuting the war, the demand for Amphipolis became ever more insistent.

There was one last deceptive success: in 357 Athens quickly seized an opportunity and brought back into the League the cities of Euboea, which had sided with Thebes

---

[74] Shared trierarchy first attested in the last years of the Peloponnesian War: Lys. 32. *Diogiton* 24–26; referred to in the 340's as normal practice before Periander's law: Dem. 21. *Midias* 154; another development was that trierarchs might avoid personal involvement by paying a contractor to do their work for them: e.g. Dem. 51. *Trierarchic Crown* 7, 21; *Midias* 80. Periander's law: [Dem.] 47. *Evergus & Mnesibulus* 21 with Dem. 14. *Symmories* 16–17; trierarchs and *symmoria*-members: MacDowell 1990: 372–373, Gabrielsen 1994: 182–199; Demosthenes in 354/353: Dem. 14. *Symmories*. Leptines' law and Demosthenes' attack on it in 355/354 (Dem. 20. *Leptines*) show that there were difficulties in finding men to perform festival liturgies too.

[75] First use of term *epidosis* 394: Isae. 5. *Dicaeogenes* 37–38; "first" appeal 357: Dem. 21. *Midias* 160–161 (MacDowell 1990: 381 suggests the first appeal for volunteers to donate ships and serve as their trierarchs).

[76] Iphicrates: Dem. 23. *Aristocrates* 129; Anaxandridas, fr. 42 Kassel & Austin; Athens and the three claimants: Dem. 23. *Aristocrates* 163–173, cf. *IG* II² 126 = Rhodes/Osborne 2003: no. 47.

[77] Argaeus and Amphipolis: Diod. Sic. 16.2.1, 2.4–3.7, 4.1, 8.3; cf. Theop., *FGrH* 115 FF 30, 42; Dem. 23. *Aristocrates* 116, 1; *Olynth.* 1. 8, 2. *Olynth.* 2. 6; [Dem.] 7. *Halonnesus* 27; Aeschin. 2. *Embassy* 33, 70, 3. *Ctesiphon* 54; Isoc. 5. *Philip.* 2; de Ste. Croix 1963 demonstrated the impossibility of a secret treaty between Athens and Philip but not the impossibility of secret talks. Pydna, Potidaea, Methone: Diod. Sic. 16.8.3–5, 31.6, 34.4–5, cf. Dem. 23. *Aristocrates* 116, 1. *Olynth.* 1. 9, 2. *Olynth.* 2. 6–7.

since Leuctra.[78] But in 356 and 355 leading members of the League – Rhodes, Chios, Cos, Byzantium – which had been approached by Thebes in the 360's and were now encouraged by Mausolus of Caria, fought against Athens in the Social War. Shockingly, the Athenians were defeated in naval battles, at Chios and at Embata; after Embata the general Chares retired into the service of the rebel satrap Artabazus, and that led to threats that Persia would give its support to Athens' rebels, so the war came to an end with Athens' rebels leaving the League.[79]

So in about fifteen years after Leuctra Athens revived former imperial practices, and tried to recover former possessions; but it could not pay for what it was trying to do, it did not achieve its major objectives, it alarmed League members even though it did not take direct action against most of them, and in the Social War it was defeated in naval battles by the rebels. Some Athenians thought that enough was enough. That reflecter of opinion Isocrates, who in his (4) *Panegyric* had defended the Delian League and advanced Athens' claim to be the leader of Greece once more, in (8) *On the Peace* at the end of the Social War urged Athens to "stop coveting a maritime empire ... which is neither just nor possible to bring about nor advantageous" – though he naïvely suggested that if the Athenians underwent this conversion other Greeks would be so impressed that they would freely grant them τὰ ἑαυτῶν (the Chersonese and Amphipolis) and more besides.[80] Xenophon's *Poroi* seems to reflect policies advocated by Eubulus after the Social War: to revive trade by making Athens more attractive to metics and visiting merchants, to invite investment in a capital fund to be spent on facilities for traders, to make more of the silver mines – and, to underpin all of this, to have peace.[81] I believe that we should attribute to Eubulus and Diophantus and date to the late 350's the creation of the theoric fund, which not only subsidised citizens' theatre tickets but built up a surplus to be spent for purposes of which its treasurer approved, and which shifted the balance of Athens' priorities by receiving not only an allowance in the *merismos* but any surplus revenue beyond the sums bespoken for the *merismos*, whereas previously it is likely that surpluses had gone to the stratiotic fund.[82] There is no doubt that between the time of the Social War and the time of Alexander Athens did once more become a prosperous state, and that this was achieved by cutting back on military expenditure as well as by increasing revenue.

This brings us to Philip of Macedon and the Athenians' responses to him. At the beginning of his reign his hints over Amphipolis weakened the Athenians' support for Argaeus and left them feeling cheated, but no Macedonian king had caused them serious trouble before: Philip had to be taken into account, just like his predecessors, but at first the Athenians still thought they would capture Amphipolis in the end. Eubulus'

---

[78]   Diod. Sic. 16.7.2; Aeschin. 3. *Ctesiphon* 85; *IG* II² 124 = Rhodes/Osborne 2003: no. 48: see the commentary of Rhodes/Osborne 2003 for the chronology of this episode and the Social War.

[79]   Diod. Sic. 16.7.3–4, 21.1–22.2; cf. Isoc. 8. *Peace* 16; Dem. 15. *Freedom of Rhodians* 3, 26. There is no other evidence that Cos was a member of the League, but it is not unlikely.

[80]   Stop coveting: Isoc. 8. *Peace* 64–66; other Greeks will grant: §§ 22–23.

[81]   Trade: Xen. *Poroi* 2–3; mines: ch. 4; peace: ch. 5.

[82]   Creation of fund: Just. 6.9.1–5; schol. Aeschin. 3. *Ctesiphon* 24 (65 Dilts); surpluses: [Dem.] 59. *Neaera* 4–6; Dem. 1. *Olynth.* 1.19–20, 3. *Olynth.* 3.10–11, 19. *Embassy* 291; Liban. *hyp. Olynth.* 1. 5. See Rhodes 1972: 105–107, cf. 235–240; and the discussions of Hansen 1976, and Harris 1996 = 2006: 121–139.

policy seems to have involved giving up such ambitions: the Athenians would still react when directly threatened, as they did in 352 when Philip advanced beyond Thessaly to Thermopylae, and Diophantus proposed the decree of thanksgiving afterwards;[83] as they did again in thinking Euboea, through which an attacker from the north could by-pass Thermopylae, more important than Olynthus in 349/348. At first Demosthenes seems to have been no more worried than anybody else about Philip; but in 352 his speech (23) *Against Aristocrates* identifies Philip as Athens' greatest enemy, and the (4) *First Philippic* followed in 351 or 350.[84] The message of that was that Athens had suffered by letting Philip make the running, and ought instead to take the initiative and make trouble for Philip as near to the heart of his kingdom as possible. In the early years of Philip's reign, when nobody yet realised the danger which he presented, that might have worked; but in those years the danger was not realised and Athens was quarrelling with the members of its League, and by the time Demosthenes advocated the policy it was too late: Philip was by then too secure in the north to be vulnerable to what Athens could do against him.

Philip was advancing eastwards into Thrace, which would take him to the Hellespont, and thanks to the Third Sacred War he was advancing southwards into central Greece, which would take him uncomfortably near to Athens.[85] In the east Cersebleptes became worried enough to grant the Chersonese to Athens, and cleruchs were sent there in 353/352; in 352, when Philip after being checked at Thermopylae switched his attention to Cersebleptes, the Athenians voted to send a relief expedition, but ran out of momentum on hearing that Philip was ill.[86] By 349/348 Olynthus, favoured by Demosthenes because to defend it would fit the strategy of the *First Philippic*, was surrounded by Philip's territory, and it is hard to think that a greater effort by Athens could have kept it safe for long. Whether Philip was involved in the Euboean affair is uncertain,[87] and how an intervention which began well ended in disaster is mysterious. Not only are the men involved in that intervention linked in various ways with Eubulus, but after Athens' failures in Olynthus and Euboea it was Eubulus who was responsible for a first series of embassies to arouse the southern Greeks against Philip.[88] In 346 Philip was expected to intervene on a large scale in the Sacred War once more, and further Athenian embassies

---

[83]   Diod. Sic. 16.38.1–2; Iust. 8.2.8–12; Dem. 19. *Embassy* 84, 86, with schol. 86 (199, 201 Dilts); for Diophantus, cf. Cawkwell 1963b: 48.

[84]   Dem. 23. *Aristocrates* 121, cf. 107–113, 116; 352/351: Dion. Hal. 725–726 *Amm.* 4; 353/352: Lane Fox 1997: 183–187; 4. *Phil.* 1. 352/351: Dion. Hal. 725. *Amm.* 4; 350/49: Lane Fox 1997: 195–199.

[85]   In the Third Sacred War Athens backed the eventual losers, the Phocians who seized Delphi in 356. The war was provoked by the Thebans' political exploitation of Delphi, against which the Athenians had reacted in 363 by harbouring men exiled from Delphi and proclaiming that their exile was "contrary to the laws of the Amphictyons and the Delphians" and invalid (*SIG*³ 175) – but Boeotia suffered badly during the war and the Thebans did not profit from being on the winning side.

[86]   Chersonese: Diod. Sic. 16.34.4; *IG* II² 1613, 297–298; Philip's campaign: schol. Aeschin. 2. *Embassy* 81 (178 Dilts); Theop., *FGrH* 115 F 101; Dem. 4. *Phil. 1.* 40–1; 3. *Olynth.* 3.4–5.

[87]   He is mentioned in the manuscript text of Aeschin. 3. *Ctesiphon* 87 and by Plut. *Phoc.* 12.1: on the basis of schol. 86 (190 Dilts) Cawkwell 1962: 129 emended Philip to Phalaecus, the Phocian leader, but Philip is upheld by [Hammond]/Griffith 1979: 318 n. 2.

[88]   Phocion and Eubulus: e.g. Aeschin. 2. *Embassy* 184; Midias and Eubulus: Dem. 21. *Midias* 205–207; Hegesilaus and Eubulus: Dem. 19. *Embassy* 290; Eubulus and embassies: Dem. 19. *Embassy* 304; these embassies rightly distinguished from those of early 346: e.g. [Hammond]/Griffith 1979: 330 n. 1.

were sent out, but after he had come to an arrangement with the Phocian leader Phalaecus the Phocians rejected Athenian help and the Athenians made peace with Philip after all.

I resist the temptation to discuss the problems of the Peace of Philocrates in detail.[89] Eubulus and his associates had been planning to resist Philip but their plans had collapsed; and now they were receptive of Philip's hints that he would end the Sacred War on terms with which they would be happy. Demosthenes, it seems, since the fall of Olynthus had been sulking: if the Athenians would not take his warnings seriously and resist Philip as he wanted, let them make peace on whatever terms they could get, and they would soon learn that Demosthenes had been right after all. Some men were opposed to peace on Philip's terms, but Eubulus insisted that the alternative was an all-out war which would have to be paid for.[90] Peace was made, but Philip's hints turned out to have been deceptive: Eubulus' associates wanted nevertheless to accept the unsatisfactory peace and make the best of it; some men clamoured for an immediate war; Demosthenes in (5) *On the Peace* wanted war but only when Philip had provided a justification for it.

What did Philip want, and what were the possibilities for Athens? I do not accept the theory that his hints were sincere, that he wanted to cooperate with Athens, but his plan was wrecked by Demosthenes. I do not accept that Isocrates' (5) *Philip* and a statement by Diodorus are sufficient evidence that Philip was already in 346 thinking of a Persian war and wanted a cooperative Greece simply to pave the way for that.[91] I think Greece was for him an objective in its own right, and the best indication of what he wanted is what he obtained after Chaeronea: a form of supremacy in which the Greeks were not conquered or directly ruled by him but were still compliant, yet were handled tactfully as subordinate allies. For most states that would be no worse than the conditions they had been accustomed to in the Greek world, but for Athens it would mean that *archein* had given way to *douleuein*. Until Philip's deal with Phalaecus, Eubulus was no less opposed to him than Demosthenes, but disagreed only on where and how to resist; and it was Eubulus' supporter Aeschines who in 348/347 reminded the Athenians of an earlier barbarian invader by reading out the decrees of Miltiades and Themistocles.[92] If a ghost was haunting Athens in the early 340's it was the ghost of the Persian Wars rather than of the empire.

In the deal with Phalaecus, and then in his hints to the envoys, Philip simply outmanoeuvred the Athenians, and even if the Athenians had been willing to abandon Eubulus' financial policy they could not in the short term have undone Philip's success. However, many Athenians were angry when it turned out that Philip's hints had been false. Demosthenes looked for trouble, and duly found it; Philip's offers to renegotiate the Peace of Philocrates were met with demands which he could not have been expected to agree to. What is remarkable is that, despite his claims that the Athenians were unwilling to accept his hard message,[93] Demosthenes succeeded in convincing not only Athens but many of the Greek states that Philip was a threat to their freedom. In 339/338 he did persuade the

---

⁸⁹ For a short account of my views see Rhodes 2010: 347–351.

⁹⁰ Dem. 19. *Embassy* 291.

⁹¹ Hints sincere: Markle 1974; envisaging Persian war: e.g. [Hammond]/Griffith 1979: 458–463, cf. Diod. Sic. 16.60.4–5, but Demosthenes shows no knowledge of such plans until 10. *Phil.* 4. 32–34.

⁹² Dem. 19. *Embassy* 303–304.

⁹³ E.g. Dem. 8. *Chersonese* 48–57, 9. *Phil.* 3.4.

Athenians that surplus revenue should go not to the theoric but to the stratiotic fund.[94] At Chaeronea Philip faced a substantial alliance, and the largest Greek army that had been assembled since Plataea in 479[95] – and the better commander and the better army won. The resistance was a valiant effort, and although Philip was not beaten it was not unthinkable that he could be beaten; I do not think more money would have made much difference; it is hard for us now to see things as the Athenians will have seen them in 340–338, but I can believe that a majority of Athenians did agree with Demosthenes that Philip represented a major threat to them.

Athens' defeat in the Peloponnesian War had not been final, and it was not obvious that Athens' defeat at Chaeronea would be final. The death of a Macedonian king often led to a disputed succession and a period of weakness – but in 336 it did not. Alexander might easily have been killed in the Balkans in 335 (when wishful thinking believed rumours that he had been killed[96]), or in Asia after that – but he was not. Demosthenes rejoiced at Philip's death in 336, supported the rising of Thebes in 335.[97] Such measures in Athens as the remodelling of the *ephebeia* show a determination not only to revive the Athenians' morale but to be ready to seize the opportunity when one arose. There was one manifestation of the ghost of empire. When Athens had been great, it had been a naval power, and it must have been shocking that in the Social War Athens was defeated in naval battles. After the Social War there was no serious threat to Athens at sea, but an enlargement of the navy was begun in the time of Eubulus, and the enlargement was continued and triremes were replaced by up-to-date quadriremes and quinqueremes in the time of Lycurgus, until in the 320's the Athenians had more warships than ever before, but no need for them and no men to row them.[98] They decided not to join in the Spartan-led rising in 331–330, when their joining in might have made the rising more serious; they did lead a rising after Alexander's death, to be defeated on land and at sea.[99]

I have argued that for the Greeks in general the hellenistic period was not noticeably worse than the classical: manoeuvring between the hellenistic kings did not differ too badly from manoeuvring between Athens, Sparta and Thebes, the kings did not often interfere directly in the internal affairs of the cities, and the Aetolian and Achaean Leagues were better than the leagues of the classical period in that they were not dominated by major cities. Athens was no longer in a position to dominate, but for half a century it did what it could to play a major role in the new world.[100] Some kings declared their commitment to the freedom of the Greeks, and in making alliances with them I dare say the

---

[94] Philoch, *FGrH* 328 F 56a.

[95] Plataea: 38,700 hoplites and more light-armed; Her. 9.28–30; Chaeronea: [Hammond]/Griffith 1979: 599 with n. 4 suggests 35,000 infantry and up to 2,000 cavalry, confronting Philip's over 30,000 infantry and 2,000 cavalry (Diod. Sic. 16.85.5).

[96] Balkans: Arr. *Anab.* 1.7.2–3; Granicus first of many occasions in Asia when Alexander's life was in danger: Arr. *Anab.* 1.15.7–8; Diod. Sic. 17.20.6.

[97] Philip's death: Diod. Sic. 17.3.2, 5.1; Plut. *Dem.* 22.1–3; Aeschin. 3. *Ctesiphon* 77–78; Thebes: Diod. Sic. 17.8.5–6; Plut. *Dem.* 23.1–2; *Alex.* 11.6.

[98] 283 ships in 357/356: *IG* II² 1611.9 (but only 120 used at Embata in 355: Diod. Sic. 16.21.1); 349 in 353/352: 1613.302; 392 triremes + 18 quadriremes = 410 in 330/329: 1627.266–269, 275–278; 360 triremes + 50 quadriremes + 2 quinqueremes = 412 in 325/324: 1629.783–812 with Ashton 1979.

[99] They used only 170 of their ships: cf. Morrison 1987.

[100] See, on the general point, Rhodes/Lewis 1997: 542; on Athens in particular, Rhodes 2006.

Athenians tried to believe that they were not (let us say) Ptolemising but Ptolemy was Atticising.[101] Except between 307 and 295 there were Macedonian garrisons in Attica; in 307 flattery required the creation of new tribes named after the "liberator" Demetrius and his father Antigonus. Nevertheless in 279/278 Athens joined in an Aetolian-led defence of Delphi against marauding Celtic tribes, and could believe that once more it was playing its part in Greek resistance to barbarian invaders. In 268/267 Athens, Sparta and other southern Greeks made an alliance with Ptolemy II against Antigonus Gonatas, to fight the Chremonidean War, and they could think of this as a Greek alliance led by the now cooperating Athens and Sparta, with the support of the friendly Ptolemy, rather than as their being caught up in a war between Antigonus and Ptolemy. But Athens and its allies were defeated in the Chremonidean War, and for a short time after that there was direct Antigonid intervention in the internal affairs of Athens. That does mark the end of Athens' attempts to be a leading city in Greece.

So what did go wrong? The ghost of empire can certainly be seen behind what happened to the Second Athenian League after Leuctra had made its original purpose irrelevant, but I do not think it can be blamed for the King's Peace before or the successes of Macedon after. (The large navy of the Eubulan and Lycurgan period was a waste of money, but money was plentiful once more and it does not seem to have been a damaging waste.) Nor should we let the orators persuade us that fourth-century Athenians were inferior to fifth-century Athenians, that everything might have been different if the poor had been more willing to give up their handouts and the rich more willing to pay *eisphora*. As for the calibre of leaders, it is certainly true that politicians and generals were seriously in danger of prosecution – the great Callistratus was acquitted in 366/365, but was condemned in absence in 361 and was put to death later when he risked returning to Athens; Hansen lists fourteen *eisangeliai* against generals between 366/365 and 356/355[102] – but there was no shortage of men willing to face the danger, and I see no reason to think that there were more able men who were frightened out of public life. After the Peace of Philocrates Demosthenes did persuade the majority of the Athenians, and many other Greeks too, that his attitude to Philip was the right attitude – but still they were beaten at Chaeronea.

There was nothing fundamentally wrong in the state of Athens. Athens' problem, as the British prime minister Harold Macmillan would have said, was "events, dear boy; events:"[103] the Spartans' success in the Hellespont in 387, which enabled them to impose the King's Peace; the chances which gave Macedon Philip II, who was too clever diplomatically and became too strong militarily for the Athenians; Alexander's succession in 336 and his success and survival in his campaigns. J. Ober in his contribution to a book of historical speculations about *What If?* suggests that, with Sparta weakened by Thebes and Thebes destroyed by Alexander, if Alexander had been killed at the Granicus in 334 Athens would once more have become the strongest state in Greece.[104] But it was not to be.

---

[101] Cf. what Agesilaus is alleged to have said about the King's Peace, see above pp. 115–116 with n. 36.

[102] Callistratus: Hansen 1975: nos. 83, 87; *eisangeliai* against generals: nos. 84, 85, 86, 88, 89, 90, 91, 93, 94, 95, 96, 100, 101, 102.

[103] Alleged reply when asked what his greatest problem was (e.g. Knowles 1998: 202 no. 8).

[104] Ober 1999.

Finally, was Demosthenes right to be afraid of Philip's supremacy? We might as well ask whether some people today are right to be afraid of the increasing power of the European Union over its member states. The benefits of belonging to what you feel to be your own unit, free to take decisions based on its own interests, have to be weighed against the benefits of belonging to a large and flourishing combination, and there may be different answers if you posit as the alternative independence for your own unit in a world in which the large combination does not exist or in a world in which the large combination does exist without you. I will say only that I can understand why the Athenians, after the history of the past hundred and fifty years, did let Demosthenes persuade them.

BIBLIOGRAPHY

Ashton, N.G. (1979): How Many *Pentereis?*, *GRBS* 20: 237–242.

Badian, E. (1991): The King's Peace, in: *Georgica ... G. Cawkwell*, (*BICS* Supp. 58), London: 25–48.

Badian, E. (1995): The Ghost of Empire. Reflections on Athenian Foreign Policy in the Fourth Century B.C., in: W. Eder (ed.), *Die athenische Demokratie im 4. Jahrhundert v. Chr. Vollendung oder Verfall einer Verfassungsform?*, Stuttgart: 79–106.

Brun, P. (1985): *IG* II² 1609 et le versement en nature de l' eisphora, *REA* 77: 307–317.

Buck, R.J. (1992): The Athenians at Thebes in 379/8 B.C., *AHB* 6: 103–109.

Buck, R.J. (1994): *Boiotia and the Boiotian League, 432–371 B.C.*, Edmonton, Alberta.

Buckler, J. (1977): On Agatharchides *F. Gr. Hist.* 86 F 8, *CQ* 2nd series 27: 33–34.

Buckler, J. (1980): *The Theban Hegemony*, Cambridge, Mass.

Buckler, J. (2000): The Phantom *Synedrion* of the Boiotian Confederacy, in: P. Flensted-Jensen, T.H. Nielsen, L. Rubinstein (eds.), *Polis and Politics ... M.H. Hansen*, Copenhagen: 431–446.

Buckler, J., Beck, H. (2008): *Central Greece and the Politics of Power in the Fourth Century B.C.*, Cambridge.

Cargill, J.L. (1981): *The Second Athenian League. Empire or Free Alliance?*, Berkeley–Los Angeles.

Cawkwell, G.L. (1962): The Defence of Olynthus, *CQ* 2nd series 12: 122–140.

Cawkwell, G.L. (1963a): Notes on the Peace of 375/4, *Historia* 12: 84–95.

Cawkwell, G.L. (1963b): Eubulus, *JHS* 83: 47–67.

Cawkwell, G.L. (1973): The Foundation of the Second Athenian Confederacy, *CQ* 2nd series 23: 47–60.

Cawkwell, G.L. (1976): The Imperialism of Thrasybulus, *CQ* 2nd series 26: 270–277.

Cawkwell, G.L. (1981): Notes on the Failure of the Second Athenian Confederacy, *JHS* 101: 40–55.

de Ste. Croix, G.E.M. (1963): The Alleged Secret Pact between Athens and Philip II Concerning Amphipolis and Pydna, *CQ 2nd* series 13: 110–119.

Gabrielsen, V. (1994): *Financing the Athenian Fleet. Public Taxation and Social Relations*, Baltimore.

Grote, G. (1869/1884): *History of Greece*, "new edition" in 12 volumes, London.

Grote, G. (1888): *History of Greece*, "new edition" in 10 volumes, London.

Hammond, N.G.L., Griffith, G.T. (1979): *A History of Macedonia*, vol. II, Oxford.

Hansen, M.H. (1975): *Eisangelia. The Sovereignty of the People's Court in Athens in the Fourth Century B.C. and the Impeachment of Generals and Politicians*, Odense.

Hansen, M.H. (1976): The Theoric Fund and the *Graphe Paranomon* against Apollodorus, *GRBS* 17: 235–246.

Hansen, M.H. (1986): *Demography and Demography*, Herning.

Hansen, M.H. (1988): *Three Studies in Athenian Demography*, Copenhagen.

Hansen, M.H. (2005): *The Tradition of Ancient Greek Democracy and Its Importance for Modern De-mocracy*, Copenhagen.

Hansen, M.H. (2006): *Polis. An Introduction to the Ancient Greek City-State*, Oxford.

Hanson, V.D. (1998): *Warfare and Agriculture in Classical Greece*, 2nd ed., Berkeley–Los Angeles.

Harding, P. (1995): Athenian Foreign Policy in the Fourth Century, *Klio* 77: 105–125.

Harris, E.M. (1996): Demosthenes and the Theoric Fund, in: R. Wallace, E.M. Harris (eds.), *Transitions to Empire ... E. Badian*, Norman, Okla: 57–76.

Harris, E.M. (2000): The Authenticity of Andokides' *De Pace*. A Subversive Essay, in: P. Flensted-Jensen, T. H. Nielsen, L. Rubinstein (eds.), *Polis and Politics ... M.H. Hansen*, Copenhagen: 479–505.

Harris, E.M. (2006): *Democracy and the Rule of Law in Classical Athens*, New York–Cambridge.

Jehne, M. (1992): Die Anerkennng der athenischen Besitzansprüche auf Amphipolis und die Chersones. Zu den Implikationen der Territorialklause ἔχειν τὰ ἑαυτῶν in den Verträgen des 4. Jahrhunderts v. Chr., *Historia* 41: 272–282.

Keen, A.G. (1995): A "Confused" Passage of Philochoros (F 149A) and the Peace of 392/1, *Historia* 44: 1–10.

Keen, A.G. (1998): Philochoros F 149 A & B. A Further Note, *Historia* 47: 375–378.

Knowles, E. (1998): *The Oxford Dictionary of Twentieth Century Quotations*, Oxford.

Krentz, P. (1995): *Xenophon, Hellenika, 2.3.11–4.2.8*, Warminster.

Lane Fox, R.J. (1997): Demosthenes, Dionysius and the Dating of Six Early Speeches, *C&M* 48: 167–203.

Lewis, D.M. (1954): Notes on Attic Inscriptions, vi. The Epistates of the Proedroi, *BSA* 49: 31–34.

Lewis, D.M. (1990): The Synedrion of the Boeotian Alliance, in: A. Schachter (ed.), *Essays in the Topography, History and Culture of Boiotia*, (*Teiresias* Supp. 3), Montreal: 71–73.

Lewis, D.M. (1997): *Selected Papers in Greek and Near Eastern History*, Cambridge.

Lewis, D.M., Stroud, R.S. (1979): "Athens Honors King Euagoras of Salamis," *Hesperia* 48: 180–193.

MacDowell, D.M. (1990): *Demosthenes Against Meidias*, Oxford.

Markle, M.M. (1974): The Strategy of Philip in 346 B.C., *CQ* 2nd series 24: 253–268.

Montgomery, H. (1983): *The Way to Chaeronea. Foreign Policy, Decision Making and Political Influence in Demosthenes' Speeches*, Bergen.

Morrison, J.S. (1987): Athenian Sea-Power in 323/2 B.C. Dream and Reality, *JHS* 107: 88–97.

Ober, J. (1999): Conquest Denied. The Premature Death of Alexander the Great, in: R. Cowley (ed.), *What If: Military Historians Imagine What Might Have Been*, New York: 37–56.

Rhodes, P.J. (1972): *The Athenian Boule*, Oxford.

Rhodes, P.J. (1981): *A Commentary on the Aristotelian Athenaion Politeia*, Oxford.

Rhodes, P.J. (1994): The Polis and the Alternatives, *CAH*[2] VI: 565–591.

Rhodes, P.J. (2006): "Classical" and "Hellenistic" in Athenian History, *Electrum* 11: 27–43.

Rhodes, P.J. (2008): Making and Breaking Treaties in the Greek World, in: P. de Souza, J. France (eds.), *War and Peace in Ancient and Medieval History*, Cambridge: 6–27.

Rhodes, P.J. (2010): *A History of the Classical Greek World, 478–323 B.C.*, 2nd ed., Chichester.

Rhodes, P.J., Lewis, D.M. (1997): *The Decrees of the Greek States*, Oxford.

Rhodes, P.J., Osborne, R. (2003): *Greek Historical Inscriptions, 404–323 B.C.*, Oxford.

Rice, D.G. (1975): Xenophon, Diodorus and the Year 379/378 B.C. Reconstruction and Reappraisal, *YCS* 24: 95–130.

Romilly, J. de (2005): *L'Élan démocratique dans l'Athènes ancienne*, Paris.

Ryder, T.T.B. (1965): *Koine Eirene. General Peace and Local Independence in Ancient Greece*, Oxford.

Samons, L.J. (2004): *What's Wrong with Democracy? From Athenian Practice to American Worship*, Berkeley–Los Angeles.

Seager, R. (1967): Thrasybulus, Conon and Athenian Imperialism, 396–386 B.C., *JHS* 87: 95–115.

Sinclair, R.K. (1978): The King's Peace and the Employment of Military and Naval Forces, 387–378, *Chiron* 8: 29–54.

Sordi, M. (1951): La pace di Atene del 370 a.C., *RFIC* 79 (= 2nd series 29): 34–64.

Spek, R.J. van der (1998): The Chronology of the Wars of Artaxerxes II in the Babylonian Astronomical Diaries, *Achaemenid History* 11: 239–254.

Thorne, J.A. (2001): Warfare and Agriculture. The Economic Aspect of Devastation in Classical Greece, *GRBS* 43: 225–253.

Tuplin, C. (1984): Timotheus and Corcyra. Problems in Greek History, 375–373 B.C., *Athenaeum*, 2nd series 62: 537–568.

Wilamowitz-Moellendorff, U. von (1893): *Aristoteles und Athen*, Berlin.

Zahrnt, M. (1971): *Olynth und die Chalkidier*, (*Vestigia* 14), München.

ELECTRUM * Vol. 19 (2012): 131–135
doi:10.4467/20800009EL.12.007.0748

How Many Companions did Philip II have?

Jacek Rzepka

Abstract: This paper deals with a famous passage by Theopompus concerning the *hetairoi* of Philip II. Athenaeus, one of the three authors who transmitted this fragment to us, states that Philip had 800 *hetairoi* in 339, which seems to be too low a number for the last years of the reign. In search of a solution which would match Athenaeus' quotation from Theopompus with other data about Macedonian cavalry under Philip and Alexander, I consider a textual corruption in Athenaeus.

Keywords: Theopompus, Athenaeus, Philip II of Macedon, Alexander the Great, *hetairoi*.

Modern scholars unanimously credit Philip II with making the Macedonian armed forces an efficient instrument of conquest. However, whereas they agree in general terms in this regard, they vary greatly in details. One such much discussed detail is the strength of the Macedonian cavalry in the reign of Philip.

The most important piece of evidence in this respect is a version of Theopompus' insulting portrait of Philip's *Friends/Companions* preserved in Book VI of Athenaeus' *Learned Banqueters* (Athen. 6.77 p. 260 D – 61 A = *FGrH* 115 F 225b). This fragment of Theopompus was notorious in Antiquity for its abusive language. A slightly differing version of it may be found in Polybius (Polyb. 8.11. 5–13 = *FGrH* 115 F 225a), and the opening sentences of the same passage are also cited by Pseudo-Demetrius of Phalerum, the author of *On Style* (Demetr. *De eloc.* 27 = FGrH 115 F 225c). The almost verbatim similarity between the texts transmitted by Polybius and Athenaeus makes it clear that both authors used the same original with the intention of reproducing it in the original wording. Polybius' version is the longest one, but it is Athenaeus, who – having removed some content preserved in Polybius – closes his quotation with a sentence suggesting that Philip II had 800 Companions or Friends, whom he awarded with land, which normally would have been cultivated by the 10,000 richest Greeks:

οἴομαι γὰρ τοὺς ἑταίρους οὐ πλείονας ὄντας κατ᾽ ἐκεῖνον τὸν χρόνον ὀκτακοσίων οὐκ ἐλάττω καρπίζεσθαι γῆν ἢ μυρίους τῶν Ἑλλήνων τοὺς τὴν ἀρίστην καὶ πλείστην χώραν κεκτημένους.

I think that these companions, who numbered at the time not more than eight hundred, enjoyed the profits of as much land as any ten thousand Greeks possessing the richest and the most extensive land.

A problem with this fragment is that the term *hetairos* was used by ancient authors for both the king's courtiers (advisers, guests and most trusted commanders and fighters or simply *court hetairoi*) and Macedonian heavy cavalrymen. We do not know who Theopompus actually meant: court *hetairoi* or cavalrymen. Since he uses the word *philoi* as a synonym for *hetairoi* in F 225, there are some scholars who tend to think that Theopompus meant the court *hetairoi*. Theopompus' figure of 800 is obviously too large for the inner circle of Philip's advisers or court *hetairoi*, and another explanation must be sought. Therefore, Michael Flower assumes that 800 might be a corruption of a smaller number, such as 80.[1]

Admittedly, Theopompus' wording is unclear (and deliberately so, I suspect) and any interpretation of who the Companions or Friends actually were may seem arbitrary.[2] However, since the historian from Chios alludes to the Companions as would-be killers (*andraphonoi*), I am tempted to agree with those scholars who think that this passage refers to the Cavalry Companions. The figure of 800 *hetairoi* must therefore be dealt with as an important piece of information about the organization of the Macedonian cavalry under Philip II.

Unfortunately, it must be said that this statement poses some problems. The digression on *hetairoi* comes from Book XLIV of *Philippika*, which focused on the events of the year 339.[3] Although it is not necessarily so that the number of 800 cavalrymen mentioned by Theopompus referred to this year, we should assume that in this highly rhetorical passage the historian from Chios gave the highest number that Philip's cavalry had ever reached. Thus this figure must be valid for 339. The "800" is a number slightly higher than the 600 horse mobilized against Bardylis in 358 (Diodorus 16.4.3). It is also significantly lower than the figures for Alexander's cavalry on the crossing to Asia in 334 (1800 Macedonian cavalrymen according to D.S. 17. 17. 4) or the overall number of Macedonian horse (3300, also including the 1500 cavalry of Antipater – Diodorus 17.17. 5).[4] This discrepancy was not overlooked by modern scholars. Some believe that the figure of Theopompus refers to the earlier years of Philip's reign, and perhaps to the time when Philip was reforming his armed forces.[5] Some others argue that the 800 were the only *hetairoi* in the strict sense of the word, and that there were other Macedonian heavy cavalrymen without that name or prestige.[6] George Cawkwell assumed that this figure

---

[1]   Flower 1994: 111–112, n. 35.

[2]   There is no doubt that this passage is a piece of exaggerated rhetoric. Still, we may assume that Theopompus based his harangues on some real facts.

[3]   Shrimpton 1991: 63.

[4]   There are a few diverging attempts at understanding the organization of Alexander's mounted forces. The most influential reconstruction is by P. Brunt (1963: 27–46), but see also J. Rzepka (2008: 39–56), arguing for six-partite division of both the Macedonian horse and foot.

[5]   Hammond 1989: 141.

[6]   Momigliano 1934: 136–137; Griffith 1979: 404.

referred to the *Companions settled by Philip in newly conquered lands* only.[7] The fourth and most courageous suggestion is that the number of Macedonian cavalry grew rapidly between 338 and 334, in the last months of Philip and the opening years of Alexander.[8]

The first of these solution is the easiest one, but at the same time not satisfactory at all. The second one seems unlikely, if we agree that a mass force of *pezetairoi* already existed under Philip. Regardless of controversies over the proper interpretation of Anaximenes (*FGrH* 72 F 4), another passage of Theopompus concerning female foot-prostitutes led by the Athenian general Chares makes it almost certain.[9] If the *pezetairoi* were already a mass army in the mid-340s,[10] we can hardly imagine a restriction of the name of *hetairoi* to a narrow elite only. Thus the most appealing solution might be a dramatic growth in both Macedonian manpower and prosperity in the early 330s. However, it is not easy to imagine how Alexander could enhance the Macedonian cavalry so quickly without becoming famous as a donor of land estates,[11] whereas Philip, who was repeatedly praised as the man who had resettled Macedonians and divided the territory of the kingdom, would have been unable to strengthen this army.

Therefore, we should look for another explanation. My guess is that perhaps the text of Theopompus in Athenaeus is corrupted. Numerals are well known to disappear from the hand-transmitted texts easily and with no trace of corruption.[12] A textual corruption

---

[7] Cawkwell 1978: 38. An alternative answer by Cawkwell is that *it was the number of the Greek adventurers who had gone to Macedon to share in Philip's largesse, which would have been in new lands.* This is, however, not likely. Theopompus underscores in F 224 that Philip's Companions or Friends were a multi-ethnic band: «εἰ γάρ τις ἦν ἐν τοῖς Ἕλλησιν ἢ τοῖς βαρβάροις»> φησί <«λάσταυρος ἢ θρασὺς τὸν τρόπον, οὗτοι πάντες εἰς Μακεδονίαν ἀθροιζόμενοι πρὸς Φίλιππον ἑταῖροι τοῦ βασιλέως προσηγορεύοντο, where *barbaroi* may well refer to the Macedonians.

[8] Sekunda 2009: 330, where he states that *Alexander III is alleged to have alienated nearly all crown lands to the Companions prior to the Asian campaign* (Plut. *Alex.* 15.3–4). Plutarch's passage may be well an allusion to the second, stage, this time Alexander's, of enhancing the Macedonian cavalry, which perhaps provided 1500 fresh horsemen's estates of Antipater.

[9] ὅς γε περιήγετο στρατευόμενος αὐλητρίδας καὶ ψαλτρίας καὶ πεζὰς ἑταίρας – *while waging war he led flute-girls, female harpists and female foot-companions* (Athen. 12.43 p. 532 C = *FGrH* 115 F 213 from Book XLV of *Philippica*). Andrew Erskine assumes that *the joke here is that Chares had a footguard of* ἑταίραι on the basis of his argument that Philip's *pezhetairoi* were an elite army (Erskine 1989, 388). However, this pun introduces a tripartite division of prostitutes in Chares' army, which should reflect some structure in the army having *pezhetairoi*. The "foot hetairai" are introduced as the last, and so occupy the least prestigious place in Chares' female army. This may indicate that Theopompus was not so consistent in depicting *pezhetairoi* as an elite unit, as Erskine and also E. Anson (1985: 246–248) insist. They may still be the bulk of the Macedonian foot-soldiers. Anson and Erskine may overestimate the meaning of *epilektos/apolektos* used to describe *pezhetairoi*, for the use of the term *epilektoi* in the sense of a well-trained mass army as opposed to a simple levée en masse; see Rzepka 2009: 18–30.

[10] Goukowsky (1987: 243–248) argues that *asthetairoi* were a subclass of *phalangitai*, next in rank to *pezhetairoi*, virtually equal to the foot *agema*, and seems not to have appreciated the real meaning of Curtius Rufus 3.9.7 presenting a *taxis* of Amyntas as *peregrini milites* who were *in societatem nuper adsciti*. Philip II used to resettle various peoples in order to merge them into one nation (Iust. 8.6.1). In the case of Amyntas' unit a mass naturalization in Macedonia was meant, and an admission *in societatem* must be equal to making them *hetairoi* of a kind, i.e. *pezhetairoi*.

[11] Alexander was, of course, active in this field, too, as a letter to Philippi and the Kallindoia dedication prove (both texts were re-edited conveniently as Hatzopoulos 1996: nos. 6 and 62).

[12] Robert Develin (1990: 31–45) tried to show that numerals were transmitted in the manuscript tradition with special care, so in manuscripts mistakes in numerals are quite rare. This, however, seems to be in discord

has already been considered by Flower,[13] but his hypothetical figure of 80 would not explain satisfactorily how the text had been corrupted.

If we look closer at the crucial sentence in *FGrH* 115 F 225b, we must notice that the number of *hetairoi* is exactly one thousand less than the actual Macedonian mounted force in the army of Alexander (800 + 1000 = 1800). I would pursue the hypothesis that we should add the numeral *thousand* in the phrase *though these companions numbered at the time not more than eight hundred*. Thus we would obtain:

οὐ πλείονας ὄντας κατ' ἐκεῖνον τὸν χρόνον <χιλίων> ὀκτακοσίων.

The possible loss of χιλίων from our manuscripts may be not so difficult to explain if we remember that the preceding word was χρόνον, which begins and ends with the same letters as χιλίων (χ, ν). Since from the 2ⁿᵈ century AD onwards the letters o and ω may have been pronounced in the same way,[14] the possibility that a copier lost one χ–word after another χ-word, both ending with ον/ων, is even more appealing.

According to this suggestion Alexander would in Asia have had the same number of Companion cavalry as his father in the last year before Chaeronea.[15] The 1500 cavalrymen left to Antipater might not have been included in Theopompus' figures because they had not been elite soldiers, as were 1800 people in Alexander's army. It is obvious that a cavalryman's military education demanded much more time than a footman's training, and perhaps, 1500 horse of Antipater were Alexander's addition to Philip's army. During Alexander's campaign the Macedonians were unable to muster cavalry in the ideal 1:10 proportion to infantry,[16] and this shows that – contrary to popular opinion – the Macedonian cavalry lacked manpower, and that this army was always developed when possibilities appeared. It is possible, therefore, that the number of Alexander's Macedonian cavalry was reflected in the description of *hetairoi/philoi* in Theopompus.

These premises may perhaps for many be insufficient to prove that we should conjecture Philip's 800 *hetairoi* in Theopompus to 1800. However, this solution seems worth considering, and as such is proposed to the scholarly community.

---

with the opinions of most modern students of textual criticism and with what the ancient Greeks themselves thought about textual corruption of numerals; see Renehan 1969, 58.

[13]   See n. 1.

[14]   Blass 1890: 37; Sturtevant 1940: 47 (stressing that the pace of changes towards the identical pronunciation of both vowels varied depending on the region of the Greek world).

[15]   We should also note that if there were just 800 *hetairoi* of Philip with estates more valuable than estates of 10,000 Greeks possessing the richest soils, the financial resources of an average Companion would be 12.5 times greater than those of the wealthy Greeks of that time. This is rather unbelievable, when we consider that usually horsemen were paid between two and three times better than heavy or elite infantrymen – there is no difference between mercenary armies and citizen ones in this respect (see the estimates of *sitarchiai*, Launey 1949, 757). The Hellenistic data of Launey cannot be misleading for the Late Classical period). The proportion of financial resources available to Philip's cavalrymen and average Greek hoplites, which we reach by assuming 1800 *hetairoi*, is far more likely, if still unusually high.

[16]   Rzepka 2008: 52–53.

BIBLIOGRAPHY

Anson, E. (1985): The Hypaspists: Macedonia's Professional Citizen-Soldiers, *Historia* 34: 246–248.

Blass, F. (1890): *Pronunciation of Ancient Greek Translated from the Third German Edition of Dr Blass with the Author's Sanction by W.J. Purton*, Cambridge.

Brunt, P.A. (1963): Alexander's Macedonian Cavalry, *JHS* 83: 27–46.

Cawkwell, G. (1978): *Philip of Macedon*, Boston.

Develin, R. (1990): Numeral Corruption in Greek Historical Texts, *Phoenix* 44: 31–45.

Erskine, A. (1989): The πεζέταιροι of Philip II and Alexander III, *Historia* 38: 385–394.

Flower, M.A. (1994): *Theopompus of Chios: History and Rhetoric in the Fourth Century BC*, Oxford.

Goukowsky, P. (1987): Makedonika, *REG* 100: 240–255.

Griffith, G.T. (1979): Part Two, in: N.G.L. Hammond & G.T. Griffith, *A History of Macedonia*, vol. II, Oxford.

Hammond, N.G.L. (1989): *The Macedonian State*, Oxford.

Hatzopoulos, M. (1996): *Macedonian Institutions under the Kings*, vol. 2: *Epigraphic Evidence*, Athens.

Momigliano, A. (1934): *Filippo il Macedone*, Firenze.

Launey, M. (1949): *Recherches sur les armeés hellénistiques*, 2 vols., Paris.

Renehan, R. (1969): *Greek Textual Criticism: A Reader*, Cambridge (Mass.).

Rzepka, J. (2008): The Units in the Army of Alexander the Great and the District Divisions of Late Argead Macedonia, *GRBS* 48: 39–56.

Rzepka, J. (2009): *The Aetolian Elite Warriors and Fifth-Century Roots of the Hellenistic Confederacy*, Warszawa.

Sekunda, N.V. (2009): Macedonian Military Forces. A. Land Forces, in: H. van Wees, P. Sabin (eds.), *The Cambridge History of Greek and Roman Warfare*, vol. I, Cambridge: 325–357.

Shrimpton, G.S. (1991): *Theopompus the Historian*, Montreal.

Sturtevant, E.H. (1940): *The Pronunciation of Greek and Latin*, Philadelphia.

ELECTRUM * Vol. 19 (2012): 137–147
doi:10.4467/20843909EL.12.008.0749

REMARKS ON ARISTOTLE'S *THETTALON POLITEIA*

Sławomir Sprawski

Abstract: This article attempts to make a critical assessment of the preserved fragments of *Thettalon politeia* as a source on the history of early Thessaly. The traces of the existence of this text come from the second half of the 2nd century CE at the earliest, but even then it was seen as one of the *Politeiai* recorded by Aristotle. As a result of this attribution, information from this text is treated as a reliable source of knowledge on the *koinon* organization of the Thessalians and their joint army. There are, however, important reasons to treat this source with the greatest caution: we have only six short quotations from the work available, and the part which refers to Aleuas' supposed reforms is very much damaged and has been subjected to a number of emendations by its various publishers. The description of the system of mobilization of the Thessalian army from *Thettalon politeia* seems anachronistic, and probably arose under the influence of information about the reorganization of the army conducted in the 370s BCE by Jason of Pherae and the propaganda that accompanied these changes.

Keywords: Aristotle, *Thettalon politeia*, Thessaly, Aleuas the Red, Jason of Pherae, peltast.

Among the most important sources concerning the history of Thessaly in the Archaic and Classical period are the preserved fragments of *Thettalon politeia*. We can assume that it may have come about as one of the studies of political systems, *Politeiai*, written around 330 BCE by Aristotle himself or one of his pupils. Aristotle's authority is such that this information is treated as a reliable source of knowledge on the organization of the Thessalians' *koinon* as well as their joint army. There are, however, important reasons to treat this source with the greatest caution. Firstly, all quotations from *Thettalon politeia* are very fragmentary. Secondly, the text of the most important one, referring to Aleuas' supposed reforms, is very much damaged and has been subjected to a number of emendations. Thirdly, the description of the system of mobilization of the Thessalian army appears to be anachronistic.

Thettalon politeia

It is worth beginning any analysis of the information provided by *Thettalon politeia* by reflecting on the state in which this source is preserved. We are in possession of just three quotations which mention the work's title and unambiguously point to its origin.

Unfortunately, the titles they give, while similar, do differ somewhat. In his *Fragmenta Historicorum Graecorum*, K.O. Müller includes only the three mentioned extracts, concluding that the work was entitled Κοινή Θετταλῶν πολιτεία, since this is the title given by Harpocration. However, in his publication of extracts of the unpreserved works of Aristotle, Valentin Rose identifies six passages which were preserved in quotations by 15 authors. He concludes, based on Photius, that the work was entitled Θετταλῶν πολιτεία.[1] Rose complemented his selection by adding to them quotations referring to Thessalian affairs, although the title of the work they come from does not crop up. A short list of the issues to which his selected extracts refer is as follows:

F 495: mention of the origin of the vine name *Aminaeos*;

F 496: explanation of the origin of the names of the place Korakas – The Crows;

F 497: information about the division of Thessaly carried out by Aleuas into four regions called moiras or tetrads;

F 498: information about the division of Thessaly carried out by Aleusas into kleroi, each of which has to provide 40 horsemen and 80 hoplites;

F 499: a mention of the wine vessel which the Thessalians called *lagynos*;

F 500: deliberations on the topic of the difference between two types of clothes: *chlamis* and *chlaina*.

The passages identified by Rose mostly do not concern political matters. This might come as a surprise to those who know the content of *Athenaion Politeia* and arouse suspicion as to whether all the quotations cited in fact come from *Thettalon politeia*. However, for some time the view has been dominant that the description of Athens's political system – the only one completely preserved from the whole collection – cannot be treated as a model when reconstructing the content of other descriptions. This doubt is also to a certain degree dispelled by the testimony of Athenaeus. Explaining the term *lagynos*, he clearly indicates that he took it from *Thettalon politeia*.[2] The situation is similar with analysis of most of the preserved extracts from other Aristotle's *Politeiai*. Research on these passages has shown that their content was very diverse, and could to a great extent contain information far from descriptions of political institutions and their evolution. Hence the conclusion that *Athenaion Politeia* in the collection *Politeiai* was rather the exception than a typical case. Such a diversity of contents makes it difficult to define what these *Politeiai* actually were. There is no information to prove that Aristotle or his pupils travelled to collect information on various cities. They must have based their conclusions on various texts available in Athens, both historiographical and geographical works as well as poetry. This may have been complemented by oral information provided by the numerous foreigners coming to Athens.[3] The content of the various works must have been very diverse, but we can say for sure that few of the books were on a par with *Athenaion Politeia*. It is hard to imagine there being a comparable amount of information in Athens on the political systems and history of any other city as the information on local history. We hear that a work called *Thettalika* was written by Hellanicus, to which Harpocration refers when explaining the division of Thessaly into

---

[1] Harpocration, s.v. τετραρχία; Photius, *Bibliotheka* 161, 104 B.

[2] K.O. Müller, *Fragmenta Historicorum Graecorum*, Paris 1878, vol. II, 151 F 145 (= Harpocration, s.v. τετραρχία); F 145 a (= Athen. 11.499b) and F 146 (= Philargyrius in Virgil. *Georg.* 2.97).

[3] Toye 1999: 235–253.

tetrads. We also have evidence of interest in its political system in the form of information that Critias, the later leader of the so-called Thirty Tyrants, stayed in Thessaly and was the author of a description of its system. Athenaeus refers to this work when writing about the Thessalians' exceptional wealth.[4] We do not know the nature of Critias' work. The evidence on his stay and activities in Thessaly are very limited and conflicting. They may, however, bear witness to Critias' interest in the social relations and political system that prevailed in Thessaly. We can assume that his work was not a systematic description of the Thessalian constitution, but rather a political pamphlet in the style of the pseudo-Xenophonic *Constitution of Athens*. It is also difficult to determine what the literary form of Aristotle's *Thettalon politeia* was. We can do this only with reference to the example of *Athenaion Politeia*, although, as mentioned earlier, this cannot be treated as a mode. Plutarch, reading the collection of *Politeiai* of unknown titles, was delighted by the pleasures this brought. These pleasures might have just been the type enjoyed only by an eccentric man of letters enamored of the distant past.[5] However, we cannot rule out the possibility that, if it was not Aristotle who was the author of all these works, then the various authors of the texts could have given them a very diverse stylistic form. Among these there may have been works which were very accomplished in literary terms. Unfortunately it is not clear whether the description of the Thessalian system was among these.

Information on *Thettalon politeiai* comes relatively late. Above all, this work is not mentioned in *Heraclidis Epitome*, the 13th century manuscript containing short summaries of descriptions of the political system. The author of these abstracts is identified as Heraclides Lembos, an Alexandrian scholar from the 2nd century BCE.[6] The catalogue of works of Aristotle passed on by Diogenes Laertius refers to 158 *Politeiai*, yet *Heraclidis Epitome* contains short extracts from just 44 descriptions of the systems. If the figure given by Diogenes is correct, then Heraclides' *Epitome* features (approximately) fragments of only a quarter of the total number. The selection of descriptions appears to have been done without any particular reason, which is why it is justified to assume that *Epitome* mentions only those which were known to Heraclides. *Thettalon politeia* was clearly not among these. Unfortunately, we do not know whether this work was one read by Plutarch. However, a summary of it was included in the 12th book of *Eklogai diaphorai* by Sopater of Apamea, writing at the beginning of the 4th century CE. Sopater's work is known to us only from a review written by Photius, who claimed to have found summaries in it: *the Constitutions of Aristotle, dealing with those of the Thessalians, Achaeans, Parians, Lycians, Chians, and of all the peoples whom he has mentioned in his political writings.*[7] The selection of the aforementioned works is a little surprising, as is the inclusion of *Thettalon Politeia* in first place. Thanks to this evidence, however, it is possible to state that at the time of Sopater a work with this title was still available. The last trace of this text's being used appears to be the Latin commentary to Virgil's

---

   [4]   Hellanicus: *FGrH* 4 F 52; Critias: *FGrH* 244 F 222 = Athen. 14.663a. On Critias' activities in Thessaly see Sprawski 1999: 31–34; Jordovic 2008: 37–46.
   [5]   Plut. *Mor.* 1093c.
   [6]   Bloch 1940: 27–39.
   [7]   Phot. 161 104b–105a (translated by J.H. Freese).

Georgics written in the manuscript as a work of Philargirius, an author of whom we do not know any more, but writing in Late Antiquity.[8]

The earliest traces of the use of *Thettalon politeia* seem to lead only to the second half of the 2nd century CE. It was at this time that Diogenianos' dictionary was produced, and the authors of the scholia on Plato put together in Late Antiquity were able to use this.[9] The work of Athenaeus of Naucratis and Harpocration, who mention the title of this work, is dated to the late 2nd century CE. The usual explanation for the clear similarities between the works of these two authors is that Athenaeus made use of the lexicon of his colleague, or that both authors, working in Egypt, may have had access to the lexica and commentaries still existing during their lifetimes and later lost.[10] It may be that the text of *Thettalon politeia*, which previously had not aroused a great deal of interest, was only noticed by Harpocration. We know that he studied the texts of ancient historians. There is no doubt that he used *Athenaion politeia*, which he cites some 50 times in his lexicon. Even if Harpocration had the text of *Thettalon politeia* to hand, we cannot be entirely sure that it was the text produced in Aristotle's school. After the philosopher's death, his library was partially dispersed. Ptolemy II Philadelphus is said to have bought Aristotle's manuscripts from various owners, accumulating a collection in Alexandria numbering over 1000 scrolls. It is entirely possible that among them were works whose authorship was only attributed to Aristotle because of the subject matter, or those which just came from his library. This is made all the more likely by the assumption that the works had not one, but many authors.[11]

Aleuas' reforms

A description of the reforms said to have been carried out in Thessaly by Aleuas seems to be the most interesting of the preserved passages from *Thettalon politeia*. Information on this subject is provided by two quotations. The first of these (F 497 Rose) comes from the explanation of the word *tetrarchia* in Harpocration's lexicon. With reference to Timaeus, the author states that Thessaly was divided into four parts (mere), i.e. tetrads. The second quotation (F 498 Rose) comes from anonymous *scholia* on Euripides' tragedy *Rhesus*:

> πολλὰ πελταστῶν τέλη· πέλτη ἀσπὶς ἐστιν ἴτυν οὐκ ἔχουσα, καθάπερ φησὶν Ἀριστοτέλης ἐν τῇ Θεσσαλῶν πολιτείᾳ γράφων οὕτως· διελὼ δὲ τὴν πόλιν Ἀλόας ἔταξε καὶ κλῆρον παρέχειν ἑκάστην ἱππέας μὲν τεσσαράκοντα, ὁπλίτας δὲ ὀγδοήκοντα ... – ἦν δὲ ἡ πέλτη ἀσπὶς ἴτυν οὐκ ἔχουσα ἐπίχαλκος αἰγὸς δέρματι περιτεταμένη – καὶ τριάκοντια οἳ καὶ μακρὸν δόρυ πάντες ἐφόρουν ὃ σχέδιον ἐκαλειτο (*Schol. Ad Eurip. Rhes.* v 307)

The author of the *scholion* concentrates on the description of *pelte* – a particular type of shield distinguished by goatskin padding and the lack of a rim reinforcing its edges.

---

[8]   Daintree 1990: 68–69.

[9]   Dickey 2007: 46–47.

[10]   Zecchini 2000: 153–160.

[11]   Sprawski 2008: 107–116. On the subject of Harpocration's knowledge of Aristotle's works see Zecchini 2000: 156. On the fate of Aristotle's library see *Diog. Laert.* 5.51–2; Athen. 1.4.3 a–b; Strab. 13.1.54; Plut. *Sull.* 26; Keaney 1963: 58–63; Lindsay 1997: 290–298.

He refers here to a passage taken from Aristotle's *Thettalon politeia* concerning Aleusas' reforms. We learn from this that Aleuas divided a *polis* into *kleroi*, each of which was to provide 40 horsemen and 80 hoplites.[12]

Almost every sentence of the scholion triggered discussion and led to attempts to make emendations to the text. Even at first glance it is not hard to notice that the mention of Aleuas' reforms does not particularly fit the remaining parts of the scholion, that is the description of the *pelte* and offensive weapons worn by unspecified warriors. There is no explanation of what connects this type of weapons with the mounted units and hoplites which the Thessalian *kleroi* were supposed to provide.

This incoherence in the text of the *scholion* has long bothered scholars. One of the first commentators on this passage, the German scholar Ludwig Preller, reached the conclusion that the text is damaged, and part of it must have been lost.[13] C.G. Cobet, meanwhile, who published *Scholia on Euripides* (1849), opted for another solution, making an emendation to the text. He replaced the expression "eighty hoplites" with "eighty peltasts,"[14] thus referring to the obvious association of the name of the shield with the name of a type of light infantry. However, Cobet's emendation was not recognized by later editors of the *scholia*.

Half a century later, the scholion became the subject of analysis of Eduard Meyer, who also reached the conclusion that the problematic part required an emendation. Evidence for this in his opinion was the fact that the Thessalian hoplites are very rarely mentioned in sources in comparison with the cavalry or light infantry. He therefore proposed two solutions. The first of these was based on the assumption that the text of the scholion was complete but damaged. In this case Cobet's emendation should be acknowledged as correct. According to the second the text is not damaged, but just incomplete, and originally – following the reference to the size of the hoplite contingent – contained information about the size of the peltast contingent. These soldiers, analogically to the army of Jason from the 370s BCE described by Xenophon, were provided by *hypekooi* or *symmachoi*, that is the neighbors of the Thessalians.[15] A proponent of the latter solution was H.D. Wade-Gery, who concluded that after the words "eighty hoplites" and before the explanation of the word *pelte* there must have been the claim that the lands belonging to the Thessalian *perioikoi* (ἐκ δὲ τῆς περιοικίδος), Aleuas had given the instruction to provide peltasts.[16] This complementation of the text has been accepted by many scholars. The only reservation has been the uncertainty as to whether the *perioikoi* at the time when this reform was conducted were subordinate to the Thessalians.[17] According to Bruno Helly, the Thessalians took control over the *perioikoi* immediately after Aleuas' reforms. Based on this assumption, he arrived at the belief at the Thessalian army could not do without the light infantry, who, as with Jason's army, constituted an inseparable

---

[12]   Helly 1995: 153–154.

[13]   Preller 1848: 138.

[14]   *Scholia antiqua in Euripidis tragoedias ex recensione C.G. Cobeti*, Lipsiae 1849, Rhesus v. 307 – πελταστὰς δὲ ὀγδοήκοντα.

[15]   Meyer 1909: 222 n. 1.

[16]   Wade-Gery 1924: 58–59.

[17]   Among those who have supported the acceptance of an emendation is Marta Sordi (1958: 67 and 319 n. 4); a more critical approach was maintained J.A.O. Larsen (1960: 237; 1968: 17).

part of it, offering crucial support to the cavalry and the hoplites. If the army could not do without the light infantry, the Thessalians could not have only comprised units provided by their neighbors. In Helly's opinion, the extract from *Thettalon politeia* cited in the scholia must have referred to the appointment of the peltasts from Thessaly itself among the *penestes* – the people of lower status who lived there. Although we do not have any direct mention of *penestes* serving as light infantry, we do hear that they were summoned for military service. Xenophon mentions that in the 370s Jason of Pherae wanted to use them as crew for warships. Demosthenes, meanwhile, invokes the example of Menon of Pharsalos, who he says provided the cavalry unit from his own *penestes*, then sending it as support for the Athenians fighting for Eion in 476/475.[18]

The above examples show the extent to which the scholion we are analyzing was the subject of the emendations of editors. Some of these corrections seem very obvious, such as Pflugk's proposal to change the name "Aloas" appearing in the manuscripts to "Aleuas." A more detailed analysis of the changes introduced by the various publishers was conducted by H.T. Wade-Gery, and it is therefore only necessary to point to a few of them here. Wade-Gery was struck in particular by the unusual use of the word *polis*. The context of the sentence suggests that the word was used with reference to the whole of Thessaly, although it would be more natural to use *ethnos* or *chora*. Here, according to him, we can make the emendation of τὴν πόλιν to τὴν πόλι<τικὴ>ν, by analogy with the description of the Spartan state in Polybius (6.45.3), where the wording ἡ πολιτικὴ χώρα appears. As he interprets it, *politike* (ἡ πολιτική), i.e. land (γῆ, χώρα), means the land in the lowlands belonging to the citizens, that is the Thessalians, comprising the tetrads, as opposed to the *perioikis* (ἡ περιοικίς), that is the lands of the Achaeans, Perrhaebeans and Magnetes. Although we do not have any evidence of the use of the term *perioikis* in reference to the lands of the Thessalian neighbors, Wade-Gery refers to the example of Elida and Sparta, in which cases they were used to describe the lands occupied by a population dependent on citizens.[19] Earlier editors such as Schwartz suggested emendations to the form τὴν πόλιτείαν, but the most widely accepted is the form τὰς πόλεις, which is supported by Rose. The use of the word *polis* to refer to the whole of Thessaly, which was hard to accept for earlier scholars, no longer arouses such resistance, as proven by the opinion of M.H. Hansen that this is a rare example of use of the term *polis* in a wider sense to designate a state. Helly, however, employed strong arguments to reject the emendations and return to the original form, assuming that the text refers to the division not of the whole of Thessaly, but only of the city of Larisa.[20]

Also unclear is the last sentence of the *scholion*. The numeral τρίακοντια has been corrected by Preller as τρί'άκοντια. This is supported by Xenophon's statement that the Thessalian peltasts were excellent spearmen – *akontistai*. Finally, there is a lack of clarity in the explanation that they carried a long spear (καὶ μακρὸν δόρυ πάντες ἐφόρουν) called a *schedion*. The name of this spear suggests that it was used for giving thrusts in direct skirmishes. However, Pflugk's emendation has gained recognition, correcting this

---

[18]   Xen. *Hell.* 6.1.11; Dem. 13. 23; Helly 1995: 184–186.

[19]   Wade-Gery 1924: 58–59.

[20]   Helly 1995: 153–154; Hansen 1997: 14; Decourt/Nielsen/Helly 2004: 667.

passage to the form καὶ μικρὸν δόρυ πάντες ἐφόρουν, which is based on the conviction that the spear in question was a short one used for hurling.[21]

The above remarks demonstrate how hard it is to reconstruct an extract from *Thettalon politeia* on the basis of a scholion. The scholia on *Rhesus* are not a homogenous text, and it is very difficult to determine their date of origin. It is thought that the *scholia vetera*, in contrast to later, Byzantine *scholia*, had their beginnings in the works of Aristophanes of Byzantium. This Alexandrian scholar of the second century BCE produced a critical publication of the text of the tragedy with comments. The next comments on the text were written by Didymus at the end of the first century BC as well as Dionysius, who is difficult to identify. We do not know which of these commentaries the *scholia* available to us are based on, but it is generally assumed that they took on their form before the mid-3rd century CE.

The information collected above shows that the *scholion* analyzed here may have been produced over a long period, of even 400 years, during which it was copied and corrected on a number of occasions.[22] Modern editors have considered this text to be so damaged that they have introduced a series of changes to it, guided by their own ideas on the subject of the political organization of Thessaly on the threshold of the Classical period as well as the organization and arming of its military. Since we know very little about this subject, each attempt to make use of this extract must be connected with the need to again decide on the correctness of the emendations made in it.

This is not the end of the problems, however. Even if it were possible to reconstruct the text of the extract of *Thettalon politeia* cited by the scholiast, there remains the question of how reliable the information about the history as well as political and military organization of Thessaly was. An analysis of such a well preserved text as *Athenaion politeia* must be accompanied by caution. Although the author without doubt possessed a considerably greater knowledge on the political system of Athens than was available at the time on the subject of any other Greek state, the reliability of the information passed on by him is still questioned. An example might be the alleged system reforms of Draco. The anachronistic nature of the solutions described there, as well as the lack of references to these reforms later on in the text, has led scholars to believe that this passage is a later interpolation.[23] This example shows that the interpretation of a text like *Thettalon politeia* requires that particular caution be exercised, especially as we know only a few short quotations from it, without any wider context. Doubts as to the historicity of the reforms of Aleuas mentioned in this work were raised as soon as the late-19th century by Friedrich Hiller von Gaertringen, who suspected a later fabrication.[24]

There are several reasons to question the reliability of the extract from *Thettalon politeia* referring to Aleuas' reforms.

First, it is very hard to pinpoint the time of Aleuas and his reforms. Marta Sordi identified this figure as Aleuas, son of Simos, said to have been the patron of the poet

---

[21]   Harpocration, s.v. σχέδιον.

[22]   Dickey 2007: 31–32.

[23]   *Athen. Polit.* 4. This discussion is covered by Rhodes 1981: 53–56.

[24]   A critical approach to the *scholia* was expressed by Friedrich Hiller von Gaertringen (1890: 1–16), who suspected that the description of Aleuas' reforms may have been a later fabrication. See also the review of Bruno Helly's book written by Jeremy Trevett (1999: 213). Cf. Hose 2002: 159–161.

Simonides in the late 6th century BCE. He was identified as the father of Thorax and his brothers, mentioned by Herodotus, who led the Thessalians at the time of the invasion of Xerxes. These were also the reasons for which Sordi pointed to the end of the 6th century BCE as the probable time when the reforms were carried out.[25] However, we cannot rule out the possibility that Aleuas was a fictitious figure who was only attributed with the introduction of these reforms. This position makes it possible to shift the time of the reforms rather freely between the beginning of the 6th and beginning of the 5th century BCE.[26]

Each of the above proposals for dating Aleuas' reforms places them in the period prior to Xerxes' invasion of Greece. If they really were introduced at the end of the 6th and start of the 5th century, they had no great significance for the consolidation of the Thessalians' military power. On the contrary, according to tradition, the Thessalians enjoyed their greatest successes at the time before the period when the reforms may have happened. The era before Xerxes' invasion must have been the time of their expeditions to central Greece, tough battles with the Photians and intervention in Attica against the Spartans.[27] In the 5th century the Thessalians did not play much of a role on the political stage in Greece. Shifting the moment of these reforms to the early 6th century makes them even less likely, as the organization of the Thessalian army described by *Thettalon politeia* appears to be anachronistic.

The information available to us making it possible to imagine how the Thessalian army must have looked in the Archaic and the Classical period is very fragmentary. Although in most of the Greek states heavily armed infantry were the core of the army, in the case of Thessaly horsemen assumed such a role; most of our sources are silent on the issue of the role of the hoplites. Without doubt, cavalry was the formation that was most closely associated with the Thessalians, and the one most often mentioned by sources. Even in the early 5th century, Thessalian horses enjoyed the reputation as the best in all of Greece. In the 4th century, apart from its excellent cavalry, Thessaly was also renowned for its outstanding peltasts, as stressed by Xenophon and Isocrates.[28] Against this background, the scantiness of information on the Thessalian hoplites is striking.

The Thessalian hoplites are mentioned sporadically in sources, and only the information of Xenophon about Jason's army confirm their large numbers. In his excurse devoted to Jason, Xenophon described the forces which he planned to accumulate as well as those which he in fact had at his disposal after acquiring power over the whole of Thessaly and his election as *tagos*. In the former case, Jason expected that after the unification of the Thessalians under his leadership he would be able to gather up to 6000 horsemen as well as over 10,000 hoplites. He was convinced that his army would have an advantage over his rivals in terms of number of peltasts. He was led to this conclusion by the observation that almost all the inhabitants of the regions around Thessaly were excellent javelinmen – *akontistai*. Referring to Jason's true forces, Xenophon claims that he had 8000 of his own and allies' horses available, not less than 20,000 hoplites and

[25] Pind. *Pyth.* 10; Herod. 9.58.1; *Schol. in Theoc.* 16.34–35 p. 327 (Wendel); Sordi 1958: 65–84.

[26] Larsen 1960: 236–237; 1968: 16–18; Helly 1995: 181–191.

[27] Herod. 5.63, 7.130, 8.29–35; Plut. *Mor.* 244 E–245 C, 706 E–761 A, 866 E; Plut. *Cam.*, 19.2; Paus. 9.14.2, 10.13–2.1; Polyaenus 6.18.1–2.

[28] Herod. 7.196; Xenoph. Hell. 6.1.8–9 and 19; Isoc. 8.118.

sufficiently numerous peltasts (*peltastikon*) to oppose every other army.[29] It is not hard to notice that the proportion between the number of hoplites and the number of cavalry correspond approximately to that which was foreseen by Aleuas' reform. On closer inspection, however, this impression of similarity may be erased. We must remember that Xenophon may have included in these numbers Jason's mercenaries, which numbered around 6000. We can only speculate as to how many of these were mounted and how many infantry. We do not know whether – speaking of allies – Xenophon has Thessalian cities in mind, or other states that were joined by alliance with Jason. We also do not hear of Jason at any point making use of all the forces which he had at his disposal. Xenophon only says that after the Battle of Leuctra in 371, on the request of the Thebans Jason came to Boeotia, leading his mercenaries and cavalry.[30] Without doubt, though, Jason's army is the first example known to us in the history of Thessaly of the use of hoplites on a grand scale. Most evidence speaking of the Thessalian infantry refers to peltasts. It is therefore difficult to explain why Aleuas' reforms refer to the mobilization of a large number of hoplites, since we do not find proof of this formation – with the exception of Jason's army – in practice playing any greater role on the battlefields trodden by the Thessalians.

The question of the use of the word "hoplites" in *Thettalon politeia* is also problematic. There is much to suggest that the term became widespread in the Greek world during the 5th century. We do not find its first usage until the *First Isthmian Ode* by Pinar, dated around 470 BCE.[31] It is therefore very unlikely that the term was used in Thessaly at the end of the 6th century to describe a contingent of foot warriors. It is a similar case with the peltasts. The first mention of warriors armed with shield named *pelte* appears in Herodotus in a description of the contingents constituting Xerxes' army in 480 BCE. Describing the weaponry of the Thracians, the historian mentions that they possessed *pelte* and javelins (*akontia*).[32] Meanwhile, the description "peltasts" was first used by Thucydides in reference to Thracian units who together with the cavalry were apparently sent as support from Sitalces for the Athenians in 431 BCE, as well as in reference to the Thracian mercenaries from the year 413. The peltast units, provided by various Greek cities lying in Chalkidiki, were also part of Brasidas' army in 423 and 422.[33] Most information on the Thessalian peltasts was given by Xenophon. However, he uses this term with a somewhat different meaning from Thucydides, for example, referring to all light infantry. He uses the term regardless of whether a shield was an element of the weaponry or not. Moreover, he makes no mention in his works about javelinmen (*akontistai*) as a military formation, let alone as a formation differing from the peltasts.

Identifying the peltasts with ordinary javelinmen does not solve the problem of interpretation of the extract of the *scholion* quoting passages from *Thettalon politeia*. The text of this *scholion* makes reference not to peltasts, but to *pelte*. Although the name of this shield is associated with the lightly armed peltasts, they are mentioned for the first time by Thucydides, as Thracian warriors, only at the time of the Peloponnese war. For-

---

[29] Xen. *Hell.* 6.1.8–9 and 19; Best 1969: 124–126.
[30] Xen. *Hell.* 6.4.22.
[31] Pind. *Isth.* 1.23; Rey 2008: 152–158.
[32] Herod. 7.75.
[33] Thuc. 2.29.5, 4.129.2, 5.6.4, 7.27.1.

mations of warriors armed following their model became widespread in the Greek world after this war ended. If we were to accept the thesis that the peltasts appeared a hundred years earlier in Thessaly, and Aleuas ordered their mobilization, this would lead to the conclusion that a feature of their weaponry must have been the *pelte*. Otherwise, it would be hard to understand why there was a description of it in *Thettalon politeia*. The question arises as to whether the army of Archaic Thessaly needed both hoplites and peltasts. An analysis of iconographic evidence shows that the hoplites from this era did not always possess complete defensive weaponry, did not fight in closed ranks and, like the light infantry, could hurl spears[34]. As a result, the hoplites at the close of the Archaic period were very similar to the peltasts armed with shield and javelins known from the later period.

It is hard to resist the impression that the so-called reform of Aleuas does not fit with the reality of Thessaly in the late 6th and early 5th century. It is tempting, however, to connect the foundation of the tradition of Aleuas' reforms with Jason of Pherae, as proposed a century ago by Hiller von Gaertringen.[35] Only in the case of Jason do we hear of attempts to conduct a mobilization of the Thessalian army efficient enough to fully exploit the demographic potential of the country. It is not without significance that only in this case was there a mobilization of such a large number of hoplites. Jason also sought the support of all Thessalians and the appearance of legality for his actions. Xenophon mentions that he referred to another figure from the past, Scopas, imposing the requirement to pay tributes on neighbors. Making reference to the past was a method for justifying the need to introduce reforms. Perhaps in order to gain greater acceptance for the introduction of a system for mobilization of the army, he invoked the past, and the alleged reforms of Aleuas. Such a paradigm could justify in particular the mobilization of the armed infantry as well as the heavily armed hoplites. This type of infantry was dominant on 4th century battlefields, and it would be hard to imagine joining a war for hegemony in the Greek world, of which Jason dreamed, without having such a formation at one's disposal. However, military service in the form of hoplites conflicted with Thessalian customs, and may also have been linked with the need to make a greater outlay to individual weaponry.

The author of *Thettalon politeia* may therefore have taken from Jason's propaganda information about Aleuas' supposed reforms. He complemented this information with his sparse knowledge on the organization of Thessaly and its army in the distant times from before Xerxes' invasion. Further confusion may have been caused by the information that the Thessalians were willing and able, at least until the mid-5th century, to make use of different shields than typical Greek hoplites. This type of shield was probably depicted in the stele of Theotimos preserved in the Archaeological Museum in Larisa recalling his death in the Battle of Tanagra in 457 BCE. Without the roundness and wide metal rim characteristic of hoplite shields, it was more similar to the shield used by the peltasts. We can assume that this may have been the reason for which the description of the *pelete* was included in *Thettalon politeia*.[36]

---

[34]   Van Wees 2000: 155–156.

[35]   Hiller von Gaertringen 1890: 14–16.

[36]   For more on this subject see my forthcoming paper "Who is represented on Theotimos' stele? Remarks on the Thessalian foot warriors."

BIBLIOGRAPHY

Best, J. (1969): *Thracian Peltasts and their Influence on Greek Warfare*, Groningen.

Bloch, H. (1940): Heraklides Lembos and his Epitome of Aristotle's Politeiai, *TPAPhA* 71: 27–39.

Daintree, D. (1990): The Virgil Commentary of Aelius Donatus – Balsk Hole or "Eminence Grise"?, *Greece & Rome* 37: 65–79.

Decourt, J.-C., Nielsen, Th.H., Helly, B. *et al.* (2004): Thessalia and Adjacent Regions, in: M.H. Hansen, Th.H. Nielsen (eds.), *An Inventory of Archaic and Classical Poleis*, Oxford: 676–731.

Dickey, E. (2007): *Ancient Greek Scholarship. A Guide to Finding, Reading, and Understanding Scholia, Commentaries, Lexica and Grammatical Treatises, from their Beginnings to the Byzantine Period*, London–New York.

Hansen, M.H. (1997): Polis as the Generic Term for the State, in: Th.H. Nielsen (ed.), *Yet More Studies in the Ancient Greek Polis*, (Historia Einzelschriften 117), Stuttgart: 9–15.

Helly, B. (1995): *L'État thessalien. Aleuas le Roux, les tétrades et les Tagoi*, Lyon.

Hiller von Gaertringen, F. (1890): Das Königtum bei den Thessalern, in: *Aus der Anomia, Archaeologische Beitrage*, Berlin: 1–16.

Hose, M. (2002): *Aristoteles. Die historischen Fragmente. Übersetzt und erläutert von Martin Hose*, Berlin.

Jorodvic, I. (2008): Critias and Democracy, *Balcanica* 39: 33–46.

Keaney, J.J. (1963): Two Notes on the Tradition of Aristotle's Writings, *AJP* 84: 52–63.

Larsen, J.A.O. (1960): A New Interpretation of the Thessalian Confederacy, *CPh* 55: 229–247.

Larsen, J.A.O. (1968): *Greek Federal States*, Oxford.

Lindsay, H. (1997): Strabo on Apellicon's Library, *RhM* 140: 290–298.

Meyer, E. (1909): *Theopompos Hellenika*, Halle.

Preller, L. (1848): Zu Aristoteles politie der Thessaler, *Philologus* 3: 138–140.

Rhodes, P.J. (1981): *A Conmentory on the Aristotelian Athenaion Politeia*, Oxford.

Rey, F.E. (2008): *Ciudadanos, Campesinos y Soldados. El Nacimiento de La Polis Griega y La Teoria de La Revolucion Hoplita* (Anejos de Gladius), Madrid.

Sordi, M. (1958): *La lega tessala fine ad Alessandro Magno*, Roma.

Sprawski, S. (1999): *Jason of Pherae*, (*Electrum* 3), Kraków.

Sprawski, S. (2008): Aristotle on the History of Euboea? Remarks on the Author of *Peri Euboias* (FGrH 423), *Journal of Classical Studies Matica Srpska* 10: 107–116.

Toye, D.L. (1999): Aristotle's Other Politeiai. Was the Athenaion Politeia Atypical?, *CJ* 94: 235–253.

Trevett, J. (1999): rev. Helly B., *L'État thessalien. Aleuas le Roux, les tétrades et les Tagoi, JHS* 119: 213.

Wade-Gery, H.T. (1924): Jason of Pherae and Aleuas the Red, *JHS* 44: 55–64.

Van Wees, H. (2000): The Development of the Hoplite Phalanx. Iconography and reality in the seventh century, in: H. Van Wees, *War and Violence in Ancient Greece*, London: 125–166.

Zecchini, G. (2000): Harpocration and Athenaeus Historographical Realtionship, in: D. Braund, J. Wilkins (eds.), *Athenaeus and His World. Reading Greek Culture in the Roman Empire*, Exeter: 153–160.

ELECTRUM * Vol. 19 (2012): 149–156
doi:10.4467/20843909EL.12.009.0750

INTERNAL POLITICS IN SYRACUSE, 330–317 BC

Ryszard Tokarczuk

Abstract: There is a certain difficulty in attempts to describe the period in Syracuse between the death of Timoleon and the coming to power of Agathocles. It was a time of great turmoil and political instability – Syracuse would reappear after 317 BC as a tyranny. This article is a review of the events and causes that shaped the final outcome. The main points of interests are: an attempt to describe a type of government present in the given period, especially the function of the group of the so-called "Six Hundred Noblest," and the career of Agathocles, an exemplary one considering the political realities of the time.

Keywords: Sicily, Syracuse, Agathocles, tyranny.

After the death of Timoleon in 333 BC democracy was restored in the *polis* of Syracuse. This period, however, was to last no longer than 13 years, with occasional bouts of oligarchy. Another tyrant, in this case Agathocles, would rise to power in 317 BC. This interim period is rife with questions and uncertainties. Modern scholars have usually concentrated on the later period, when Agathocles seized ultimate power, or just before then (Berve 1953). Still, even partial answers can shed light on our understanding of internal politics in Syracuse in general.

However, before I can deal with the events of that period, I need to review in brief the results of Timoleon's actions and decisions, as they clearly had an impact on subsequent events. The "Timoleontic revival" (Talbert 1975; Smarczyk 2003) in Syracuse meant first and foremost an increase in the number of citizens, which was certainly important for a city ravaged by continuous fighting between Dionysius the Elder's successors. Nevertheless, the expansion of the citizenry had its consequences: "new" citizens could be exiles returning to the city, some of them attempting to reclaim property acquired by others. Furthermore, newly arriving citizens would expect to be granted a share of the land. These were not new problems for Greek *poleis*. However, as Timoleon did not resolve tensions and inequalities between groups of old and new citizenry before his death, Agathocles was subsequently able to exploit these divisions in his attempts to gain power. Around this time, Syracuse's population also became quite diverse, as volunteers were gathered from many other areas and settlements.

All the above gives an impression of the situation of Syracuse's society at the moment of Timoleon's death. Before continuing, it is necessary to consider two important questions, both of them resulting from a critical approach to written sources (mainly Diodorus Siculus). Namely: where was the power to govern the city? Did the *demos* hold it, or did some other group take it for themselves? Secondly, anyone researching this period also needs to consider the exemplary career of Agathocles before he became a tyrant – how was it possible for him to gain such influence in Syracuse at that time?

Let us deal with the first question – it is generally assumed that the main result of Timoleon's activities in Sicily was to overthrow tyrannies on the island and to restore democratic governments. In Syracuse, turning away from the past was marked by demolition of buildings connected with Deinomenid rule – especially Dionysius' palace on the isle of Ortygia. Similarly, the temple of Zeus Eleutherios (Zeus the Liberator, whose cult was of special significance for democratic *poleis*) was built.

On the other hand, one particular group of citizens seems to have gained influence quickly in the city – the so-called Six Hundred Noblest. It is easy to connect the members of this group with the Syracusan military leadership of that time, as we are given names – Heraclides and Sosistratus – which are simultaneously the names of chief commanders during the campaign to relieve the city of Croton, which was being besieged by Bruttians. It is more difficult to point to its beginning. Was it created as a council (*sunedrion*), for example, during Timoleon's reforms? Later in Diodorus' narrative, however, the group is called *hetaireia*. Could it have been just a "political club" of the most rich and influential citizens? Uncertainty is caused partly by the terminology used by Diodorus (Galvagno 2011). The answer is clearly connected with the form and function of government during the period between Timoleon and Agathocles. Based on Aristotle's set of definitions, it would be a "mixed" constitution – unfortunately, this does not give us a clear picture, as nowhere in the surviving sources can we find solid information on the capabilities of such a "council." Still, the presence of the Six Hundred alone would suggest that the Syracusan constitution at this time was not a pure democracy (Hüttl 1929: 128–130; Sordi 1980: 280–282).

Without doubt, the Six Hundred had political weight, and certainly such a group could function under a democratic government. Careful scrutiny of Diodorus will show that the aforementioned leaders, Heraclides and Sosistratus, were chosen for the Croton campaign. At that time, Croton was led by an oligarchy. Why should democratic Syracuse help oligarchical Croton? One could look for the answers in the work of Thucydides, who in one passage remarks that kindred constitutions of different *poleis* are likely to give support to each other (Thuc. 3.82). Naturally, Croton was an important city, both politically and economically, in Magna Graecia, but it was also a target of the campaigns of Dionysii and Agathocles. A democratic *polis* may have found it necessary to maintain good relations with such a city. Later events however – the takeover of the Syracuse by Heraclides and Sosistratus after their return from campaigning – lead the reader to question the motives behind the intervention in the siege of Croton. First, an oligarchical party was saved in Croton, and soon afterwards oligarchical rule took hold in Syracuse. Of course, oligarchs would be inclined to support oligarchy in other cities, and it seems reasonable to assume that such support is likely to have been reciprocated. Yet foreign support could not have been the sole reason for the success of the Six Hundred and their ability to stay in power.

It is possible that the answer can be found in the role of Heraclides and Sosistratus as commanders during the campaign. Their campaign was at least a moderate success – as can be discerned from a later passage (Diod. Sic. 19.10.3) – and victorious ancient war leaders increased their influence in their respective states. Moreover, as their own soldiers gained spoils from military success, their allegiance to their leaders increased. It can be assumed that part of Syracusan society also welcomed the outcome. Such newly found support in the end would only help elevate the influence of the Six Hundred even further, eventually leading to oligarchical domination of Syracuse.

This does not mean that the Syracusan people were completely unaware of the impending danger of oligarchical power, nor that they made no attempt to resist it in some way. Still, it was Agathocles who bore the brunt of the accusations that led to him being exiled (Diod. Sic. 19.4). It is unclear whether this exile was self-imposed, yet it is clear that other participants of the Croton campaign also remained in Italy because of political changes in Syracuse. This is another indication of the ongoing power struggle within Syracuse at that time. Agathocles' departure from the city could only strengthen the power of the victorious party. In the narrative of Diodorus this point marks the beginning of open conflict between the oligarchs and Agathocles.

Later, oligarchic rule weakened and eventually fell – we can only wonder whether subsequent military defeats had anything to do with this turn of events. It was the exiles led by Agathocles who helped prevent the capture of Rhegium by the Six Hundred. If indeed the foundation of power for the Six Hundred was military prowess and the spoils of a victorious war, such a rebuff must have been a significant setback. However, the conflict was not a short one, and it took more than one campaign to decide it. However, written sources are silent on any constitutional changes made by oligarchs during their rule – democracy appears to have re-established itself without too much difficulty.

Nevertheless, the fall of the Six Hundred had several implications for the immediate future. Diodorus' *sunedrion* of the Six Hundred became the *hetaireia* – the political terminology of this Greek historian certainly leaves much open to discussion. Still, an explanation of what he meant may be possible. The end of oligarchy, exile and eventually a pardon would certainly have led to a loss of influence in the city. On the other hand, attempts at reconciling the conflicting parties and the return of exiles clearly prove a fear of continued conflict like the one before Timoleon's intervention, marked by a lack of well-faring citizens. Unfortunately such attempts had also clearly failed to mitigate the inequalities that were the root cause of internal divisions in Greek *poleis* so many times before and after.

Democracy returned, and it seems that, in order to settle old internal divisions, the city turned to a traditional solution – an invitation to its mother-city, Corinth, to send an impartial man to adjudicate on disputes between its citizens. The mission of Acestorides in Syracuse is not clearly stated (other than that he was an "elected general" – Diod. Sic. 19.5.1; cf. Plut., *Timoleon* 38.2; Westlake 1949). As noted by Westlake, it is possible that the main aim of inviting foreigners to one's own city was to solve internal, not necessarily external problems. That reason would explain why the *strategos* would be fearful of influential citizens (a group to which Agathocles certainly belonged) and would send assassins to kill them. There is a telling silence in our sources about Acestorides – only a mention of conflict with Carthage (without a word about his participation in it) and an assassination attempt instigated by the Corinthian. It is no help that after these brief episodes we do not hear anything about him – his mission was probably deemed fulfilled, either by exiling Agathocles – in fact for the second time – thus restoring the political balance in Syracuse, or by making peace with Carthaginians.

The Six Hundred returned once more to centre-stage when Agathocles, having been allowed to return from exile under oath, plotted their downfall. This was also the moment when Diodorus let us know that the political composition of Syracuse was more complex than he had earlier led us to believe – there are many *hetaireiai*, and at least some of them are against Agathocles (Diod. Sic. 19.5.6). Yet the main conflict seems to have been driven by a struggle between Agathocles and the Six Hundred. The outcome of the subsequent bloodbath and the number of casualties – more than 4000 killed, more than 6000 exiled – raise more questions. This brutal action was taken against the Six Hundred and their supporters. It is difficult to be clear about the exact numbers, as we have only a general description. Similarly, it is impossible to say whether all of them should be accounted for as being killed or exiled. The example of Deinocrates, *philos* of Agathocles (*sic!*), may prove otherwise.

The opinions of scholars as regards the coup are not unanimous. Some see the role of Agathocles as a leader of radical democrats and poor, disenfranchised Sicilians (Consolo Langher 1980); some just stress the conflict against the oligarchical group of the Six Hundred (Berger 1992: 49–50). It cannot be maintained, however, that it was anything but a purge by Agathocles before he took ultimate power in Syracuse. The main victims seem to have been Syracusan aristocrats, people with property and power. Yet the number of casualties probably suggests that the Six Hundred and their supporters were not the only targets of the purge. This leads to another question: to what degree was that violence controlled? Diodorus tells us that amongst the people involved in the slaughter were soldiers and poor citizens. After the leaders of the Six Hundred were dealt with, we also learn of an angry, armed mob, inspired by Agathocles himself. Suddenly the soldiers – the group that should at least theoretically have been the most trusted and reliable in such situations – vanish from the narrative and are replaced by an unruly mob. In the confusion many innocent people – individuals, families and small groups with no political allegiance – were probably harmed. Still, it was probably also an opportune moment for Agathocles to deal with any individuals or groups that he deemed to be likely opponents in the future.

How was it possible for Agathocles, an individual of no distinctive background that we know of, to reach such a position of power? He was an outsider – his family did not originate from Syracuse. His father, Carcinus, brought him into the city when Timoleon was repopulating Syracuse and other Greek cities on the island of Sicily. It is not easy to discern the facts of the young Agathocles' upbringing and wealth. It may have been true that he was the son of a potter or a prostitute – or both – but such information could equally have been a slur, designed especially to denigrate political enemies (Polyb. 12.15; Diod. Sic. 19.2.7; Iust. 22.1.4–5). If such a lowly, working-class background was indeed his, it is difficult to explain how he would have developed relationships with men of high-standing, such as the one with Damas, one of the Syracusan *strategoi*. It is more probable that father and son owned a pottery workshop and thus were at least middle-class businessmen rather than mere craftsmen. Even more, we learn later that

Agathocles' brother, Antander, served the city as a *strategos*. This brings us to the matter of Heraclides, the leader of the Six Hundred. Agathocles had an uncle called Heraclides – is this a mere coincidence, or is it the same person? There is not enough evidence to support such a hypothesis or to reject it entirely. If it were true, it would, among other things, be a compelling argument against the tyrant's low birth.

Even with just his family wealth behind him, it would have been almost impossible for a son of Carcinus to reach such a prominent, high-status position. Somehow, a friendly or perhaps even intimate relationship with *strategos* Damas (or Damascon, as mentioned by Justin) began. Such a turn of events is not in itself as remarkable as the fact that Agathocles married the widow of Damas, enriching himself in the process. Diodorus passes over this marriage with a few words, but behind those words more conundrums are hidden. There was apparently no one to contest Agathocles' right to the hand of a widow – neither from the family of the deceased husband nor from the soon-to-be bride's family. Moreover, it seems that the entire property of Damas became that of Agathocles.

According to what is known about both the marriages of widows and their inheritances from their deceased husbands, it becomes clear that Athenian tradition could not have been applied in the case of Agathocles. The ease of remarrying in this case and the transfer of all the property of Damas' widow to Agathocles brings to mind Dorian women and their relative liberty in matters of marriage and ownership of property. The closest example available to us would be the Gortyn Law and its passages about brides. It is likely that a contract similar to that mentioned in this law took place here (Davies 2005: 319–322). Nevertheless, it is remarkable that no mention is made of any resistance to the second marriage of Damas' widow. One of our sources even describes an affair happening before the death of Damas, which would support the supposed licentiousness of Agathocles (Iust. 22.1.12). On the other hand, it makes this explanation somewhat suspect – as it is in the case of a young tyrant prostituting himself.

Having dealt with questions of wealth and marriage, it seems probable that money, relationships and licentiousness were not the main reason for Agathocles' power. First and foremost he was a military leader, having started his career as a soldier at an early age. He participated in several campaigns and seemingly excelled in martial prowess. Several times he had proven himself on the battlefield, yet the Croton campaign of 330 BC was the first step in the conflict with the influential Six Hundred, as mentioned above.

The reason for the subsequent exile of Agathocles is astounding. As an officer, he reported to the people of Syracuse that Heraclides and Sosistratus planned to overthrow democracy in the city. It is testament to the power and influence of the Six Hundred that the accuser himself is exiled. Later, democracy is indeed overthrown, as Agathocles had warned. The reason for the conflict between the leaders of the Six Hundred and Agathocles, according to Diodorus, was a personal one – a disagreement about the division of the reward for service during a campaign. It can be assumed that Agathocles was officially deemed "a poor soldier," even if this were to denigrate his real achievements and undermine his influence.

Following the actions of Agathocles can give us some insight into his ambitions and aims – he tries in several cities of Southern Italy to achieve a superior position by military service, and every single time he is exiled on the same grounds. His attempts at becoming a tyrant can be explained somewhat if we remember that each time he had no status as a citizen in each of those cities. So any attempt to advance one's position socially or politically can be described as being *neoterikos*, which itself is a term with a certain political weight.

The turning point was finally reached when the Syracusans under the Six Hundred attacked Rhegium. Agathocles joined with an assortment of exiles to fight in defense of his father's city. As before, this deed was carried out under the banner of the anti-oligarchy movement. It is difficult to say if, according to one hypothesis (Consolo Langher 2000), this clearly makes Agathocles and his supporters defenders of democracy. Naturally, the opposition to the Six Hundred could easily be called such, and it is possible to see Agathocles as a radical politician. After the fall of the Six Hundred, there was a period of personal danger for Agathocles, marked by conflict with Carthage and the presence of Acestorides of Corinth, as *strategos* in Syracuse. We can guess that this must have led to a struggle between the Corinthian and Agathocles, a renowned military leader with impressive achievements behind him. After all, the latter was a hero, having fought against the oligarchs, and it can be assumed that his influence had risen significantly after returning to Syracuse from exile. This could be reason enough for some citizens to suspect Agathocles of holding ambitions of tyranny. If so, Acestorides' his decision to eliminate this danger to stability may have been Agathocles' reason for action he took against them. One needs also to consider the official position held by Agathocles during the *strategia* of Acestorides. Their rivalry could have arisen because Agathocles was either made a subordinate of Acestorides or given no position at all.

Once again, the future tyrant of Syracuse became a rootless one and turned to a life of brigandry. His actions became damaging to Carthaginians and Greeks alike. Finally, for better or worse, the resolution of the conflict with Carthage put an end to his exclusion from Syracuse. All exiles were brought back to the city – Agathocles among them. In his case, however, he was expected to make a special gesture. He was ordered to make an oath in the sanctuary of Demeter not to plan anything against democracy. He later took the office of "protector of the peace" (Diod. Sic. 19.5.5: *phylax tes eirenes*). The status of this position can be disputed – one may wonder if it was not similar to a position held earlier by Acestorides, namely to protect the city from strife, until all exiles returned to Syracuse. This was usually seen as one of the first steps necessary – or expected – on the way to becoming a tyrant, a voluntary act whereby the politician imposed his will on the citizens through shrewd persuasion (Meister 1984: 402). Yet it can also be seen in a different light, as compensation for him after the conflict with Acestorides. If the office of *strategos* could have been expected to be given to Agathocles, then making him, a recent exile, defender of the city, acknowledged his importance, awarded him a publically acknowledged status and removed the need for his hostility against his fellow citizens. Placing such trust in a person such as Agathocles can be seen by us as a mistake, yet we have to remember that he was bound by an oath sanctioned by religion. Moreover, the city of Syracuse lacked capable and influential citizens like him. Every once in a while a *polis* tried to return exiles and to end internal strife as soon as possible. Such a policy could not provide a long-term solution – the bloody end of the struggle between the Six Hundred and Agathocles is the ultimate proof in this regard.

Even this final episode in the history of democratic Syracuse finds an explanation in the defense of liberty. One can note that it is not the first time that Agathocles appeared as a supporter of democracy – he was, after all, the person that warned Syracuse of the plans of the Six Hundred. He campaigned against them during his exile. He had made an oath to do no harm to Syracuse. Of course, each of these acts furthered his own goals – with success, one must add. Because of the instability and periods of strife, the safest position in the Sicilian *polis* was the highest one – above the rivalry shared by holders of office or political opponents.

All solutions to the problems that haunted Syracuse after the death of Timoleon were rather unsuccessful – the banishment of citizens endangering internal peace could only be temporary. The ever-present need for social advance caused by inequalities and division between citizens can be seen both in the career of Agathocles himself and in the readiness of his supporters to acquire the properties of rich families. In this light, his tyranny seems to have been inevitable, because as one of the influential citizens he needed to secure his position in the city.

The instability of democracy during that period is also underlined by the manner in which the oligarchy triumphed temporarily until tyranny finally won domination. It was not achieved by implementing new laws or institutions – rather simply by one part of the whole system gaining ascendancy over another in power and influence. It can be ascertained from the sources that even before the Croton campaign the Six Hundred were held in high regard. Similarly, one may wonder how much Agathocles' position as a "defender of peace" differed from that of the Six Hundred after he had ordered death or exile for the representatives of Syracusan democracy. Those subtle but important shifts in influence are not usually marked by any significant changes in the institutions functioning in a *polis* during this period. On the other hand, the remaining literary sources present a particular point of view which serves particular goals but also emphasizes personal relationships and their role in shaping the turn of events.

A gap in our sources on the details of constitutional changes potentially made by either the Six Hundred or by Agathocles could be the result of intended omission. However the decision to help the city of Croton, supported by oligarchs, would prove that such changes were not necessary. The influence of victorious leaders could easily sway the general opinion of a city's citizens.

Diodorus version of the discussed events does not provide us with clear-cut political positions of Agathocles and the Six Hundred. Was their conflict – oligarchy against democracy – the driving force for the events during the period between 330 and 317 BC? It is difficult to accept either personal vendetta or being a radical democrat as a correct explanation in that case. The need for personal advancement can both be seen in the career of Agathocles and explain the motives of the participants in the bloody coup. It is a telling thing that the future tyrant, at first a relatively wealthy newcomer to Syracuse with one of his kin serving as a prestigious official, later himself one of the first citizens because of his marriage, is compelled to advance his position even further. Only after reaching a supreme position in the *polis* did personal safety seem to be guaranteed. The Timoleontic constitution, a "mixed" one, had not been able to maintain the peace in Syracuse. Stability, paradoxically – and even then only temporary – could be achieved under first a tyrant and later a king. At the same time, the lack of stability in the period before Agathocles grasped power makes describing the Syracusan constitution a very problematic task.

BIBLIOGRAPHY

Berger, S. (1992): *Revolution and Society in Greek Sicily and Southern Italy*, Stuttgart.

Berve, H. (1953): *Die Herrschaft des Agathokles*, München.

Consolo Langher, S.N. (1980): La Sicilia dalla scomparsa di Timoleonte alla morte di Agatocle. L`introduzione della «Basileia», in: *La Sicilia antica II, 1. La Sicilia greca dal VI secolo alle guerre puniche*, Napoli: 291–296.

Consolo Langher, S.N. (2000): *Agatocle. Da capoparte a monarca fondatore di un regno tra Cartagine e i Diadochi*, Messina.

Davies, J. (2005): The Gortyn Laws, in: M. Gagarin (ed.), *The Cambridge Companion to Ancient Greek Law*, Cambridge: 319–322.

Galvagno, E. (2011): Timoleonte e le costituzione siracusana, in: M. Congiu, C. Micciche, S. Modeo (eds.), *Atti del VIII Convegno di studi. Timoleonte e la Sicilia della seconda meta del IV sec. a.C.*, Caltanisetta: 217–234.

Hüttl, W. (1929): *Verfassungsgeschichte von Syrakus*, Prag.

Meister, K. (1984): Agathocles, *CAH²* VII,1: 384–390.

Smarczyk, B. (2003): *Timoleon und die Neugründung von Syrakus*, Göttingen.

Sordi, M. (1980): Il IV e III secolo da Dionigi I a Timoleonte (336 a.C.), in: *La Sicilia antica* II, *1. La Sicilia greca dal VI secolo alle guerre puniche*, Napoli: 280–282.

Talbert, R.J.A. (1975): *Timoleon and the revival of Greek Sicily, 344–317 B.C.*, London.

Westlake, H.D. (1942): Timoleon and the Reconstruction of Syracuse, *Cambridge Historical Journal* 7: 73–100.

Westlake, H.D. (1949): The purpose of Timoleon's Mission, *AJPh* 70: 65–75.

ELECTRUM * Vol. 19 (2012): 157–163
doi:10.4467/20843909EL.12.010.0751

Notes on a Stratagem of Iphicrates in Polyaenus and Leo *Tactica*

Everett L. Wheeler

Abstract: Proper understanding of Iphicrates' stratagem at Polyaenus 3.9.38, marred by a lacuna, can be derived from Leo *Tact.* 20.196, where anchoring a fleet off a harborless coastline is described. Emending Polyaenus' text from the reading of a later MS also clarifies the anecdote's meaning. Leo knew the full text of Polyaenus, since Polyaenus 3.9.38 does not occur in the abbreviated *Excepta Polyaeni*, which some recently suggest replaced the *Strategica* in Byzantine use of Polyaenus.

Keywords: Iphicrates, Polyaenus, Leo, *Strategica*.

Artaxerxes II's attempt to recover Egypt in 374–373 B.C. with a combined force of Greek mercenaries and Persians fell victim to the bickering of its commanders, Iphicrates and Pharnabazus. A major joint military and naval expedition it was. From 377 or 376 B.C. there assembled at Ace (Acco, Acre, Ptolemais) in Phoenicia (allegedly) 200,000 Persians, 20,000 Greek mercenaries, 300 triremes and 200 triaconters.[1] Diodorus (15.41–45) provides the fullest narrative (from Ephorus?), to be supplemented by tidbits of Trogus (*Prol.* 10), Nepos (*Iphic.* 2.4), Plutarch (*Aratax.* 24.1), and Polyaenus' *Strategica*.[2] Iphicrates, the most rusé of all generals in Polyaenus with 63 stratagems to his credit, distinguished himself in four *exempla* from this campaign in the stratagem collector's compendium (3.9.38, 56, 59, 63).[3] Polyaenus 3.9.38, marred by a lacuna and misinterpreted in two recent translations, demands re-examination.[4] Although a complete history of the campaign cannot be recovered on present evidence, filling the lacuna at Polyaenus 3.9.38 can offer a proper understanding of the anecdote and contribute to an aspect of the *Nachleben* of Polyaenus' text.

---

[1] Diod. 15.41.3; Nepos (*Iphic.* 2.4) reduces the Greeks to 12,000.

[2] On Diodorus' use of Ephorus for fourth-century events, see most recently Bianco 2010 with references to earlier bibliography; Parke (1933: 105–106) and Bianco (1997a: 189–191) provide modern overviews of the campaign.

[3] For studies of Iphicrates' career see Pritchett 1971–1991, II: 59–72; Bianco 1997a; on Iphicrates' ranking as no. 1 in use of stratagems in Polyaenus, see Wheeler 2010: 37–38.

[4] Melber's discussion of Iphicrates in Polyaenus (1885: 565–573) omits treatment of 3.9.38.

I

Polyaenus 3.9.38 reads:

Ἰφικράτης βασιλεῖ στρατηγῶν μετὰ Φαρναβάζου, πλέων ἐπ' Αἰγύπτου, τῆς χώρας οὔσης ἀλιμένου, παρήγγειλε τοῖς τριηράρχοις 'τεσαράκοντα σάκκους ἕκαστος ἐχέτω'. Προσορμιζομένων δὲ τοὺς σάκκους ἄμμου πλήσας ἑκάστης κεφαλίδας ἐξῆπτεν ἑκάστης νεὼς καὶ οὕτως ἀνείλκυσεν αὐτὰς τεταρσωμένας.

Krentz translates the passage as:

When Iphicrates was serving the King as a general with Pharnabazus, he sailed to Egypt. Since the land had no harbors, he ordered the captains, "Let each have forty sacks." After they came to anchor, he filled the sacks with sand * * * fastened them to the bow of each ship, and in this way he dragged the ships up complete with oars.

For Bianco the passage reads:

Ificrate, mentre svolgeva funzioni di stratego per conto del re di Persia insieme a Farnabazo, salpò alla volta del'Egitto; poiché la regione era priva di porti, ordinò ai trierarchi che ciascuno avesse con sé quaranto sacchi. Ormeggiatisi, fece riempire i sacchi di sabbia +++ e li fece attaccare alle sartie di prua di ciascuna nave: così riuscì a tirare a terra le navi, fornite di remi.[5]

Both interpretations of the text are essentially identical: forty sacks of sand attached to the prow of each ship (or "shrouds of the prow" pace Bianco) are somehow used as a means of dragging the ships (onto the shore?) at a harborless coastline. How forty sacks of sand on a ship's prow can aid in dragging (ἀνείλκυσεν) the vessel is unclear, although such is the usual nautical meaning of ἀνέλκω (LSJ[9] *s.v.*). Paradoxically, the additional weight of forty bags of sand would seem to add weight and thus to increase the difficulty of hauling the ships ashore.

Clarification of the lacuna and the stratagem's meaning comes from Leo VI's *Tactica* (c. 900 A.D.), where a version of Polyaenus' *exemplum* appears. Leo *Tact.* 20.196 reads:

Ἱστορήσω σοι καὶ ναυτικοῦ στόλου στρατήγημα. ὅταν γὰρ εἰς ἀλιμέμους καὶ ψαμμώδεις τόπους τὴν ἀπόβασιν μέλλης ἐν καιρῷ ναυτικῆς στρατηγίας, εἰ οὕτω τύχοι, ποιήσασθαι σάκκους πολλοὺς πληρώσας ἄμμου, καὶ τοῖς σχοινίοις προσδήσας ἀπὸ ἑκάστου δρόμωνος ἐκκρεμάσεις τοὺς ἀρκοῦντας οἱονεὶ σιδηρᾶς ἀγκύρας, καὶ οὕτως τὸν λεγόμενον πελαγολιμένα ποιήσας, εὐκόλως κατὰ τὸν τόπον νυκτὸς ἐξελθὼν τὴν βεβουλευμένην σοι καταδρομὴν ποιήσεις.

I will tell you of a stratagem for the naval fleet. When, in the course of a naval expedition, it happens that you wish to disembark in a sandy place without a harbor, fill a large number of sacks with sand, tie them with ropes, and hang a sufficient number of them from each dromon like iron anchors. Thus, having made what is called a harbor at sea, you will easily disembark at that place at night and make the raid you had planned.[6]

At first glance the two passages seem to resemble each other only in the reference to a harborless coast and the practice of hanging bags of sand from a ship's prow, as the function of the sandbags differs: in Polyaenus for somehow dragging the ships (onto

---

5   Krentz, in Krentz/Wheeler 1994, I: 259, 261; Bianco 1997b: 94–95.
6   Tr. Dennis 2010: 607; the text with English translation is also to be found at Pryor/Jeffreys 2006: 516–517.

shore?); in Leo for anchoring the ships off shore. Polyaenus' κεφαλίδας ἐξῆπτεν would correspond to Leo's τοῖς σχοινίοις προσδήσας ... ἐκκρεμάσεις. κεφαλίδας, a *hapax* in Polyaenus (LSJ⁹ *s.v.* IV), are ropes suspended from a ship's prow and, contrary to Krentz's interpretation, not the prow itself; hence the equation of Polyaenus' κεφαλίδας with Leo's τοῖς σχοινίοις. The difference in the sandbags' function can be removed, if the reading εἴλκυσεν, found in *Monacensis gr.* 401 (dated to 1581–1596), be accepted.[7] The sense of ἕλκω here is not "to drag" but "to weigh down," as in weighing items on a scale (LSJ⁹ *s.v.* A.9). Although Woefflin's favorable view of the great authority of *Monacensis gr.* 401 as a witness is now disputed by Schindler, who finds this tradition contaminated, in this case the reading of *Monacensis gr.* 401 seems preferable.[8] Schindler failed to note the significance of **M**'s reading (his **M**1) at 3.9.38, as argued here, for the real meaning of the *exemplum* and even the alternative reading. Iphicrates substituted sandbags for anchors or supplemented anchors with sandbags to stabilize a fleet's position offshore from a harborless coastline, to create what Leo calls a "harbor at sea" (πελαγολιμένα).

Identification of the relevance of Leo *Tact.* 20.196 to Polyaenus 3.9.38 derives from Karl Ludwig Roth (1790–1868), who apparently communicated the suggestion to Woefflin privately, as Melber did not cite Roth's own publication of the idea. Melber retained it in the *apparatus criticus* of his 1887 edition and wisely did not attempt to reconstruct the lost portions of Polyaenus' text.[9] Leo clarifies the meaning of Polyaenus' anecdote without permitting such a reconstruction. The vocabulary of Leo's text differs significantly from that of Polyaenus and more than just a few words may be missing. Indeed Leo may have known a longer version of the text, unless Leo has considerably reworked Polyaenus' *exemplum* for his own purposes – an unlikely view for the section of a book like his Constitutio XX, which offers an *exempla* collection even repeating material from earlier parts of the *Tactica*, just as Frontinus reproduced *exempla* from his first three books in his *Strat.* 4.[10] In any case, the significance of Polyaenus' concluding words, αὐτὰς τεταρσωμένας, referring to ships having their complete row(s) of oars, is not clear and seems irrelevant to Leo's version. The obscurity may derive from Polyaenus' own abbreviation of his source or offer further proof that a longer version of the *exemplum* has not survived.[11]

Placement of the stratagem of 3.9.38 within its specific context during the 374–373 B.C. campaign could also enlighten, but such must remain problematic. Tempting is a connection with Iphicrates' amphibious assault described at Polyaenus 3.9.63, where Iphicrates commanded 100 triaconters, a type of vessel used in the 374–373 B.C. expedition (Diod. 15.41.3). But these ships are explicitly stated to have anchors at their sterns (ἄγκυραν ἀφιέναι κατὰ πρύμναν), whereas in 3.9.38 Iphicrates is concerned with

---

[7] *Monacensis gr.* 401 is the **M** of the Teubner editions of Woefflin (1860) and Melber's revision (1887) of Woefflin's text, but **M**1 in Schindler's study of the manuscript tradition: 1973: 129–137.

[8] Melber 1887: xv; Schindler 1973: 265–267.

[9] Melber 1887, reprinted in Krentz/Wheeler 1994, I: 260; the connection is also noted in the translation and commentary of Nefedkin 2002: 397 n.122.

[10] E.g., *Tact.* 20.21 = 11.21; 20.45 cf. 19.40; 20.80 cf. 6.5, 11.41; 20.87 = 17.91; 20.110 cf. 12.57, 14.101; 20.139 cf. 18.132; on the authenticity of Frontin. *Strat.* 4, see Wheeler 2010: 33 with n.102, 39 n.122.

[11] Polyaenus' abbreviation and modification of *exempla* in his sources is discussed at Schettino 1998: 97–107.

weighing down the ships from the prow. More troubling, however, in 3.9.63 Iphicrates is attacking Phoenicians in Phoenicia, but the hostilities of 3.9.38 concern joint Persian-Greek operations against Egypt and the expedition had its base at Ace (Ptolemais) in Phoenicia. Bianco attractively suggests that 3.9.38 describes a training exercise – a view that can be neither refuted nor confirmed.[12] A third possibility is the expedition's landing at the Mendesian mouth of the Nile – a surprise attack from the open sea after Egyptian fortifications and preparations blocked a landing at the Pelusiac mouth (Diod. 15.42.4). Diodorus mentions an extensive beach but not a harbor. The versions of both Polyaenus and Leo imply the need for a "harbor at sea," a situation in which the beaching of the ships was impossible or unadvisable.[13] Little more can be done with Polyenus 3.9.38 on present evidence.

<h1 style="text-align:center">II</h1>

Surprisingly, Leo's version of Polyaenus 3.9.38 at 20.196 substantiates a significance aspect of the *Strategica's Nachleben.* Constantine VII Porphyrogentius (r. 912–959), son of Leo VI (r. 886–912), recommended to his own son Romanus II (r. 959–963) what books to take with him when campaigning: these should include the historical works of Polyaenus and Syrianus Magister.[14] Constantine's encyclopedic efforts had included the collection of ancient and earlier Byzantine military treatises – manifest in the famous manuscript of the Greek tacticians, *Laurentianus* LV-4 of c. 985.[15] This collection included the *Excerpta Polyaeni* (*Hypotheseis*), the earliest Byzantine abbreviation of the *Strategica*, in which Polyaenus' c. 900 stratagems were reduced to 356 and reorganized from the original prosopographical-ethnographic order into a topical arrangement by military categories as in Frontinus' *Strategemata.*[16] Dates of composition for the *Excerpta* range from 500 to 850, but all are conjectural. Thus the earliest witness of the *Excerpta, Laur. gr.* LV-4, antedates the earliest manuscript of the complete text of the *Strategica, Laurentianus gr.* LVI-1 (c. 1295) by three centuries.[17]

The prominence accorded to the *Excerpta* by its inclusion in the *Laur. gr.* LV-4 and the relatively late date of the earliest manuscript of the *Strategica* have often led to an assumption that the *Strategica*'s text was not available or not used, but rather in the time

---

[12] Bianco 1997a: 189 n. 34.

[13] Pryor/Jeffreys (2006: 516 n. 65) disparage Leo's *exemplum* at 20.196, since a Byzantine *dromon* (like a trireme) could be beached and thus a "harbor at sea" was unnecessary. They do not consider the situation of an assault on an occupied coast in the face of an enemy and are unaware of the connection of Leo 20.196 with Polyaenus 3.9.38. On amphibious operations in Antiquity see Tucci 2004: a selection of case-studies and in no way a comprehensive discussion. Polyaenus 3.9.38, 63 and Leo 20.196 are not treated.

[14] Haldon 1990: 106–107 (C198–99); on Syrianus see Rance 2007 with references to bibliography besides the recent edition (with translation) of his relatively inaccessible *Rhetorica militaris*: Eramo 2010.

[15] On this MS see Dain/Foucault 1967: 382–385; Schindler 1973: 216–218. The impulse to compile this military encyclopedia certainly antedates Constantine's death in 959, but the hand(s) of the *Laur.* LV-4 point(s) to a date over twenty years later.

[16] See Wheeler, in Krentz/Wheeler 1994: xx–xxi; Dain/Foucault 1967: 337.

[17] On the *Laur.* LVI-1 see Schindler 1973: 15–18.

of Leo VI and Constantine VII the *Excerpta* had replaced the *Strategica*.[18] Exclusion of the *Strategica* from the *Laur. gr.* LV-4 – and thus the codicological tradition of the Greek military theorists – has also produced skepticism about Polyaenus' prominence as an inspiration of Byzantine military thought, although the concept of stratagem as a *Schwerpunkt* of Byzantine doctrine is indisputable.[19] Such pessimism about Polyaenus' Byzantine fate, however, excessively, if not mechanically, emphasizes the chance survival of manuscripts – one but not the only source of intellectual history. Constantine VII, if he had in mind the collection of the *Laur. gr.* LV-4 in his advice to this son, could not have meant the *Excerpta* when he mentioned Polyaenus, because Polyaenus' name is missing from the superscript of the *Excerpta* in that manuscript. Polyaenus name was only added to the *Excerpta* in the sixteenth century, when the *Parisinus gr.* 2522 was copied from the *Laur. gr.* LV-4.[20]

Further, and more significantly, Leo knew the complete text of Polyaenus' *Strategica* directly and Polyaenus' collection seems to have been a major source for Leo *Tact.* 20. A scribe of the late tenth-century (?) *Vindobonensis phil. gr.* 225, one of the earliest witnesses to the *Tactica*, included Polyaenus in a marginal note to Prolog. 6.55–59 on earlier writers.[21] But better evidence comes from Leo's use of Polyaenus 3.9.38. Leo must have drawn this *exemplum* directly from the *Strategica*, as this anecdote is found neither in the *Excerpta* nor in the so-called *Stratagems of the Emperor Leo*, 118 *exempla* from the *Excerpta* further abbreviated, stylistically revised, and inserted in the mid-tenth century *Sylloge Tacticorum*.[22] Indeed Leo apparently drew on Polyaenus frequently in composition of *Tact.* 20: of the 221 *exempla* included, Polyaenus is a potential source for twenty-seven and many, like 3.9.38, are not found in the *Excerpta* or possibly used through [Maurice]'s *Strategicon*. Leo's reliance on [Maurice] noticeably decreases as *Tact.* 20 progresses (see Appendix). Clusters of Polyaenian material appear at *Tact.* 20.78–87, 144–68, 193–98, and 216–220.[23] Leo's failure to mention Polyaneus explicitly comes from his desire to rework material from "the ancients" as a collectivity rather than from ignorance of Polyaenus' complete text. As in 3.9.38 he updated the vocabulary and eschewed verbal reminiscences. Polyaenus' direct influence on Byzantine military thought was still flourishing in the tenth century.[24]

---

[18]   Trombley 1997: 267, 272; Schettino 1998: 21 n. 2; Rance 2007: 736 n. 99.

[19]   Rance 2011; but cf. Wheeler 2010: 48–54.

[20]   Wheeler 2010: 335 n. 110; on the *Paris. gr.* 2522, see Dain 1941.

[21]   Dennis 2010: 7, n. 4. The list includes Arrian, Aelian, Pelops, Onasander, Menas, Polyaenus, Syrianus, and Plutarch. Pelops and Menas, otherwise unknown, may be inventions or pseudonyms.

[22]   On the *Stratagems of the Emperor Leo* see Wheeler, in Krentz/Wheeler 1994: xxi–xxiii, 850–1075 (text and translation); the text of the *Sylloge*: Dain 1938; see Dain/Foucault 1967: 357–358 for commentary.

[23]   Cf. the meager list at Rance 2011: n. 3.

[24]   John Haldon reaches (independently) the same conclusion as this paper on Leo's use of the full text of Polyaenus. See his *The Taktika of Leo IV 'the Wise': Critical Commentary*, forthcoming.

Appendix

The following table lists *exempla* in Leo *Tact.* 20, which derive directly or indirectly from Polyaenus, or for which Polyaneus was one of the possible sources. Comprehensive citations of the anecdotes from all possible sources are not given.

L = Leo, P = Polyaenus *Strategica*, *Exc.P.* = *Excerpta Polyaeni*, M = [Maurice] *Strategicon*

L	P	M	L	P	M
20.27, 97[25]	3.9.17	8.1.26, 2.36	20.158	2.3.11	x
20.46	3.9.35	8.2.15	20.162	2.10.5	x
20.76	cf. 3.9.10	x	20.163	2.20	x
20.78	4.3.4; 4.20	x	20.168	3.9.18 (*Exc.P.* 46.4)	x
20.80	8.16.1–2	x	20.193 (cf. 20.159)	3.9.22	x
20.87 (cf. 17.91)	8.16.8	x	20.196	3.9.38	x
20.108	6.38.4 (*Exc.P.* 23)	x	20.197	cf. 3.9.47	x
20.136	1 *praef.* 3	x	20.198	3.10.2	x
20.144	5.40 (*Exc.P.* 58.3) 5.41, 44.5 (*Exc.P.* 28.3)	x	20.216 (= 17.89)	3.13.1	x
20.146	cf. 1.39.3[26]	x	20.217	3.11.1	x
20.154	2.1.17 (*Exc.P.* 15.2), 4.4.3	x	20.218	2.3.2 (*Exc.P.* 14.4)	x
20.156	2.3.4	x	20.220	4.7.2 (*Exc.P.* 57.14)	x
20.157	2.3.6	x			

[25] See also Plb. 10.32.11–12 and Wheeler 1988: 164–65 with n. 37–38.

[26] On the prominence of battles of desperation in Polyaenus, see Wheeler 2010: 39–42, where Puuap. fr. 44 Blockley should be added at n. 128.

BIBLIOGRAPHY

Bianco, E. (1997a): 'Ificrate, ῥήτωρ καὶ στρατηγός, *MGR* 21: 179–201.

Bianco, E. (tr.) (1997b): *Gli Stratagemmi di Polieno*, Torino.

Bianco, E. (2010): The Third Book of Polyaenus and Ephorus, in: Brodersen 2010: 69–84.

Blockley, R. (ed./tr.) (1983): *The Fragmentary Classicizing Historians of the Later Roman Empire*, vol. II, Liverpool.

Brodersen, K. (ed.) (2010): *Polyainos, Neue Studien – Polyaenus. New Studies*, Berlin.

Dain, A. (1938): *Sylloge Tacticorum, quae olim "Inedita Leonis Tactica" dicebatur*, Paris.

Dain, A. (1941): Le Parisinus 2522, *RPh* 41: 21–28.

Dain, A. and Foucault, J.-A. de (1967): Les stratégistes byzantins, *T&MByz* 2: 317–392.

Dennis, G. (ed./tr.) (2010): *The Taktika of Leo VI*, Washington, D.C.

Dennis, G. (ed.), Gamillscheg, E. (tr.) (1981): *Das Strategikon des Maurikios*, Vienna.

Eramo, I. (ed./tr.) (2010): *Siriano, Discorsi di Guerra*, Bari.

Haldon, J. (ed./tr.) (1990): *Constantine Porphyrogenitus. Three Treaties on Imperial Military Expeditions*, Vienna.

Haldon, J. (forthcoming): *The Taktika of Leo VI 'the Wise': Critical Commentary*, Washington, D.C.

Krentz, P., Wheeler, E.L. (eds./trs.) (1994): *Polyaenus, Stratagems of War*, 2 vols., Chicago.

Melber, J. (1885): Über die Quellen und den Wert der Strategemensammlung Polyäns, *Jahrbücher für classische Philologie* (Suppl. 14), Leipzig: 417–688.

Melber, J. (ed.) (1887): *Polyaeni Strategematon*, Leipzig.

Nefedkin, A.K. (ed./tr.) (2002): *Polien, Strategemi* (in Russian), St. Petersburg.

Parke, H.W. (1933): *Greek Mercenary Soldiers*, Oxford.

Pritchett, W.K. (1971–1991): *The Greek State at War*, 5 vols., Berkeley/Los Angeles.

Pryor, J.H. and Jeffreys, E.M. (2006): *The Age of the ΔΡΟΜΩΝ. The Byzantine Navy ca. 500–1204*, Leiden.

Rance, P. (2007): The Date of the Military Compendium of Syrianus Magister (formerly the Sixth-Century Anonymous Byzantine), *BZ* 100: 701–737.

Rance, P. (2011): review of Brodersen 2010, *BMCR* 2011.06.07.

Schindler F. (1973): *Die Überlieferung der Strategemata des Polyainos*, (Österreichische Akademie der Wissenschaften, Phil.-hist. Klasse, SB, Bd. 284.1), Vienna.

Schettino, M.T. (1998): *Introduzione a Polieno*, Pisa.

Trombley, F. (1997): The *Taktika* of Nikephoros Ouranos and Military Encyclopaedism, in: P. Binkley (ed.), *Pre-Modern Encyclopedic Texts. Proceedings of the Second COMERS Congress, Groningen, 1–4 July 1996*, Leiden: 261–274.

Tucci, J. (2004): *Terra marique. Amphibious Warfare in the Ancient World* (= diss. University of Wisconsin 2003), Ann Arbor.

Wheeler, E.L. (1988): Πολλὰ κενὰ τοῦ πολέμου. The History of a Greek Proverb, *GRBS* 29: 153–184.

Wheeler, E.L. (1994): Introduction, in: Krentz/Wheeler 1994, I: vi–xxiv.

Wheeler, E.L. (2010): Polyaenus: *Scriptor Militaris*, in: Broderson 2010: 7–54.

Woefflin, E. (ed.) (1860): *Polyaeni Strategicon*, Leipzig.

DISCUSSIONS

ELECTRUM * Vol. 19 (2012): 167–178
doi:10.4467/20800909EL.12.011.0752

LA TESTA MOZZA DI CRASSO (PLUT., *CRASS*. 32–33).
A PROPOSITO DI UN LIBRO RECENTE SULLA BATTAGLIA DI CARRE[1]

Federicomaria Muccioli

A differenza di altre epoche storiche, quella antica è particolarmente selettiva dal punto di vista storiografico. La storia (o, meglio, le storie) dei Greci e l'*imperium Romanum*, con la sua cultura bilingue, operarono di norma un processo di selezione e talora manipolazione delle fonti, anche quando furono soccombenti in campo militare. Eccezioni marginali sono i casi in cui la storiografia e, in modo talora parallelo o addirittura antecedente, la retorica si esercitarono, anche con un certo successo, su episodi di storia controfattuale (o ucronìa): il dilagare dei Persiani in Grecia nel 480, se gli Ateniesi non si fossero opposti[2], e l'ipotetica conquista di Alessandro in Occidente[3] ne costituiscono gli episodi più noti. Oltre a ciò, niente di più che giochi letterario-storiografici vanno considerate opere come la *De excidio Troiae historia* di Darete Frigio, presunta traduzione latina di Cornelio Nepote, dedicata a Sallustio, dell'originale di un sacerdote troiano; testo che rappresenterebbe gli avvenimenti troiani dalla parte dei vinti.[4]

La scrittura della storia operata dai vincitori del mondo classico, anche quando costoro subirono cocenti sconfitte, è favorita almeno in parte da una diversa prospettiva culturale dei popoli altri, che non conoscono forme storiografiche simili o comparabili a quelle greco-latine.[5] Questi infatti privilegiano la cultura materiale e le forme di comunicazione orale (anche di tipo epico-folclorico) o monumentale (con un particolare tipo, spesso stereotipato, di scrittura esposta e di comunicazione di messaggi).[6] Non coltivano generi letterari in tutto e per tutto assimilabili a quelli del mondo greco-romano, a meno di 'piegarsi' ai suoi canoni (si pensi a Manetone di Sebennito ovvero a Berosso Caldeo, rispettivamente in ambito egizio e babilonese, per quanto discusse siano le finalità e la

---

[1] G. Traina, *La resa di Roma. 9 giugno 53 a.C., battaglia a Carre*, Laterza Editore, Roma–Bari 2010, pp. 212 (= Traina 2010); ora anche in edizione francese: *Carrhes, 9 juin 53 av. J.-C. Anatomie d'une défaite*, Préface de G. Brizzi, Les Belles Lettres, Paris 2011.

[2] Hdt. 7.139.4.

[3] Vd., ad es., *Rhet. ad Her*. 4.31; Liv. 9.17–19; Plut. *De fort. Rom*. 326a–c.

[4] Vd. ora Garbugino 2011.

[5] Un'eccezione è evidentemente costituita dagli Ebrei, che trasferiscono nei testi sacri la propria memoria storica, anche di stampo cronachistico-storiografico.

[6] Cfr., indicativamente, i contributi contenuti in Gabba 1999. Per una messa a fuoco di una forma del tutto particolare di storiografia monumentale nell'Egitto faraonico cfr. Pernigotti 2001.

struttura stessa delle loro opere), ovvero sfruttando forme di comunicazione di tipo oracolare.

Un caso emblematico, se non addirittura il più emblematico, a conforto delle considerazioni sopra esposte è costituito dallo scontro tra Romani e Parti il 9 giugno 53 a.C. Manca infatti sostanzialmente una storiografia partica o filopartica incentrata proprio sulla *clades* romana. Infatti i *Parthika* di Apollodoro di Artemita (e forse di tutto un filone storiografico a lui collegato), quantunque di datazione incerta, non sembrano essere arrivati fino all'avvenimento in questione. È poi significativo come Strabone, noto autore filoromano e lettore di Apollodoro, non abbia inteso approfondire l'episodio, nonostante egli sia perfettamente consapevole che l'ecumene è divisa in due, tra Roma e gli Arsacidi.[7] Una consapevolezza che peraltro si diffonde a macchia di leopardo nella pubblicistica classica (ma anche in un autore come Flavio Giuseppe), una volta esaurita e ridimensionata la spinta propulsiva dei regni macedoni.[8]

La storiografia filopartica o attenta alle dinamiche sociali, politiche e culturali del regno degli Arsacidi, filtrata da Strabone e, presumibilmente, da fonti non strettamente 'organiche' alla propaganda romana (come Timagene e Pompeo Trogo/Giustino) non è riuscita a ribaltare la prospettiva interpretativa nel mondo classico, portato a presentare i Parti in chiave negativa.

Ciò si riverbera, inevitabilmente, anche nello scontro di Carre, che a torto o a ragione è divenuto un *turning point* nel rapporto tra Oriente e Occidente (soprattutto per merito, o per colpa della narrazione di Plutarco nella *Vita di Crasso*), e oggetto di un attento e brillante studio di Giusto Traina, che accomuna agilità espositiva ad apprezzabile rigore metodologico (pur con l'intento di arrivare a lettori non specialistici, a giudicare dalla collocazione editoriale del volume). Un libro che indaga sia lo scontro militare (mettendo in luce debolezze ed errori romani), sia la genesi del suo mito, dall'antichità in poi, in cui trovano ampio spazio e adeguata sistemazione considerazioni già avanzate dallo studioso in studi preliminari.[9]

L'autore è da tempo attento ai fenomeni di intersezioni culturali, avvezzo a frequentazioni 'pericolose' per classicisti di stretta osservanza, come attestano, se non altro, i suoi fondamentali lavori su Mosè di Khorene e la storia armena. Frequentazioni che dimostrano come sia necessario guardare con occhio diverso alle altre realtà politiche, sociali e culturali coeve a quelle greco-romane, anche da una prospettiva di storico dell'antichità classica (quale è quella del Traina, con frequenti e salutari interazioni con la sfera archeologica, fin dagli esordi del suo percorso di studi e accademico). Infatti tale sensibilità a fenomeni e culture di frontiera o marginali tiene conto di una tendenza, ormai imprescindibile, portata a riconsiderare profondamente le culture iraniche, anche per chi ha un approccio legato a una forma mentis di stampo classicistico.

La necessità di rivedere consolidati e invecchiati stereotipi interpretativi è tanto più pressante sia dal punto di vista scientifico, ovviamente, sia anche in presenza di pericolose cadute di stile mediatiche (si pensi ad una pellicola come *Trecento*, con tutte le polemiche che ne sono seguite), e che ancora si insinuano in chi, per professione, indaga

---

[7]   Strabo 6.4.2; 11.9.2; 16.1.28.

[8]   Vd. Alex. Polyhist., *FGrH* 273 F 81a; Ioseph. *Ant. Iud.* 18.46; Tac. *Ann.* 2.2 e 56; Iust. 41.1.1; cfr. 43.1.1, nonché Manil. 4.674–675. Cfr. Muccioli 2007: 107–115.

[9]   Vd., per tutti, Traina 2009: 235 e nota * (con gli articoli ivi segnalati).

o legge le fonti (per tutti, Erodoto) con un certo strabismo interpretativo, ovvero con attenzione rivolta solo al *côté* greco.[10]

Se dunque può avere senz'altro un senso leggere la spedizione di Alessandro riconsiderando uno dei grandi reietti della storia, quale fu Dario III[11], è ancora più stringente la necessità di riconsiderare il rapporto tra le monarchie ellenistiche, in particolare i Seleucidi, e le nascenti regalità di ceppo iranico, come quella partica.

Infatti la *scholarship* sui Parti ha sofferto per lungo tempo di un pregiudizio, che ha limitato anche la comprensione della società e della regalità arsacide. Un pregiudizio teso a considerare quello partico come un regno solo parzialmente ellenizzato, in una contrapposizione tra cultura e barbarie, a tutto vantaggio della superiorità del mondo greco-romano. Emblematiche di questa tendenza sono le pagine di studiosi di cose ellenistiche del calibro del Breccia e del Meyer, che segnano senz'altro un passo indietro rispetto a certa critica ottocentesca, protesa invece, nelle sue personalità più aperte, a cogliere le intersezioni culturali (vd., ad es., una figura come A. von Gutschmid e la sua *Geschichte des Irans*).[12]

Il Breccia così scriveva nel 1905, a proposito dell'appellativo ufficiale Philhellen, adottato dai Parti a cominciare da Mitridate I, in un articolo dedicato a questo sovrano: «Il cognome φιλέλλην dimostra che Mitridate iniziò una politica volta ad attirare le simpatie della popolazione greco-macedonica, e dimostra pure la grande forza dell'Ellenismo che agiva tanto potentemente su popolazioni non da molto uscite dalla barbarie».[13]

Ancora più famoso e riecheggiato nella storia degli studi il giudizio del Meyer, secondo cui la morte del re seleucide Antioco VII nel 129 a.C. nello scontro contro gli Arsacidi rappresentò una vera e propria catastrofe per la cultura ellenistica nel continente asiatico, oltre che per il regno dei Seleucidi.[14]

Un'interpretazione di questo tipo appartiene ormai all'archeologia degli studi (anche se talora continua a riscuotere qualche credito, più o meno surrettiziamente, in pubblicazioni di tipo specialistico e non). Infatti da tempo la critica più accorta ha messo in luce i processi di interazione e di acculturazione, anche reciproca, tra mondo greco e mondi altri, in un'analisi di ampio respiro. Se è vero che ormai i fenomeni di acculturazione reciproca valgono per ambiti di studio come la grecità coloniale, tanto maggiore è la loro validità nell'Oriente ellenistico e iranico, se non addirittura ellenistico-iranico. È noto il tentativo di Antioco I di Commagene di fondere le diverse anime culturali del suo regno, mentre è meno rilevante quanto messo in atto tra gli Arsacidi, in particolare a partire da Mitridate I.

Nella storia della ricerca il *turning point* a riguardo è senz'altro costituito dalla produzione di Jósef Wolski, autore di una lunga serie di studi dal 1937 al 2007 sul mondo

---

[10]   Sulla necessità di leggere lo storico di Alicarnasso con sensibilità interpretativa attenta anche alla cultura iranica cfr., per tutti, i saggi contenuti in Rollinger/Truschnegg/Bichler 2011.

[11]   Vd. Briant 2003, nonché Briant 2008.

[12]   von Gutschmid 1888.

[13]   Breccia 1905: 52. Sull'epiteto Philhellen da intendersi soprattutto nel suo significato propagandistico (con risvolti politico-economici), e non certo come forma di sudditanza o riconoscimento di una superiorità culturale, cfr. Muccioli 2013: 257–261.

[14]   Meyer 1921: 270–273, partic. 272 («Die Niederlage des Antiochos Sidetes im Jahre 129 ist die Katastrophe des Hellenismus im kontinentalen Asien und zugleich die des Seleukidenreichs»).

partico[15], e proseguita dalla sua scuola, in particolare l'allievo e successore all'Università di Cracovia, Edward Dąbrowa.[16]

Il libro del Traina, dunque, si riallaccia idealmente a questo filone di salutare 'revisionismo', che conosce ora anche importanti strumenti di lavoro sulle fonti partiche[17], cercando, per quanto possibile, di dare voce anche allo "sguardo del regno arsacide" (sia pure evanescente e comunque filtrato dalla tradizione iranica posteriore), spesso eluso dalla storiografia classica.[18]

Lo fa con occhio attento a tutta la produzione bibliografia, anche quella eccentrica o meno frequentata, 'disseppellendo' ad es., il libro di Pietro Manfrin sulla cavalleria partica.[19] Una produzione che comprende evidentemente i lavori di matrice classica, ma che abbraccia anche la produzione meno accessibile o comunque poco nota ai cultori di *classics* di stretta osservanza. Uno sforzo davvero meritorio, in cui rare e, direi, inevitabili sono le lacune (o, meglio, le integrazioni bibliografiche che si possono suggerire).[20]

Uno dei pregi principali del libro è senz'altro quello di mettere a fuoco, con argomenti importanti e convincenti, gli aspetti strettamente attinenti alle questioni belliche, che determinarono, insieme a errori tattici e strategici, la sconfitta romana a Carre, al di là del diaframma e del fraintendimento imposti dalle fonti. Spiccano, in particolare, le osservazioni sui catafratti e sugli arcieri partici, nonché un'adeguata analisi topografica del campo di battaglia, situato nell'attuale Turchia.

La conclusione a cui arriva il Traina è che, in buona sostanza, la battaglia di Carre va sottratta alla mitizzazione letteraria e storiografica, anche se senz'altro si trattò del primo grande scontro di una guerra continua, praticamente mai conclusa, fra Roma e l'Iran.

Vi sono alcuni punti specifici che meritano una discussione, che concernono proprio la testimonianza plutarchea della biografia di Crasso, fonte principale insieme a Cassio Dione.[21] La critica, soprattutto negli ultimi tempi, si è esercitata spesso sul duplice livello di lettura delle *Vite parallele*, intravedendo connessioni talora bizzarre se non del tutto improbabili, nel tentativo, spesso forzato, di attualizzazione del racconto plutarcheo. Ed è certo un dato di fatto che il Cheronese, nella ricostruzione biografica (ma sarebbe più corretto a mio avviso intendere storico-biografico), miri ad una cristallizzazione etica dei personaggi: costoro, pur inseriti nelle coordinate spaziali e temporali della loro epoca, tendono quasi a diventare personaggi astorici, paradigmi etici (positivi, ma talora anche negativi) valevoli per il lettore reale, ma anche quello ideale di Plutarco.

Ha dunque senz'altro ragione il Traina a sottolineare la doppia chiave di lettura della battaglia di Carre nel Cheronese, storica e attualizzante, in rapporto alla spedizione partica di Traiano. Come spesso capita con Plutarco, i contorni cronologici della stesura delle sue opere rimangono forzatamente indeterminati, ma vi è un certo generalizzato

---

[15]   Biliografia completa in Dąbrowa *et al.* 2010: 5–17.

[16]   Vd. ora i lavori raccolti in Dąbrowa 2011.

[17]   Vd. Hackl/Jacobs/Weber 2010 e, pur con qualche riserva, l'analisi di Lerouge 2007.

[18]   Traina 2010: XI–XII, 126–128.

[19]   Manfrin 1893.

[20]   Cfr. Frendo 2003 [2007]; Hartmann 2008 e, per quanto attiene propriamente alla *Vita di Crasso* plutarchea e alle sue tecniche compositive, Braund 1993 (comunque opportunamente citato nel volume); Zadorojniy 1997; Schettino 2003; Chlup 2009 (ma la bibliografia su Plutarco e le sue biografie ormai tende pericolosamente a dilatarsi).

[21]   Plut. *Crass.* 16–33; Dio 40.21–27.

consenso nel ritenere che la coppia Nicia-Crasso vada appunto datata al 114.[22] All'epoca la questione partica costituiva ancora un problema scottante, solo parzialmente risolto poi con Traiano.

L'attenzione a questo nervo scoperto nell'impero romano è comunque in Plutarco particolarmente distratta e priva di reale approfondimento, geografico, culturale e politico. Il che può solo apparentemente sorprendere, nel quadro degli orizzonti culturali di II secolo e, più specificatamente, dell'autore in questione. Se è vero che non abbiamo gran parte delle biografie dei Cesari, dal resto dell'opera si evince che Plutarco è autore legato ancora sostanzialmente alla polis di matrice classica, incapace di avere una visione di stampo geopolitico che possa davvero abbracciare tutta l'ecumene sotto l'*imperium* romano.[23] L'espansione partica, nelle sue diverse fasi evolutive, è da lui generalmente ignorata così come ne è ignorato il lignaggio, in linea con un *misunderstanding* costante nei confronti delle regalità greche (o grecizzate) dell'Oriente ellenistico.[24]

Non si sottrae poi alla riproposizione di un topos consolidato, riguardo alla assoluta inaffidabilità dei Parti, citando le parole di Teofane di Mitilene. Costui, a Pompeo in fuga dopo la battaglia di Farsalo e tentato di rifugiarsi presso gli Arsacidi, sconsigliò vivamente di recarsi presso i Parti, in quanto costoro erano il più infido dei popoli e misuravano il potere solo in base all'insolenza e alla lussuria.[25] Anche se Plutarco si limita a riportare il giudizio della fonte, è comunque evidente il carattere negativo di questa rappresentazione, peraltro confermata dalla scena – probabilmente una delle più famose nelle *Vite* – in cui viene portata la testa mozza di Crasso, alla presenza dell'arsacide Orode e dell'armeno Artavasde, durante il banchetto di nozze del figlio del primo Pacoro e della sorella del secondo.

Proprio questo episodio, assai noto, chiude l'ultima parte della biografia del Romano, tutta dedicata all'infausta spedizione contro gli Arsacidi. Cruciale si dimostra un'indagine sulla *Quellenforschung*, affinata con il progresso della dottrina sul metodo di lavoro plutarcheo, quantunque questa sia complicata dal fatto che il Cheronese non cita pressoché nessun autore direttamente in questa sezione, limitandosi all'uso di fonti indeterminate.[26]

Il Traina passa diligentemente in rassegna tutte le principali suggestioni, alcune in realtà fantasiose e prive di reali riscontri, circa la possibile fonte (diretta o indiretta) dello

---

[22]   Traina 2010: VIII–IX, 129. Cfr. Schettino 2003: 274–275.

[23]   Cfr. la posizione, fortemente intrisa di pregiudizi, di Luciano, su cui vd. Gangloff 2007.

[24]   Vd., esemplarmente, il misconoscimento di una figura come Menandro, protagonista dei *Milindapañha*, testo fondante del Buddismo. Costui è definito «un certo Menandro» (*Praec. ger. reip.* 821d–e), a sottolineare tutta la distanza culturale, prima ancora che geografica, che separava lo scrittore di Cheronea da una realtà come quella della grecità asiatica. Pur in considerazione di questo scarso interesse, risulta comunque significativo che Plutarco, certo del tutto meccanicamente, abbia raccolto una versione antitetica a quella buddista e sostanzialmente più attendibile. Se per la tradizione indiana il sovrano si sarebbe convertito al Buddismo e avrebbe abbandonato la vita terrena, abdicando in favore del figlio, dai *Praecepta* invece sappiamo che costui morì nel corso di una spedizione militare e le città gli resero in comune onori funebri; successivamente vennero a contrasto e se ne contesero le ceneri e ognuna eresse un monumento in onore del sovrano. Per un approfondimento vd. Muccioli 2012: 42.

[25]   *Pomp.* 76.7–9.

[26]   Sul problema nella biografia cfr. Garzetti 1987: 213; Angeli Bertinelli 1993: XLV–XLVI. Più in generale, sull'uso delle fonti indeterminate, rimando a Muccioli 2012: 52.

scontro di Carre nella *Vita di Crasso* plutarchea: Gaio Cassio Longino, Timagene, Nicolao Damasceno, Asinio Pollione, Apollonio (liberto di Crasso) o addirittura il sovrano armeno Artavasde (Artawazd), cultore delle *litterae* greche.[27] A queste ipotesi, preferendola pur con estrema cautela, accosta l'uso di una monografia sull'invasione dei Romani nella regione, ad opera di un anonimo greco di Mesopotamia, che sarebbe stato dunque un testimone oculare degli avvenimenti.[28] L'idea di un utilizzo di una fonte diretta degli avvenimenti è stata peraltro talora prospettata nella *scholarship*. Basti ricordare come il Desnier ritenga che Plutarco abbia utilizzato Antioco Filopappo, i cui avi commagenici potevano avere conoscenza diretta dell'accaduto, ovvero aver assistito a qualche *performance* poetica a corte a celebrazione/ricordo dello scontro.[29] Una fonte comunque che ben difficilmente potrà essere stata romana, a giudicare dalla perentoria affermazione plutarchea. Infatti l'autore, a proposito dell'uccisore di Crasso e del particolare della testa e della mano destra mozzate quando costui ormai giaceva a terra, pronuncia un chiaro giudizio negativo. Si tratta di un particolare improbabile, scrive, frutto più di congettura che di reale conoscenza: dei presenti alcuni fuggirono, altri risalirono sul colle. Sappiamo comunque che, tra quanti furono catturati, alcuni sopravvissero.[30]

Dal canto suo, un buon conoscitore di Plutarco (peraltro forse troppo spesso e troppo presto dimenticato) come Albino Garzetti, a suo tempo aveva individuato nei capitoli 16–33 un'unitarietà del racconto, tale da risalire in ultima analisi al libro CVI di Livio (pur con inserzioni di altri autori, in particolare Nicolao Damasceno). Una dipendenza basata sul confronto tra la *Periocha* relativa e le fonti che dal Patavino sostanzialmente dipendono (Cassio Dione, ma anche Floro, Eutropio, Rufio Festo, Giulio Ossequente, Orosio). Accanto a Livio, sulla scorta di suggestioni del Flacelière (e del Pareti), il Garzetti riteneva plausibile l'esistenza di *Memorie* del questore Cassio, figura che viene presentata positivamente in più passi della biografia.[31] Quanto agli ultimi due capitoli, secondo lo studioso «appartengono sicuramente al patrimonio aneddotico plutarcheo, da una tradizione che vedeva le cose d'Oriente con gli occhi dell'Ellenismo».[32]

A fronte di questo ventaglio di ipotesi va registrata pure la posizione del Magnino, tendente sostanzialmente all'atetesi, anche se lo studioso riconosceva che i capitoli 16–33 «costituiscono un *unicum* compatto e organico».[33]

Il Pelling, invece, ha individuato almeno due fonti importanti a proposito della spedizione partica (difficilmente determinabili e opportunamente mediate da Plutarco), salvo poi ritenere, in un successivo contributo, che quella di Crasso sia «a peculiarly

---

[27] Plutarco ricorda come costui avesse scritto tragedie, opere in prosa e storiche, alcune delle quali sono conservate (*Crass.* 33.2: quest'ultima notazione, visto l'uso del presente διασῴζονται, sembra risalire direttamente al Cheronese). La menzione di opere storiche indica, evidentemente, un'omologazione alla forma di tradizione della memoria storica (o almeno un compromesso) di cui si è detto *supra*.

[28] Traina 2010: 105–106. Sulla presenza di Greci nel corso della spedizione testimonia esplicitamente Plut. *Crass.* 25.12.

[29] Desnier 1995: 131–144. Sui rapporti, spesso ambigui, tra regalità commagenica e Arsacidi cfr., per tutti, Facella 2010 (con rimando ai suoi studi precedenti).

[30] Plut. *Crass.* 31.8; *Ant.* 37.2; Hor. *Od.* 3.5.5–12; Dio 40.27.4. Cfr. Zadorojniy 1997: 171–172.

[31] *Crass.* 18.4; 20.4; 22.3–4; 23.3; 28.6–7.

[32] Garzetti 1987: 215–216. Parzialmente concorde anche Angeli Bertinelli 1993: XLIII–XLIV (che si pronuncia per un uso di Livio, a cui si aggiunge, come fonte complementare, Nicolao Damasceno).

[33] Magnino 1992: 258–259.

lightweight and anecdotal Life», vista l'impossibilità di scrivere «a serious historical biography».[34]

A mio avviso, se pure è possibile ammettere una pluralità di fonti o comunque l'assenza di una fonte guida usata in tutta la sezione relativa alla spedizione partica, occorre in qualche modo scindere il racconto dagli ultimi due capitoli, che paiono invece configurarsi come un *unicum* compatto, in cui è peraltro ben tangibile il filtro plutarcheo. Infatti, come opportunamente sottolinea il Traina, Crasso è anche un grande personaggio tragico che subisce la giusta punizione per la sua *hybris*.[35] Una tragicità che si adatta sì al genere biografico, come rimarca l'autore, ed è perfettamente in consonanza con il linguaggio e le metafore usate da Plutarco (qui come altrove nelle *Vite* e nei *Moralia*), aspetto su cui ha sovente insistito la critica specialistica.[36] Del resto, proprio il famoso capitolo in cui la testa del Romano rotola, macabro trofeo, con grande divertimento del re partico e di quello armeno impegnati ad ascoltare la *performance* di Giasone, costituisce, agli occhi del biografo, l'ἐξόδιον della tragedia della spedizione di Crasso. Si tratta di una scena assai forte, in cui il Cheronese, pur indugiando su particolari a forti tinte, evita di scivolare nel raccapricciante, mantenendo, peraltro non senza qualche difficoltà, un giusto equilibrio narrativo.[37] In particolare, non ricorda la notizia, tràdita invece da Cassio Dione (e da altre fonti), dell'oro fuso colato nella bocca del Romano, macabro contrappasso della sua cupidigia di ricchezza.[38]

Il passo plutarcheo è sicuramente interessante sotto diversi aspetti, non da ultimo per il grado dell'ellenizzazione alle corti partica e armena.[39] A questo proposito il Traina scrive pagine importanti sulla cultura orale armena e sull'importanza delle *performances* teatrali, ispirate al mondo greco, nel regno di Artavasde. La cultura greca infatti è un collante non irrilevante anche a livello teatrale, in Armenia come nell'Oriente dominato dagli Arsacidi, ad es. a Babilonia.[40]

È inoltre indubbio che Plutarco, nel presentare tale scena simposiaca *sui generis*, sia vittima di un *misunderstanding* sostanziale nei confronti dell'apertura alla cultura greca (o addirittura acculturazione) dei sovrani partici e armeni, ben rappresentata nel passo. Una barriera mentale del Cheronese dovuta anche all'accentuazione della mancanza di *philanthropia* nel banchetto partico, visto in antitesi del banchetto classico.[41] Un frain-

---

[34]   Pelling 2002: 15 con nota 96; 208, rispettivamente (i due articoli ivi riprodotti sono stati pubblicati originariamente nel 1979 e nel 1986).

[35]   Traina 2010: 128.

[36]   Nello specifico cfr. Braund 1993; Zadorojniy 1997; Schettino 2003. Più in generale, punto di partenza fondamentale (e spesso negletto dalla critica più recente) rimane Fuhrmann 1964: 241–244.

[37]   Sul problema delle concessioni plutarchee ad una narrazione con elementi di tipo 'tragico' (o, meglio, drammatico), nonostante l'esplicita critica agli esponenti della storiografia denominata, non senza qualche arbitrio, appunto tragica (Duride e Filarco), cfr. Muccioli 2012: 73–78 (con la bibliografia ivi addotta), nonché Candau Morón 2011.

[38]   40.27.3; cfr. Flor. 1.46.11; Serv. ad *Aen.* 7.606; Fest. *Brev.* 17.3, con Angeli Bertinelli 1993: 419 e, soprattutto Traina 2010: 87–90 (per opportuni confronti con analoghe prassi nelle culture iraniche). Vd. anche la reminiscenza e rielaborazione di Dante (*Purg.* 20.116–117).

[39]   Vd., esemplarmente, Wiesehöfer 2000.

[40]   Cfr. Potts 2011 (con una dettagliata analisi delle varie fasi e ricostruzioni del teatro greco a Babilonia, in particolare sotto la dominazione partica, prendendo spunto proprio dal passo in questione della *Vita di Crasso*).

[41]   Parla di «grotesque details» Chlup 2009: 185, sulla scorta di Zadorojnyi 1997: 180.

tendimento peraltro attestabile anche per il simposio alla corte achemenide descritto nella *Vita di Artaserse*, indipendentemente dall'uso colà di fonti dirette o che riflettono testimonianze dirette e oculari.[42]

Ammettendo nei capitoli 32–33 la presenza di un non altrimenti noto autore/testimone greco di ambito locale, è preferibile pensare non ad un utilizzo diretto, bensì ad una mediazione da parte di una fonte di più ampio respiro (preferibilmente greca piuttosto che romana): una fonte che è sì interessata al mondo greco (la macabra sorte della testa di Crasso) ma anche alle sorti della dinastia partica (la morte in battaglia di Pacoro, l'avvelenamento di Orode ad opera dell'altro figlio Fraate IV). Un interesse che si mescola con l'intenzione plutarchea (già nella fonte?) di creare una sorta di contrappasso alla violenza e alla crudeltà partica.

Tenendo conto di questi elementi, assurge ad un ruolo di spettatore attivo, se non quasi da coprotagonista, la città di Seleucia sul Tigri, in alcune delle sue principali componenti (la γερουσία τῶν Σελευκέων e gli stessi Σελευκεῖς intesi genericamente, ma implicitamente considerandone e valorizzandone la matrice greca).[43] È infatti evidente che notazioni come quella sul giudizio negativo degli abitanti di Seleucia nei confronti della sfrontatezza di Surena nel criticare le *Favole milesie* lette dai Romani durante la spedizione (a fronte della dissolutezza dei Parti)[44] tradiscono una sensibilità greca o comunque grecizzante, di stampo tipicamente ellenistico, nonostante contatti e 'compromissioni' con le regalità iraniche e possibili inserti plutarchei.[45]

Per un'individuazione della fonte e della sua tendenza occorre analizzare il luogo anche in rapporto con quanto affermato in precedenza nella biografia, circa il primo errore commesso da Crasso. Questi, si afferma, non volle spingersi fino a raggiungere Babilonia e Seleucia (*scil.* sul Tigri), città che erano state sempre ostili ai Parti.[46] Si tratta di una prospettiva ben diversa da quella di Tito Livio, che, non senza enfatizzazioni e il ricorso a luoghi comuni (fors'anche retorici), arriva a stigmatizzare la degenerazione, ovvero la barbarizzazione, dei Macedoni in città come Alessandria e appunto Seleucia e Babilonia.[47] Una prospettiva che va confrontata con quella espressa da Tacito: negli *Annales*, a proposito dell'adulazione nei confronti dell'armeno Tiridate da parte degli abitanti di Seleucia, questi scrive che la loro città non era stata corrotta da costumi barbari e manteneva il carattere distintivo del suo fondatore Seleuco I. Lo storico latino ricorda poi esplicitamente un consiglio di trecento membri, da lui paragonato al senato (*trecenti opibus aut sapientia delecti, ut senatus*).[48] Un consiglio forse identificabile con la βουλή civica attestata, sia pure in modo sporadico, nella documentazione numismatica della prima metà del I secolo d.C.,[49] anche se non è questa la sede ovviamente per delineare un quadro dei fenomeni di continuità e di discontinuità nell'amministrazione

---

[42]   *Artox.* 15, su cui cfr. Almagor 2009.

[43]   *Crass.* 32.4–5.

[44]   *Crass.* 32.5–6.

[45]   Forse tangibili in *Crass.* 32.6.

[46]   *Crass.* 17.8.

[47]   Liv. 38.17.11.

[48]   Tac. *Ann.* 6.42; cfr. Plin. *NH* 6.122.

[49]   *BMCArabia, Mesopotamia and Persia*: CXVI–CXVII.

delle città fondate dai Seleucidi sotto i Parti, dal momento che qui interessa soprattutto l'aspetto storiografico.

La prospettiva raccolta e filtrata a sua volta da Plutarco, dal canto suo profondamente contrario a forme di *Mischung* etnica, è dunque quella di chi vede con una certa benevolenza la grecità orientale. È una visione greca o grecizzante, come aveva ben visto Garzetti. L'ipotesi di Nicolao Damasceno è senz'altro quella più praticabile, come è stato adeguatamente sottolineato dagli studiosi, dato che ha riscontri in Ateneo (a proposito del traditore Andromaco).[50] Evidentemente tale autore, originario appunto di Damasco, poteva avere una sensibilità particolare nei confronti della grecità d'Oriente, delle sue dinamiche (anche politiche) e dei suoi rapporti con altre culture, che autori romani non avevano (indipendentemente dall'utilizzo di·fonti locali).[51] Infatti nel succitato luogo de *I Deipnosofisti* si ricorda che Andromaco ebbe dai Parti come ricompensa del suo tradimento nei confronti di Crasso la signoria della sua città natale, Carre, che esercitò con crudeltà. A prescindere dal richiamo della punizione divina, materializzatasi nell'incendio causato dai suoi esasperati concittadini, non può sfuggire come l'assegnazione di tale potere monocratico rifletta precisi *patterns* nella gestione delle città d'Asia da parte dei Parti, già dal II secolo a.C.[52] Non si può peraltro dimenticare anche un altro autore, la cui ombra compare spesso a proposito dei Parti: Timagene di Alessandria. È inevitabile a questo proposito ricordare il noto passo liviano sui *levissimi ex Graecis*, favorevoli al *nomen* partico, in cui bisogna rintracciare proprio il nome dello scrittore alessandrino.[53]

Tranne qualche eccezione, la critica non è propensa a individuare la traccia diretta di questo autore nella *Vita di Crasso*, in particolare a proposito dello scontro con i Parti.[54] L'ipotesi timagenica, come fonte guida o anche sussidiaria non va peraltro scartata a priori, anche in una riconsiderazione più generale del problema partico nel I secolo a.C. negli autori di età imperiale.[55]

Se è sensato suggerire, come si è detto, che la *Vita di Crasso* possa avere una lettura attualizzante, questa chiave di lettura rimane sostanzialmente sottintesa nella biografia e le connessioni e le sovrapposizioni sono tutte lasciate al lettore. Conseguentemente, sono tanto più rimarchevoli i luoghi in cui è individuabile una polemica *ad personam*, o comunque una discussione critica che trascenda il personaggio in questione. Plutarco, nel confronto finale tra Nicia e Crasso, afferma che coloro che lodano la spedizione militare di Alessandro Magno e invece biasimano quella di Crasso sono in errore, perché giudicano gli inizi dall'esito finale.[56] Il passo va senz'altro inteso come un riconoscimen-

---

[50] Vd. Athen. 6.252d–e (= *FGrH* 90 F 79), dal libro CXIV delle *Storie*, a proposito di Andromaco e la sua fine (vd. Plut. *Crass.* 29). Cfr. la rassegna di Scardigli 1979: 108–109 e relative note; più recentemente, Zadorojniy 1997: 171 (comunque incerto sull'uso di Nicolao o di Asinio Pollione) e i riferimenti citati *supra*.

[51] Sui Parti in Nicolao, nel quadro degli scontri con i Seleucidi (in particolare Antioco VII) vd. Ioseph. *Ant. Rom.* 13.250–251 (= *FGrH* 90 F 92; cfr. FF 66, 130, per i riferimenti nella *Vita di Augusto*). Cfr. L. Thommen, in Hackl/Jacobs/Weber 2010, II: 293–294 (*ibid.*: 335–339, sui capitoli in questione della *Vita di Crasso*).

[52] Sulla questione cfr. Muccioli c.s.

[53] In proposito cfr. Muccioli 2007; Desideri 2010: 20–21.

[54] Cfr. Regling 1899; Frendo 2003 [2007]: 73.

[55] Cfr. le ipotesi di Clementoni 1985–1986, riguardo al possibile utilizzo dello scrittore alessandrino (fonte comunque scomoda in una prospettiva strettamente filoromana).

[56] *Nic.-Crass.* 4.4; cfr. *Crass.* 16.2 (sulla possibile *imitatio Alexandri* di Crasso, peraltro discussa dai moderni). Per quanto segue riprendo, con integrazioni, quanto affermato in Muccioli 2009: 72–73.

to, quasi simpatetico, dell'autore con il personaggio descritto, tenendo conto anche del problema, spesso surrettizio, dell'*imitatio Alexandri* nei protagonisti romani di I secolo a.C. (in particolare Pompeo e Cesare) e il punto di vista di Plutarco.

Uno degli elementi che non vanno sottovalutati è infatti il giudizio finale del Cheronese nei confronti di Crasso, che probabilmente è meno ambiguo di quello espresso nei confronti del suo omologo greco, Nicia.[57] La scelta di scriverne la biografia non sembra tanto motivata dall'interesse per il personaggio in sé, e dalla volontà di chiudere idealmente con Alcibiade il V secolo, quanto dall'esigenza di trovare un *pendant* ad una figura come quella del Romano. E, almeno sotto l'aspetto della superstizione (*deisidaimonia*), concetto che è metro fondante di giudizio nell'ottica dello scrittore, Nicia si dimostra superiore a Crasso.[58]

Nella biografia di quest'ultimo, proprio per mantenere un certo tono narrativo, Plutarco rinuncia deliberatamente a inserire notazioni marginali ed osservazioni personali, che possano creare esplicitamente un rapporto tra passato e presente. Il diverso registro narrativo della *comparatio* gli permette invece di inserire una notazione che può essere adeguatamente spiegata solo tenendo conto di tutta la tradizione storiografica greca sui Parti, e con tradizione storiografica si intende sia quella filoromana sia quella ostile o critica nei confronti di Roma.

Quello che Plutarco dunque afferma è che vi erano delle fonti che tendevano a confrontare e a contrapporre la spedizione di Alessandro a quella di Crasso, ricorrendo a una sovrapposizione etnolinguistica tra Persiani e Parti (peraltro frequente nella tradizione).[59] È difficile ritenere che qui si alluda ad autori di I–II secolo d.C., coevi o di poco anteriori a Plutarco (periodo in cui della *clades* di Crasso ormai si aveva sempre più labile traccia), mentre è più sensato supporre un'eco delle fonti di età tardo-repubblicana e augustea. Dal passo plutarcheo si evince che la spedizione di Alessandro viene fortemente depurata degli aspetti negativi. È un tema questo che può senz'altro ricordare la contrapposizione tra virtù e fortuna (con, di rimando, presentazione negativa del personaggio) particolarmente viva nella pubblicistica, greca e latina, soprattutto di I secolo d.C. e di cui lo stesso Plutarco era stato non trascurabile esponente.[60] Tra i diversi nomi che possono essere proposti a riguardo (Potamone di Mitilene, Apione, Dione Crisostomo)[61], senz'altro Timagene si fa preferire, considerata anche la sua 'benevola' attenzione verso il mondo partico.

---

[57] La critica discute se Plutarco abbia espresso una valutazione negativa o almeno parzialmente positiva nei confronti dell'Ateniese, pur stigmatizzando la sua *deisidaimonia*; cfr., per tutti, Nikolaidis 1988; Paganelli 2000; Titchener 2008; Vanotti 2011.

[58] *Nic.-Crass.* 5.3, su cui cfr. Stoffel 2005: 311–312.

[59] Cfr. la rassegna di Paratore 1966; le osservazioni di Spawforth 1994 e, con prospettiva divergente, di Schneider 2007; Oudot 2010.

[60] Vd. la duplice orazione *De Alexandri Magni fortuna aut virtute*, che comunque non rispecchia appieno il pensiero più maturo del Cheronese sul figlio di Filippo II (espresso invece nella biografia sul personaggio).

[61] *FGrH* 147 F 1 (= *FGrH* 1085 T 4a); *FGrH* 616; *Suda* s.v. Δίων, ὁ Πασικράτους, nonché *P.Oxy.* LVI, 3823v.

BIBLIOGRAFIA

Almagor, E. (2009): A "Barbarian" *Symposium* and the Absence of *philanthropia* (*Artaxerses* 15), in: J. Ribeiro Ferreira, D. Leão, M. Tröster, P. Barata Dias (eds.), Symposion *and* Philanthropia *in Plutarch*, Coimbra: 131–146.

Angeli Bertinelli, M.G. (1993): Introduzione e note alla *Vita di Nicia*, in: M.G. Angeli (edd.) Bertinelli, C. Carena, M. Manfredini, L. Piccirilli, Plutarco, *Le Vite di Nicia e di Crasso*, Milano.

Braund, D. (1993): Dionysiac Tragedy in Plutarch, *Crassus*, *CQ* n.s. 43: 468–474.

Breccia, E. (1905): Mitridate I il Grande, di Partia, *Klio* 5: 39–54.

Briant, P. (2003): *Darius dans l'ombre d'Alexandre*, Paris.

Briant, P. (2008): *Lettre ouverte à Alexandre le Grand*, Arles.

Candau Morón, J.M. (2011): Plutarco y la historiografía trágica, in: J.M. Candau Morón, F.J. González Ponce, A.L. Chávez Reino (Dirs.), *Plutarco Transmisor. Actas del X Simposio Internacional de la Sociedad Española de Plutarquistas*, Sevilla: 147–169.

Chlup, J.T. (2009): Crassus as symposiast in Plutarch's *Life of Crassus*, in: J. Ribeiro Ferreira, D. Leão, M. Tröster, P. Barata Dias (eds.), Symposion *and* Philanthropia *in Plutarch*, Coimbra: 181–190.

Clementoni, G. (1985–1986): Cassio Dione, le guerre mitridatiche ed il problema partico, *InvLuc* 7–8: 141–160.

Dąbrowa, E. (2011): *Studia Graeco-Parthica. Political and Cultural Relations between Greeks and Parthians*, Wiesbaden.

Dąbrowa, E. *et al.* (eds.) (2010): *Hortus historiae. Studies in Honour of Professor Józef Wolski on the 100th Anniversary of his Birthday*, Kraków.

Desideri, P. (2010): Il mito di Alessandro in Plutarco e Dione, in: S. Bussi, D. Foraboschi (edd.), *Roma e l'eredità ellenistica*, Pisa–Roma: 19–31.

Desnier, J.-L. (1995): *De Cyrus le Grand à Julien l'Apostat. Le passage du fleuve: essai sur la legitimité du souverain*, Paris.

Facella, M. (2010): Advantages and Disadvantages of an Allied Kingdom: The Case of Commagene, in: T. Kaizer, M. Facella (eds.), *Kingdoms and Principalities in the Roman Near East*, Stuttgart: 181–197.

Frendo, D. (2003) [2007]: Roman Expansion and the Graeco-Iranian World: Carrhae, its Explanation and Aftermath in Plutarch, *Bulletin of the Asia Institute* 17: 71–81.

Fuhrmann, F. (1964): *Les images de Plutarque*, Paris.

Gabba, E. (ed.) (1999): *Presentazione e scrittura della storia: storiografia, epigrafi, monumenti*, Como.

Gangloff, A. (2007): Peuples et préjugés chez Dion de Pruse et Lucien de Samosate, *REG* 120: 64–86.

Garbugino, G. (2011), *Darete Frigio. La storia della distruzione di Troia*, Alessandria.

Garzetti, A. (1987): Introduzione alla *Vita di Crasso*, in: *Plutarco. Nicia-Crasso*, Milano.

Hackl, U., Jacobs, B., Weber, D. (Hgg.) (2010): *Quellen zur Geschichte des Partherreiches*, Bd. I–III, Göttingen.

Hartmann, U. (2008): Das Bild der Parther bei Plutarch, *Historia* 57: 426–452.

Lerouge, C. (2007): *L'image des Parthes dans le monde gréco-romain. Du début du Ier siècle av. J.-C. jusqu'à la fin du Haut-Empire romain*, Stuttgart.

Magnino, D. (1982): *Vite di Plutarco*, vol. II, Torino.

Manfrin, P. (1893): *La cavalleria dei Parthi nelle guerre contro i Romani*, Roma.

Meyer, E. (1921): *Ursprung und Anfänge des Christentums*, Bd. II, Stuttgart–Berlin.

Muccioli, F. (2007): La rappresentazione dei Parti nelle fonti tra II e I secolo a.C. e la polemica di Livio contro i *levissimi ex Graecis*, in: T. Gnoli, F. Muccioli (edd.), *Incontri tra culture nell'Oriente ellenistico e romano*, Milano: 87–115.

Muccioli, F. (2009): Letterati greci a Roma nel I secolo a.C. Elementi per una riconsiderazione di Alessandro Poliistore e Timagene, in: S. Conti, B. Scardigli (edd.), *Stranieri a Roma*, Ancona: 59–84.

Muccioli, F. (2012): *La storia attraverso gli esempi. Protagonisti e interpretazioni del mondo greco in Plutarco*, Milano–Udine.

Muccioli, F. (2013): *Gli epiteti ufficiali dei re ellenistici*, Stuttgart.

Muccioli, F. (c.s.): *OGIS* 254, l'ἐπιστάτης et le στρατηγὸς καὶ ἐπιστάτης τῆς πόλεως, in corso di stampa.

Nikolaidis, A.G. (1988), *Is Plutarch fair to Nikias?*, *ICS* 13: 319–333.

Oudot, E. (2010): «Marathon, l'Eurymédon, Platées, laissons-les aux écoles des sophistes!» Les guerres médiques au second siècle de notre ère, in: P.-L. Malosse, M.-P. Noël, B. Schouler (éds.), *Clio sous le regard d'Hermès. L'utilisation de l'histoire dans la rhétorique ancienne de l'époque hellénistique à l'Antiquité Tardive*, Alessandria: 143–157.

Paganelli, L. (2000): Nicia secondo Plutarco. Una proiezione dell'antico in età imperiale, in: *Tradizione enciclopedica e divulgazione in età imperiale*, (*Serta Antiqua et Mediaevalia* 2), Roma: 73–86.

Paratore, E. (1966): La Persia nella letteratura latina, in: *La Persia e il mondo greco-romano*, Roma: 505–558.

Pelling, C. (2002): *Plutarch and History. Eighteen Studies*, London.

Pernigotti, S. (2001): La più antica storia d'Egitto e le origini della storiografia, in: *Storiografia locale e storiografia universale*, Como: 23–39.

Potts, D.T. (2011): The *politai* and the *bīt tāmartu*: The Seleucid and Parthian Theatres of the Greek Citizens of Babylon, in: E. Cancik-Kirschbaum, M. van Ess, J. Marzahn (Hgg.), *Babylon. Wissenskultur in Orient und Okzident*, Berlin–Boston: 239–351.

Regling, K. (1899): *De belli Parthici Crassiani fontibus*, Diss. Berolini.

Rollinger, R., Truschnegg, B., Bichler, R. (Hgg.) (2011): *Herodot und das Persische Weltreich – Herodotus and the Persian Empire*, Wiesbaden.

Scardigli, B. (1979): *Die Römerbiographien Plutarchs. Ein Forschungsbericht*, München.

Schettino, M.T. (2003): Modello storico, eroico e tragico in Plutarco: il caso della Vita di Crasso, in: A. Barzanò, C. Bearzot, F. Landucci, L. Prandi, G. Zecchini (edd.), *Modelli eroici dall'antichità alla cultura europea*, Roma: 265–280.

Schneider, R.M. (2007), Friend and Foe: The Orient in Rome, in: V. Sarkhosh Curtis, S. Stewart (eds). *The Age of the Parthians*, London: 50–86.

Spawforth, A. (1994): Symbol of Unity? The Persian–Wars Tradition in the Roman Empire, in: S. Hornblower (ed.), *Greek Historiography*, Oxford: 233–247.

Stoffel, É. (2005): La divination dans les *Vies* romaines de Plutarque: le point de vue d'un philosophe, *CGG* 16: 305–319.

Titchener, F.B. (2008): Is Plutarch's Nicias Devout, Superstitious, or Both?: in: A.G. Nikolaidis (eds.), *The Unity of Plutarch's Work: 'Moralia' Themes in the 'Lives,' Features of the 'Lives' in the 'Moralia,'* Berlin: 277–283.

Traina, G. (2009): Note in margine alla battaglia di Carre, *Electrum* 15: 235–247.

Vanotti, G. (2011): L'*Ermocrate* di Plutarco (e/o di Timeo?), in: R. Scuderi, C. Zizza (edd.), *In ricordo di Dino Ambaglio*, Pavia: 91–102.

von Gutschmid, A. (1888): *Geschichte Irans und seiner Nachbarländer von Alexander dem Grossen bis zum Untergang der Arsaciden*, Tübingen.

Wiesehöfer, J. (2000): "Denn Orodes war der griechischen Sprache und Literatur nicht unkundig...." Parther, Griechen und griechische Kultur, in: R. Dittmann, B. Hrouda, U. Löw, P. Matthiae, R. Mayer-Opificius, S. Thürwächter (Hgg.), *Variatio Delectat. Iran und der Westen. Gedenkschrift für Peter Calmeyer*, Münster: 703–721.

Zadorojniy, A.V. (1997): Tragedy and Epic in Plutarch's 'Crassus', *Hermes* 125: 169–182.

REDAKCJA
Jadwiga Makowiec

KOREKTA
Małgorzata Szul

SKŁAD I ŁAMANIE
Wojciech Wojewoda

Wydawnictwo Uniwersytetu Jagiellońskiego
Redakcja: ul. Michałowskiego 9/2, 31-126 Kraków
tel. 12-631-18-81, tel./fax 12-631-18-83